NATIONAL GEOGRAPHIC
TRAVELER
Berlin

NOV 9-89

BIRGIT KINDER

NATIONAL GEOGRAPHIC
TRAVELER
Berlin

By Damien Simonis
Photography by Pierre Adenis

National Geographic
Washington, D.C.

Contents

Page 1: The "Trabi," East Germany's
standard car, as depicted at the East
Side Gallery stretch of the Berlin Wall
Pages 2–3: All that glitters at the
entrance to Schloss Charlottenburg
Page 4: Cellular phones at the
Museum für Kommunikation

How to use this guide

See back flap for keys to text and map symbols.

The *National Geographic Traveler* brings you the best of Berlin, in text, pictures, and maps. Divided into three main sections, the guide begins with an overview of Berlin today, its history, and culture.

Following are eight area chapters with featured sites selected by the author for their particular interest. Each chapter opens with its own contents list for easy reference. A map introduces the parameters covered in the chapter, highlighting the featured sites and locating other places of interest. Walks (and, in the Excursions chapter, a drive), plotted on their own maps, suggest routes for discovering the most about an area. Features and sidebars offer intriguing detail on the area.

The final section, Travelwise, lists essential information for the traveler—pre-trip planning, special events, getting around, practical advice, and emergency contacts—plus provides a selection of hotels and restaurants arranged by area, shops, activities and entertainment.

To the best of our knowledge, information is accurate as of press time. However, it's always advisable to call ahead when possible.

Color coding

158

Each area of the city is color coded for easy reference. Find the area you want on the map on the front flap, and look for the color flash at the top of the pages of the relevant chapter. Information in **Travelwise** is also color coded to each region.

Visitor information

Alte Nationalgalerie
www.smb.museum
Map p. 83
Bodestrasse 1–3
030 20 90 55 77
Closed Mon.
$$$
U-Bahn & S-Bahn: Friedrichstrasse

Practical information for most sites is given in the side column (see key to symbols on back flap). The map reference gives the page number of the map and grid reference. Other details are address, telephone number, days closed, entrance charge in a range from $ (under $5) to $$$$$ (over $25), and U-Bahn and/or S-Bahn stop. Other sites have information in italics and parentheses in the text.

Hotel & restaurant prices

An explanation of the price bands used in entries is given in the Hotels & Restaurants section (beginning on p. 241).

TRAVELWISE

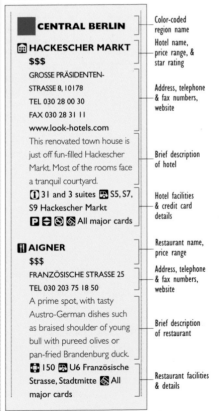

Color-coded region name

Hotel name, price range, & star rating

Address, telephone & fax numbers, website

Brief description of hotel

Hotel facilities & credit card details

Restaurant name, price range

Address, telephone & fax numbers, website

Brief description of restaurant

Restaurant facilities & details

AREA MAPS

Point of interest

District name

- A locator map accompanies each area map and shows the location of that area in the city.

Important featured site

WALKING TOURS

Building outline

Numbered bullets link sites on map to descriptions in the text.

Start point

Walk route

Direction of route

Parking

- An information box gives the starting and ending points, time and length of walk, and places not to be missed along the route.

REGIONAL/EXCURSION MAPS

S-Bahn station

Map reference

Important point of interest

Place of Interest

U-Bahn station

- Cities and sites described in Chapters 2 through 8 (pp. 51–206) and the Excursions chapter (pp. 207–232) are highlighted in gray on the map. Other suggested places to visit are shown with a red diamond symbol.

NATIONAL GEOGRAPHIC

TRAVELER

Berlin

About the authors & photographer

Damien Simonis, raised in Sydney, Australia, has had a little trouble settling down since he took a one-way flight to Cairo in 1989. In his baggage was a degree in languages and seven years' experience on some of Australia's leading dailies, including the *Australian* and *The Age.* Since landing in the Egyptian capital, Damien has lived, studied, and worked all over Europe and the Middle East. In 1992 he started writing guidebooks and travel articles for publications in Australia, the U.K., and North America. He hasn't stopped since. His wanderings have taken him from the Ukraine to Sudan, from the Alps to the Red Sea. Even before that flight to Cairo, Damien had had his first taste of foreign travel in Germany in the 1980s. Repeated study trips brought him back and he frequently visited Berlin at the height of the Cold War. Although he now lives in the warmer climes of Barcelona, Spain, his affection for Germany, and Berlin in particular, has never waned. He'll be back again soon.

Photographer **Pierre Adenis**, born in Toulon, France, studied in Nice, Lille, and Paris before moving permanently to Berlin in 1987. In 1990, he began his career as a press photographer and became the Berlin correspondent for Paris Sipa Press photo agency. He became a partner in Berlin's GAFF agency in 1992, and has been represented worldwide by LAIF since 2000. In addition to his work in his current home country of Germany, Pierre has traveled to and photographed the United States, France, Russia, the Middle East, and Greece. He has been published in numerous books and magazines, mostly in France and Germany.

Jeremy Gray wrote the Travelwise section. Born in Louisiana, this experienced travel author and photographer has penned a dozen guidebooks including bestselling titles to Amsterdam, Montreal, and Munich, and contributes images to publications worldwide. Having worn through several European cities, Jeremy now lives in the pulsing heart of Berlin's Mitte district.

History & culture

Wings of victory: The triumphant Siegessäule statue stands high above Berlin's Tiergarten.

Berlin today

"IT IS BERLIN'S DESTINY NEVER TO BE, BUT ALWAYS TO BE IN THE PROCESS of becoming." The phrase belongs to art historian Karl Scheffler (1869–1951) and is as true today as when he wrote it in the 1920s. Berlin is the most changeable city in Europe. Its physical face has been repeatedly torn asunder and reassembled. Its restless populace is as fickle as it is creative, making for an ever-evolving cultural and nocturnal scene, much as it was in the 1920s. A city of paradoxes, it exerts a magnetic charm that few can resist.

Munich may be richer and Hamburg more of a commercial powerhouse, but neither attracts the attention Berlin does. A colorful army of *Zuzügler* (newcomers) from all over the world and all walks of life have come and seem unable to leave. The number of tourists visiting the city has rocketed since 2000, placing Berlin in third place in Europe after

London and Paris. Some 6.5 million overnight visitors were registered in 2005.

Berlin has something for everyone. In few places is the drama and tragedy of 20th-century European history so deeply etched into the fabric of a city. Berlin's grand galleries are world class and the cultural calendar is jammed. With three opera houses, the Berlin Philharmoniker, and a thriving local gallery scene, Berlin is busy year-round.

Night owls have myriad opportunities to test their staying power in the restaurants, bars, and clubs of several different districts.

Even working-class Friedrichshain, once a dour East German neighborhood, now has its own lively scene to rival the well-established nocturnal offerings of the Kreuzberg and Prenzlauer Berg areas. As local party animals will tell you, it is virtually impossible to keep up with the bars and clubs that open and close across a city where there is no regulated closing time. And Berlin is one of the continent's gay magnets, especially now that the legendary summer Love Parade has been resurrected.

THE PHOENIX RISES

Bombed to the ground in World War II and divided in two on the Cold War front lines for 40 years, this indomitable phoenix continues to rise from its ashes. The scars of war, cold or otherwise, have yet to be completely healed, but progress has been breathtaking. Lack of money and simple neglect had left much of East Berlin in decay. Infrastructure was poor (few East Berlin households had telephones), and the no-man's-land on both sides of the Berlin Wall had left vast tracts of the city center as wasteland.

But from 1990 on, Berlin became one of the biggest construction sites in the world. The city had to sew its two halves together, which meant creating citywide transportation, telecommunications, and utilities. A bevy of international architects flocked to the city to fill the gaps with imaginative new buildings, many of which constitute sights in their own right in 21st-century Berlin. Potsdamer Platz, one of the busiest squares of prewar Germany and a desert from 1945 to 1990, is again a bustling, urban nerve center.

Much of the city disappeared in the 1940s bombings and postwar demolition, but the solution hasn't simply been to build from scratch. Many of Berlin's grandest buildings have been restored to their former glory. Some are an exciting crossbreed of old and new. The remodeling of the Reichstag, once again the seat of Germany's

Berlin's new skyline includes the Sony Center, Bahntower, and Killhoff buildings at rejuvenated Potsdamer Platz.

national parliament, is perhaps the most startling architectural symbol of this attempt to marry the city's (at times) glorious past with a more optimistic look into the future.

Controversy is never far away. Now, as decades ago, arguments rage over what should be restored, demolished, replaced, or rebuilt from scratch. Icons of western Berlin, such as Schloss Charlottenburg and the ruined Kaiser-Wilhelm-Gedächtniskirche, were due to be finished off by the wrecking ball in the 1950s, but have now been saved. On the east side, the damaged but intact Berliner Schloss, onetime residence of Germany's emperors, was destroyed in a cynical demonstration of ideological willfulness. To the communists, it had been a symbol of German imperialism. Its successor, the Palast der Republik, the East German parliament building, was due to be torn down in 2007.

To many Germans, it was a symbol of dictatorship. To others, however, it was a piece of German history and should have been left in place. Why, they cried, should this building go when so many erected under Adolf Hitler's regime (such as the former Aviation and Propaganda ministries and Tempelhof airport) have been left standing? What made the Nazi's Olympic Stadium worthy of protected status and the communist parliament worthy of destruction? As the campaign to

Sound and light at the Sage Club in Mitte; young Berliners enjoy some of the wildest, and latest, nightlife in Europe.

rebuild the original Berliner Schloss gathers speed (but not funds), heated debate is likely to go on for years.

A CULTURAL CRUCIBLE

Berlin's value as a tourist destination was long restricted to the curiosity of the Berlin

Wall, the fortified ideological frontier that separated West from East. Indeed, in the early 1990s, tourism to the city collapsed. With the same tenacity that distinguished Berliners as they rebuilt their city after World War II, the city's residents set about rebuilding their reputation as a destination for art lovers.

The extraordinarily costly business of restoring the central Museumsinsel (Museum Island) to its former glory and turning it into one of the world's biggest and most modern museum complexes is symbolic of the city's efforts to renew itself. Much has already been done, but in the coming years all of Berlin's collections of antiquities as well as much of its European art through the 19th century will be housed here.

The Kulturforum, which arose in West Berlin in the 1960s as a new pole of the arts, is also undergoing change, but it will

remain home to such major collections as the Neue Nationalgalerie (20th-century art) and Kunstgewerbemuseum (applied arts). Schloss Charlottenburg, along with its surrounding museums, and the Dahlem Museen complex in the city's southwest are further cultural magnets.

Other signal museums have emerged from nothing. A once glorious—and then bombed out—railway station is now at the core of the Deutsches Technikmuseum

The Brandenburg Gate, long a symbol of the division between West and East, marks the start of chic Unter den Linden.

(German Museum of Technology), one of the world's great homages to human creativity. Nearby, a daring design has given life to the Jüdisches Museum, dedicated to German Jewry. The Berlinische Galerie has established itself as a major stop on the modern and contemporary art circuit.

Another former railway station, Hamburger Bahnhof, is now an enormous contemporary art gallery. In all, the city counts around 175 museums.

HISTORY HOUNDS

For many, though, the fascination of Berlin lies in its historical resonance. So many of its buildings, monuments, streets, and districts are redolent of the events of the 20th century. Those seeking to come to grips with the horrors of the Nazi period can try to do so in countless ways. The Denkmal für die ermordeten Juden Europas, a controversial site in the heart of the city, is a broad, open-air monument dedicated to the memory of the Jews killed under Hitler. The Sachsenhausen concentration camp just outside Berlin is enveloped in a terrifying quiet on a cold winter's day. A stroll around the Scheunenviertel, the main Jewish quarter in prewar Berlin, has

an eerie quality. Similarly, a walk around Wilhelmstrasse, the old government district, will bring back memories of the Nazi era, especially in the Topographie des Terrors, on the site of the former SS (Schutzstaffel) headquarters.

Berlin's history has many other layers, however. Parts of the wall that cut the city in two from 1961 to 1989 are still in place. Checkpoint Charlie continues to be visible. On the eastern side of the city, you can visit

Berlin is surrounded by scenic lakes, among them Wannsee (above), where locals flock to summer beer gardens.

the former Ministry for State Security (Stasi) and its horrifying jail. In Karlshorst you can visit a museum dedicated to the fighting on the Eastern Front that's housed in the former Soviet military headquarters in Berlin. Soviet war memorials, especially in Treptower Park, recall not only the huge sacrifices made by the Soviet Union during World War II, but also the imposition of Soviet control on East Germany.

Schloss Charlottenburg, Berliner Dom (Berlin Cathedral), the Brandenburg Gate, and Gendarmenmarkt, all heavily restored, evoke seemingly more innocent times under the kings of Prussia and emperors of the German Reich from 1871. Unter den Linden, Potsdamer Platz, and Alexanderplatz, however altered down the years, are still powerfully evocative of times before the Nazi nightmare.

EAST MEETS WEST

Berlin and its people manage the neat trick of living with the city's often painful history without allowing themselves to be dragged down by it. Time, however, will be needed to heal all the wounds. In spite of the frantic pace of reconstruction, the city's western and eastern halves have yet to fully blend.

Catch the U1 train from Uhlandstrasse, in the west of the city, to Warschauer Strasse in the east and observe the subtle changes as you travel. At early stops you will see locals reading the *Berliner Morgenpost* or western German dailies such as the *Frankfurter Allgemeine Zeitung.* By the time you reach Warschauer Strasse, most will be reading East Berlin's *Berliner Zeitung.* A few may even be flipping through *Neues Deutschland,* the old Communist Party organ. On your way, through Kottbusser Tor, you may hear more Turkish spoken than German, and by the end of the line it might well be Russian. The city's central districts (such as Mitte, Prenzlauer Berg, and Kreuzberg) have largely been taken over by Germans from other parts of the country and by foreigners. Berliners stick to the periphery. East Berliners prefer Pankow or Karlshorst. West Berliners congregate in Charlottenburg, Wilmersdorf, and beyond. It would hardly occur to them to move east, just as an East Berliner would feel like a fish out of water in, say, Dahlem.

The division manifests itself in other ways. While West Berlin is for the most part solidly bourgeois, the eastern half exerts an ongoing fascination for a younger, alternative set. Much of what is thought to be hip

happens on the east side, and young Berliners will tell you that 90 percent of the best bars, clubs, and entertainment venues lie east of the former Berlin Wall—quite a change from the years before 1989.

THE SPIRIT OF BERLIN

Locals are known for their *Schnauze,* the Berlin version of attitude. Yes, Berliners can have a curt and grouchy side, pretty much like any big-city folk. They also have a limitless sense of humor and self-deprecation. Berliners will be the first to smile and admit that they forever *meckern* (grumble) about

almost everything (another big-city malady).

One thing that attracts so many other Germans to Berlin is that the city is, well, so un-German. To many, it is a mysterious East European city, far removed from the center of things and having more in common with Warsaw or Moscow than with the former capital, Bonn, or the banking city of Frankfurt.

It can be untidy and easygoing. Berlin in the 1920s was an anything-goes town, and so it is today. Nowhere else in Germany will police turn such a blind eye to minor infractions such as jaywalking. The trains and trams don't always run exactly on time. The city can seem grubby and shabby in places. And the myriad Bohemian taverns look like they would be more at home in Madrid or Barcelona.

Berlin is the biggest college town in Germany, with three universities, various other higher education centers, and more than 130,000 students. The city's mostly left-leaning governments pour money into

Art looks at art in Kreuzberg's Berlinische Galerie, one of a phalanx of world-class galleries in Berlin.

the arts. Berlin is one of the cheapest cities in the country for renting, dining, or entertaining yourself. All of this has contributed to the energized feeling in Berlin. Art galleries and alternative theater thrive. And Berlin has gotten itself firmly on the map as a design center, from fashion to interiors. In January 2006, UNESCO (United Nations Educational, Scientific, and Cultural Organization) named Berlin a Design City, praising it as a crossroads of creativity in building, the arts, interior design, fashion, and other applied arts.

Almost half a million of the city's population of 3.45 million comes from abroad. Leading the major groups are the Turks, with about 118,000, followed by about 38,500 Poles. Australians, who number 1,100, bring up the rear. These immigrant groups have added still more color to the cityscape and variety to local eating habits.

...THE TOUGH GET GOING

Not all is well, however. Berlin's vitality and creativity are palpable, but the city's present is as rich in tension and contrast as its past.

Berlin is a city, but is also at the heart of a tiny *Land* (federal state), not unlike Washington, D.C. Covering 343 square miles (889 sq km), about the area of London, Berlin is cradled by the Spree and Havel Rivers and lies 112 feet (34 m) above sea level. It was capital of Prussia until 1945, and of the German *Reich* (empire) from 1871 to 1945. East Berlin was capital of East Germany from 1949 to 1990. The united city was made capital of a reunited Germany in 1990, but the *Bundestag* (federal parliament) and government moved from Bonn only in 1999. Under an agreement designed to protect Bonn from collapse, six ministries remained behind and various other bodies moved into the small West German town. Curiously, while Berlin struggles economically, Bonn is today booming more than ever.

After reunification, many speculated on a rapid resurrection of Berlin as Germany's capital. The greatest enthusiasts dreamed of the city becoming a grand metropolis at the crossroads of Eastern and Western Europe.

The dreamers may have been a mite too ambitious. Many real estate speculators who bought up big in Berlin in the 1990s have had their fingers burned. The reunification euphoria of 1990 has evaporated. In its wake, much of the heavy industry that had kept East Berliners employed collapsed. Federal subsidies to West Berlin dried up. Certain planners saw the new Berlin, which had been an industrial powerhouse in pre-war Germany, as a sparkling government, services, and media center. All those sectors are growing, but have yet to stave off massive unemployment, which stands at just under 18 percent (almost double the national average). And the Berlin state government is 60 million euros in debt.

In spite of such problems, the city continues to pour money into its own transformation. In mid-2006, the city's first central train station, the Hauptbahnhof, was opened. It is Europe's biggest rail junction, and transportation planners predict 50 million long-distance rail passengers will pass through this hub annually by 2010, turning Berlin into one of Europe's central transportation nerve centers.

Berlin is not out of the woods, but perhaps a corner has been turned. The challenges for Berlin's gay, Socialist *Regierende Bürgermeister* (governing mayor), Klaus Wowereit (in power since 2001), are considerable, but he meets them with unfettered optimism in one of Europe's most

At the East Side Gallery, the longest surviving stretch of the Berlin Wall, locals create a summer beach bar.

inspiring, happening, and magnetic cities. The reorganization of older museums and the creation of many new ones are beginning to pay off. Tourism has skyrocketed in Berlin since 2000, and its burgeoning intellectual, café, and restaurant life gives the city a unique dynamism. Berlin is gaining a Europe-wide name for design as well as some cutting-edge industrial sectors. The high unemployment notwithstanding, there is an unmistakable buzz in the air. And Berlin has weathered far greater storms with grit and humor. ■

History of Berlin

FEW OF EUROPE'S CAPITALS HAVE HAD SUCH A ROLLER-COASTER RIDE IN SO short a time. From imperial metropolis to bombed-out, walled-in Cold War hostage and on to hip new capital, Berlin tells a story whose high drama few cities can match. And few could have seemed less destined to play a significant role in world affairs in the early days of their existence. London, Paris, and Rome all had more than a thousand years of history behind them when Berlin was little more than a huddle of muddy, medieval huts on the Spree River.

ON THE EDGE OF CIVILIZATION

Chronicles from 1237 are the first to mention a settlement called Kölln on a tiny island in the Spree River. The town was in the wild and woolly territory that came to be known as the Mark Brandenburg (a *Mark,* or March, was a frontier territory). Another settlement, called Berlin, was founded close by about the same time. The surrounding thinly populated, marshy land was hotly contested by rival Slav and German counts and princes.

Invasions from the east, including those by the Mongols in the 13th century, threatened the existence of the two communities. In 1307 Berlin and Kölln joined forces in mutual defense. Through much of the 13th and 14th centuries, no one controlled the Mark Brandenburg. Plundering robber knights roamed at will, extorting what they could from towns and country folk.

THIRTY YEARS' WAR & BERLIN'S REBIRTH

Into the Brandenburg power vacuum stepped Friedrich Hohenzollern (1371–1440), a German noble who imposed the rule of (his) law on the Mark and the entire region and became Kurfürst (Elector) Friedrich I in 1415. Seven electors—among them archbishops, a duke, a margrave, a count, and a king—elected the Holy Roman Emperor, who had at least nominal control over much of what is today Germany, Austria, and central Europe; he was supposed to be the secular counterpart of the pope. Berlin-Kölln was brought to heel in 1448 and then made the elector's capital.

After two relatively stable centuries, disaster befell the twin towns when they were overrun by marauding troops during the Thirty Years' War (1618–1648) and hit by

plague, leaving them with only 7,000 inhabitants. Friedrich Wilhelm (*R.*1640–1688), who became known as the Great Elector, made it a priority to regain control of Brandenburg and repopulate the city. Protestants expelled from Catholic Austria were welcomed, as were wealthy Jewish families ordered to leave the Austrian capital, Vienna, in 1670. Around the same time, French Protestants (Huguenots) fleeing per-

secution also began to arrive. Other immigrants came from Poland, Holland, Sweden, Switzerland, and Bohemia. By the end of the century, what would from 1710 be known simply as Berlin had a population of 30,000, a third of them Huguenots.

In 1701, Kurfürst Friedrich III (R.1688–1713), whose territories included Prussia to the east, named himself King Friedrich I of Prussia. He opened the purse strings to embellish his now royal capital, financing the rebuilding of the central *Schloss* (palace), the creation of the Friedrichstadt quarters, the *Zeughaus* (armory), and Gendarmenmarkt square. A country palace was built for Queen Sophie Charlotte (1668–1705) and, after her death, named Charlottenburg.

His successor, King Friedrich Wilhelm I (R.1713–1740), curtailed spending on construction and arts (except for the rapid expansion of Potsdam into a second royal residence), concentrating instead on raising a powerful standing army. The soldier-king was, by all accounts, a man of little humor and of odd tastes. His particular obsession was "collecting" unusually tall men *(lange Kerls)* to fill his regiments.

FREDERICK THE GREAT

Friedrich Wilhelm I was not missed by ordinary Berliners, who hoped for less austere times under his son, Friedrich II (R.1740–1786), later known as Friedrich der Grosse (Frederick the Great).

A philosopher-king, Friedrich II enacted a policy of religious tolerance, attracted

The goddess of peace dominates the Brandenburg Gate, but Prussia acquired a warlike reputation under 18th-century ruler Frederick the Great.

French philosophers (such as Voltaire) and artists to his court, banned the most excessive forms of torture, and even dropped censorship for a while. Such freedoms were unheard of in 18th-century Europe.

Friedrich II, known to mouthy Berliners as Der Alte Fritz (Old Fred), was also the warrior-king of a draconian military state. The people of Prussia (and Berlin) were considered not citizens, but subjects whose duty it was to obey their superiors unquestioningly. In the army, it was policy that soldiers should fear their (often brutal) non-commissioned officers more than the enemy. In a series of clashes culminating in the Seven Years' War, which he came within an ace of losing, Friedrich established Prussia as a major military player in Europe.

Friedrich II sought to augment Prussia's population and modernize the state by attracting immigrants from across Europe. At the end of the Seven Years' War in 1763, he expressed the wish: "May the French and Turks populate Berlin." By the time he died in 1786, Berlin had 150,000 inhabitants, a burgeoning arms industry, and thriving cultural life.

Friedrich I proclaimed himself the first king of Prussia in 1701.

REVOLUTION & NAPOLEON

Three years after the death of Friedrich II, the French Revolution rocked Europe. By the time Napoleon Bonaparte (1769–1821) crowned himself emperor of France in 1804, he was at war with much of the continent. After an initial stint in a Europe-wide coalition against France, Prussia opted for neutrality. Having crushed an Austrian-Russian army at Austerlitz in December 1805, Napoleon created a Rhine Federation of occupied German states, modernizing the political and legal structure of these formerly feudal mini-states.

Egged on by the military, Friedrich Wilhelm III (R.1797–1840) demanded in

October 1806 that Napoleon vacate southern Germany. It was just the excuse Napoleon needed. After routing the Prussians at Jena, he entered Berlin on October 27. The Berliners welcomed the French at first, but soon found the cost of occupation onerous: The city would not pay off the debts incurred until 1861.

Napoleon allowed a shrunken Prussian state to remain, but the king had to watch as French-style reforms were pushed through. These included the (theoretical) end of rural serfdom, the creation of city councils, including one for Berlin, and the modernization of the army (though the French kept its numbers limited). Berlin's first council of deputies was elected (by limited suffrage) in 1809.

In 1810, the von Humboldt brothers, Wilhelm and Alexander, intellectuals from a Huguenot family, founded the university that would later take their name on Unter den Linden. In these years of French control came the first stirrings of a pan-German nationalism. Intellectuals and the bourgeoisie began to dream openly of uniting all the German states in a single, free nation.

The dreamers would have to wait. After joining Napoleon in his ill-fated assault on Russia in 1812, Prussia switched sides and began a "War of Liberation" that saw the French ousted from Berlin in 1813. With Napoleon defeated, the Congress of Vienna redrew the map of Europe. Most of the continent returned to the old order, though Prussia gained important territory in western Germany.

RESTORATION & EMPIRE

In Berlin, rulers rolled back the reforms of earlier years and tightened press censorship. The city quickly developed as an industrial hub. It got its first railway line (to Potsdam) in 1838 and by 1870 counted more than one

Prussian guns bombard Paris into submission in 1870. Bismarck's victory in the Franco-Prussian War brought disaster to France and led to the unification of Germany.

thousand factories. The working class grew just as quickly. Chronic housing shortages were solved in 1820 by the creation of *Mietskasernen* (rental barracks), high-density tenements stretching over several inner courtyards. Most of the population lived on starvation wages and conditions in the factories were appalling, so the first major working-class riots in 1830 should have come as no surprise.

In 1848, as in many other European cities, a short-lived revolt was repressed without delicacy. A Prussian parliament (*Landtag*) was created, but within a year a voting system was imposed that concentrated votes and power in the hands of the wealthy, conservative minority.

In 1862, King Wilhelm I (*R.*1861–1888) appointed a chancellor from that parliament. He was a *Junker* (Prussian landed noble) by the name of Otto von Bismarck (1815–1898), whose motto was that the important questions in life could only be settled with "iron and blood." His ambition was a Germany united under Prussia, and he achieved this with breathtaking alacrity using a wily combination of dirty tricks and warfare (against Denmark in 1864, Austria in 1866, and France in 1870). In January 1871, in the Palace of Versailles, Bismarck dictated peace terms (involving hefty reparations payments from Paris) and announced the creation of the German Reich (Empire). All the hitherto independent German states came together under Prussia, with Berlin as capital. King Wilhelm I became Kaiser (Emperor) Wilhelm I.

Four years later, the press took rather less notice of the founding of the Sozialistischen Arbeiterpartei Deutschlands (Socialist Workers Party, or SAP); it became the Sozialdemokratische Partei Deutschlands (SPD) in 1890. Its political program was aimed at defending the interests of the burgeoning proletariat. By the beginning of the 20th century, the SPD would be the most important party in Berlin and a major force throughout Germany.

Berlin, meanwhile, was in the grip of a boom. Now the capital of a united Germany, and with 5 billion gold francs in war reparations due from Paris, it grew rapidly. New factories opened, housing projects blossomed, and land speculation was rife. The first electrically powered city railway lines began to operate and electric street

Kaiser Wilhelm II led Germany to a costly defeat in World War I.

lighting was introduced (although most street lighting remained gas-powered until the 1930s). By the 1880s, Berlin counted 1.5 million inhabitants.

KAISER WILHELM II & WORLD WAR I

The young Kaiser Wilhelm II (*R.*1888–1918) ascended the throne with big plans. He embarked on what he considered a beautification program of the city, adding dozens of monuments and more than 30 new churches in his first 20 years on the throne. One of

these was the Kaiser-Wilhelm-Gedächtnis-kirche, dedicated to the memory of his grandfather, Kaiser Wilhelm I, which gets more attention now as a bombed-out war memorial than it ever did as a church.

The bulk of Berliners thought little of the kaiser's monuments. Their interests lay with other priorities. When one of the founding fathers of the SPD, Paul Singer, died in 1911, his funeral cortege was accompanied by almost a million red-flag-bearing mourners. For several years, Berlin's unionized workers had been campaigning and striking for improved conditions and wages, women's rights, and an end to Kaiser Wilhelm II's saber rattling.

As early as 1905, the kaiser had written to Chancellor Bernhard von Bülow: "First render the Socialists harmless, in a blood-bath if necessary, and then war abroad!" Singer's funeral and the 1912 Reichstag (national lower house of parliament) elections, in which the SPD emerged as the strongest party with 110 seats—in spite of rigged voting regulations—showed that the Socialists were far from "harmless."

On June 28, 1914, the heir to the Austrian throne, Archduke Franz Ferdinand was assassinated. In August, the kaiser launched a war that initially pitted Germany, Austria-Hungary, and Turkey against France, the United Kingdom, and Russia. The Socialists joined the right-wing parties and voted for war credits.

At first, many Berliners enthusiastically greeted the news of war, believing firmly in a quick victory and that the boys would be home by Christmas. But it was only after more than four years of some of the most frightful slaughter humankind had ever witnessed that the war finally ended with Germany's defeat in November 1918. The kaiser abdicated and fled to Holland. Some called for the establishment of a republic; in the confusion, militants of the so-called Spartacist League (a precursor to the German Communist Party) under Karl Liebknecht (1871–1919) took virtual control of Berlin. The SPD under Friedrich Ebert (1871–1925) sent in right-wing para-military Freikorps (Free Corps) troops to put down the Spartacist Revolt in early

1919. The anti-republican troops went a step further, assassinating Liebknecht and the cofounder of the league, Rosa Luxemburg (1871–1919). Their deaths set the tone for the years of tit-for-tat political assassinations that would bloody the streets of Berlin in the coming years.

As Germany struggled with its internal chaos, the Allies dictated drastic peace terms at Versailles in 1919. Enormous reparations, attempt in Berlin in early 1920 was strangled by a general strike. Shortly thereafter, various communist uprisings also took place in Berlin, all bloodily put down.

In 1920, a city law was passed expanding Berlin's municipal boundaries to include independent satellite districts (such as Charlottenburg, Wilmersdorf, Spandau, and Köpenick). This action took the city's total population to just short of four mil-

Karl Liebknecht speaks before his supporters. The militant communist politician was a major force in post–World War I Berlin, but was assassinated by right-wing troops in 1919.

the reduction of the armed forces to 100,000 men, huge territorial losses—in the toughness and humiliation of the peace treaty terms lay the germ of the unimaginable tragedy that would follow.

THE WEIMAR REPUBLIC

In the quiet town of Weimar, a national parliamentary assembly came together and by August 1919 had approved Germany's first parliamentary democratic constitution.

Trouble was never far away in those years. An anti-republican military coup lion (it reached its high point in 1942, with 4.48 million).

The spluttering German economy came close to disintegration under the weight of reparation payments to the Allies. French troops occupied the industrial Ruhr area and the currency collapsed. A U.S. dollar had bought 8.9 Reichsmarks in 1919. By November 1923, one dollar bought 4.2 billion Reichsmarks.

A coalition government under right-wing chancellor Gustav Stresemann (1878–1929) carried out a painful currency reform that wiped out most of the middle class's savings but saved the country from implosion. Reparation payments were rescheduled and foreign (mostly U.S.) loans pumped capital into the economy.

THE GOLDEN TWENTIES

To the Berliners, they were Die Goldenen Zwanziger (The Golden Twenties), that manic period separating the end of the nightmare of World War I, with its immedi-

constitution in place and the worst shocks of the postwar years surmounted, the 1920s, and especially the brief period from 1924 to 1929, saw an unprecedented explosion in all fields of the arts and a flowering of social freedoms.

Artists, poets, and musicians, whether they had been at the front or not, could not accept the old order and cast everything into doubt. Satirical writing flourished as it had never before, with the acid pens of Kurt

Nowhere did the twenties roar more than in the cabarets and bars of interwar Berlin.

ate postwar misery, and the rise of the Nazis in 1933. It was not a period of great prosperity. But after the horrors of World War I, an electric energy rippled through the city, and nothing could be like it was before 1914. With an almost utopian republican

Tucholsky (1890–1935) and Erich Kästner (1899–1974), or the socially critical plays of Bertolt Brecht (1898–1956), leading the way. Max Reinhardt (1873–1943) and Erwin Piscator (1893–1966) animated Berlin's theater and cabaret world with stinging, satirical work. The dada movement and the expressionists painted and formed images of the world and society that sought to tear down ingenuous formalisms. Atonal music, seemingly trying to break free from bourgeois bonds, led the experimental way. German cinema lived its moment of glory.

Where the arts and the people came together most often, perhaps, was in the city's more than one hundred cabarets. Here political satire mixed with saucy entertainment in smoke-filled, steady-drinking bars that spanned the range from

the luxury affairs along Kurfürstendamm (Ku'damm) to the less reputable spots around Friedrichstrasse.

A certain social and sexual emancipation accompanied it all. Hemlines rose and men and women mixed in bars and restaurants as they never had before. That they were eating in restaurants at all was a novelty, but as the economy steadied in 1924,

Berliners seemed to unload all the tension of the previous years.

Berlin soon acquired a name for itself as Europe's anything-goes pleasure palace; it became one of the continent's biggest tourism drawing cards. The city liked to sell itself as the *Stadt der Musik und des Theaters* (city of music and theater), but many came for more dubious pleasures. And come they did. Up to 180,000 foreigners, especially Americans and Britons, visited the city every month. That figure might not seem much by modern standards, but it was a veritable flood at the time.

Some came to party. Sex was no longer as taboo a subject as it had been, and Berlin was seen as a loose town. Homosexuality, while not open, was widespread. The bar scene, including drag-queen shows, was particularly busy around Nollendorf-Platz. It attracted the likes of Anglo-American Christopher Isherwood (1904–1986), who lived just off the square and who later wrote *Goodbye to Berlin*, the novel that would inspire the musical *Cabaret*.

The film not only depicts the manic looseness and nightlife of Berlin of the twenties; it also portrays the growing presence of a dark new force in the city and across the country. The party was soon to be over.

THE THIRD REICH & WORLD WAR II

The fragile social peace came unstuck on October 25, 1929, the day of the Wall Street crash. The effects were felt in Germany almost immediately. By 1930, the unemployed totaled a record half million in Berlin. Protests were again the norm.

In the following years, parliamentary democracy ground to a halt as the crisis led the president, Field Marshal Paul von Hindenburg, to intervene with emergency decrees. The atmosphere led to the rapid rise of extremist parties at both ends of the political spectrum. In Berlin, the Communist Party gained ground at the expense of the SPD. At the September 1930 elections, the previously insignificant, Bavaria-based Nazionalsozialistische Deutsche Arbeiterpartei (National Socialist German

Workers Party: NSDAP, or Nazis), led by an Austrian World War I corporal by the name of Adolf Hitler (1889–1945), won 107 seats. Street fighting between communist militants and the thugs of the Nazi Sturmabteilung (SA, Stormtrooper Department) increased, and Hindenburg, in an effort to bring stability, finally appointed Hitler chancellor on January 30, 1933.

The violence of the brown-shirted SA, years of virulent anti-Jewish campaigning, and the existence of Hitler's political manifesto, *Mein Kampf (My Struggle)*, were all ample signs of the anti-democratic nature of the Nazis, but few could imagine just how far Hitler was prepared to go, including his conservative and moneyed backers.

Under the cover of emergency decrees signed by Hindenburg after the Reichstag was set on fire on February 27, 1933, Hitler grabbed full power. He banned the Communist Party and so created for himself a de facto majority in parliament. Persecution of left-wing opponents began in earnest. In Köpenick alone, 91 were murdered in a week. On March 23, 1933, the Reichstag virtually voted itself out of existence with the Enabling Law, which gave dictatorial powers to Hitler.

This act opened the way to *Gleichschaltung* (literally "bringing into line"). In December 1933, the government banned all political parties but the NSDAP and all trade unions. On April 1, 1934, a total boycott of Jewish shops was declared; on May 10 the Nazis staged the *Bücherverbrennung* (burning of the books) in Opernplatz (Bebelplatz today) and other cities across the country. Books by authors considered perverted or in any way dangerous to the party and state were tossed onto enormous bonfires. On August 1, 1934, Hitler proclaimed himself *Führer* (leader) of the German state. At the same time, he brought a sense of prosperity to Germany with a massive public works program (including steady rearmament) that wiped out unemployment in just three years.

The 1935 Nuremberg race laws, which deprived German Jews of citizenship and most rights, affected about 170,000 Berlin Jews (and as many as 40,000 foreign Jews

resident in the city). By 1939, about half the city's Jewish population had fled, leaving behind all their property, taken by the state as an "emigration tax." On the night of November 9, 1938, in what came to be known as *Kristallnacht* (night of broken glass), SA troopers in civilian clothing destroyed synagogues, shops, offices, houses, and other Jewish properties across the city and around Germany. In the war years to come, 50,000 Berlin Jews would be deported to concentration camps, where at least two-thirds perished. In June 1943, a report declared Berlin to be *judenfrei* (free of Jews).

Hitler's foreign policy aims were becoming clear by 1935. By the time he announced the invasion of Poland on September 1, 1939, he had already reoccupied the demilitarized Rhineland (1936), absorbed Austria

and the Czech Sudetenland (1938), and occupied Prague (1939), all without having fired a shot.

Public reaction in Berlin to the start of hostilities in Poland had been muted, but the military parade beneath the Brandenburger Tor in the summer of 1940, after Hitler's lightning victories in a few short months over Denmark, Norway, Holland, Belgium, and France, was greeted with greater enthusiasm.

Until 1943, Berlin remained largely unscathed by the war. From that point on, however, Allied bombing raids increased in intensity. By the end of the war, some 50,000 civilians had died in more than 360 air raids. Starting in November 1943, the government evacuated up to one million civilians to "safe areas," some located in

Hitler's gift for rousing oratory helped him to power in 1933.

occupied Poland and Czechoslovakia.

By the time Hitler returned to Berlin from the Eastern Front on January 16, 1945, most people could see that the war was lost. Berliners working in munitions factories around the city put in 60-hour weeks on increasingly tight rations. All the city's parks had been cleared of trees and turned into fields of potato and cabbage crops.

The final Soviet assault on Berlin, with three armies totaling 1.5 million men, began on April 16, 1945. By April 25 the city was encircled; it finally surrendered to the Soviets two days after Hitler committed suicide in his *Führerbunker* on April 30. Soviet troops celebrated with days of raping and looting throughout the ruined city. On May 8, German forces signed an unconditional surrender in the Berlin suburb of Karlshorst, where the Soviets had set up their headquarters.

More than half of Berlin's buildings had been destroyed in the fighting, as well as a third of its industry. The population stood at about 2.5 million. In all, more than 120,000 Berliners had lost their lives in air raids and the final battle.

THE CITY DIVIDED

Soviet-occupied Berlin was a smoldering ruin, but the Berliners were soon working to get basic services running again. The U-Bahn (*Untergrundbahn*, or subway) was running again on May 14, and six days later the first trams were operating. On May 26, the Berlin Philharmoniker gave its first free concert. On June 10, political parties with anti-fascist credentials were allowed to begin their activities again.

Five days earlier, the Allies had agreed to divide the country into four occupied sectors (American, British, French, and Soviet). Significantly, the Soviets picked up large tracts of eastern Germany (western Saxony, Thuringia, and Mecklenburg) in exchange for the division of Soviet-occupied Berlin into four Allied sectors. By mid-August, U.S., British, and French troops had arrived in Berlin. It is tempting to speculate that a separate East German state might never have arisen in the following years had the western Allies not ceded those territories.

At war's end, as much as two-thirds of the population in Berlin was women. They set about clearing more than 2.6 billion cubic feet (75 million cu m) of rubble in

A neighborhood just south of Potsdamer Platz lies in ruins after six years of war. Allied bombing and street fighting in 1945 destroyed more than half of Berlin's buildings.

German children greet an Allied transport plane during the 1948 Soviet blockade of Berlin. During the height of the blockade, an Allied plane landed with supplies every 90 seconds.

the city center, becoming known as *Trümmerfrauen* (rubble women). Rations were scarce and considerable resources went to the occupying Soviet forces. In the western sectors the black market flourished, with Allied soldiers exchanging supplies for anything from jewels to sex (despite an initial strict nonfraternization policy). Prostitution and street crime soared. To top it off, the winter of 1946 was one of the coldest on record.

The fighting had not finished when Walter Ulbricht (1893–1973) and other German communist comrades were flown in from Moscow to set up a German administration. In April 1946, these authorities attempted to force the two main parties in Berlin, the resurrected SPD and the Stalinist KPD (Kommunistische Partei Deutschlands) to fuse into one, the Sozialistische Einheitspartei Deutschlands (German Socialist Unity Party, or SED). SPD members opposed the fusion; some were arrested and tortured for their trouble by Soviet secret police. In the first free city-wide elections to be held after the war, in October 1946, the rump SPD (in the western Allied occupied sector of the city) won

48.7 percent of the vote, with the SED trailing behind with 19.8 percent.

The Soviets and western Allies were soon at loggerheads. When SPD leader Ernst Reuter (1889–1953) was elected mayor of Berlin in 1947, the Soviets blocked his nomination (he finally became mayor of West Berlin in 1948). As cooperation between the Soviets and western Allies faltered, so the divisions between east and west deepened. In 1948, the Allies introduced a new currency (the *Deutsche Mark,* or D-Mark) in the western zones and prepared the way for the creation of a German government in their zones. The Soviets reacted by creating an East German mark *(Ostmark);* in late June 1948 they imposed a blockade on West Berlin. The Allies circumvented this with an air bridge, ferrying in vital supplies around the clock until the blockade was lifted in May of the following year (see p. 184).

Under the circumstances, the division of Germany was inevitable. In 1949, the three western sectors became the Federal Republic of Germany (FRG), while the Soviet sector became the German Democratic Republic (GDR), headed by

SED party boss Ulbricht. Fatefully for Berlin, the western half shifted its capital to Bonn, inducing many industries to shut down and head west too. East Berlin was worse off still. More heavily bombed than the western half of the city, it had lost virtually all its industry—dismantled and shifted to the U.S.S.R. in lieu of official reparations.

On June 17, 1953, massive strikes and violent protests in East Berlin against the communist regime were put down by Soviet tanks, costing more than 250 lives. Playwright Bertolt Brecht, who lived in East Berlin, wrote that the East German government had distributed leaflets after the June 17 rising "in which you could read that the people had lost the government's confidence…. Would it in that case not be simpler if the government dissolved the people and elected another?"

Whether out of dislike for the Soviet-backed SED government or simply because life was clearly harder in East Germany, many East Germans streamed westward, half of them through Berlin, where it was easy to move between the Soviet and Allied sectors. West Berlin itself was becoming an attractive option. The West German government pumped billions of D-Marks (DM) into the city. From 1945 to the summer of 1961, 2.7 million Germans fled from east to west. More than 200,000 made the move in just the first six months of 1961. On August 12 of that year, the East German People's Army closed all but 12 of the 80 sector crossing points and began to build what soon became a nearly impenetrable wall around West Berlin. Patrols had orders to shoot to kill anyone trying to cross.

West Berlin's SPD mayor from 1957 to 1964, Willy Brandt (1913–1992), kept the lines of communication open with the East Berlin authorities, procuring permission for West Berliners to make brief visits to the east side in late 1963. As West German chancellor (1969–1974), Brandt went further with his *Ostpolitik* (eastern policy), managing to sign various agreements with East Germany's Erich Honecker (1912–1994), in power since 1971, to ease travel restrictions from west to east. In the other direction, access was restricted for all but

senior citizens and the disabled.

By 1980, traffic into East Berlin from West Berlin was fully regulated. Foreigners could visit on a day visa that expired at midnight. Compulsory exchange of DM25 at a one-for-one rate (the real exchange rate was more like ten East German marks for DM1) represented a source of hard currency for the East German government.

The two Berlins could not have looked any different. Even in the 1980s, many of the surviving historic buildings in East Berlin had been left more or less as they were in 1945. Austere apartment buildings had gone up in much of the city. Traffic was almost nonexistent, consisting of locally produced Wartburg and Trabant cars. Soldiers patrolled quiet streets in which nightlife was anything but scintillating. It was a gray city.

The bright lights of West Berlin presented a rather different picture. The Ku'damm had become the city's center, lined with shops, restaurants, and bars. Nearby Bahnhof Zoologischer Garten won an unhappy reputation as a hangout for the city's young heroin addicts, many of whom resorted to street prostitution to survive.

Life in Berlin could be surreal. Every day, West Berlin commuters on U-Bahn lines that passed below East Berlin would glide through dimly-lit "ghost stations," patrolled by heavily armed East German soldiers, on their way to work. No one could have imagined what was in the offing.

BERLIN REUNITED

If Honecker and his SED party pals could have done anything about it, the status quo would have remained indefinitely. But events were moving beyond their control. The arrival of reformer Mikhail Gorbachev (born 1931) to power in the U.S.S.R. in 1985 marked a significant change. Poland and Hungary were also beginning to loosen their Communist Party shackles. For the GDR, the real trouble came from Hungary, which in May 1989 opened its border to Austria, allowing a limited number of East Germans to cross to the West.

An East German border guard greets a West Berliner atop the Berlin Wall in 1989.

The situation snowballed in the following months, with East Germans streaming into Hungary and taking refuge in West German embassies in various East European capitals. At home, a protest movement quickly gained momentum. On November 4, half a million people demonstrated against the communist government in Alexanderplatz. Overtaken by events and with no help coming from Moscow, the East German government tried to ingratiate itself with its people by announcing on November 9, 1989, that East Germans could travel freely to the West.

Incredulous, the first Berliners crossed the wall into West Berlin that evening. What started as a trickle of visitors turned into a flood, and spontaneous parties erupted at Brandenburger Tor, where West and East Berliners came together. The first breaches were hacked into the wall on November 10. On November 11 and 12, an incredible 2.7 million exit visas were issued at East Berlin checkpoints. *Die Wende* ("the change") had begun.

From the fall of the wall, it was a surprisingly short step to the collapse of the East German state. Conservative West German chancellor Helmut Kohl (born 1930 and in power since 1982) declared that his aim was a united Germany. As East Germans visited the western half of the country and realized how much better off their western cousins were, the idea of maintaining a separate, socialist state quickly lost attractiveness for most of them. Making what proved to be imprudent promises of a prosperous future just around the corner, Kohl moved to accel-

Berlin celebrates its multiculturalism with the annual Karneval der Kulturen (carnival of cultures) in Kreuzberg.

on *Wessis* (West Germans) created ill feeling toward *Ossis* (East Germans). Easterners felt increasingly patronized by the better-off Westerners. They resented long-lasting differences in pay and job opportunities.

Unemployment in both sides of the city rose as heavy industry and unprofitable businesses in former East Berlin went belly up. With the wall gone, tourism to Berlin declined sharply. And people began to vote with their feet. Berlin's city administration made much of the fact that, in 2005, for the first time since reunification, the city's population of 3.45 million did not decrease.

All the while, city and federal governments, together with private enterprise, have poured money into Berlin. Aside from the huge task of linking the two halves of city (including transportation, utilities, and administration), billions have been spent on the restoration of old landmarks and the creation of new ones. A who's who of local and international architects has had a field day in Berlin, for years described as the biggest construction site in Europe.

In the process, the city has gone deep into the red. The unexpectedly high economic and social costs of unification (around 600 billion dollars was spent on modernizing East German industry and business from 1990 to 2000) have sharply dented Germany's economy since the early 1990s. Unemployment remains at 18 percent in the former East Germany (and Berlin), an area that still soaks up around 70 billion euros in federal subsidies a year. Many of the region's disillusioned young are heading west.

On the other hand, a stream of creative people is pouring into the capital from around Germany and the rest of Europe. Drawn by Berlin's vibrant and uninhibited cultural scene, they are helping to propel the city to the forefront of European capitals. In terms of annual visitors, Berlin has leapt into third spot behind London and Paris. It is a rough diamond, but glittering nonetheless. ■

erate the process. Elections in March 1990 in East Germany brought victory for Kohl's CDU (Christian Democratic Union) party. By July, both governments had agreed upon a unified currency and political union. In September, the four World War II allies ended formal occupation of Germany (with the last troops leaving Berlin in September 1994). On October 3, administrative unity in the city was restored and the following year the German national parliament *(Bundestag)* decided to make Berlin the capital. The Bundestag moved to the imaginatively renovated Reichstag building in April 1999.

After the initial partying, reality set in. The huge national subsidies that had long propped up West Berlin were gradually dropped. Special unification taxes imposed

The ingredients for many a meal come from markets like this one at **Winterfeldplatz.**

Food & drink

ASK A BERLINER WHAT THE CITY'S GREATEST CONTRIBUTION TO WORLD cuisine is, and you may well be told: *Currywurst*. Germans just love a snack of *Wurst* (sausage) with *eine Portion Pommes* (a serving of fries). Berlin's specialty is this lightly spicy sausage bathed in a tangy sauce; just about any *Imbiss* (snack stand) will serve this treat up, along with a variety of other sausage options. Bratwurst (grilled sausage with ketchup or mustard) is another universal German favorite.

You don't have to live on sausages and fries, however. In the days of the wall, Berlin's culinary reputation was not the stuff of Michelin stars, but things have changed. Top chefs are at work in Berlin (now home to nine Michelin-star restaurants). Leading the way (and reestablishing a pre–World War II tradition) is the Lorenz Adlon restaurant in the resurrected Hotel Adlon on Pariser Platz, considered one of the best eateries in the capital. With thousands of options, eating in Berlin is a treat.

International cuisine abounds, servings are generous, and prices reasonable. Of all the world cuisines on offer, the most deeply rooted in Berlin is Turkish. The big Turkish population introduced *döner* (meat slow-grilled on a vertical rotating spit) to Berlin

palates in the 1970s, and these filling rolls jammed with meat, salad, and spices are nowadays as popular as Wurst.

Traditional German cooking has a reputation for being heavy, and Berlin's specialties are no exception. Local food is meaty and hearty and, while you may not want to indulge every night, it is worth trying some authentic dishes.

Boulette (or *Bulette*) is a kind of meatball, usually served with mixed vegetables and a shot of mustard. Order a serving of *Berliner Eisbein* (pork knuckle) and you'll be in for a shock. What seems like a whole leg of corned-beef-style meat will appear, on the bone and covered by the skin (which you don't eat). It comes with sauerkraut and, sometimes, mashed peas. *Kalbsleber Berliner*

Art (calf liver, served with, say, glazed onions and oven-cooked apple) is another classic. Much beloved are the variations on veal that generally come from southern Germany. *Kalbsgeschnetzeltes* is sliced, breaded, and fried (similar to Wiener Schnitzel) and best served in a hearty mushroom sauce. Popular national dishes include *Kassler Rippen,* a feast of sliced smoked pork rib meat with a vaguely hammy flavor.

Pork dominates traditional menus, but things change in mid-November when the Feast of St. Martin arrives. This means goose feasts. Such a banquet might involve a cooked goose with sauce, trimmings, and a bottle of red wine for around €50 a head.

Beer is the Berliner's tipple of choice. The city once teemed with breweries. Several local lagers, such as Berliner Kindl, continue to keep the after-hours conversations well oiled. The local specialty is *Berliner Weisser mit Schuss* (Berliner White with a shot). The shot is raspberry (red) or woodruff (green) syrup.

Many locals prefer a good *Weizenbier* (wheat beer that can be *Hefe,* yeasty, or *Kristall,* filtered). You can order it *hell* (light) or *dunkel* (dark). A weightier option is a *Schwarzbier,* a dark, porterlike ale. Light and refreshing is *Weinschorle,* a glass of white wine with sparkling water, or the nonalcoholic *Apfelsaftschorle* (apple juice with same).

Marzipan pigs reflect the German fondness for pork in all its guises.

Dessert plays a big role in German eating. You should not leave Berlin without indulging in a chunky slice of *Apfelstrudel* (apple pie), preferably drowned in dollops of vanilla sauce. Berlin's most famous pastry, a jam-filled donut, is known worldwide as a Berliner—but ask for a Berliner in Berlin and you will be stared at blankly, as here it is called a *Pfannkuchen* (literally "pancake").

Remember to save room for brunch. On weekends in particular, cafés and restaurants around the city feature set-price, all-you-can-eat buffet brunches over which locals will linger for hours.

Most restaurants offer a varied international wine list, but it is possible (and worthwhile) to try wines from closer to home. The nearest decent winemaking area is in Saxony, Germany's smallest and most northerly wine region. Both whites and reds are produced here along a 34-mile (55 km) strip of the Elbe River from Diesbar-Seusslitz to the Czech border. Output is dominated by the Müller-Thurgau (20 percent of production) and Riesling (15 percent) varieties. Among the reds, the dry Grauburgunder (Pinot Grigio) is popular; the fruitier Ruländer is harder to come by. ∎

The arts

BERLIN BEGAN TO REGISTER ON THE EUROPEAN MAP OF THE ARTS IN THE Age of Enlightenment. By the 19th century, the rapidly growing metropolis acted as a magnet for writers, artists, musicians, and thinkers from all over Germany. But it was amid the chaos of the Weimar Republic that the city reached its creative apogee in literature, film, theater, music, and painting. Today Berlin again seethes with activity. Most visible in the breadth of its daring new architecture, the artistic renaissance is equally dramatic in the city's theaters, literary circles, and art galleries. The numbers alone speak volumes: In Berlin there are 3 opera houses, about 150 theaters, 175 museums, and 300 art galleries. The city is reinventing itself in a fashion barely even imaginable in any other Western capital, and in the process fostering an electrifying creative dynamism.

ARCHITECTURE

Until the 18th century, Berlin was rarely thought of as more than a fairly grubby, unprepossessing town. Since then, the city has shed its skin several times, most spectacularly in the energetic years since its reunification.

Little remains to remind us of the first five centuries of Berlin's existence. Most of what you see standing in central Berlin was built after World War II. Among the oldest standing

buildings in Berlin are those of the central Nikolaikirche (with tapering 19th-century twin towers) and Heilig-Geist-Kapelle, both churches built around the late 13th century. The slightly later Marienkirche and Klosterkirche (the latter left in its ruined wartime state) are also Gothic churches, typical of north Germany. Renaissance reminders come in Spandau's Zitadelle fort and, to a lesser extent, the Jagdschloss Grunewald.

The first wave of serious building came with Great Elector Friedrich Wilhelm. His master architects embellished his capital, largely in a sober baroque style. Dutchman Johann Arnold Nering (1659–1695) designed the Zeughaus (armory) on Unter den Linden. Hamburg-born Andreas Schlüter (1660–1714) decorated its internal courtyard and designed the heart of the nearby Berliner Schloss, the

central royal residence (demolished after World War II). The Swede Johann Friedrich Eosander von Göthe (1669–1728) and Parisian Huguenot Jean de Bodt (1670–1745) were among Schlüter's competitors. Eosander had a major hand in Schloss Charlottenburg and de Bodt completed the Zeughaus. Shortly after, Gendarmenmarkt was graced with the Französischer Dom and Deutscher Dom churches.

The next building spurt came under Friedrich II, who dreamed of a rococo Forum Fridericianum along Unter den Linden. Under architect Georg Wenzeslaus von Knobelsdorff (1699–1753), various elements of Friedrich's plan were carried out, among them the Staatsoper, Altes Palais, and Sankt-Hedwig-Kathedrale. His greatest work was, however, the Schloss Sanssouci, a jewel of Prussian rococo, in Potsdam. If baroque was a sensuous outgrowth of the sterner, clean-lined Renaissance, rococo was baroque on a sugary high, all swirls and curls, best admired in the palaces of Schloss Sanssouci.

The prolific Karl Friedrich Schinkel (1781–1841) and his students, especially Friedrich August Stüler (1800–1865) dominated the first half of the 19th century. Schinkel's Neue Wache and Altes Museum are masterpieces of neoclassicism, which represents a return to a more sober style. Stüler designed the temple-like Alte Nationalgalerie and Matthäuskirche. The century closed on what might be considered a fanciful note, with buildings such as the Reichstag and Berliner Dom built in grandiose (even bombastic) neo-Renaissance form.

Major undertakings were not the order of the day in the cash-strapped postwar Weimar Republic. Nevertheless, the infectiously creative spirit of the city spilled over into individual building projects, often well in advance of their time. The Shell-Haus just south of Tiergarten remains a telling example, as is the Hufeisensiedlung, a horseshoe-shaped residential project in the Neukölln District, designed in part by the city's town planner, Martin Wagner (1885–1957). Wagner attracted a flock of avant-garde architects, such as

The late 19th-century Berliner Dom is a salute to the Italian High Renaissance.

the founder of the Bauhaus movement, Berlin-born Walter Gropius (1883–1969), and Ludwig Mies van der Rohe (1886–1969), to the city. They and others dedicated most of their efforts to residential and industrial projects. Berlin's best example of Bauhaus, the Bauhaus Archiv, was built in 1976 to 1979 to a Gropius design meant for another city.

The Nazis brought a monumental approach to city architecture and, largely under the direction of Albert Speer (1905–1981), Hitler's favorite architect, added buildings designed to last centuries and make impressive ruins. They cooked up plans to tear up much of Berlin and build the *Welthauptstadt Germania* (World Capital Germania). Two axes, one east-west from the Brandenburger Tor to Charlottenburger Tor and the other north-south from the Reichstag to Tempelhof airport, would define the core of this thousand-year capital.

An imposing but austere style marked those buildings completed, especially Hitler's New Reich Chancellery. Major reminders of the Nazi period include the 1936 Olympiastadion, the former Aviation Ministry (nowadays the Finance Ministry), and Tempelhof.

Massive destruction during World War II gave the city an unwelcome opportunity to embark on new architectural adventures. In East Berlin, Hermann Henselmann (1905–1995) dominated the scene and was responsible for the city's highest structure, the Fernsehturm (TV tower), as well as the master plan for the showcase boulevard, Stalinallee (now Karl-Marx-Allee). For much of the city's rebuilding, ugly *Plattenbau* (prefabricated concrete slabs) were used.

Meanwhile, West Berlin was preoccupied with residential construction, but had room for modern monuments, too. In the center, key postwar buildings are Mies van der Rohe's Neue Nationalgalerie and the Philharmonie designed by Hans Scharoun (1893–1972).

Reunification in 1989 was the starting shot for a race to sew the wounded city back together. For a look at what has been built and a glimpse into the future, see pp. 122–23.

PAINTING & SCULPTURE
Berlin was late off the starting blocks in the visual arts, but you would hardly know that

today. Berlin is where the heart of Germany's art beats loudest. Between its grand collections of everything from old masters to Picasso and its thriving contemporary scene, Berlin is the place to be.

When Prussian king Friedrich I decided to embellish his now royal city at the outset of the 18th century, Berlin was a provincial backwater. Nearby Dresden, thanks to the extravagant art acquisitions of its ruler, Augustus the Strong (R.1694–1733), was just one of many European cities that eclipsed Berlin.

Architect Andreas Schlüter was also a gifted sculptor; he created the statue (restored after World War II) of the Great Elector Friedrich Wilhelm that now stands in front of Schloss Charlottenburg. Friedrich I had Antoine Pesne

(1683–1757) brought from France as court painter in 1711. A master of frescoes, he dominated Berlin's artistic development in the first half of the 18th century. Some of his paintings can be seen in the Gemäldegalerie.

Nineteenth-century Berlin was dominated by its sculptors, among them Johann Gottfried Schadow (1764–1850), known for his classicist Quadriga sculpture atop the Brandenburger Tor (which had to be remade from scratch after World War II), and Christian Daniel Rauch (1777–1857), who produced the equestrian statue of Friedrich II on Unter den Linden. Other works by both can be seen in the Friedrichwerdersche Kirche. Reinhold Begas (1831–1911) made the statue of Friedrich Schiller in Gendarmenmarkt

The brilliance of Berlin's cinematic glory years unfolds before visitors at the modern Filmmuseum Berlin in the Sony Center.

square and the Neptune fountain by the Marienkirche in Alexanderplatz.

In painting, Berlin failed to shake off its academic provincialism. Schinkel was a capable landscape artist, and we owe a debt to Eduard Gärtner (1801–1877) for his prolific production of Berlin panoramas. Adolph Menzel (1815–1905), who tended toward realism, dominated the latter half of the century. Cottbus-born romantic painter Carl Blechen (1798–1840) concentrated on landscapes and indeed was professor of landscape painting at the Berliner Akademie.

Kaiser Wilhelm II rather fancied himself an art critic. As far as he was concerned, the work of Berliner Max Liebermann (1847–1935) or Norway's Edvard Munch (1863–1944) was "gutter art." To combat such official rejection, Liebermann, who became one of Germany's leading impressionists and

A 1913 oil-on-canvas portrait of author Gerhart Hauptmann painted by his friend, Berlin artist Max Liebermann

head of the Prussian Art Academy in 1920 (resigning in 1933 after the Nazis came to power), launched the Berliner Secession of contemporary artists in 1898. Leading artists to join included Lovis Corinth (1858–1925) and Käthe Kollwitz (1867–1945), one of Germany's finest expressionists.

The horrors of World War I produced radical reactions in Berlin art. The first was the outlandish dada movement (which had started in Zurich). Its leading painter was Berlin's George Grosz (1893–1959), who later went on to lead the Neue Sachlichkeit (New

Objectivity) movement and some of whose works can be seen in the Neue National-galerie's collections. Dada's key message was the wholesale rejection of convention, in society and art. It favored an anarchic approach, in which collage and montage were favored and subjects were deliberately provocative.

Dada quickly fizzled and the 1920s were dominated by expressionists, whose art was dedicated to the expression of emotion rather than strict realism. They included Otto Dix (1891–1969), who is also identified with Neue Sachlichkeit, Max Beckmann (1884–1950), and Ernst Ludwig Kirchner (1880–1938). The latter was a leading light in the Brücke art movement, to which a museum is now dedicated. They were abetted by a bevy of foreign artists, notably Wassily Kandinsky (1866–1944), Paul Klee (1879–1940), and Marc Chagall (1887–1985). The first two were leading figures of the Bauhaus movement.

To the Nazis, most of this was *entartete Kunst* (degenerate art). Their arrival in power in 1933 put an almost immediate stop to the artistic ferment in Berlin.

The post–World War II years saw realist painter Karl Hofer (1878–1955) squaring off against what he saw as the self-indulgent abstract artists of the West Berlin Zone 5 group, which included Hans Thiemann (1910–1977) and Heinz Trökes (1913–1997). Werner Heldt (1904–1954) was the artist of ruined Berlin, combining realism with an expressionistic twist in, for instance, his "Berlin am Meer" ("Berlin at the Seaside") series.

East Berlin artists who managed to carve a path away from imposed socialist norms include Harald Metzkes (born 1929) and Manfred Böttcher (born 1931), part of the Berlin school. In the 1970s and 1980s, an artistic subculture evolved in semi-legal galleries in Prenzlauer Berg, which showed artists whose individualistic work clashed with the ruling ideology's concepts of real socialist art. In West Berlin, the focal point of creativity, a potpourri of conflicting movements and styles, shifted to Kreuzberg. The experimental sculptures of Bernhard Heiliger (1915–1995) are a feature of Berlin life. Several remain scattered around the city's public spaces today, such as his bronze "Die Flamme" ("The Flame") on Ernst-Reuter-Platz or his iron

"Echo I" and "Echo II" at the Philharmonie.

Today, a dynamic contemporary scene in the reunited capital keeps a plethora of small, precarious galleries (especially in Prenzlauer Berg and Mitte) in business, with a restless local populace of artists hard at work.

LITERATURE

Berlin's literary career started with the Enlightenment. Friedrich II, who declared himself the "first servant" of the state, was attracted by the musings and writings of French thinkers like Voltaire (1694–1778), who spent some time at the court in Berlin.

Friedrich had little time for his own subjects' writings. Towering above the rest of Berlin's writers was Gotthold Ephraim Lessing (1729–1781), whose classic play *Minna von Barnhelm* was a box-office hit in Berlin theaters and despised by the king.

The Romantic period in the early 19th century that followed the Enlightenment saw myriad poets working in Berlin. They included Heinrich von Kleist (1777–1811), whose work won little favor in his lifetime and who died in a suicide pact with his lover on the Wannsee shore near Potsdam; Joachim Ludwig Achim von Arnim (1781–1831); and Clemens Brentano (1778–1842). Ernest Theodor Amadeus Hoffmann (1776–1822) penned stories rich in fantasy.

The post-Napoleonic restoration managed to muzzle Berlin's literary scene. Alone, Adolf Glasbrenner (1810–1876), a cheeky pamphleteer, regaled Berliners with sparkling prose in his reviews and fell frequent victim to censorship. The tail end of the 19th century was dominated by two quite different figures. Theodor Fontane (1819–1898) wrote a series of grand novels (among them *Effi Briest*) depicting the strictures of bourgeois Berlin society. Gerhart Hauptmann (1862–1946) caused upheaval with his social drama, encapsulated in *Die Weber (The Weavers)*, a play about the misery of Silesian weavers. Kaiser Wilhelm II canceled his box at the Deutsches Theater when the play premiered there in 1894.

Berlin reached a peak of literary genius in the 1920s. The manic interwar capital was a magnet for writers, thinkers, and charlatans from all over Germany and beyond.

Alfred Döblin (1878–1957), by trade a doctor, wrote the quintessential (if opaque) Berlin novel with *Berlin Alexanderplatz,* the story of a released jailbird, Franz Biberkopf, trying to make good. Heinrich Mann (1871–1950), Lübeck-born brother of Thomas and a diehard anti-Nazi, penned one of the most biting satires of German society, *Der Untertan (The Subject)* in 1919. Dresden-born Erich Kästner also poured forth volumes of mostly satirical poetry. He later watched as his

Playwright Bertolt Brecht chose to live in East Berlin, becoming one of the icons of modern German and European theater.

books were burned in Bebelplatz in 1933. The plays of Bertolt Brecht, who staged *Die Dreigroschenoper (Threepenny Opera)* in the 1920s, were laced with social criticism. He continued to write during a 15-year exile and became an icon in 1950s East Germany, where he founded the Berliner Ensemble theater.

Brecht was the greatest figure writing in immediate postwar Berlin. On the eastern side, party control made it difficult for writers who did not toe the line to prosper. One of the best who did was (and remains) Christa Wolf (born 1929), whose novel *Der Geteilte Himmel (Divided Heaven)* was the first in a line that dealt with the hopes and realities of living in communist Germany. That the reality

Writer Günter Grass towered over the literary scene in postwar West Berlin.

was not always pleasant was demonstrated by the fate of rambunctious singer-songwriter Wolf Biermann (born 1936). In 1953 he moved to East Berlin on ideological grounds but in 1976 was stripped of East German citizenship because of his regime-critical lyrics.

West Berlin's literary life was long dominated by Günter Grass (born 1927). His novels include the powerful *Die Blechtrommel* (*The Tin Drum,* 1959). In it the hypocrisy and horrors of the Nazi years and postwar West Germany are seen through the honest eyes of a man with the mind of a child.

At the dawn of the new century, the writer of the moment is Moscow-born Wladimir Kaminer (born 1967), whose *Russendisko, Karaoke,* and *Schönhauser Allee* are all set in the capital. Foreign writers have also used Berlin as a backdrop. A Cold War classic is John Le Carré's (born 1931) 1963 thriller *The Spy Who Came In from the Cold.* More recent is Ian McEwan's (born 1948) *The Innocent,* another twisting Cold War tale. Edinburgh-born Philip Kerr (born 1956) has written countless detective novels, among them the Berlin Noir trilogy. The city's Turkish community is beginning to make itself heard, too, with writers like Emine Sevgi Özdamar (born

1946) and Yadé Kara (born 1965). Kara's *Selam Berlin* has a Turkish perspective on the changes in Berlin since the wall came down.

CINEMA

Had history taken another turn, the mecca of global filmmaking might have been Babelsberg. The 1920s was a period of deep political and social unrest in Germany, but in that cauldron was born some of the greatest cinema of the day. Classics, from *The Blue Angel* to *Metropolis,* are as admired today as they were then.

In the late 1890s, film houses began to spring up along Friedrichstrasse, but things got serious when the Deutsche Bioskop company set up film studios in Babelsberg, near Potsdam, in 1911. Taken over by Universum Film AG (UFA) after World War I, it was Europe's leading film production center and second only to Hollywood. Stars of the 1920s included Swedish actresses Greta Garbo (1905–1990) and Zarah Leander (1907–1981), Emil Jannings (1884–1950), and the Danish-born superstar, Asta Nielsen (1881–1972).

Among UFA's masterpieces was *Das Kabinett des Dr. Caligari* (*The Cabinet of Dr. Caligari,* 1919–1920), a hallucinatory horror story by Robert Wiene that still mesmerizes audiences. Others followed, such as Ernst Lubitsch's *Madame Dubarry* (1919) and Friedrich Wilhelm Murnau's *Nosferatu* (1922) and *Der Letzte Mann* (*The Last Man,* 1924), a psychological drama. Fritz Lang's (1890–1976) futuristic fantasy *Metropolis* (1926) was UFA's biggest attempt to outdo Hollywood, with a suitably dark, German Gothic touch. It was restored, edited, and brought out with a modern soundtrack in 1987. Lang was back with plenty of twisted social and psychological drama in *M–Eine Stadt Sucht einen Mörder* (1931), a thriller known simply as *M* in English and starring the inimitable Peter Lorre. Berlin-born Marlene Dietrich (1901–1992) got her big break with *Der Blaue Engel* (*The Blue Angel,* 1930), based on Heinrich Mann's 1905 novel *Professor Unrat* and directed by Josef von Sternberg (1894–1969). Dietrich plays a nightclub star who seduces

and destroys a schoolteacher. Von Sternberg shot German and English versions of the film simultaneously.

The heady pre-Hitler years in Berlin, a mix of bubbling creativity, louche nightlife, and political violence, were captured years later in the film musical *Cabaret* (1972), starring Liza Minnelli (born 1946).

Moviemakers in California didn't have to deal with the economic and political chaos that assailed Germany; in the early 1920s, talent had already started to slip away from Babelsberg. Directors Erich von Stroheim (1885–1957) and Lubitsch were among the first to flee to Hollywood, followed by Jannings, Murnau (both in 1926), and von Sternberg (1930). Dietrich packed her bags the following year. The rise of the Nazis to power in 1933 turned the trickle into a flood. Polish-born Billy Wilder (1906–2002), for instance, who had lived in Berlin since 1926,

Fritz Lang stunned audiences in 1926 with *Metropolis,* his disturbing futuristic fantasy film.

fled to Paris and then the United States. There he became known for such classics as *A Foreign Affair* (1948), which he shot amid the ruins of postwar Berlin, *The Seven Year Itch* (1955), and *Some Like It Hot* (1959).

The arrival of the Nazis sounded a sudden, if temporary, death knell for German film-making. Much of Babelsberg production in this period ranged from crude propaganda to technically brilliant propaganda. *Der Triumph des Willens* (*The Triumph of the Will*, 1934) and two films on the 1936 Olympic Games by

government came to exercise full control over most aspects of East German cultural life, some promising films were produced. Among them was Wolfgang Staudte's (1906–1984) *Die Mörder sind unter uns* (*The Murderers Are among Us*, 1946), which was Germany's first postwar film. This DEFA production tells the story of a doctor who returns home to a Berlin in ruins and encounters an officer who had ordered the execution of innocent hostages. It tackled the Nazi issue openly and predated a long phase in the 1950s and 1960s

2003's *Good Bye, Lenin!* takes a lighthearted look at East Berliners' adjustment to reunification.

Berlin-born Leni Riefenstahl (1902–2003) were masterpieces of the latter. The first captured the atmosphere of Hitler's carefully orchestrated sixth party congress rallies at Nuremberg, winning the gold medal at the 1937 universal exposition in Paris. The Olympics films were also brilliantly executed and won an award from the International Olympic Committee in 1939.

The postwar division of Berlin led to a split film industry. The East Germans eventually took over Babelsberg. Under the umbrella of the DEFA film institute, they churned out a steady diet of mostly party-loyal, but occasionally good-quality, drama. It was not all bleak and, in the early years before the central

when the issue was not discussed.

In the West, the center of production migrated to Munich and Hamburg, although some of Germany's most creative directors worked in West Berlin (and in some cases continue to work in the now united city). Among them were Wim Wenders (born 1945), Rainer Werner Fassbinder (1945–1982), Volker Schlöndorff (born 1939), and Werner Herzog (born 1942). Overall, however, Berlin has struggled to get back onto the cinema map, except as host to the Berlinale, the city's prestigious annual film festival, held in February.

Postwar Berlin has been a lead player in several key films. Italy's Roberto Rossellini

(1906–1977) made use of destroyed Berlin as a set for his moving *Germania, Anno Zero* (*Germany, Year Zero*, 1948), a masterpiece of black-and-white Italian neorealism. Wenders's ethereal *Der Himmel über Berlin* (*Wings of Desire*, 1987) placed, for a moment, both German cinema and the city center stage. Bruno Ganz (born 1941) and Otto Sander (born 1941) star as two good-natured angels posted to Berlin. They range across the city, listening in to the lives of mortals and, in the case of Ganz, falling in love with one of them.

A delightful farce, *Good Bye, Lenin!* (2003) by Wolfgang Becker (born 1954), managed the trick of dealing compassionately with the trials of adjustment for East Berliners at the time of reunification. Altogether different is Fatih Akin's (born 1973) *Gegen die Wand* (*Against the Wall*, 2004), a tough film about the difficulties facing Turks born in Germany (and particularly Berlin). Andreas Dresen's *Sommer vorm Balkon* (*Summer in Berlin*, 2005), set mostly in the hip district of Prenzlauer Berg, is a delightful trip into the tribulations of two Berlin women one summer.

Bruno Ganz returned to Berlin not as an angel, but something approaching the opposite, in the lead role of Bernd Eichinger's (born 1949) *Der Untergang* (*The Downfall*, 2004). Ganz's performance as Hitler during his last weeks in the Berlin bunker in 1945 is a tour de force that reveals a human side to the Führer, along with his unfathomable cruelty.

The Babelsberg studios are alive and kicking. One of the most expensive European films in history, the 70-million-dollar blockbuster about the battle of Stalingrad, *Enemy at the Gates* (2001), was shot here.

MUSIC

One name says it all: Herbert von Karajan (1908–1989). The authoritarian figure graced countless millions of record sleeves and CD covers down the decades. Von Karajan ruled the Berlin Philharmonisches Orchester (aka Berlin Philharmoniker), the city's top musical calling card, from 1955 until his death in 1989. The orchestra is one of the world's finest, but it is just the tip of the iceberg. Berlin's musical offerings range from chamber music to opera, and from jazz to "click house."

King Friedrich Wilhelm I, no music lover,

cut the royal budget for court orchestras and choirs. Indeed, Berlin was long musically overshadowed by cities such as Leipzig and Vienna. Friedrich II was a different matter. In 1743 he opened Berlin's first opera house, what is today the Staatsoper, on Unter den Linden. Along with the Komische Oper and Deutsche Oper, it is one of three opera houses in the city.

The Berlin Philharmoniker came into being in 1882 with 50 musicians (today it numbers around 130). Until Wilhelm Furtwängler (1886–1954) arrived as conductor in 1922, the orchestra worked under various people, including guest conductors such as Peter Tchaikovsky, Gustav Mahler, and Richard Strauss. Alongside the classics, Furtwängler supported experimental composers working in Berlin, including Paul Hindemith (1895–1963) and the Viennese Arnold Schönberg (1874–1951), both of whom left the capital in the 1930s.

Punk diva Nina Hagen's rebelliousness led to both notoriety and success in the 1980s.

Sir Simon Rattle, a successor to the legendary Herbert von Karajan, directs the Berlin Philharmoniker at its home, the Philharmonie, at the edge of Tiergarten.

Schönberg was particularly interested in atonal music, and support of this kind of "degenerate art" got Furtwängler into hot water with the Nazis. He stayed on as artistic director but was forced to resign his other positions with the orchestra, which from 1934 on became a vehicle of Nazi propaganda. Furtwängler, after a period of "de-Nazification," resumed his position fully in 1952. His successor, von Karajan, combined genius at the podium with a sense of marketing that took him and "his" orchestra to hitherto unattained heights of world renown. In 1938, as director of the Staatskapelle, he conducted the first stereo music recording in the world. Today, the Philharmoniker is flourishing under the direction of Britain's Sir Simon Rattle (born 1955) and is one of five city orchestras (all subsidized by the state).

There was musical life in Berlin before the Philharmoniker. Carl Maria von Weber (1786–1826) premiered his opera *Der Freischütz* to acclaim in Berlin in 1821, while Berliner Felix Mendelssohn Bartholdy (1809–1847) proved a virtuoso composer and conductor from an early age. His most enduring work is the opera *A Midsummer Night's Dream* (1843). Giacomo Meyerbeer (1791–1864) was made Prussian general director of music in 1842, at which time he was one of Europe's most successful opera composers. The works of Leipzig-born Richard Wagner (1813–1883), however, who wrote an anti-Semitic pamphlet against

Meyerbeer, didn't even get a hearing in Berlin until the 1890s.

A night at the opera is not everyone's idea of fun; in the 1920s most Berliners could be found hanging out in cabarets and jazz clubs. Today, too, the jazz scene in Berlin is humming. The annual five-day Jazzfest Berlin in November is one of Europe's top jazz festivals. Among the big names to look for in Berlin are Ed Schuller, Till Brönner, Ernst Bier, Walter Norris, and David Friedman. Plenty of new talent is emerging, with outlets in venues around the city. The Berlin Voices are four divine vocalists (none from Berlin) who fuse modern jazz elements with pop and soul. M&M are a pair of Berlin-based guitarists whose band performs mostly original material in a modern jazz context.

The '80s were big for music in Berlin and West Germany. Led by East Berlin–born Nina Hagen, the queen of German light punk, the decade was marked by the *Neue Deutsche Welle* (German new wave), a phalanx of poppy-punky bands that, however, got little attention outside Germany.

More successful on a broader stage has been Berlin's techno scene. The city was the launchpad for European electronic music and retains its primacy today. Clubs across town pump it out late into the night (there is no official closing time on bars and clubs in Berlin) and locals love it. House, hip-hop, electrojazz, R&B, breakbeat, and most other electronic variants are on Berlin's menu. ■

The great avenue of Unter den Linden is the central stage for centuries of Berlin's history. Near it, the Reichstag, a mix of old guard and avant-garde, is the symbol of Germany's modern political rebirth.

Unter den Linden & Potsdamer Platz

Detail of the Apollo hall in the Staatsoper

Unter den Linden & Potsdamer Platz

THE MOST WIDELY KNOWN BOULEVARD IN GERMANY, UNTER DEN LINDEN IS Berlin's central artery. With more than three centuries' history, this avenue "under the linden trees" has witnessed the city's greatest and most harrowing moments. Around it, signs of Berlin's past exist uneasily next to the modern creations of a city reborn.

After the trauma of decades of division, the city has quickly recovered its equilibrium, and the center of attention has shifted inevitably back to this part of the central Berlin district known, appropriately enough, as Mitte (the Middle). Much of Unter den Linden and the surrounding area was destroyed in World War II. The creation of the Berlin Wall, beginning in 1961, rendered Unter den Linden an aimless, dowdy boulevard that lost itself in an ignominious dead end at its west end, the Brandenburger Tor (Brandenburg Gate).

It is hard to appreciate any of this decay today. Many fine buildings along Unter den Linden have been restored or even rebuilt from scratch. New life has been breathed into the stately avenue.

The single greatest symbol of the city's rebirth is the Reichstag building northwest of the avenue. Here a united national parliament again proudly sits in a building that, since its architectural transformation at the hands of Sir Norman Foster (born 1935), combines the pomp of the past with a vision of the future.

It is a leitmotif heard all over the area. The Brandenburger Tor, already patched up after World War II, has been repaired and its square, Pariser Platz, restored to its former elegance. The embassies that once stood here are returning, and the ritzy Hotel Adlon has risen from its ashes.

At the opposite end of Unter den Linden, its most sumptuous edifices (such as the Altes Palais, Staatsoper, and Opernpalais) bask again in glory. Following the lead of the Reichstag, the 18th-century Zeughaus (and its German history museum) has been restored and equipped with a daring 21st-century extension.

Potsdamer Platz, once one of Berlin's busiest squares—and after World War II an enormous vacant lot—has been transformed. A veritable laboratory for the best in international architecture, it again teems with life. And while the pretty Gendarmenmarkt square remains true to its origins, Friedrichstrasse has won new life as a shopping artery, helped by the creation of imaginative new department stores in the Friedrichstadtpassagen. The scars and reminders of the city's troubled past also make their presence felt. A vast memorial to the victims of the Holocaust lies just south off Pariser Platz, close to the location of Adolf Hitler's wartime bunker and the government district of Wilhelmstrasse. Little remains of the monumental architecture of the Nazi regime, except for painful memories in places such as the Topographie des Terrors, an open-air display located on the site of the Gestapo's former headquarters.

The scars of more recent history are equally apparent. A stretch of the Berlin Wall still stands outside the former Gestapo headquarters, and nearby is Checkpoint Charlie, the former U.S. Army crossing point where for decades Westerners would stream into and out of the East under the watchful gaze of armed guards. ■

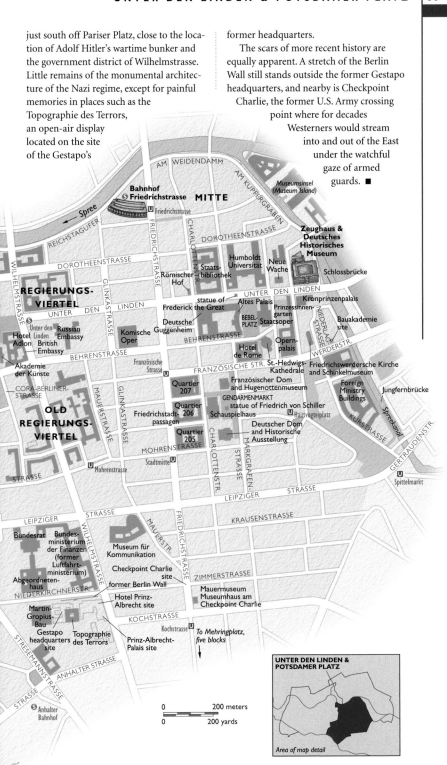

0   200 meters
0   200 yards

UNTER DEN LINDEN &
POTSDAMER PLATZ

Area of map detail

Sir Norman Foster created a people's dome for the Reichstag, again home to the national parliament since unification.

Reichstag

THERE IS PERHAPS NO MORE FITTING WAY TO BEGIN AN acquaintance with Berlin than at its symbolic epicenter, the national parliament building. Used by Hitler on his rise to power, bombed but not destroyed in World War II, the Reichstag sits right next to the path of the of the Berlin Wall, for nearly 29 years the dividing line between East and West.

The Reichstag (Imperial Parliament) has inspired strong reactions. Kaiser Wilhelm II liked to refer to the building, completed from a design by Paul Wallot (1841–1912) in 1894, as the "imperial monkeys' cage." He worried that its apparent grandeur might overshadow that of his official Berlin residence, the Schloss, at the eastern end of Unter den Linden. In the end, he

have happened had it, for example, voted against war credits at the outbreak of World War I. In 1916, as that war was grinding on, the words *Dem Deutschen Volke* (To the German People) were added to the facade.

Although Hitler used the fragile interwar parliamentary system to achieve power in the early 1930s, he never actually entered the Reichstag building, which was seriously damaged by fire under suspicious circumstances in 1933. The Nazis didn't bother to restore the building, which was further damaged in the final months of World War II. The remains of Wallot's dome were dynamited in 1954, but the rest of the edifice, on the west side of the Berlin Wall, was restored in the 1960s. Although used by parliamentary work groups, a 1971 accord prohibited the Bonn-based West German federal parliament (*Bundestag*) from sitting in the Reichstag (and competing with East Germany's government).

Everything changed with reunification in 1990. The federal parliament voted in 1991 to move to Berlin, and British architect Sir Norman Foster won the bid to make over the building. He retained the grave exterior but gutted the inside. The most spectacular element is his **glass dome.** Visitors should expect to wait in line for an hour before taking the elevator that whisks you up to dome, which lies directly above parliament's plenary hall. At the center of the dome, a funnel seemingly armored with mirror plates spreads upward. Around its base you can read a little of the building's tumultuous history. Then climb the spiral ramp to the top of the dome for ever better views across central Berlin. There's a

could do nothing about its dimensions and contented himself with harrumphing that it was the "height of bad taste." Wallot's daring iron-and-glass dome, however, awakened especial admiration among public observers at the time.

Although executive powers when the Reichstag was built lay with the kaiser and his ministers, in particular the chancellor, the parliament did exercise some influence over the affairs of state. One can only wonder what might

Reichstag

www.bundestag.de

▲ Map p. 52

✉ Besucherdienst, Platz der Republik 1

☎ 030 22 73 21 5; fax 030 22 73 00 27

🕐 Dome 8 a.m.–midnight; last admission 10 p.m.

🚇 S-Bahn: Unter den Linden

rooftop café there, as well.

Parliament moved here from Bonn in 1999. Visitors can sit in on a session of parliament and tour the **Plenarsaal** (the gray semicircular hall, dominated by the enormous eagle that symbolizes the federal republic, where parliament sits) and other parts of the building. To do so requires advance planning. Most organized visits are conducted in German, but tours in English are generally held at noon on Tuesdays. Details of tour days and times are available on the Bundestag's website. You must fax or write to apply for a time and a day to visit.

East of the Reichstag stands

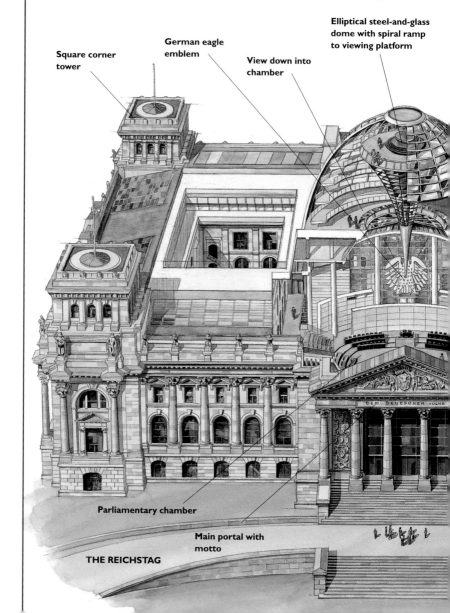

Square corner tower

German eagle emblem

View down into chamber

Elliptical steel-and-glass dome with spiral ramp to viewing platform

Parliamentary chamber

Main portal with motto

THE REICHSTAG

Past and present dovetail in the Reichstag, with its grand 19th-century exterior intact.

Internal courtyard

Rusticated pedestal facade

the Jakob-Kaiser-Haus, a modern complex that houses half the offices of members of parliament. It was built around 1904 as the Reichstagspräsidentenpalais, which was the office of the parliamentary president until 1933 and now houses offices.

The bare square in front of the Reichstag was, until World War II, altogether different. Known as Königsplatz (King's Square) until the 1920s, when it became **Platz der Republik** (Republic Square), it hosted the Siegessäule, the winged golden symbol of victory that Hitler moved to its present lofty location in Tiergarten (see p. 121) in the 1930s. Previously the golden statue had rested on a rather modest pillar, but Hitler changed that, too, when he made the move. From 1961 on, the square was the scene of frequent massive demonstrations demanding freedom for East Germany and the removal of the wall. ■

Brandenburger Tor & Pariser Platz

UNTIL THE BERLIN WALL TUMBLED DOWN IN 1989, MOST Western visitors to the city could not meander beneath the grand Brandenburger Tor (Brandenburg Gate) that had been the key pre-war landmark for Berlin's weekend strollers.

Pariser Platz and its trademark Brandenburg Gate have been mostly restored to their prewar glory.

In the postwar decades, the pock-marked gate could be observed only across the wall. Those who made the day trip to East Berlin were generally dissuaded from getting too close by troopers patrolling Unter den Linden. The buildings around the once elegant square to its immediate east, Pariser Platz, had all been demolished after the war, allowing Unter den Linden boulevard to peter out in a desolate plain.

That was then. Since reunification, the gate has been restored to its initial splendor and the Pariser Platz has regained much of the style it once knew.

The rectangular Pariser Platz was laid out in 1734 to cap the western end of Unter den Linden on its way from the now vanished royal Schloss (palace). It was part of a careful town-planning exercise under Philipp Gerlach (1679–1748) that included the circular Mehringplatz (then called the Rondell), completed two years earlier, and the octagonal Leipziger Platz (now reconstructed), which was also laid out in 1734.

Each square was meant to have a city gate, and in 1791 the Brandenburger Tor was opened to public acclaim on Pariser Platz. Its designer, Carl Gotthard Langhans (1732–1808), found that "the location, in its way, is without doubt the most beautiful in the world," even if he did say so himself. A low-slung, broad affair, not at all attempting to mimic the grandeur of Roman triumphal gates, it is graced with simple Doric columns.

Indeed, the gate was supposed to symbolize the triumph of peace rather than arms. In 1795, the gate was topped by the 18-foot-high (5.5 m) copper **Quadriga** statue depicting the goddess of peace, Eirene (or the goddess of victory, according to other versions), riding into the city on a chariot drawn by four horses. To drive the peace message home, a sculpture of the war god, Mars, at the southern end of the gate shows him sheathing his sword.

The Quadriga was created by Johann Gottfried Schadow, a Berliner born into a tailor's family. At 20 he eloped with the daughter of a rich jeweler, who eventually consented to their wedding and paid for his art studies in Italy. What you see now is a copy made in West Berlin in the 1960s in a rare gesture of East-West cooperation. The original was largely destroyed in World War II (having also been kidnapped by Napoleon for a stint in Paris from 1806 to 1814).

If running around central Berlin has you gasping, pop into the **Raum der Stille** (Silence Room) in the north flank of the gate *(daily 11 a.m.–4 p.m.)*. This room, with its spotlighted wall hanging and artistically situated rock, is a place in which to meditate in silence.

Since 1992, generous European Union funding has allowed Pariser Platz to be transformed into a close approximation of its former self. The grand early 20th-century **Hotel Adlon** again stands proudly on the southeast corner. Opened in 1997, some 90 years after the original, it is attracting as much attention now as then. New buildings also house the embassies of France, the United States (its building still under construction), and the United Kingdom (with a playful main

facade on Wilhelmstrasse) in their prewar locations. Graceful gardens, closely modeled on those planted in 1880, have been laid out. Even the square's lampposts are replicas of the 1888 originals.

Much of the glittering, glass **Akademie der Künste** (Arts Academy) building—one of several the academy has dotted around town—is given over to archives and administration, but temporary exhibitions are also held there. The academy also stages exhibitions across the square in the reconstructed **Max Liebermann** building.

Canadian-born U.S. architect Frank O. Gehry (born 1929) designed the **DG Bank,** located between the Akademie der Künste and the U.S. Embassy. The sober facade belies Gehry's mad interior. Beneath the spiderweb steel-and-glass ceiling seems to hover a gelatinous creature from the deep, which is in fact a conference room. The wavy rear facade plastered with metal-framed outward-jutting windows is also eye-catching. ∎

Rebuilt from scratch, the Hotel Adlon is once again a drawing card for international VIPs.

Akademie der Künste
www.adk.de
🅼 Map p. 53
✉ Pariser Platz 4
☎ 030 200 57 0
🕐 Closed Mon.
💲 Free–$
Ⓢ S-Bahn: Unter den Linden

Denkmal für die ermordeten Juden Europas

Denkmal für die ermordeten Juden Europas
www.stiftung-denkmal.de
- Map p. 52
- Cora-Berliner Strasse 1
- 030 26 39 43 36
- Closed Mon.
- S-Bahn: Unter den Linden

FOR MORE THAN A DECADE, THE DEBATE RAGED IN AND out of parliament. Should a Monument to the Murdered Jews of Europe, the six million victims of Hitler's Holocaust, be built in the heart of a newly reunited Berlin? And if so, what form should it take? Only in 1999 did the Bundestag, the federal parliament, vote in favor of a memorial. In late 2005, 15 years after the debate kicked off, the monument was a reality.

Berlin is not short on sites that evoke the history of Nazi persecution of the Jews. From the country villa in Wannsee (see pp. 203–04) where the Final Solution was devised, to the Sachsenhausen concentration camp outside of town (see p. 217), Berlin offers the attentive visitor plenty of opportunity to explore this path of darkness. The debate that erupted in the 1990s, however, was about the creation of a public place of remorse and recognition in the core of the old-new capital of a reunited Germany.

Clearly no ordinary monument would do. The choice of location is itself symbolic. A stone's throw from the Reichstag, Brandenburger Tor, and course of the former Berlin Wall, it lies at the city's center. Its inclusion in the new government district is silent testimony to the

A dense forest of concrete pillars, the heart of Berlin's monument to victims of the Holocaust, is complemented by an underground display.

German people's recognition that the genocide is an inescapable part of their national history.

For all the importance of the monument's placement, no sign tells passersby what it is. And it is by no means obvious. The New York architect Peter Eisenman (born 1932) designed a field of 2,711 concrete pillars, all leaning slightly off-center but otherwise different from one another only in their height—varying from 8 inches to 15 feet (0.2 m–4.7 m). The monument rests on an undulating and deepening field of concrete slabs. The view across this petrified forest is different from every angle.

This gray stone field is sliced by a grid of paths so narrow that visitors can see only the path they are following and the ones that cross their path. It elicits reactions as varied as its visitors, from the claustrophobia of those who know what it

is about to the merry laughter of kids chasing one another through the labyrinth.

On the eastern side of the monument is the entrance to the **Ort der Information** (*entry recommended only to visitors 14 yrs. and older*), a poignant introduction to the horror of the Holocaust. Get here in good time, as lines and tight security can slow down entry considerably. The first of a series of rooms holds an overview of the persecution of the Jews in Nazi Germany and in conquered Europe from 1933 until 1945. Along a corridor a series of texts and images provide an unsentimental introduction to this unfathomable history. From here, one is led to the **Dimensions Room,** in which 15 victims from different parts of Europe express themselves in letters and diary entries. Writes one journalist in his diary: "If something like this [the persecution and extermination] was possible, what else is there? For what reason is there war? For what reason hunger? For what reason the world?"

The **Families Room** that follows uses text, pictures, movie reels, and audio to illustrate the lives and destinies of 15 Jewish families across Europe—most of whom did not survive the war. Then comes the **Names Room.** An audio loop reads names and short biographies of murdered and missing Jews from those years in German and English—a task that would take more than six years if all six million were read. An annex allows access to data on about three million victims from the pages of testimony held by the Yad Vashem Holocaust Memorial in Israel. The **Places Room,** the last, depicts (in pictures and film) some 200 locations in Europe connected to the Holocaust, from ghettos to concentration camps. ■

Along Unter den Linden

Restored to its rightful place at the heart of reunited Berlin, Unter den Linden is dotted with cafés.

IN 1646 THE AVENUE WAS A ROYAL ROAD FROM THE Berliner Schloss, home to Prussia's rulers, to their hunting grounds in what is now the Tiergarten. By the end of the 19th century it had become Berlin's Champs Elysées. Pounded to smithereens during World War II, neglected by the East Germans, and deprived of its central-city status by the division of Berlin, it has regained much of its former glory since reunification.

Just east of Pariser Platz stretches the compound of the **Russian Embassy.** Through all the turbulent history of Berlin and Russia, this embassy has remained like a rock in a storm. The embassy of tsarist Russia in the 19th century, what was then Unter den Linden 7 became the Soviet Embassy in 1918. Destroyed in World War II, the present structure (Nos. 63–65) was built by the Soviets in 1949–1952, and it has all the Cold War gravity of the period. Nevertheless, the building had little trouble transforming itself into the Russian Embassy to the Federal Republic of Germany when the Cold War faded in 1991.

Across Glinkastrasse is the drab **Komische Oper** (*Behrenstrasse 55–57, tel 030 47 99 74 00 for tickets, www.komische-oper-berlin.de*), whose main entrance is on Behrenstrasse. The opera house may not look like much from the outside (the result of postwar rebuilding), but it has pedigree. A theater has stood on this site, with interruptions, since 1764. The plush neobaroque interior of the theater was largely untouched by Allied bombs and is today a protected monument. The best way to get a look is to take in one of the shows , which range from light classics to contemporary performances.

Diagonally across the road at Unter den Linden 10 is the **Römischer Hof** shopping and office center, built into the restored shell of the former Hôtel de Rome. Opened in 1867, the hotel was converted into public offices in 1910.

Two blocks east from the Komische Oper, the **Deutsche Guggenheim** is a bit of a disappointment, with two limited rooms for temporary exhibitions.

Directly across Unter den Linden is the **Staatsbibliothek.** In this central branch of the German state library *(Unter den Linden 8, tel 030 26 60, http://staatsbibliothek-berlin.de),* which is still being renovated, lie extraordinary treasures. In its map archives, for instance, is a 1664 world atlas—the biggest in the world. The library moved here in 1914 from the Altes Palais on Bebelplatz (see next column), where it had been since 1784.

On the median strip in Unter den Linden, a proud equestrian **statue of Frederick the Great** could almost be directing traffic. He was only restored to his position here in 1981, having languished in Potsdam in the postwar decades. In late 2005 he got a fright when a 1,100-pound (500 kg) bomb dropped by the British Royal Air Force in World War II was found buried nearby and had to be destroyed in a controlled detonation.

Next door to the library is the seat of the **Humboldt Universität** *(Unter den Linden 6, tel 030 2 09 30, www.hu-berlin.de),* founded in 1810 and still a center of excellence, with buildings scattered across the city. The main edifice was raised in the 18th century as the palace of Prince Heinrich of Prussia (1726–1802) and was extended in 1920.

Directly across the road from the university is the curvaceous **Altes Palais,** also known as the Alte Bibliothek, on Bebelplatz. Built in 1780 and once home to the Staatsbibliothek, it is now part of Humboldt University. Berliners, who just love to give their buildings sobriquets, dubbed this one the Kommode because it looks like an antique chest of drawers *(Kommode).*

Facing the Altes Palais across the square is the neoclassic **Staatsoper** *(tel 030 20 35 45 55)* built by Knobelsdorff in 1743 and Berlin's first theater, which was damaged in air raids in 1945. Daniel Barenboim, the opera's artistic director, donated

Deutsche Guggenheim
www.deutsche-guggenheim.de

🅰 Map p. 53
✉ Unter den Linden 13–15
☎ 030 202 09 30
💲 $, Mon. free
🚈 S-Bahn: Unter den Linden

Burning the books

O n the night of May 10, 1933, Bebelplatz (then Opernplatz) became the site of an enormous bonfire. In front of the Altes Palais, which for more than a century had been the city's main library, thousands of books by authors considered undesirable by the Nazis were heaped onto the flames. Karl Marx, Sigmund Freud, Thomas and Heinrich Mann, and Bertolt Brecht were just a few of the writers whose works had to be "cleaned out." The scene, organized by student associations as an "action against un-German thinking" and attended by university rectors and professors, was repeated in university cities across the country. Berlin's Erich Kästner, one of the undesirables, watched as his works went up in flames. Condemned to silence, he nevertheless remained in Berlin throughout the years of the Nazi regime. ■

St.-Hedwigs-Kathedrale

www.hedwigs-kathedrale.de

🅼 Map p. 53

✉ Behrenstrasse

☎ 030 203 48 10

🚇 U-Bahn: Französische Strasse

The Friedrichswerdersche Kirche was one of the few monuments in central Berlin to survive World War II.

€100,000 for its renovation in 2006.

The broad copper dome at the southeast corner of Bebelplatz belongs to the city's main Catholic church, **St.-Hedwigs-Kathedrale.** The church, completed in 1773 by Knobelsdorff, was inspired by the Pantheon in Rome. Next door, the luxury Hotel de Rome opened in 2006 in a restored late 19th-century former bank headquarters.

Back on the main drag, Unter den Linden is graced by the **Opernpalais,** across a park from the Staatsoper. It houses a couple of restaurants and the opulent Operncafé, where you can enjoy a thick slice of strudel (see p. 243). The park itself is occupied by

several martial statues of Prussian generals who fought against Napoleon. Leading the way is Gerhard von Scharnhorst (1755–1813). Behind him line up Count Johann Yorck (1759–1830), Gebhard von Blücher (1742–1819), who led the Prussians against Napoleon at Waterloo, and August von Gneisenau (1760–1831). After World War II, the East German regime removed the statues, judging that the generals personified the imperial past of Germany and were thus politically incorrect. However, the regime changed its mind in 1963 and brought the generals back.

Next door, the restored **Kronprinzenpalais** (*Unter den Linden 3*) dates to the mid-17th century. Once a private residence and later an art gallery shut down by the Nazis for showing "degenerate art" (such as expressionism), it opens only occasionally for exhibitions or other events.

Anyone who visited East Berlin prior to 1990 will remember the **Neue Wache,** across Unter den Linden. Here, goose-stepping sentries would change the guard outside what had become a memorial to the victims of World War II and, in particular, of the Nazi war machine. Karl Friedrich Schinkel built it in 1818 as a barracks for the King's Watch troops. Since 1993 it has become Germany's central memorial to all the victims of World War II and, pointedly, of the East German regime. Next door is the Zeughaus museum (see pp. 66–67).

Just behind the rebuilt Kronprinzenpalais rises one of the rare buildings to have survived the bombing of Berlin more or less intact. Schinkel built the **Friedrichswerdersche Kirche,** a neo-Gothic redbrick

caprice topped by slender pinnacles and imitating 19th-century English retro tastes, in 1831. Since 1987 the building has housed the **Schinkelmuseum.** Downstairs is scattered a sculpture collection, with works by such important Berlin sculptors as Johann Gottfried Schadow and Christian

Kirche is, or rather isn't, yet another Schinkel effort, the **Bauakademie,** a 19th-century architecture school that Schinkel liked so much he chose to live there. It survived the war but not the East German regime, which demolished it in 1962 to make way for its foreign office. This

Schinkelmuseum

www.smb.spk-berlin.de

🗺 Map p. 53

✉ Werderscher Markt

☎ 030 208 13 23

🚇 U-Bahn:
   Hausvogteiplatz

Daniel Rauch. Emil Wolff (1802–1879) had a penchant for restoration, and there are several examples of ancient statues that he worked on here, including one of Hermes from the fifth century B.C. Schinkel himself is immortalized in a statue on the right as you enter, created by his friend and sculptor Friedrich Tieck (1776–1851). The architect's life and work is displayed in documents and images along the upper gallery.

Just across Niederlagstrasse from the Friedrichswerdersche

building was itself torn down in 1995, leaving a huge vacant lot. Since 2001, a private group has been campaigning to have the Bauakademie reconstructed; to lend the campaign more weight, they have created a tarpaulin imitation on the site.

The restored **Schlossbrücke** marks the end of Berlin's best known boulevard. Schinkel designed the bridge, which was completed in 1824, although the sculptures were added in 1849. Destroyed in the war, it was restored in 1950. ■

The elegant Operncafé in the Opernpalais recalls the grandeur of another era.

**Zeughaus &
Deutsches
Historisches
Museum**
www.dhm.de

🏛 Map p. 53

✉ Unter den Linden 2

☎ 030 20 30 40

💲 $

🚇 U-Bahn & S-Bahn:
Friedrichstrasse

Zeughaus & Deutsches Historisches Museum

IN THE REMARKABLY ORNATE BUILDING THAT ONCE HELD the city's armory *(Zeughaus)*, the past, present, and future all seem to flow together. Housing the Deutsches Historisches Museum (German History Museum), the building is an engaging voyage through the nation's history; with its ultramodern extension, it symbolizes a forward-looking vision in its presentation of the past.

ES HISTORISCHES MUSEUM

I. M. Pei's glass spiral stairway is part of his dynamic extension of the Deutsches Historisches Museum.

Completed in 1706, the vaguely pink-hued facade on Unter den Linden is more suggestive of a baron's mansion than a weapons depot. One of the earliest buildings to grace the fairly new boulevard, the Zeughaus has since gone through repeated transformations. Only its heady facade has remained impervious to change. Originally designed by Johann Arnold Nering, with continued work by Andreas Schlüter and Jean de Bodt, it was finished in 1729 and served as an armory until the late 19th century. By 1829, however, some top floor rooms had been remodeled to display the national collection of Prussian war booty (mostly weapons, ensigns, flags, and the like). By the 1880s, the entire building had been transformed into a military museum.

On entering from Unter den Linden today, the visitor seems to travel through time. The **entrance hall,** with its sober pillars encased in travertine marble and oval ceiling lights, is a faithful restoration of the East German design of the 1950s.

From here you proceed to the inner courtyard, commonly known as the **Schlüterhof** because of the masks of dying warriors, carved by Andreas Schlüter, that frame the windows. The gently vaulted glass ceiling, which stretches like a sheet of bubble wrap over the grand hall, was designed by the Chinese-American architect I. M. Pei (born 1917). It takes its cue from the late 19th-century steel-and-glass roof destroyed in World War II. The elegantly curving stairwells in the Schlüterhof are among the few surviving details from the original baroque building.

Where Pei really went to town, however, was behind the Zeughaus. From the Schlüterhof you proceed down escalators to the underground passage that leads to his **extension** of the museum. The building itself, as well as the exhibitions it holds, is worth a close look. The bright beige limestone walls, all smooth surfaces and straight lines, transport you to a wonderfully orderly flight of fancy. Four floors open up before you. The limestone continues to dominate, along with concrete overpasses, a gentle curving rear glass wall, and a cheeky, glassed-in spiral stairway. Arrowhead angles and broad bow shapes combine to create a unique open space that allows visitors to observe all floors at once. Behind closed doors on each floor are generous exhibition spaces set aside for the museum's temporary expositions.

The museum's core exhibition is in the Zeughaus. It starts in the west wing of the upper floor, with collections and displays taking you from the earliest days of Germanic tribal history through the Middle Ages to about 1500. You then proceed around the rest of the top floor for a look at events from the Renaissance until World War I and the collapse of the German Reich in 1918.

Down on the first floor, the collection picks up again with the Weimar Republic. The main following sections are devoted to the rise of Nazi Germany, World War II, and the parallel histories of East and West Germany. Another area deals with Reunification and the final withdrawal of wartime occupation troops from Berlin and the rest of the country. The last rooms are given over to contemporary history and are likely to change regularly with events.

In the I. M. Pei building, temporary exhibitions treat specific areas related to German history or draw on the museum's massive archives. The museum also has a cinema, where classic films, generally from the early decades of film, are shown. ■

Interlocking planes and daring open spaces make the Pei building an impressive setting for temporary exhibitions.

The twin
churches of
Gendarmenmarkt
make the square
one of Berlin's
prettiest.

Gendarmenmarkt & around

THIS 17TH-CENTURY MARKET SQUARE EMERGED AS PART of the city-planning effort still known as Friedrichstadt, and it is arguably the prettiest such space in central Berlin. Kurfürst Friedrich III (from 1701, King of Prussia Friedrich I), commissioned the district's construction beginning in 1688. In the next decades the square came to host the buildings that still give it beauty.

Französischer Dom
www.franzoesischer-dom-berlin.de

🗺 Map p. 53
✉ Gendarmenmarkt 5
☎ 030 229 17 60
🕐 Closed Mon.
💲 $
🚇 U-Bahn: Stadtmitte

Hugenotten-museum
www.franzoesischer-dom-berlin.de

🗺 Map p. 53
✉ Gendarmenmarkt 5
☎ 030 229 17 60
💲 $
🚇 U-Bahn: Stadtmitte

Gendarmenmarkt square took its name both from the regiment of Gens d'Armes—men at arms—stationed here and from the fact that it was, until the 1880s, Germany's biggest weekly produce market.

On either side of the square stand two virtually identical baroque churches. The one on the north side was raised for the city's burgeoning French Huguenot population, many of whom moved into the area and opened luxury stores along Friedrichstrasse in the 18th century. A simple church, the **Friedrichstadt Kirche,** built here in 1705, was modeled on the French Protestants' main church in France at Charenton.

It is overshadowed by the grand baroque tower next to it, which was completed in 1785 by Carl von Gontard (1731–1791). Capped by a dome, it came to be known as the **Französischer Dom** (French Dome), a confusing appellation as *Dom* in German also means "cathedral," which this building is not. The climb to the top of the tower is rewarded with fine views.

At the tower's base, the **Hugenottenmuseum** tells the story of the persecution of the Protestants in France, their flight into exile, and their role in the history of Berlin. The church is frequently used for concerts and boasts a 60-bell carillon.

The town's German Lutheran community built a church in 1708

at the southern end of the square. In 1785, von Gontard raised a tower there nearly identical to the French one. It was inevitably dubbed the **Deutscher Dom** (German Dome) and was heavily damaged in World War II.

In the 1980s, the East Germans started to convert the church into an arts center, filling the main tower and dome with a cement interior. Much of this was retained when the united Berlin decided to turn it into a museum **(Historische Ausstellung)** on the history of German democracy—a worthy if rather dry introduction to this subject. It starts in the basement with a look at German parliamentary democracy today. The revolts of 1848 and parliamentary history are covered on the next two levels as you head upstairs. The following level is devoted to the Nazi and GDR states, followed by exhibits on women's role in politics and on Germany in the European Union.

Between the two churches, the rather more lighthearted **Schauspielhaus** (aka Konzerthaus Berlin) was yet another Karl Friedrich Schinkel creation. Its opulent interior is the result of restoration, as the theater was gutted during World War II. The Berlin Symphony Orchestra calls it home, and it is the scene of a busy program of classical music concerts. Outside on the square stands a **statue of Friedrich von Schiller** (1759–1805), one of the giants of 18th-century German literature.

One block to the west of Gendarmenmarkt runs Friedrichstrasse, one of the city's principal arteries until the end of World War II and coming back to life with a vengeance now. Once it was famous for its cafés, chic stores, and bars. The bars and

the cafés are gone, and now Friedrichstrasse is quiet at night, but shopping is back.

Some of the new stores are architectural gems. In the early 1990s, an international team of architects created an intriguing shopping promenade, the **Friedrichstadtpassagen.** The

stores, or Quartiers, start to the north with **Quartier 207,** designed by France's Jean Nouvel (born 1945) and home to a branch of Paris's Galeries Lafayette (check out the basement gourmet food section). This curvy glass cathedral is dominated inside by two inverted glass funnels that pierce all floors. Next is **Quartier 206,** an intensely angular building designed principally by U.S. architect Henry Cobb (born 1926). Cologne-based architect Oswald Matthias Ungers (born 1926) finishes with his cubic **Quartier 205.**

Two blocks east of the Gendarmenmarkt loom the **Foreign Ministry buildings.** The main one was the Nazi Reichsbank, and in GDR times, SED party headquarters. It has a grand, open atrium on Werderstrasse, built in 2003. ■

France invades Berlin with gourmet shopping at Galeries Lafayette.

Deutscher Dom
www.deutscherdom.de
⚑ Map p. 53
✉ Gendarmenmarkt 1
☎ 030 22 73 04 31
🕐 Closed Mon.
🚇 U-Bahn: Stadtmitte

Schauspielhaus
www.konzerthaus.de
⚑ Map p. 53
✉ Gendarmenmarkt 2
☎ 030 20 30 90
💲 $
🚇 U-Bahn: Stadtmitte

A mural at the former Aviation Ministry commemorates the 1953 uprising against the GDR.

A walk around Wilhelmstrasse & Old Regierungsviertel

Standing on the corner of Unter den Linden and Wilhelmstrasse, you can well believe that this area was once a center of government activity. Wilhelmstrasse was Germany's powerhouse, known as the Regierungsviertel (Government District) and it was lined with ministries and government offices from the early 19th century until Hitler's heyday. Today, with few exceptions, it is all gone, sucked up in the whirlwind of war. This walk is a ghost tour.

Start at the Russian ❶ and British ❷ embassies, which lie within a few feet of the street corner in their historic locations. The next stop is an unprepossessing office building just off Wilhelmstrasse that is home to **Stasi—Die Ausstellung** ❸**,** a permanent display on the secret police of communist East Germany *(Mauerstrasse 38, tel 030 23 24 79 51, closed Sun., www.bstu.de).* Through documents, photos, and videos (in German only), the display demonstrates the extent of the security network. (The East German Ministry for State Security had 91,000 employees and 175,000 *Inoffizielle Mitarbeiter,* or civilian informants.) Among the more alarming objects are jars with bits of material that contain the scent of potential enemies of the state, given to dogs who would search out their presence. More

amusing are the clunky old listening devices, hidden cameras, and other tricks that belong to another age of espionage.

A block down, at No. 54 Wilhelmstrasse, which in those days was No. 64, the **Prussian State Council** ❹ had its office between World War I and the arrival of the Nazis. The then-president of the Prussian State Council and later first president of West Germany, Konrad Adenauer (1876–1967), lived here in 1932–33, until the Nazis abolished the federal states and centralized power in Berlin. The building then became the headquarters of Rudolf Hess, Hitler's deputy, until Martin Bormann moved in as his replacement. The building now houses the Berlin branch of the federal ministry of consumer protection, nutrition, and agriculture.

Next door to the south was the office of the **Prussian prime minister** ⑤. When Nazi chief Hermann Göring (1893–1946) took up that position, he moved the office to Leipziger Strasse and Hess took over this building, too. Directly across the road was the **Foreign Ministry** ⑥, run by the Nazi Joachim von Ribbentrop (1893–1946) from 1938 until the end of the war.

On the same western side of Wilhelmstrasse was the **old Reich Chancellery** ⑦, the residence and offices of the German chancellor from 1878 to 1939, when Hitler's **new Reich Chancellery** ⑧ was completed on Vossstrasse. Nothing remains of either, or of the bomb-proof **Führerbunker** ⑨ in between, in which Hitler and company cowered in the last days of the war. Although these buildings are gone, panels with information about them in German and English

are scattered along Wilhelmstrasse.

Opposite the original Reich Chancellery, at Wilhelmstrasse 49 (a side lane), you can see Joseph Goebbels's (1897–1945) **Propaganda Ministry** ⑩, now the country's Health and Labor Ministry. It is best seen from Mauerstrasse.

See area map pp. 52–53
▶ Unter den Linden
🔁 2 miles (1.5 km)
🕐 1.5 hours
▶ Kochstrasse

NOT TO BE MISSED
• Stasi—Die Ausstellung
• Luftfahrtministerium
• Topographie des Terrors

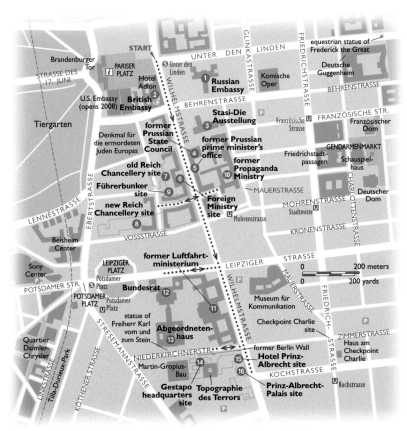

The Bundesrat sits in what was once the upper house of the Prussian parliament.
Below: The faces of Nazi victims at the Topographie des Terrors, the site of the Gestapo
secret police headquarters

Return to Wilhelmstrasse and continue south. Göring's **Luftfahrtministerium ⑪**, or Aviation Ministry, which lines Wilhelmstrasse (No. 97) between Leipziger Strasse and Niederkirchnerstrasse, was the first of the Nazis' megalomaniacal public buildings to be built (1936). It was used in the GDR's time as the House of Ministries, and was the scene of the workers' protest that launched the June 17, 1953, uprising. Today it is the federal Finance Ministry. Next door along Leipziger Strasse is the **Bundesrat ⑫,** the upper house of the federal German parliament, located in what was the upper house of the Prussian parliament until 1933.

Berlin is at the same time the capital city and one of 16 federal states. Its state parliament, the **Abgeordnetenhaus ⑬,** has its home in what was from 1899 to 1934 the Prussian state parliament lower house on Niederkirchnerstrasse. Standing proudly before the parliament building is a much restored 1869 **statue of Freiherr Karl vom und zum Stein** (1757–1831), a statesman who was instrumental in the implementation of a wide-ranging series of reforms in Prussia in the early 1800s. These novelties were greeted with gritted teeth by the Prussian monarchy and nobility, who would later roll most of them back and prefer instead to recall the reformer's patriotism in fighting Napoleon's army.

Virtually across Niederkirchnerstrasse from the Abgeordnetenhaus at what was once No. 8, behind a more or less intact stretch of the former Berlin Wall, is a vacant lot with a shudder-inducing history.

In 1933, the Third Reich commandeered the neobaroque building that once stood on the lot and converted it into the Reichssicherheitshauptamt, the umbrella body for Nazi Germany's police state apparatus. In the same building was lodged the scariest of Hitler's security tools, Heinrich Himmler's (1900–1945) Geheime Staatspolizei (Secret State Police), or **Gestapo** for short. Opponents of Hitler's regime wound up here for interrogation and torture in the cellars. Standing sentry on this infamous site are panels with text and photos detailing the sordid history of Hitler's security apparatus. Pick up an audioguide in English. The display's name, **Topographie des Terrors** ⓮ (*Niederkirchnerstrasse 8, tel 030 25 48 67 03, www.topographie.de)*, is well chosen, as you will see.

Next door, in the former **Hotel Prinz-Albrecht** ⓯ at No. 9, was the SS (Schutzstaffel, a paramilitary security organization) headquarters, while the SD (Sicherheitsdienst, or Security Service), run by Reinhard Heydrich (1904–1942), moved into the **Prinz-Albrecht-Palais** ⓰, around the corner at Wilhelmstrasse 102. The buildings were heavily damaged during World War II and demolished in the 1950s. The site is partly given over to an open-air display, with panels indicating what was where. The rest has become a wasteland. ∎

Potsdamer Platz

Filmmuseum Berlin

www.filmmuseum-berlin.de

🅰 Map p. 52

✉ Potsdamer Strasse 2

☎ 030 300 90 30

🕐 Closed Mon.

$ $$

🚉 U-Bahn & S-Bahn: Potsdamer Platz

ONE OF THE BUSIEST SQUARES IN PREWAR BERLIN, POTS-damer Platz was largely razed in World War II and then sliced off from West Berlin by the wall. It was here, close to where the sparkling Bahntower (the German railway's national headquarters) now soars above the square, that the first hammers were taken to the wall on November 10, 1989. Remains of the wall mark the spot. Since then, a wasteland has been propelled into the 21st century by reconstruction that is still underway in adjacent Leipziger Platz.

The most exciting project on the square is the **Sony Center,** designed by German-American architect Helmut Jahn (born 1940). Made up of eight buildings and completed in 2000, it has become a symbol of modern Berlin. The centerpiece is the oval Forum, a warren of restaurants, bars, an IMAX cinema, and offices beneath a stunning glass-and-steel big top. Lit up at night in ever changing colors, it is a beacon to Berliners (including those who gather with laptops to benefit from the free Wi-Fi hot spot).

Cunningly built into the glass structure is the old-world **Kaisersaal** *(Bellevue Strasse 1, tel 030 25 75 14 54),* a gourmet restaurant that was the only part of the once elegant late 19th-century Esplanade Hotel to survive World War II. The adjacent 26-floor **Bahntower** is the tallest building on the square.

Inside one of the angular buildings of the complex is the **Filmmuseum Berlin,** which covers the history of film in Germany from the early days of the fabled Babelsberg studios to contemporary German cinema. The exhibition starts on the third floor with a marvelous mirror game. You wander along a silver-lit path past screens showing snippets of classic films and see yourself reflected to infinity in the mirrors that constitute

ceiling, floor, and walls. The exhibition proper starts off with the earliest stars of the German screen, including Henny Porten (1890–1960, the "white goddess of the masses") and Danish-born Asta Nielsen.

From there you are taken through the heady days of the Weimar Republic, an era that produced masterpieces such as Josef von Sternberg's *Der Blaue Engel (The Blue Angel,* with Marlene Dietrich) and Fritz Lang's landmark sci-fi film *Metropolis.* Several rooms are dedicated to Berlin-born star Dietrich herself, and others to the steady exodus of German directors and actors to Hollywood in the 1920s and 1930s. The Nazi era is treated briefly, with a room on Leni Riefenstahl's *Olympia* but no film clips. The remainder of the exhibition deals with the work of Germans in the United States and German cinema (east and west) to the present. The museum is part of the **Filmhaus,** which contains cinemas, the city's film archives, and, beginning in 2006, the **Fernsehmuseum** (TV Museum).

Not as immediately arresting as the spectacular Sony Center is the labyrinthine **Quartier DaimlerChrysler** *(www .potsdamerplatz.de)* across Potsdamer Strasse to the south. The two complexes turn their

The Sony Center Forum is a nocturnal beacon in the heart of Berlin.

Panoramapunkt
www.panoramapunkt.de

📍 Map p. 52

✉ Potsdamer Platz 1

☎ 030 25 29 43 72

🕐 Closed Mon. &
   Nov.–March

💲 $

🚇 U-Bahn & S-Bahn:
   Potsdamer Platz

backs to one another on either side of this windy canyon. The Quartier DaimlerChrysler represents the single greatest urban construction project in European history. Under the direction of Italian architect Renzo Piano (born 1937), a total of 19 new buildings, 10 streets, and 2 squares were created in just four years from 1994. It is a mix of office space, hotels, casino, shopping center, apartments, and entertain-

A summertime drink is just the thing for weary wanderers inside the DaimlerChrysler complex.

ment center. Among the world-class architects to go to town here were Japan's Arata Isozaki (born 1931), Britain's Sir Richard Rogers (born 1933), and Spain's Rafael Moneo (born 1937), as well as several Germans. The signature building is the dark, peat-fired tiled office block at Potsdamer Platz 1, designed by Hans Kollhoff (born 1946). Reaching 338 feet (103 m) and climbing in three layers toward its peak, it has a whiff of Manhattan about it.

Inside the Kollhoff building, you can take what is said to be Europe's fastest elevator (a 20-second whoosh) to the **Panoramapunkt** on the 24th and 25th floors for some of the best views to be found in Berlin.

Haus Huth–Sammlung DaimlerChrysler
www.sammlung.
daimlerchrysler.com

📍 Map p. 52

✉ Alte Potsdamer
   Strasse 5

☎ 030 25 94 14 20

🚇 U-Bahn & S-Bahn:
   Potsdamer Platz

The third tower on the square (after the Bahntower and Kollhoff's building) is a daring work by Renzo Piano. The ocher-tinted 18-story office culminates in an acutely angled glass structure that, seen head on, seems a razor-edged rocket.

The only building on the square to survive World War II intact was **Haus Huth,** a six-story building raised in 1912 by architects Conrad Heidenreich (1873–1937) and Paul Michel (1877–1938). Their decision to use a steel skeleton in construction, revolutionary at the time, gave it the strength to withstand Allied bombs. A restaurant and winery from the time it opened until well into World War II, it is now restored and again home to a fine restaurant, Diekmann (Potsdamer Strasse 5, tel 030 25 29 75 24). The fourth floor holds the **Sammlung DaimlerChrysler,** a constantly changing display of some of the DaimlerChrysler collection of more than a thousand works of contemporary minimalist and conceptual art.

Scattered about inside the DaimlerChrysler mini-city are eight pieces of street sculpture, the most striking being **"Balloon Flower"** by controversial American artist Jeff Koons (born 1955) on Marlene-Dietrich-Platz. It looks likes a series of navy blue sausage balloons twisted together to form, well, a fat flower.

The last of the three big projects on the square is the **Beisheim Center** (www .beisheim-center.de), rising on the triangle of land between Ebertstrasse and Bellevuestrasse. Financed by German tycoon Otto Beisheim, it comprises three top hotels, offices, and luxury apartment buildings created by local and international architects. ■

Checkpoint Charlie

FOR YEARS, MOST FOREIGN DAY-TRIPPERS TO EAST BERLIN crossed here at the U.S. Army's Checkpoint Charlie. A replica of the American checkpoint was erected on the spot in 2001, along with a copy of the sign: YOU ARE LEAVING THE AMERICAN SECTOR. That this Cold War memorial exists at all is due to Rainer Hildebrandt (1914–2004), the man who started and long ran the adjacent Haus am Checkpoint Charlie museum.

Checkpoint Charlie was the best-known Cold War crossing point from West to East Berlin.

A higgledy-piggledy collection begun in a building right next to the Berlin Wall in June 1963, the museum has been an organic affair, growing in haphazard fashion since then to document each new escape and tragedy associated with the wall.

With photos, videos, and models, the meandering museum is full of engrossing details. Several cars used to smuggle people over the border are surpassed by more astounding methods of escape. One woman was taken out of East Berlin inside a big stereo system speaker, another between two hollowed-out surfboards. The most daring escape was that undertaken by two families of four, who sailed across the border in 1979 in Europe's biggest ever hand-made balloon . On show are its fuel tanks and the sewing machine used to assemble 13,450 square feet (1,250 sq m) of material.

In a curious room with communist-era paraphernalia you will espy a red wax candle of Stalin. In the same room are odds and ends that belonged to the former head of the Stasi (secret police), Erich Mielke (1907– 2000), including a tiny telephone book listing the GDR regime's bigwigs. It's opened at the page of GDR president, Erich Honecker, with his phone numbers at home, at the SED party's central committee, and in the Staatsrat (State Council).

Plenty of material is devoted to those who died trying to cross the East German border, much of it presented in personal and heartbreaking fashion—but not all East German soldiers shot to kill. One photo in the collection shows a banner erected on the west side in 1971 that thanks "the many GDR border guards who had no wish and will have no wish to fire on escapees." ∎

Mauermuseum Museumhaus am Checkpoint Charlie

www.mauermuseum.de

🅼 Map p. 53

✉ Friedrichstrasse 43–45

☎ 030 253 72 50

💲 $$$

🚇 U-Bahn: Kochstrasse or Stadtmitte

With the exception of a few last pieces, the Berlin Wall is turning into a distant memory.

The Berlin Wall, then & now

It happened around midnight. Units of the National People's Army stationed in East Berlin (the Soviet sector of the occupied city) went on alert late on August 12, 1961, and by early morning had improvised a wall of barbed wire and tank traps along the 96-mile (155 km) border with West Berlin. U-Bahn and S-Bahn transit between the two halves of the city was shut down.

East Germans had been voting with their feet for years. In the first half of 1961 alone, 200,000 had left for the West. The exodus threatened to destroy the country's economy. SED party chief Walter Ulbricht had declared in June: "No one has any intention of building a wall." He was lying. In agreement with the other countries of the Soviet-controlled Warsaw Pact, East Germany decided to "settle the Berlin problem" with a physical barrier.

On the morning of August 13, hundreds of East Berliners made a last break for freedom. By the end of the day, provisional strips of brick wall were being hastily built, ditches dug, and people forcibly removed from houses overlooking the border. Of 81 crossing points, 69 were permanently shut. Until 1963, virtually no one was allowed to cross in either direction.

In the coming years, the "Anti-Fascist Protection Wall" was perfected. In 1975, a 27-mile (43 km) concrete wall was put into place between the western and eastern halves of city. Made of 2.75-ton (2.5 tonne) prefabricated sections, it was 11.5 to 14 feet (3.5–4 m) high. It often cut through the middle of streets or houses. Behind the wall was a strip of no-man's-land, the "death strip," followed by a ditch and then a roadway for military vehicles. The remaining 69 miles (112 km) of Berlin's boundary with the state of Brandenburg were sealed off with heavily fortified fences. Along the length of the boundary were 300 watchtowers with searchlights and machine-gun openings. Then came a guard-dog run, trip wires, and, later, automatic weapons. Finally an inner fence was erected.

The wall's first fatality, Günter Litfin, fell on August 24, 1961. The last victim, Chris Gueffroy, died on February 5, 1989. About 5,000 people tried to get through the wall and more than 3,000 were arrested. Eighty would-be escapees died and 115 were wounded.

Isolated strips of the wall have been left standing. The longest is along the Spree River and is known as the East Side Gallery (see p. 185). Shorter strips include Niederkirchnerstrasse on the corner with Wilhelmstrasse (see p. 73) and the Gedenkstätte Berliner Mauer (see p. 114) along Kielerstrasse north of the Hamburger Bahnhof. Several watchtowers have been retained, including ones at Kielerstrasse and Am Schlesischen Busch (see p. 185). Memorials to the dead include one on the Tiergarten side of the Brandenburger Tor and another on the Spree River just north of the Reichstag. ■

One August night in 1961, East Germany decided to wall off West Berlin (below). Watchtowers (above) were later installed along its entire length.

More places to visit in Unter den Linden & Potsdamer Platz

BAHNHOF FRIEDRICHSTRASSE

Once the halfway station on the direct train route from Paris to St. Petersburg, Bahnhof Friedrichstrasse has played a lead role in the city's history. After the Berlin Wall went up in August 1961, the station became one of the most important, and surreal, of the city's border crossing points. The multilevel shopping mall in here now makes it impossible to imagine the atmosphere in the station until 1989. People queued for passport control in a glass-and-steel building virtually attached to the station, known as the Tränenpalast (Palace of Tears), now used as a music venue. This is where those returning to the West would take leave of friends and family in the East, most of whom could not obtain a permit. One minute you were in the gray reality of communist East Berlin, the next in a U-Bahn train hurtling back to the lights of the West.
🅰 Map p. 53 ✉ Friedrichstrasse 🚇 U-Bahn & S-Bahn: Friedrichstrasse

MARTIN-GROPIUS-BAU

A russet red noble relic from 19th-century Berlin, the Martin-Gropius-Bau was restored in the late 1970s largely at the insistence of Walter Gropius, a great-nephew of the man after whom this museum space is named. Built in 1881 by Martin Gropius as the Renaissance-style home for the Kunstgewerbemuseum, it housed various of the city's museum collections until World War II. It narrowly escaped the wrecking ball and, since its restoration, sponsors a variety of art exhibitions.
🅰 Map p. 53 ✉ Niederkirchnerstrasse 7 ☎ 030 25 48 60, www.gropiusbau.de ⏱ Closed Tues. 💲 $$ (depends on exhibition) 🚇 U-Bahn & S-Bahn: Potsdamer Platz

MUSEUM FÜR KOMMUNIKATION

This modern successor to an 1898 postal museum is the logical extension of the original. The communication museum's collections are spread out over three floors gathered in a V around an internal courtyard, whose ceiling glows cobalt blue at night. The ground floor is used for temporary exhibitions. Around here you may be intercepted by one of three good-humored robots (although they don't seem to speak English). On the first floor, exhibits are mostly dedicated to postal history and include a collection of German post office signs, as well as an equally curious collection of mailboxes from around the world (with an 1891 example from the United States and another from Russia from 1910). You have probably never seen so many telephones in one exhibition room, complemented by the collection of old-time switchboards and other telecommunications paraphernalia of the not-so-distant past. The top floor's core exhibits involve radio and TV, including some of the first (huge) sets with small screens. The 1936 upright TV, whose horizontal screen was viewed through a mirror, is the most bizarre model of all.
🅰 Map p. 53 ✉ Leipziger Strasse 16 ☎ 030 20 29 40 ⏱ Closed Mon. 💲 $ 🚇 U-Bahn: Stadtmitte ∎

Miniature glass globes add to the visual spectacle at the Museum für Kommunikation.

Next to the high-dosage concentration of art in the Museumsinsel—five halls of high culture—stretches the one-time showcase square of East Berlin, Alexanderplatz. Short strolls from the square bring you to the historic Nikolaiviertel and the once Jewish Scheunenviertel neighborhoods.

Central Berlin

Translucent sea life swims in the AquaDom.

Central Berlin

THIS IS WHERE BERLIN STARTED, HUDDLED AROUND AN ISLAND IN the middle of the Spree River in the 13th century. Where thatched huts of the dark and dank Middle Ages once stood, proud museums built in the early 20th century house extraordinary royal and imperial art collections.

On the same island were the symbols of royal and (from 1871) imperial power. Opposite one another stood the Berliner Schloss, official Berlin residence of Prussian kings and German kaisers, and the late 19th-century Berliner Dom (Berlin Cathedral), its equally impressive, if gaudy, religious counterpart. Both Schloss and Dom were severely damaged in World War II. Schlossplatz became the showplace center of German Democratic Republic (GDR) power between 1949 and 1990, and what will be done with the square remains in doubt.

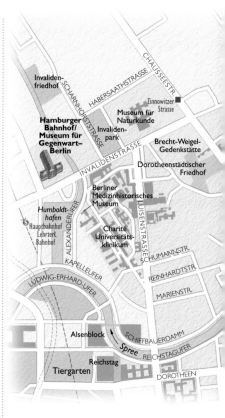

Prussian king Friedrich Wilhelm IV (*R.*1840–1861) originally designated the area north of the Lustgarten as a "free zone for art and science." He could not have imagined how it would develop. The Museumsinsel (Museum Island) lodges five museums whose seemingly endless collections take you from the Babylonian Ishtar Gate to the French Impressionists. It was declared a UNESCO World Heritage site in 1999, and restoration and modernization work is set to continue for years. Work on two of the five—the Bode-Museum and the Alte Nationalgalerie—has been completed; the Neues Museum will reopen in 2009. The Pergamonmuseum and Altes Museum are open but will be renovated in later years.

It will not stop there. The neo-Renaissance Alexander-Kaserne Quartier Am Kupfergraben, west across the Spree from the Bode-Museum, was built in 1898–1901 and used as barracks by the kaiser and again by the East Germans. Beginning in 2009, it will be converted into the administrative headquarters of the Stiftung Preussischer Kulturbesitz (Prussian Cultural Heritage Foundation). A new wing will be built on the site of a now-demolished 1950s barracks to create the Museumshöfe (Museum Courtyards), which will one day host the Gemäldegalerie (see pp. 126–28). This will mostly complete the plan to bring Berlin's classic collections, from ancient Egyptian art to the old masters, together.

East over the Spree sprawls Alexanderplatz, "Alex" to the locals and home to the unmistakable East Berlin TV tower, the rebuilt City Council building, and, maybe one day, a forest of mid-level high-rises.

To its south is a little corner of old Berlin. The Nikolaiviertel, largely a restoration effort of the latter years of the GDR and in some respects not badly executed at all, is as close as World War II–battered Berlin comes to evoking its centuries-old past.

Alexanderplatz was an intermediate station between the high-minded showiness around Schlossplatz and the inner-city slums to its north, in the Scheunenviertel. The bulk of Berlin's poorer Jewish community lived in this colorful quarter. The most obvious trace

of their presence is the Neue Synagoge on Oranienburger Strasse. After a long GDR winter, the area is now again exploding with life.

Farther north and west lies diverse material for the curious, ranging from playwright Bertolt Brecht's former house to the Hamburger Bahnhof exhibition space. ■

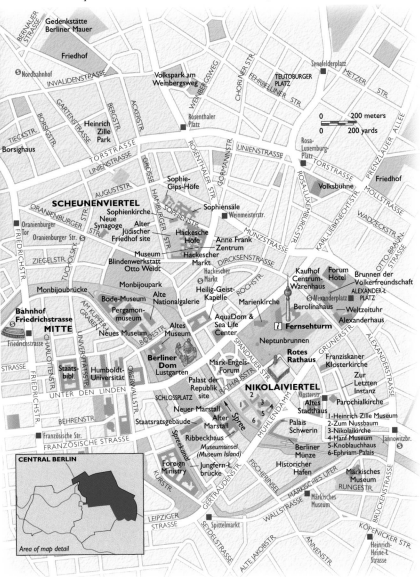

The ruins of the Greek Pergamon Altar have been reassembled and completed inside this museum of ancient art.

Pergamon-museum
www.smb.museum
- Map p. 83
- Am Kupfergraben
- 030 20 90 55 77
- Closed Mon.
- $$$
- S-Bahn: Hackescher Markt

Pergamonmuseum

IT WAS THE LAST OF THE FIVE MUSEUMS TO BE BUILT in the Museumsinsel (1930) and easily the most imposing. The Pergamonmuseum, Berlin's most visited, was built with airs of a Babylonian temple and is the city's most monumental art space, in every sense. The three grand wings loom in intimidating fashion as you approach the entrance to this haven of ancient art across a broad courtyard. The exhibits are equally impressive. Home to three extraordinary collections, it is best known for its re-creation of ancient sites, from Babylon's Ishtar Gate to the ancient Greek Pergamon Altar after which the museum is named.

Throughout the 19th century and up until World War II, German archaeologists were busy in the Middle East, from Turkey to Iran, digging up everything from pottery to whole buildings. You could spend hours in this treasure chest. A handful of its highlights are mentioned below.

In each of the museums of the Museumsinsel, an audio guide in English is available and recommended, as many of the written explanations are in German only or, at best, are more detailed in German than they are in English.

There is no slow lead-up to the first of the big stars. With tickets in hand, you wander straight into a vast room containing the re-creation of the **Pergamon Altar,** a combination of original ruins shipped to Berlin, then reassembled and completed inside the museum. The mostly destroyed altar was unearthed with other parts of the Acropolis in the Greek town of Pergamon (today Bergama) in western Turkey in the 1870s and 1880s. The most important finds were sizable chunks of the friezes that surrounded the altar. What we see today in the hall is the re-creation of the west side of the altar, originally built around 170 B.C. The friezes from the north, south, and east sides of the altar hang on the exhibition room's walls. They depict battles pitting the gods against the giants, allegorical stories representing the struggle between good and evil in which the gods (the good guys) come out on top, although, like any good drama, only just.

Upstairs, inside what would have been the altar courtyard, is another series of friezes. These pieces tell the life story of Telephos, the mythical founder of Pergamon who, as a boy, was cast out into the desert and then led a

Tickets please

Entry to each of the museums on the Museumsinsel can be purchased separately *($$)*, but a general ticket for all of them is also available *($$$)*. Better value still is the three-day ticket *($$$, ask at tourist office; half price for students and children)* that gives entry to a long list of museums across the city, including those of the Museumsinsel. Note that in many museums entry is free on Thursdays beginning four hours before closing time. ∎

life of adventure and warfare to wind up a hero.

Passing from here into the (south) **right wing** of the museum, the visitor is confronted by another enormous monumental removal job: the Roman market gate of Milet, an originally Greek town on the west coast of modern Turkey, about 50 miles (80 km) south of the city of Izmir. Built about A.D. 120, the massive gate, 95 feet (29 m) wide

Roman statues show strong Greek influences.

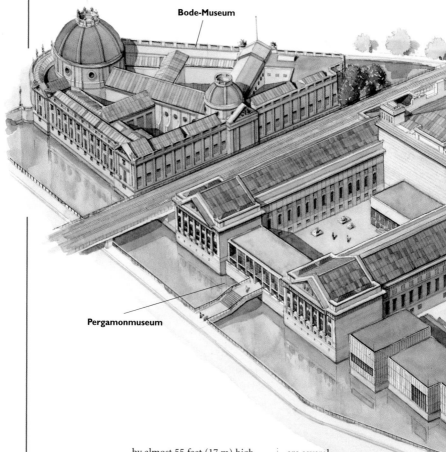

Bode-Museum

Pergamonmuseum

by almost 55 feet (17 m) high, was in fact a rather modest part of the cityscape of ancient Milet when it was a major Mediterranean trading port. Judge for yourself from the model of the town. Mostly destroyed by an earthquake in the Middle Ages, the gate was reconstructed by German archaeologists and then again damaged in Allied bombing raids in World War II. The gate here is surrounded by other items of Roman architecture.

To stick with the classical theme, cross back past the Pergamon Altar to the **north wing.** In the first main room are several items of powerful Greek architecture, including the propylon to the temple to Athena, the goddess of wisdom. This structure usually preceded or was incorporated into a gate. It will also be hard to miss the giant columns from the temple to Artemis, the goddess of the hunt.

From here stretches a series of nine rooms jammed with Greek and, more generally, Hellenistic art. They are followed by a few rooms dedicated to Roman art, often copies of Hellenistic greatness. Among the most beautiful works of statuary here is the one depicting a goddess on

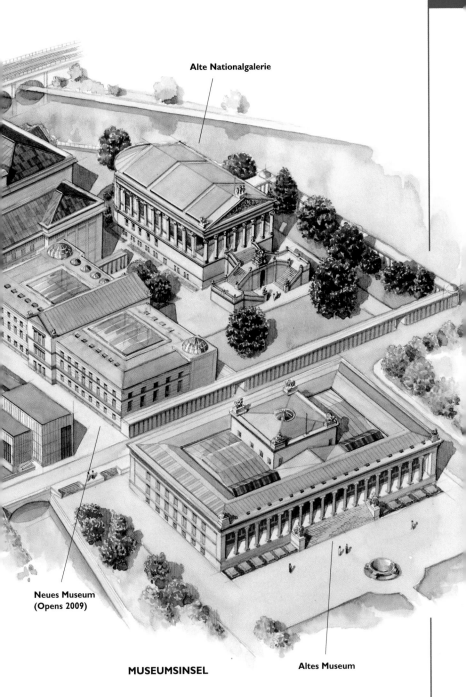

Alte Nationalgalerie

Neues Museum
(Opens 2009)

MUSEUMSINSEL

Altes Museum

her throne, found near the southern Italian city of Taranto (which started life as an ancient Greek settlement). The Romans were great engineers but couldn't touch the Greeks for artistic flair. They pragmatically recognized this flaw themselves, and **Room 14** is full of Roman statues copied from Greek originals.

To head into another world altogether, return to the Milet gate and cross it to be transported to the **Vorderasiatisches Museum** (Museum of the Ancient Near East). It could hardly begin in more overwhelming fashion, for in this area has been reconstructed the fabulous Ishtar Gate of Babylon, built in the sixth century B.C. under Nebuchadnezzar II (*R.*605–562 B.C.). The gate is adorned with glazed blue ceramic bricks and reliefs of dragons and bulls. The central corridor leading away from it is lined by equally blue walls and adorned with images of marching lions. All the animal figures were symbolic of Babylonian gods.

The original processional way was much longer and wider, and the gate you see is actually only a small precursor to a grander affair that lay inside the city of Babylon. Of the reconstruction, the lower levels and most of the animal reliefs are originals shipped by German archaeologists to Berlin in the late 19th and early 20th centuries. To complete the picture, experts then rebuilt the rest of the gate as it probably once appeared.

There is plenty more to explore in this collection. In **Room 7,** the glazed decorative theme continues with colorful reliefs, depicting soldiers, that once graced palaces in the ancient Persian cities of Perseopolis and

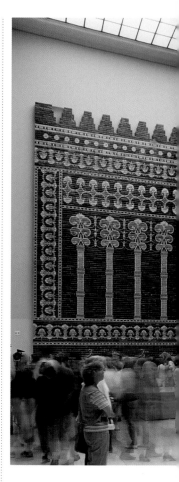

Susa (in present-day Iran). **Room 6** contains clay tablets with texts in cuneiform script dating as far back as 2300 B.C., making them some of the earliest examples of written documents.

Room 2, at the western end of the hall, contains impressive finds from ancient Syria. They include the partial re-creation of a stretch of the citadel wall, built in about the eighth century B.C., from Samal, a northern Syrian city. Its four basalt lion sculptures (one a copy) were designed to ward off evil. It is also hard to miss the huge statue of an

ancient Syrian god, Hadad.

Rooms 10 to **12** contain a welter of original and copied Assyrian reliefs. Ancient Assyria emerged as a power in northern Mesopotamia and took in parts of modern Syria, Turkey, Iraq, and Iran from around 2400 B.C. to the sixth century B.C.

From the ancient Near Eastern world, you travel upstairs to the third collection, the **Museum für Islamische Kunst** (Museum of Islamic Art). At its core is a collection of precious oriental carpets. Before reaching this area, however,

there are other moments to savor. **Room 4** is dominated by a stunning ceramic *mihrab* (prayer niche), which was removed from the Maidan Mosque in Kashan, Iran, in the 19th century. The British general consul in Isfahan bought it in 1897 and had it sent to his family home in London. German officials then purchased it in 1927 for the Berlin museum.

Still more stunning is the 13th-century turquoise faience mihrab in **Room 5,** from the Beyhekim Mosque in Konya, Turkey.

The museum's oriental carpets

The glory that was Babylon unfolds before you with the startling, ceramic-covered Ishtar Gate, one of the star attractions of the Pergamon-museum.

were accumulated by the founder of what is now the Bode-Museum (see pp. 96–97), Wilhelm von Bode. Some of the best of them, early Ottoman rugs from Turkey, are on view in **Room 12.**

But the Islamic art collections grew quickly from the late 19th century. The single biggest item, found in **Room 9,** was a present from the Turkish sultan, Abulhamid II, to Kaiser Wilhelm II in 1904. It was nothing less than the base of the facade and towers of an eighth-century prince's palace in Mshatta, about 19 miles (30 km) from Amman in present-day Jordan. It bears complex geometrical decoration within triangular fields along its length and is a stunning piece of reconstruction. The palace, part of which still stands in Jordan, was one of a series of desert castles that were once strung across the Jordanian desert. They belonged to the early Damascus-based Umayyad caliphs who ruled at the beginning of the Muslim Arab conquests of the Middle East in the eighth century.

The last item of the Islamic collection is the **Aleppo Room,** a whole reception room removed from the house of a wealthy Christian businessman in the northern Syrian town of Aleppo. Reconstructed here, it is an extraordinary example of marquetry work, rich in the geometric design typical of Muslim art in the Arab world and adopted by Arab Christians.

The Pergamonmuseum and its companions on the Museumsinsel will undergo more change over the coming years. A walkway linking all but the Alte Nationalgalerie will give rise to an archaeological promenade bringing all Berlin's ancient collections together. Gardens will also be laid out between the Pergamon and its sister museums. At any given time in the near future, parts of the museum's collections may be closed or moved. Take a look at www.museumsinsel-berlin.de to see how the Museumsinsel will appear in 2015. ∎

Joining a tour

Why join a standard walking or bus tour in Berlin when you can float along the Spree River? **Reederei Bruno Winkler** (tel 030 349 95 95, www.reedereiwinkler.de) is one of several companies offering leisurely boat tours.

Ever dreamed of driving the standard East German commuter car, the Trabant? Probably not, but here's your chance to get behind the wheel and join a convoy on a spin through central Berlin with **Trabi Tour** (tel 030 70 20 94 94, www.trabi-x.de).

Land, water ... and air! Climb aboard a Douglas Dakota of the kind used in the Berlin Airlift in 1948–49 and take off from Tempelhof airport for a 45-minute flight over the now united city. Contact **Air Service Berlin** (tel 030 53 21 53 21, www.rosinenbomber. com).

Berlin is fascinating underground. The people from **Berliner Unterwelten** (tel 030 49 91 05 17, www.berliner-unter welten.de) will show you bunkers past and present, ghost U-Bahn stations of the divided Berlin, and escape routes from East to West (some tours in English). ∎

Alte Nationalgalerie

The Alte
Nationalgalerie
forms an
impressive
backdrop for
summer outdoor
films.

DESIGNED BY FRIEDRICH AUGUST STÜLER, THE NEOCLASSIC
building that houses the Old National Gallery of 19th-century art
opened in 1876. For most visitors, the highlight of its collection is the
selection of French Impressionists on the third floor. The museum
also has an extensive display of the works of Adolph Menzel, one of
the most important Berlin artists of the century.

You reach the **second floor** by a
flight of stairs from the ticket desk.
The large first room is lined with
19th-century sculptures, including
Johann Gottfried Schadow's
"Prinzessinen Luise und Friedrike
von Preussen" and a bust of Johann
Wolfgang von Goethe (1749–1832),
one of Germany's greatest poets.

    Rooms 1.02 and **1.03** harbor
a mixed group of early 19th-
century realist works, mostly
landscapes, by the likes of John
Constable (1776–1837), Gustave
Courbet (1819–1877), Eugène
Delacroix (1798–1863), and even
one by the Spaniard Francisco de
Goya y Lucientes (1746–1828).

    Adolph Menzel, Berlin's painter
and a favorite with the royal court,
dominates **Rooms 1.05** to **1.12**.
In **Room 1.06** are some of his
bigger canvases, including the well-
known "Flötenkonzert Friedrichs
des Grossen in Sanssouci," which
depicts Frederick the Great giving a
flute concert in the Sanssouci summer palace in Potsdam. His smaller
paintings from **Room 1.08** on-
ward show that he was no mere
court painter and was happy to
portray things beyond royal reach.
"Hinterhaus und Hof" ("Rear
House and Courtyard"), for
instance, is a typical city landscape.

    You access the **third floor** by
an atrium graced with statues by
Reinhold Begas depicting mytho-
logical figures. In **Room 2.02** and
a few others are displayed works of
the so-called German Romans, a
group of young German and
Austrian artists who lived in Rome
in the early 19th century.

    The French Impressionists are
gathered in the central hall on the

**Alte
Nationalgalerie**
www.smb.museum

🄰 Map p. 83

✉ Bodestrasse 1–3

☎ 030 20 90 55 77

🕒 Closed Mon.

💲 $$$

🚇 U-Bahn & S-Bahn:
Friedrichstrasse

third floor **(Room 2.03)**. Here flourishes a potpourri of France's best. These paintings, glistening like jewels, were acquired mainly around the turn of the 20th century amid much controversy in Berlin's conservative circles, which thought little of Impressionism.

"Le Jardin d'Hiver" ("Winter Garden") by Édouard Manet (1832–1883) depicts two of the artist's friends in a florid southern French garden. Paul Cézanne (1839–1906), Auguste Renoir (1841–1919), and Claude Monet (1840–1926) are each represented

The three figures dominating the top floor are Karl Friedrich Schinkel, Caspar David Friedrich (1774–1840), and Carl Blechen. Although Schinkel **(Room 3.05)** was principally active as an architect, he had an eye for canvas, too. His attention to architectural detail in this series of mostly fantasy landscapes is notable.

Fine though his paintings are, the emotions are stirred more by Friedrich **(Room 3.06)**. This Romantic painter, who worked in Dresden, evoked the power, majesty, and mystery of nature,

A visitor ponders frescoes by the "German Romans," German artists who lived and worked in Rome in the 19th century.

with three works. Edgar Degas (1834–1917) and Camille Pissarro (1830–1903) also have works on this floor. To finish is a couple of bronzes by Auguste Rodin (1840–1917).

The other star of the third floor is Berlin's own Max Liebermann, whose large canvases **(Room 2.13)** depict realistic scenes of everyday, working life. These include "Flachsscheune in Laren" ("Flax Barn in Laren") and "Gänserupferinnen" ("Women Plucking Geese").

whether on land ("Der Watzmann—A mountain peak") or on the coast ("Zwei Männer am Meer—Two Men by the Sea").

In Blechen's works, look for the change that occurs on his voyage to Italy **(Rooms 3.07–3.08)**. While "Felsenlandschaft mit Mönch" ("Monk by Cliffs") exudes the shadowy textures of his northern homeland, his Italian paintings, such as "Fischer auf Capri" ("Fishermen on the Island of Capri") are flooded with Italian summer sunlight. ∎

Altes Museum

ONE OF THE MOST HARMONIOUS NEOCLASSIC BUILDINGS in Berlin, the Altes Museum might normally be considered one of the lesser members of the Museumsinsel team. Its primary collection, the Antikensammlung (Collection of Classical Antiquities), is made up principally of ancient Greek artifacts on the first floor. Until 2009, however, the museum also houses Berlin's renowned Ägyptisches Museum and Papyrussammlung (Egyptian Museum and Papyrus Collection) on the upper floor.

The Altes Museum is temporary home to the city's ancient Egyptian treasures.

Altes Museum

www.smb.museum

🅰 Map p. 83

✉ Lustgarten

☎ 030 20 90 55 77

🅂 $$$

🚇 U-Bahn & S-Bahn: Friedrichstrasse

Yet another product of architect Karl Friedrich Schinkel, the building was completed in 1830 under the orders of King Friedrich Wilhelm III. As a frieze in the **Säulenhalle** (Hall of Pillars) proclaims, he "donated this museum for the study of every kind of antiquities and the free arts."

Badly damaged in World War II, the museum remained closed until 1966. The facade has 18 fluted Ionic columns facing the Lustgarten. Inside, the theme continues with more Ionic columns in the Hall of Pillars at the entrance and inside the **Rotunda,** a circular chamber inspired by the Roman Pantheon. Only the Rotunda was restored faithfully after the war, down to the 18 Roman statues copied from Greek originals.

Looping around the Rotunda are two floors of exposition space. The **Antikensammlung** on the first floor starts with objects from ancient Crete, Mycenae, and the Cyclades, with simple statuettes and pottery dating as far back as 3000 B.C. The collection proceeds in loose chronological order; it is divided into 30 sections, each dedicated to a theme. **Section 4** contains a battalion of bronze helmets, figurines, and weaponry from Olympus. The decoration and forms of pottery (amphorae, pots, jars, plates, and more) become more elaborate as you proceed.

A detour in **Section 8** takes you through a collection of ancient gold and jewelry. Greek, Etruscan, Persian, and Roman items dominate. A golden fish that apparently decorated a warrior's shield is eye-catching. The beautifully decorated amphorae in **Sections 12** and **13** show sporting scenes, from wrestling to running.

other items constitutes one of the most important such finds in the world. How this collection wound up where it was found, 174 miles (280 km) east of the Roman world's ancient frontier with Germany, remains a mystery.

Giant amphorae from Greek settlements in southern Italy, especially Taranto, fill **Section 23,** and the glass example (150–80 B.C.)

Ghosts of classical warriors seem to stare at visitors in the collections of the Altes Museum.

The high point in **Section 14,** halfway through the floor, is "Der Betende Knabe" ("The Praying Boy"), an extraordinarily graceful bronze statue from 300 B.C.

Section 17 contains ceramics with decoration depicting festivals and orgies (including a merry group of satyrs). **Section 20** is home to silver treasures, principally the Hildesheimer Silberfund. This collection of 70-odd pieces of Roman silverware had been carefully buried near Hildesheim and forgotten for centuries until an army unit stumbled across it in 1868. The remarkable collection of plates, vases, trays, goblets, and

from the Greek colony of Olbia on the Black Sea in **Section 25** is unique, if only because it survived through all these centuries.

Roman sculpture inspired by Greek models dominates the last few rooms. The most curious items are the portraits on wood placed on Roman mummies in Egypt in the first two centuries A.D., after Egypt had been absorbed by the Roman Empire.

All this pales when compared with the display of ancient Egyptian treasures upstairs in the **Ägyptisches Museum and Papyrussammlung.** Here, since mid-2005, the city's extraordinary collection of Egyptian artifacts has again been brought under one roof.

Upon entering you are greeted by an imposing granite statue of Pharaoh Amenenhet III (1840–1800 B.C.), surrounded by myriad smaller busts including one of Queen Hatshepsut (1517–1484 B.C.), one of Egypt's few female pharaohs. The statues, seated and standing, accompanied in

tuted the monotheistic worship of the sun god, Aten.

The star of the collection, and one of Berlin's most famous artistic possessions, is the 1340 B.C. bust of Akhenaten's wife Nefertiti. This remarkably preserved painted limestone bust, found in an Egyptian sculptor's workshop, shows her as an exceptionally beautiful woman.

burial the person they depicted. Standing versions, with one foot forward and apparently ready to set off on a brisk walk, were meant to give the dead person dynamism and strength in the afterlife.

The statues are made of granite, quartzite, limestone, bronze, and timber. Some are in exquisite condition. Other statues, often covered in hieroglyphs, were typically placed in temples.

Sections 2–5 deal with the brief period of royal eccentricity under Akhenaten (*R.*1353–1336 B.C.), the pharaoh who abandoned Thebes, created a new capital (at what is now Amarna), and insti-

Following these sections is a selective exhibit from the Berlin papyrus collection, one of the most extensive in the world. Documents on display range from fairy tales to court rulings, from a wedding contract to instructions from a general on the execution of two wayward policemen. The documents are not only in hieroglyphics, but in later derivative scripts as well. Others are in Greek, Latin, Aramaic, and even Arabic.

Next up comes a display of coffins and mummies. The Egyptian collection ends with two human-size statues of the lion-headed god Sakhmet. ■

The stunning bust of Queen Nefertiti is the most exquisite item displayed in the Altes Museum.

Bode-Museum & Neues Museum

Bode-Museum

www.smb.museum

🅰 Map p. 83

✉ Am Kupfergraben
(entrance on
Monbijoubrücke)

☎ 030 20 90 55 77

🕐 Closed Mon.

💲 $$$

🚇 U-Bahn & S-Bahn:
Friedrichstrasse

Neues Museum

www.smb.museum

🅰 Map p. 83

✉ Bodestrasse 4

☎ 030 20 90 55 77

🕐 Opens in 2009

💲 $$$

🚇 U-Bahn & S-Bahn:
Friedrichstrasse

IN 2006 ANOTHER MAJOR PIECE IN BERLIN'S AMBITIOUS plan for museum renewal fell into place with the reopening of the Bode-Museum, home to the city's main sculpture and coin collections, as well as to a section on Byzantine art. The renewal scheme will come a step closer to completion when the Neues Museum reopens in 2009 and the Egyptian collection returns there.

Ridiculed by the local press when it opened in 1904 and dubbed the "Cul de Berlin" (Berlin's Arse), the neobaroque Kaiser-Friedrich-Museum (as it was originally called) forms the graciously curving northern bow of the Museumsinsel that splits the Spree River in two. Designed by Ernst Eberhard von Ihne (1848–1917), it lay half destroyed by the end of World War II. In 1956 it was renamed after Wilhelm von Bode (1845–1929), long the city's most prominent museum director and a key supporter of this museum in particular. Two late 19th-century Monbijou bridges (blown up by the SS in the dying days of World War II) were also rebuilt in 2006, giving access to the museum from both banks of the Spree.

On entering, you meet a copy of the equestrian statue of Great Elector Friedrich Wilhelm (the restored original, by Andreas Schlüter, now stands before Schloss Charlottenburg). Gilded busts of other Prussian rulers line the walls below the splendid dome. The main hall proceeds south, its second part known as the basilica and graced with a coat of arms of the long-ruling medieval Medici dynasty of Florence. It terminates in another circular hall and dome. The museum's collections are spread out over several branch corridors

on two floors, along with a brand-new underground level.

The prime collection is the **Skulpturensammlung** and **Museum für Byzantinische Kunst** (Sculpture Collection and Museum of Byzantine Art). Among the jewels of sculpture here are the 12th-century "Madonna des Presbyter Martinus" ("Father Martin's Madonna"), an archetypical Romanesque Virgin Mother and Child figure from central Italy; the 15th-century polychrome walnut "Dangolsheimer Muttergottes" statue of the Virgin and Child; and German reliefs and works by the Bavarian Ignaz Günther (1725–1775). Other works in stone and wood span a period from Byzantine times to the 18th century.

Also important is the Museum für Byzantinische Kunst, containing art from the dying years of the ancient world and the Byzantine Empire. Items from the latter include some remarkable mosaics, including a late 13th-century representation of the Crucifixion of Christ, flanked by the Virgin Mary and Apostle John. It is one of only three such mosaics in the world (the others are at Mount Sinai, Egypt, and in a monastery on Mount Athos, northern Greece).

The **Münzkabinett** (Coin Cabinet), a collection of more

than 500,000 coins and medallions from all historical eras, is one of the most important of its kind in the world. The Soviet Army made off with it after World War II, but the collection was handed back to East Germany in 1958. You can examine coins from the ancient world (especially Greece and Rome), pieces from medieval Europe, Byzantium, Asia, and the Muslim world, as well as a host of more modern coins from Europe and the Americas. Most are stored in 82 cabinets with nearly 11,500 display drawers in the museum's basement. Modernized in 2004, the coin cabinet was created in 1904 and is the best preserved exhibition space of the Museumsinsel. Portions of the coin collection will eventually go on display on the first floor. Some selected works from the Gemäldegalerie (see pp. 126–28) and Kunstgewerbemuseum (see p. 125) will also be moved here.

Designed by Friedrich August Stüler and completed in 1855, the Neues Museum (New Museum) was one of the most advanced museums in the world when it was built. It was the original home of the Egyptian collection. After World War II, the museum was still standing, but in bad shape, and the collection resided in the Bode-Museum. In the early years after World War II, as most of the Museumsinsel museums were shut down, the Egyptian collection was moved to Charlottenburg, where it remained until 2005. Now in the nearby Altes Museum (see pp. 93–95), it will return to its original home in 2009 when restoration is complete. ■

Elegant stairways grace the Bode-Museum, home to most of the city's medieval sculpture collections.

Built as a place
of worship for
the Kaiser and
his family, the
Berliner Dom
came close to
demolition after
World War II.

Berliner Dom & Lustgarten

IT IS HARD TO BELIEVE THAT THIS GRAND, POWERFUL
cathedral, symbol of turn-of-the-20th-century imperial power at the
heart of Germany, was gutted in World War II, or that East Berlin's
communist regime considered pulling it down completely in the 1950s.

Berliner Dom
www.berliner-dom.de

🅰 Map p. 83

✉ Am Lustgarten

☎ 030 20 26 90

💲 $$

🚇 S-Bahn: Hackescher
Markt

The Italian Renaissance–style
church was erected from 1894 to
1905, replacing an earlier, 1750
cathedral that itself had been
reworked by Karl Friedrich
Schinkel in 1822. Just across the
road from the imperial Schloss, this
was the Hohenzollern court church
and main family burial place.
Restoration work began in 1975
and continues today. Since the mid-
1990s, the grand, octagonal
Predigtkirche (main church build-
ing) has become the scene of regu-
lar choir performances.

Some of the cathedral's finest
decorative elements come from
its predecessor. They include the
white marble and yellow onyx
altar by Friedrich August Stüler,
the Schinkel-designed candelabra,
and the gilded lectern, probably
created by Andreas Schlüter.
Across the church from the altar

is the *Kaiserempore,* or imperial
gallery, where the kaiser sat.

Magnificent Schlüter-designed
decorative sarcophagi for King
Friedrich I and his second wife
Sophie Charlotte rest in niches
on the south flank of the church.
The monarchs are now buried
downstairs in the **Hohen-
zollerngruft** (Hohenzollern
Crypt), home to 94 coffins of
members of the royal family.

Long flights of stairs from the
cathedral's south side take you
past the Dom's **museum,** with
19th-century scale models of pro-
posed cathedral designs, on to an
external gallery around the top of
the copper **dome** (follow the
signs *Zur Kuppel*).

In front of the church
stretches the Lustgarten, an
unadorned park today but once
a splendid baroque garden. ■

Schlossplatz & around

THIS SQUARE WAS ONCE THE SYMBOLIC CENTER OF Berlin. On one side stood the Berliner Schloss (palace) and on the other its counterweight, the Berliner Dom. The palace is now but a memory, but many in Berlin hope to make it reality again and wipe out the gray memories of the former communist regime.

Schlossplatz
Map p. 83

Berlin's first princely castle, built in the 15th century, was replaced by a Renaissance palace in the 16th century. In 1699, Andreas Schlüter turned this royal residence into a fine baroque palace. His successor, Johann Friedrich Eosander von Göthe, doubled its size but mostly respected Schlüter's lines. The work was completed in 1716.

The palace took direct hits in air raids on February 3, 1945. Although badly damaged, it succumbed not to bombs but to ideology. Despite an international outcry, Walter Ulbricht's communist regime decided in 1950 to replace what he considered a vile symbol of German imperialism with a parade ground for "spontaneous" demonstrations.

In the 1970s a steel, concrete, and copper-colored-glass monstrosity was built on the site as the GDR's rubber-stamp parliamentary seat. This **Palast der Republik** (Palace of the Republic) will be demolished by 2007. A new complex called Das Humboldt-Forum, which includes a facade based on the original Schloss, is planned for the location (though financing remains unclear). Until that is built, the area is likely to be reshaped as public gardens until at least 2012.

Across the now desolate Schlossplatz stands the 1964 **Staatsratsgebäude,** another onetime GDR government building that, in this case, has become a business school. Some of the old GDR national symbols have been kept in two lecture halls of this protected monument.

Facing it across Breite Strasse is the 1670 **Alter Marstall,** once the royal stables and Berlin's oldest baroque structure. An extension from 1901, **Neuer Marstall,** is now home to a music school. South of the Alter Marstall is the Renaissance **Ribbeckhaus,** notable for its pretty gables. About 300 yards (275 m) west, the city's oldest bridge, the **Jungfernbrücke,** crosses the Spree to the Foreign Ministry. ∎

Save the Ampelmännchen!

Berlin's first pedestrian lights were introduced in 1957, but four years later, after the city was split by the wall, new lights were installed in East Berlin: a green man with a flat hat, decisively stepping out (go), and a red fellow with his arms outstretched (wait). With reunification in 1990, it was planned to replace these with standard West Berlin lights, but fans launched a campaign to save the Ampelmännchen (little traffic-light man), which had become a cult figure. Most of the lights were saved and new ones have even appeared in the western half of the city. Ampelmännchen key rings, mugs, fridge magnets, and stickers now take up as much space in souvenir stores as Berlin Wall memorabilia. ∎

The old East German crosswalk lights have been given the green light to stay on the street.

A walk around Red Berlin

The working class and left-oriented intellectual circles have always had an influence on Berlin's politics, and for 40 years East Berlin was capital of the communist GDR, so it doesn't take long to uncover reminders of the city's socialist and communist past.

The Fernsehturm tower, Berlin's tallest structure, rises over Alexanderplatz.

Begin in the Tiergarten with the **Sowjetisches Ehrenmal ❶** (see p. 120), a memorial to the Soviet liberation of Berlin in 1945. (The mini-revolt of June 17, 1953, in East Berlin protested this "liberation.") Head east to Brandenburger Tor on Strasse des 17. Juni, which takes its name from that unsuccessful uprising.

A block north of the gate, on the corner of Ebertstrasse and Scheidemannstrasse, is a makeshift **Berlin Wall memorial ❷** honoring those killed attempting to cross the wall between 1961 and 1989.

A stroll east along Dorotheenstrasse into what was East Berlin leads to the **corner of Friedrichstrasse ❸**, where Friedrich Engels (1820–1895), coauthor of the *Communist Manifesto*, lived for a year (1841). A plaque marks the spot but the house was destroyed in World War II.

Walk south to Unter den Linden and turn left (east). Vladimir Ilyich Lenin

(1870–1924), who led the Russian Revolution, studied at the **Staatsbibliothek ❹** on your left before World War I. One building east, Karl Marx (1818–1883) studied at **Humboldt Universität ❺**, where he forged his early ideas for communism, from 1836 to 1841.

On the east side of the university is the **Neue Wache ❻** (see p. 64), the central memorial to victims of Nazism under the East German regime. Walk south along the Spree until you come to the current **Foreign Ministry ❼** (see p. 69) in the Nazi-era Reichsbank. In 1958, it housed the Central Committee of East Germany's Sozialistische Einheitspartei Deutschlands (SED, German Socialist Unity Party).

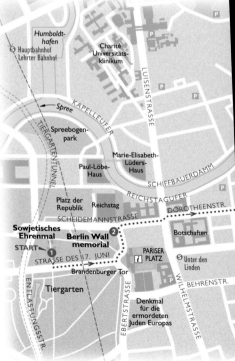

Cross the Jungfernbrücke and turn left for the Schlossplatz. A monumental doorway and balcony salvaged from the Schloss, the palace destroyed by the East Germans (see p. 99), remains on the former **Staatsratsgebäude** 8, or State Council building, on the north side of the square. From this doorway Karl Liebknecht proclaimed (in vain) the socialist republic in 1918, setting off the Spartacist revolt (see p. 26). Those events are commemorated in reliefs on the **Neuer Marstall** 9. The East German parliament was in the now demolished **Palast der Republik** 10 built over the Schloss site.

Walk east and cross the Spree again. In the square behind the Palast der Republik site stands a stiff statue to Marx and Engels in the **Marx-Engels-Forum** 11 (see p. 104). Continue east to reach concrete-laden Alexanderplatz, East Berlin's showcase square, topped by the city's tallest building, the **Fernsehturm** 12 (see p. 102). A little way north, along Spandauer Strasse, the

location of the **German Communist Party (KPD)** headquarters 13 until 1926 is marked by a plaque at Rosenthaler Strasse 38. The party then moved to the bigger **Karl-Liebknecht-Haus** 14 at Kleine Alexanderstrasse (a zigzag walk northeast via Münzstrasse), just off Rosa-Luxemburg-Platz, until banned by the Nazis in 1933. ∎

> See area map pp. 82–83
> Sowjetisches Ehrenmal, Strasse des 17. Juni
> 3.4 miles (5.5 km)
> 2 hours
> Rosa-Luxemburg-Platz

NOT TO BE MISSED
- Sowjetisches Ehrenmal
- Neue Wache
- Staatsratsgebäude
- Fernsehturm

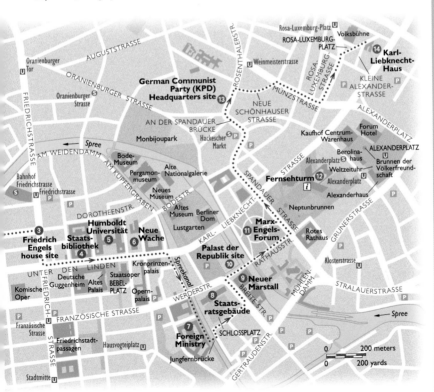

Alexanderplatz & around

Fernsehturm
www.berlinerfernsehturm.de

🅰 Map p. 83

✉ Panoramastrasse 1a

☎ 030 242 33 33

💲 $$$

🚇 U-Bahn & S-Bahn: Alexanderplatz

Marienkirche

🅰 Map p. 83

✉ Karl-Liebknecht-Strasse 8

☎ 030 242 44 67

🚇 U-Bahn & S-Bahn: Alexanderplatz

Rotes Rathaus

🅰 Map p. 83

✉ Rathausstrasse 15

☎ 030 9 02 60

🕐 Closed Sat.–Sun.

🚇 U-Bahn & S-Bahn: Alexanderplatz

ANYONE WHO HAS READ (AND MANAGED TO UNDERSTAND!) Alfred Döblin's *Berlin Alexanderplatz* cannot help being drawn to what was in the 1920s one of the busiest corners of the city. But Döblin's square ceased to exist after World War II. Heavily damaged, it was converted into a shadow of its former self by the communist authorities from the 1950s on. For all that, this onetime showplace of socialism is full of interest and, with the symbolic golf-ball TV tower soaring from its heart, an obligatory stop.

This onetime animal market was turned into a square and named after Russian tsar Alexander I (1777–1825) in 1805, when he paid Berlin a state visit. In the 1848 revolt, workers clashed violently with police and erected barricades here. In 1882 a train station was built across the middle of the square, and a U-Bahn station was added in 1913.

Döblin described the square in the 1920s, when it hosted department stores such as Wertheim (since 1910) and Tietz (opened in 1904), as a playground for "delinquents, prostitutes, and the penniless."

The square got the beginnings of a facelift in 1931–1932 with the construction of the Alexanderhaus and Berolinahaus by leading architect and designer Peter Behrens (1868–1940). Considered the height of modern architecture at the time, they remain standing today. In GDR times came the Interhotel Stadt Berlin (the now rather worn-looking Park Inn) and Centrum-Warenhaus (which is now part of the German Kaufhof chain of department stores). Most impressive of all was the Fernsehturm (TV tower) southwest of the train station, the tallest structure in all Berlin at 1,207 feet (368 m). Less impressive are the rather sad **Weltzeituhr** (World Clock), a popular meeting place in

East Berlin, in front of the Alexanderhaus, and the neglected **Brunnen der Völkerfreundschaft** (Friendship of the Peoples Fountain), just behind the Berolinahaus. Ambitious plans to transform the square and surrounding area with ten 492-foot-high (150 m) buildings may fall short, although one tower may be built as part of a huge entertainment and commercial center.

The 1969 **Fernsehturm,** pride and joy of the GDR and highest structure in Germany, has become a symbol of the city. The 28,660-ton (26,000 metric ton) concrete shaft supports a distinctive ball-shaped structure holding an observation deck and a revolving café at 666 feet (203 m). In the heyday of East Berlin, you could enjoy propaganda films in the tower's information center on the joys of life in the "Capital City of the GDR."

At the foot of the tower lies the only hint of Berlin's centuries of history in this part of town. The **Marienkirche** is a Gothic church rebuilt in 1380 after fire destroyed its predecessor. Inside, the main work of art is the faded 15th-century "Totentanz" ("Dance of Death"), a macabre 72-foot-long (22 m) frieze along the walls on your left as you enter by the main door. Andreas Schlüter designed the pulpit.

Amid flowerbeds south of the Marienkirche sits the **Neptunbrunnen** (Neptune Fountain), a neobaroque effort by Reinhold Begas, commissioned in 1891 by city hall. It originally stood on Schlossplatz. The people who commissioned it worked in the **Rotes Rathaus** (Red City Hall), off the southeast corner of Alexanderplatz. Finished in 1870 and rebuilt from scratch from 1951 through 1956, the neo-Renaissance building is the political heart of Berlin. Its name comes from the red-hued brick used, but could easily refer to the city's politics. In spite of a

Berlin's cylindrical AquaDom, near Alexanderplatz, may be the strangest aquarium in the city.

Children find refuge in the neobaroque folds of the Neptunbrunnen (Neptune Fountain).

AquaDom & Sea Life Center
www.sealifeeurope.com/de/berlin

Map p. 83
Spandauerstrasse 3
030 99 28 00
$$$
U-Bahn & S-Bahn: Alexanderplatz

complex electoral system that unashamedly favored the ruling noble class, Berliners regularly voted en masse for left-wing candidates in mayoral elections from the late 19th century on. The first fully free municipal elections (in which women had the vote for the first time) took place in 1919. The Nazis dissolved the council in 1933 and hounded many of its members into exile or concentration camps. It is again home to united Berlin's city council, known as the Senat (Senate).

Up the grand staircase and on the right is the **Säulensaal** (Hall of Pillars), used for special events and occasional exhibitions. The **Wappensaal** (Hall of Coats of Arms), also used for special occasions, is farther in on the right.

Across the road in front of the Rotes Rathaus are statues to the memory of those who cleared rubble and rebuilt Berlin after World War II. Most were women, who came to be known as *Trümmerfrauen* (rubble women). Their memory is preserved in one of the statues. The other, *Aufbauhelfer* (rebuilding helper), is of a construction worker.

An orderly green space south across Spandauer Strasse from Alexanderplatz has as its focal point the rather stylized (not to say poor) pair of statues of Karl Marx and Friedrich Engels. This leftover from GDR days gives the square its name, the **Marx-Engels-Forum.** Other GDR art includes eight steel pillars bearing suitably edifying images of life in the communist world.

Quite indifferent to Marx and Engels are the seahorses, starfish, and small sharks flitting about inside the fish tanks of the **Sealife Center.** Thousands of other critters are on show here in some 30 tanks, but don't expect too many brightly colored tropical creatures, as most come from Germany's rivers and lakes, as well as the Baltic Sea and the northern Atlantic. The most original part of the display is the **AquaDom,** a cylindrical tank filled with fish through which an elevator slowly rises.

A surprising and lonely relic of old Berlin stands a block up Spandauer Strasse from the Sealife Center. First built in about 1300 as a hospital chapel, the **Heilig-Geist-Kapelle** (Chapel of the Holy Spirit; *Spandauer Strasse 1*) has remained standing throughout the city's troubles and is, after the Nikolaikirche (see opposite), central Berlin's oldest surviving building. In about 1520, the chapel was remodeled into its present form, although much has been restored. In 1906 someone had the bright idea of tacking a school onto the chapel. It is now part of Humboldt University's economics department, through whose foyer one must enter to glimpse the chapel's interior. ∎

Nikolaiviertel & around

JUST SOUTH OF RATHAUSSTRASSE UNWINDS A COMPACT piece of old Berlin. Narrow, cobbled streets are lined with houses from another era, some hosting cozy restaurants and cafés. At the very center rise the twin, tapered towers of the gothic Nikolaikirche (St. Nicholas Church). It can be hard to believe that, with a few exceptions, none of this dates back farther than the 1980s.

The gothic Nikolaikirche was heavily damaged in World War II. It now houses a museum.

Largely destroyed by Allied bombs and then finished off by the communist GDR regime, this area had pretty much ceased to exist. As the 750th anniversary of Berlin's foundation approached in 1987, the authorities seemed to make an act of contrition by deciding to re-create the quarter rather than building still more socialist realist office blocks. A couple of houses in the Nikolaiviertel (St. Nicholas District), on the south side of Rathausstrasse, are the genuine, restored articles. The rest are no more than 20 years old. The effort had mixed results. Some, especially those south of the Nikolaikirche, look like the real McCoy. Others don't fool anyone much.

The **Nikolaikirche**, built about 1230, was restored and now contains the **Nikolaikirche-museum,** a modest museum dedicated to the story of the church and its remaking. The towers were added late in the 19th century (and also remade after World War II). Inside, the ceiling frescoes, based on the originals, lend a surprising splash of color.

Virtually across the road from the church is **Knoblauchhaus,** an 18th-century upper-bourgeois house whose museum is dedicated to the Knoblauch clan, a rich silkmaker family. It provides some insight into how wealthy families lived in Berlin a little over two centuries ago. Downstairs is a 19th-century restaurant, the **Historische**

Weinstuben (*Poststrasse 23, tel 030 24 24 107*). This is one of the few buildings that was restored but not redone from scratch.

Ephraim-Palais, a few steps south, had a more bizarre fate. The corner mansion was built in 1766 for Veitel Heine Ephraim, court banker to King Friedrich II. The rococo-era structure was to be demolished under the Nazis in

Nikolaikirche-museum
www.stadtmuseum.de
- Map p. 83
- Nikolaikirchplatz
- 030 24 72 45 29
- Closed Mon.
- U-Bahn & S-Bahn: Alexanderplatz; U-Bahn: Klosterstrasse

Knoblauchhaus
www.stadtmuseum.de
- 🅰 Map p. 83
- ✉ Poststrasse 23
- ☎ 030 23 45 99 91
- 🕐 Closed Mon.
- 💲 $
- 🚇 U-Bahn & S-Bahn: Alexanderplatz; U-Bahn: Klosterstrasse

Ephraim-Palais
www.stadtmuseum.de
- 🅰 Map p. 83
- ✉ Poststrasse 16
- ☎ 030 24 00 21 21
- 🕐 Closed Mon.
- 💲 $
- 🚇 U-Bahn & S-Bahn: Alexanderplatz; U-Bahn: Klosterstrasse

Heinrich Zille Museum
www.heinrich-zille-museum.de
- 🅰 Map p. 83
- ✉ Propststrasse 11
- ☎ 030 24 63 25 00
- 💲 $
- 🚇 U-Bahn & S-Bahn: Alexanderplatz; U-Bahn: Klosterstrasse

Hanf Museum
www.hanfmuseum.de
- 🅰 Map p. 83
- ✉ Mühlendamm 5
- ☎ 030 242 48 27
- 🕐 Closed Mon.
- 💲 $
- 🚇 U-Bahn & S-Bahn: Alexanderplatz; U-Bahn: Klosterstrasse

A sign recalling Nikolaiviertel's medieval origins contrasts with some classic concrete Plattenbau.

1935 to allow road-widening work. Locals protested so much that the facade was dismantled and put into storage. In 1983 East Berliners began to reconstruct it. Its elegant rooms now host temporary art exhibitions.

Also resurrected from the ashes was **Zum Nussbaum** (Am Nussbaum 3), a historic 16th-century eatery that stood across the Spree on Fischerinsel and was replicated, complete with walnut

tree, as part of the 1980s effort. One of its regular guests is said to have been local artist and character Heinrich Zille (1858–1929), to whom the nearby **Heinrich Zille Museum** is dedicated. He was known for his satirical sketches, some on display here.

You wouldn't know it now, but the thundering boulevard of Mühlendamm runs through what was once the Molkenmarkt, the oldest marketplace in medieval Berlin. The **Hanf Museum** is tucked away on its northern flank. It is dedicated to the serious business of hemp, its production, practical uses, and known medicinal (even dizzying) effects.

On the south side of Mühlendamm is a long, bombastic building (not open to the public). The older half was the **Palais Schwerin** (built for a minister of Friedrich I); the newer half housed the **Berliner Münze** (mint). The entire building was occupied by the Ministry of Culture under the GDR.

The 1911 **Altes Stadthaus,** a mighty edifice with a mightier tower on Jüdenstrasse, was and remains a government administration building, now for the city of Berlin. On Klosterstrasse, which runs behind the Stadthaus, stand the ruins of the 13th-century **Franziskaner Klosterkirche,** left in a parlous state by the flames of war. Behind the Stadthaus on the corner of Parochialstrasse is the **Parochialkirche,** which in turn leads one to Waisenstrasse, an old Berlin lane that survived the war and is home to the city's oldest restaurant, **Zur Letzten Instanz** (Waisenstrasse 14–16, tel 030 24 25 528). It is close to a modest strip of Berlin's other wall, the medieval one that encircled the then tiny town. ■

Hackescher Markt & around

THE HACKESCHER MARKT S-BAHN IS ONE OF THE MOST beautiful, and one of the best restored, of a series of train stations built east to west across the city in the late 19th century. The brick-and-tile station, completed in 1882, is also for many the introduction to one of the most curious corners of central Berlin, the Scheunenviertel (Barns District).

Back in the mid-17th century, Elector Friedrich III ordered all crops to be stored in barns outside the city center. King Friedrich Wilhelm I then ordered Jews who did not own property to move in among the barns. The area, enclosed by Karl-Liebknecht-Strasse, Torstrasse, and Rosenthaler Strasse, thus became Berlin's main Jewish quarter.

Much of the horror of the Nazi persecution of Jews was played out here and in the neighboring, better-off Spandauer Vorstadt District west of Rosenthaler Strasse. Here and there, especially in Rosenthaler Strasse, are scattered *Stolpersteine,* little brass plaques with the names of Jewish deportees and concentration camp victims set in the pavement before the houses where they lived.

The area is known for its turn-of-the-20th-century housing blocks with interlocking internal courtyards *(Höfe).* The renovated **Hackesche Höfe,** a prime example and something of a tourist attraction, is a series of buildings that house a mix of apartments, trendy boutiques, cafés, restaurants, and a cinema gathered around eight courtyards. The facades of the first courtyard are coated with a glazed tile decor in the best example of Berlin art nouveau, as executed by one of the architects behind the complex, August Endell (1871–1925).

Down an alley off Rosenthaler Strasse is a touching piece of anti-Nazi history, the **Museum Blindenwerkstatt Otto Weidt.** Weidt ran a small factory for the deaf and blind here during the Nazi period, in which Jews and non-Jews were employed making brooms and brushes. For years, he managed to protect his employees in this "essential war industry"; in 1942 he bribed the Gestapo into returning workers arrested for deportation. This story is told in original rooms in pictures and text. The display is limited and best understood when you watch the 20-minute video (in English or German). More rooms of the original workshop have been acquired and will be devoted to the stories of other "silent heroes" who worked against the Nazi regime.

Down the same alley is the **Anne Frank Zentrum,** a small multimedia exhibition on the life and sad times of Anne Frank (1929–1945), the German-Jewish girl whose years in hiding in Amsterdam were made famous when her diary was published in 1947.

The Sophienstrasse, which mostly survived the war, runs west off Rosenthaler Strasse. It is one of the prettiest streets in the area. Halfway along in a quiet yard is the **Sophienkirche,** which has the only original baroque bell tower in Berlin. The

Hackesche Höfe
www.hackesche-hoefe.com
- Map p. 83
- Rosenthaler Strasse 40–41
- S-Bahn: Hackescher Markt

Museum Blindenwerkstatt Otto Weidt
www.blindes-vertrauen.de
- Map p. 83
- Rosenthaler Strasse 39
- 030 28 59 94 07
- S-Bahn: Hackescher Markt

Anne Frank Zentrum
www.annefrank.de
- Map p. 83
- Rosenthaler Strasse 39
- 030 30 87 29 88
- Closed Mon.
- $
- S-Bahn: Hackescher Markt

Sophienkirche
www.sophien.de
- Map p. 83
- Grosse Hamburger Strasse 29
- 030 30 87 92 21
- U-Bahn: Weinmeisterstrasse

Sophiensäle

www.sophiensaele.de

⚠ Map p. 83

✉ Sophienstrasse 18

☎ 030 27 89 00 30

🚇 U-Bahn:
Weinmeisterstrasse

Sophie-Gips-Höfe

⚠ Map p. 83

✉ Sophienstrasse 21

☎ 030 28 49 91 21

🚇 U-Bahn:
Weinmeisterstrasse

Neue Synagoge

http://mysql.snafu.de/
cjudaicum

⚠ Map p. 83

✉ Oranienburger
Strasse 28–30

☎ 030 88 02 83 00

🕐 Closed Sat.; Dome
closed Oct.-March

💲 $

🚇 S-Bahn:
Oranienburger
Strasse

church was built in 1713 but did not get its 226-foot (69 m) sandstone tower until 1735.

Across the road, peer inside the courtyards of the **Sophiensäle,** a typical series of brick houses with inner courtyards that survived war, the GDR, and, so far, renovation. Built in 1905 for the Handwerkerverein (the sign remains carved into the facade), a 19th-century workers' club, today it is home to a theater and cultural center. In its post–World War I heyday, the great figures of German communism, Karl Liebknecht, Rosa Luxemburg, and later GDR president Wilhelm Pieck (1876–1960), harangued the workers in its halls. Under the Nazis, the building became a print shop manned by forced labor from France, Holland, and the Ukraine. A few steps up Sophienstrasse is the **Sophie-Gips-Höfe,** a classic early 20th-century three-courtyard housing block with art galleries and a café.

Sophienstrasse runs into Grosse Hamburger Strasse, until World War II an elegant street where comparatively well-off Jews lived. At its Hackescher Markt end lay the **Alter Jüdischer Friedhof** (Old Jewish Cemetery), destroyed by the Gestapo in 1943. Founded in 1672 and closed in 1827, as many as 10,000 Jews may have been buried there. After it was turned into a temporary sports field by the Gestapo, it was used as a makeshift cemetery for almost 3,000 people killed in street fighting in the last days of World War II. A memorial to Enlightenment philosopher Moses Mendelssohn (1729–1786) is all that remains.

The vacant lot next door at No. 26 was the site of a Jewish seniors home. It was used by the Gestapo

from 1942 on as a collecting point for the last of Berlin's Jews to be deported to the East European concentration camps.

Just southwest, Oranienburger Strasse was long one of the main streets of Jewish Berlin, dominated since the mid-19th century by Germany's biggest synagogue. Opened in 1866, the **Neue Synagoge** (today also known as the Centrum Judaicum) was designed by Edouard Knoblauch (1801–1865), a student of Karl Friedrich Schinkel. The building had room for 3,000 worshippers.

The beautiful facade, with its Moorish airs and gold-encrusted dome, became a Berlin landmark. It suffered relatively little when assaulted by the Stormtrooper Department (SA) on *Kristallnacht* in 1938, because the local police chief chased the thugs off and so allowed the fire brigade to save the building. He was transferred the next day. The last religious services were held in 1940 and Allied bombing in 1943 did heavy damage. The main hall was demolished in 1958 and what remained was restored in 1995.

Of the city's 14 synagogues prior to 1939, the ruins of 12 were demolished after the war.

The restored building is as impressive as the original, and the security measures more so. Inside, you can climb up into the dome. In the first-floor exhibition room below is a cutaway model of the original building, as well as a *ner tamid* (eternal lamp) saved from destruction. The exhibition is split into two parts, one on the history of the building, and the second on life in Berlin's Jewish community, then and now. ■

An unkempt alley leads to the Museum Blindenwerkstatt Otto Weidt and the Anne Frank Zentrum.

Oranienburger Tor & around

THE TOWER THAT MARKED THE OLD TOWN EXIT FROM Berlin at the intersection of Oranienburger Strasse and Torstrasse is long gone. Just beyond this junction, playwright Bertolt Brecht lived and worked in his last years. Nearby are branches of the city's Humboldt University and main city hospital, the Charité, both with curious museums. A more contemporary touch comes in the Hamburger Bahnhof train station-turned-gallery.

Dorotheenstädt-ischer Friedhof

🅰 Map p. 82

✉ Chausseestrasse

🚇 U-Bahn:
Oranienburger Tor

Brecht-Weigel-Gedenkstätte

www.lfbrecht.de

🅰 Map p. 82

✉ Chausseestrasse 125

☎ 030 282 20 03

🕐 Closed Mon.

💲 $

🚇 U-Bahn:
Oranienburger Tor

Wandering up Chausseestrasse, you come across the **Dorotheen-städtischer Friedhof,** a small-ish cemetery with more than its fair share of Berlin luminaries. They range from author Heinrich Mann and philosopher Georg Hegel (1770–1831) to towering figures of 19th-century art and architecture, including Karl Friedrich Schinkel, Friedrich August Stüler, Johann Gottfried Schadow, and Christian Daniel Rauch. Also resting here are Brecht and his actress wife Helene Weigel (1900–1971).

From 1953, the couple lived next door on Chausseestrasse in apartments overlooking the cemetery in what is now the **Brecht-Weigel-Gedenkstätte.** You can

visit some of the rooms they lived in, three of which have been left much as they were in Brecht's lifetime—but visits are by guided tour only, and are in German. Brecht wrote to a friend: "It really is advisable … to live in former capitalist surroundings, until we finally have socialist ones."

He might also have had in mind the grand-looking 19th-century mansion, the **Borsighaus** (*Chausseestrasse 13*), across the road, where the industrialist August Borsig (1804–1854) established the administration offices of his nearby factories.

Around the corner on Invalidenstrasse, in aging buildings of

Humboldt University, is the **Museum für Naturkunde,** an extensive if fusty old natural history museum, with loads of stuffed animals, fish, fossils, and a mineral section. The star attraction, in storage until a museum overhaul is complete in 2007, is the giant skeleton of a brachiosaurus.

West down Invalidenstrasse past the military hospital, a canal-side walkway north leads to the **Invalidenfriedhof,** a military cemetery where generals and senior officers lie. Memorial plaques recall civilians and soldiers buried in mass graves here after air raids, as well as executed conspirators in the July 1944 plot to kill Hitler (see sidebar p. 132). After 1961, the Berlin Wall ran right through the cemetery.

Trains don't run to the nearby **Hamburger Bahnhof/ Museum für Gegenwart– Berlin** anymore. Converted into an enormous exposition space, it hosts contemporary art exhibitions and a permanent display. The backbone of the collection consists of works by Andy Warhol (1928–1987), Anselm Kiefer (born 1945), Joseph Beuys (1921–1986), and Cy Twombly (born 1929). It also holds art from Roy Lichtenstein (1923–1997), Jeff Koons (born 1955), Damien Hirst (born 1965), and others. The range is broad, from Warhol's "Mao" portrait (1973) to the "Berlin Circle" from Richard Long (born 1945).

The complex of restored buildings comprising the central clinics and research departments of Berlin's Charité teaching hospital is home to the oddly interesting **Berliner Medizinhistorisches Museum** (Berlin Medical History Museum; *Schumantrasse 20–21, tel 030 450 536 122, closed Mon, $$*). Shudder at the old

Bertolt Brecht

Bavarian-born Bertolt Brecht made his name as a playwright in Berlin with his 1928 musical drama, *Die Dreigroschenoper (Threepenny Opera),* a satire on capitalism. His works were marked by his Marxist beliefs and a theatrical practice he called "alienation"; he wanted his audiences to remain aware that they were watching a vehicle for social messages. In his 15-year exile from Germany beginning in 1933, Brecht wrote many of his best plays, such as *Der Kaukasische Kreidekreis (The Caucasian Chalk Circle)* and *Mutter Courage und Ihre Kinder (Mother Courage and Her Children).* Only after his return to East Berlin was he able to stage them at his Deutsches Ensemble Theater. ∎

dentist tools; be thankful if you can't read the German explanation of ancient gallstone treatments; and see what you make of the bottles floating with cancerous brains and sick lungs. ∎

Museum für Naturkunde
www.museum.hu-berlin.de
- 🗺 Map p. 82
- ✉ Invalidenstrasse 43
- ☎ 030 20 93 85 91
- 🕐 Closed Mon.
- 💲 $
- 🚇 U-Bahn: Zinnowitzer Strasse

Hamburger Bahnhof/ Museum für Gegenwart– Berlin
www.smb.museum
- 🗺 Map p. 82
- ✉ Invalidenstrasse 50–51
- ☎ 030 39 78 34 39
- 🕐 Closed Mon.
- 💲 $$
- 🚇 U-Bahn: Zinnowitzer Strasse

The Museum für Naturkunde boasts an eclectic collection of nearly 25,000,000 specimens.

Berlin's Jewish community past & present

Berlin's Jews look forward to events such as this street festival in Oranienburger Strasse.

On August 30, 1929, the *Central Verein Zeitung* (a Berlin paper "for Germanness and Jewishness") published a special edition for the 200th anniversary of the birth of Berlin Enlightenment philosopher Moses Mendelssohn. It was dedicated to the "first German Jew, the spiritual father of our equal rights." Ten years earlier, Germany's Jews had been guaranteed full equality by the Weimar Republic's constitution. These rights would hold for less than 14 years.

Jews were present in Germany as early as the 8th century and in Berlin from the 13th century. Here, as elsewhere, they were subjected to restrictions. Residence permits could be revoked at any time, and Jews were barred from most trades. Money-lending, street peddling, medicine, and later banking were among the few options for Jewish businesses.

Although Jews were expelled from the territory of Brandenburg in 1573, they returned to the area in 1671 when Jewish families were expelled from Austria. Berlin from the 17th century was a relatively open city; its patchwork of regulations and edicts both benefited and hindered the city's Jews over the years.

The Enlightenment brought hopes of equality and, in spite of prejudice against them, many Jews identified closely enough with the "Fatherland" to march to their deaths in the carnage of World War I. Others were active in left-wing movements.

Berlin's Jewish society brought forth plenty of stars. Among Mendelssohn's descendants was the musician Felix. For centuries, trade had been one of the few avenues open to Jews, and some had great success. Adolf Jandorf (1870–1932) founded his KaDeWe store in west Berlin in 1907. Other famous Jewish stores before World War II included Wertheim and Tietz.

Then came the nightmare of the Nazis. When Hitler came to power in 1933, at least 170,000 Jews lived in Berlin, many in slum conditions in the largely Jewish

Scheunenviertel north of Alexanderplatz. The Scheunenviertel area and neighboring streets were a tough district, where pimps and petty criminals gathered.

More than 100,000 Berlin Jews went into exile before World War II, and more than 50,500 perished in the Auschwitz and Theresienstadt death camps. On February 27 and 28, 1943, the last Jews in Berlin were rounded up for deportation. Around 2,000 who were married to non-Jews were herded into a former Jewish welfare office at Rosenstrasse 2–4. In an act of courage, their spouses and several thousand others, mostly women, demonstrated around the clock for their release. On March 6 they were set free. As many as 6,000 Jews in Berlin survived in hiding.

Today, Berlin's Jewish community numbers at least 11,500, two-thirds of them migrants from the former Soviet Union. It is the largest Jewish community in Germany (where the total Jewish population is about 100,000). Tensions among different immigrant groups has created ill feeling; the native Berliner Jews feel outmaneuvered by the newcomers. There is no shortage of high drama as the two sides argue. ∎

Dark times: SA stormtroopers put up anti-Jewish posters in prewar Berlin.

Students behold Berlin in miniature at the Märkisches Museum.

More places to visit in central Berlin

GEDENKSTÄTTE BERLINER MAUER

This monument to the memory of the victims of the Berlin Wall is one of the best spots in which to confront the history of the barrier. The wall was built along the south side of the street. As it was perfected, houses were demolished to create a no-man's-land. A stretch of the main wall, death strip, and inner wall remain as a memorial on the corner of Ackerstrasse. A late 19th-century church, painstakingly restored after World War II, was left isolated in the death strip until finally demolished by the GDR regime in 1985. In 2000, a memorial chapel was built in its stead. Across the road, the documentation center offers a permanent exhibition on the first floor. Documents, photos, and audio and video material bring Berlin Wall history to life.

🅜 Map p. 83 ✉ Bernauer Strasse 111 ☎ 030 464 10 30, www.berliner-mauer-dokumentationszentrum.de 🕒 Closed Mon. 🚇 U-Bahn: Bernauer Strasse

HISTORISCHER HAFEN

Across the southeastern tip of Museumsinsel is this floating reminder that Berlin's trade was once largely riverborne. At the turn of the 20th century more than 400 vessels arrived in Berlin daily with goods from all over the country. This Historical Harbor is a huddle of some 20 different river vessels. One operates as a summer café and another

has a small museum aboard.

🅜 Map p. 83 ✉ Märkisches Ufer ☎ 030 21 47 32 57, www.historischer-hafen-berlin.de 🕒 Closed Mon. 💲 $$, free Wed. 🚇 U-Bahn: Märkisches Museum

MÄRKISCHES MUSEUM

Possibly one of the city's most eclectic museums, the Märkisches Museum presents a voyage through the history of Berlin, from the Stone Age tribes who settled in thatched huts around the Spree to the late 20th century. Starting in the cellars (which you reach after crossing the Grosse Halle), you learn about the modest medieval evolution of the originally Slavic riverside settlements. Some rooms on upper floors are jammed with household items, furniture, toys, and other memorabilia from bourgeois homes of 18th- and 19th-century Berlin. The rooms dedicated to the 1920s and Nazi period are curious, if only for the lack of material on the Nazis (although a strange board game with a swastika at its heart is a definite oddity). A room on the top floor contains automatophones (barrel organs and their more mechanized successors) from the late 18th to early 20th centuries. The museum staff cranks these up around 3 p.m. on Sundays. Labeling is in German.

🅜 Map p. 83 ✉ Am Köllnischen Park 5 ☎ 030 24 00 21 62, www.stadtmuseum.de 🕒 Closed Mon. 💲 $$, free Wed. 🚇 U-Bahn: Märkisches Museum ∎

Berlin's central green lung is much more than a pretty park. In and around it lie the center of German political life, a major concentration of art collections, a string of embassies, and Germany's oldest zoo.

Tiergarten & around

Cooling off in leafy Tiergarten

Tiergarten & around

THIS PEACEFUL PARK IN THE CENTER OF BERLIN IS PERFECTLY NAMED. The "animal garden" was once the favorite hunting ground of Prussian kings living on Unter den Linden in the Berliner Schloss. Those days are long gone, but in the southwest corner of the Tiergarten the city's main zoo is full of all sorts of critters, while the park's northern edge is home to Germany's parliament and other government buildings, which at times can seem like a bit of a zoo as well.

The Gedächtniskirche looks over the zoo.

As the city spread westward in the 18th and 19th centuries, the royal hunting ground gradually became what it is today, a public park laced with walking paths and strings of pretty lakes and streams. Through its middle the asphalt scar of Strasse des 17. Juni runs east and west, intersected at the Grosser Stern circle by a busy north-south thoroughfare. A monument to military victories past, the Siegessäule, rises from the circle. Strangely enough, these roads don't disturb the peace deeper inside the park. On summer nights, different fauna come out to play, as prostitutes and other sexual adventurers cruise the park.

Art lovers will be drawn to this part of town for the concentration of galleries and museums in the Kulturforum, which hangs on to the southeast rim of the Tiergarten. In the Gemäldegalerie awaits a cornucopia of old masters and other classics collected over the past couple of centuries. Nearby in the Kunstgewerbemuseum (Museum of Decorative Arts) is a diverse presentation of the best in European arts and crafts down the centuries. Here you can find anything from Meissen porcelain and Renaissance silverware to art deco objects and Bauhaus furniture. A musical note is sounded in the Philharmonie and

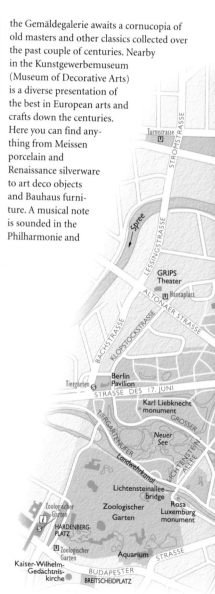

Musikinstrumenten-Museum. For a major injection of modern art, taking in anyone from Pablo Picasso to local hero George Grosz, head for the Neue Nationalgalerie's collection (which is due to transfer to the Gemäldegalerie in upcoming years). The Neue Nationalgalerie building, a key contribution to the city from Ludwig Mies van der Rohe, will itself draw fans of modern architecture. A short walk away are the innovative buildings around Potsdamer Platz (see pp. 74–76). The imaginative new buildings

of the Regierungsviertel (Government District) spread out to the north.

With a short stroll to the west of the Neue Nationalgalerie you can take a leap into pre-Nazi Berlin with a visit to the wavy facade of the Shell-Haus. Those with a taste for walking will continue through the heart of the Diplomatenviertel (Diplomatic District), where some wonders of contemporary architecture can be admired. This promenade can be rounded off with a visit to the Bauhaus Archiv. ■

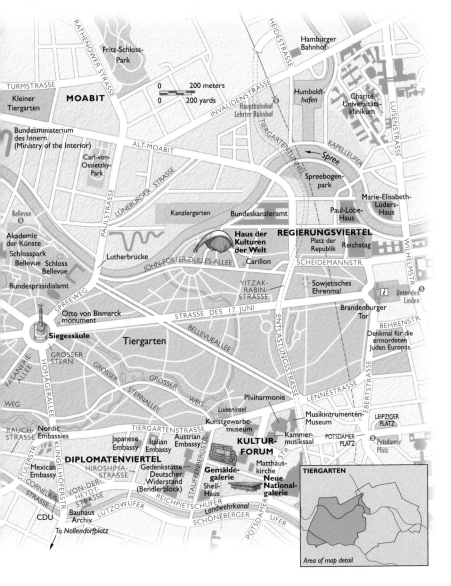

Regierungsviertel

THE 1991 DECISION TO RETURN BERLIN TO ITS STATUS AS capital of a united Germany opened the way for an architectural revolution in the city. A new Regierungsviertel (government district) had to be created. There was no possibility of a return to the pre–World War II concentration of ministerial buildings on and around Wilhelmstrasse, although some buildings there are still in use.

Sir Norman Foster's design for the modernized Reichstag (see pp. 54–57) as seat of parliament was only the beginning. Already considered too small when built in the late 19th century, it now required annexes. These arose north of the Reichstag on either side of what is known as the Spreebogen (Bend in the Spree).

The **Paul-Löbe-Haus** and **Marie-Elisabeth-Lüders-Haus,** named after prominent Weimar parliamentarians and Nazi opponents, house conference rooms and offices used by members of parliament and other Reichstag staff. The buildings, which face each other over the Spree, are laden with symbolism. The Berlin Wall divided the city here at the river; the Marie-Elisabeth-Lüders-Haus stands in what was East Berlin. In the shadow of the Paul-Löbe-Haus, on the bend in the river 164 feet (50 m) north of the Reichstag building, is a silent memorial—a series of white crosses—to those who were killed while trying to cross the wall. These two buildings of the united Germany are linked across the former border by two footbridges.

Of the two buildings, both designed by Stephan Braunfels (born 1950), the seven-story Paul-Löbe-Haus is the more striking. A series of giant glass cylinders is divided by sharp-edged, implacable-looking concrete shafts. Light pours in from all directions and the central atrium opens up like a gleaming grand canyon. The Marie-Elisabeth-Lüders-Haus contains a tapering internal stairway. The flat roof juts out as a precipice over a public square below. The detached giant cube with the huge circular windows contains the parliamentary library.

Subterranean passages connect the two buildings with the Reichstag. Organized tours must be booked in advance through the Reichstag.

West of the Paul-Löbe-Haus stands what Berliners like to call the "washing machine." They might snicker, but the chancellor who presided over reunification, Helmut Kohl, thought this new home for the H-shaped **Bundeskanzleramt** (Office of the Federal Chancellor; *Willy-Brandt-Strasse 1*) was wonderful. The nickname comes from its appearance, in which cubic forms are contrasted with large circular openings. It was designed by Berlin architects Axel Schultes (born 1943) and Charlotte Frank (born 1959) and completed in 2002. The **Kanzlergarten,** a modest garden, lies west across the river.

Just southwest of the Bundeskanzleramt along the Spree River rises the **Haus der Kulturen der Welt** (House of World Cultures). Built in 1957 by American Hugh Stubbins for that year's Interbau architecture exhibition, it has known good times and bad. The revolutionary parabolic roof collapsed in 1980 and was restored nine years later. Since then the place has been used for concerts, expositions, and other international cultural events. Outside, in adjacent gardens, the 68 bells of the carillon ring regularly in concert from a black tower.

About 2,000 feet (600 m) farther west along John-Foster-Dulles-Allee you come before the gates of **Schloss Bellevue** *(Spreeweg 1)*, which is as far as you will get. This late 18th-century summer residence for the Prussian royal family has been the prime reception palace for the German president (who resides in a villa in Dahlem) since 1994. Restored in 2005, it is set in lush, private gardens that link it with the gray, elliptical **Bundespräsidialamt,** which houses presidential staff offices.

The arrival of the federal government in Berlin has begun to change the face of the Moabit District north across the Spree. Many public servants now live in the remarkable, snake-shaped apartment block built especially for government employees at Paulstrasse, just over the Lutherbrücke from Schloss Bellevue.

Some of those employees doubtless work about a 1,640-foot (500 m) walk to the west in the glass-fronted, riverside edifice of the **Bundesministerium des Innern** (Ministry of the Interior) at Alt Moabit 98–101. This multi-story building looks like a giant magnet with two cooling towers at the river end. ∎

Haus der Kulturen der Welt

www.hkw.de

⚠ Map p. 117

✉ John-Foster-Dulles-Allee 10

☎ 030 39 78 70

🕐 Closed Mon.

💲 Exhibitions $–$$, Haus free

🚌 Bus: 100

A statue of a
Soviet soldier
stands watch over
the Sowjetisches
Ehrenmal, raised
shortly after
World War II.

Tiergarten

BORDERED TO THE NORTH BY THE SPREE RIVER, THE
Tiergarten is Berlin's Central Park: a great place to walk or cycle off
the stress of a hard day's sightseeing. The park, established as the
Prussian royal family's private hunting ground in the mid-17th
century, bristles with reminders of Berlin's tumultuous past.

South of the Regierungsviertel
buildings along the park's northern
edge, marked by John-Foster-
Dulles-Allee, the Tiergarten invites
exploration. Follow Strasse des 17.
Juni from the Brandenburger Tor
and stroll about 1,000 feet (300 m)
west until you stumble across an
historical conundrum. The
Sowjetisches Ehrenmal is a
memorial erected by the Soviets
shortly after they conquered the
city in the Battle of Berlin in 1945.
The two T-34 tanks are said to have
been the first to enter Berlin; the
red marble for the monument purportedly came from the ruins of
Adolf Hitler's chancellery. That the
locals thought of the Soviets as lib-
erators is doubtful, and the name of
this avenue commemorates an
uprising in East Berlin in 1953

against the Soviet-backed communist regime.

The broad boulevard,
which used to be known as
Charlottenburger Chaussee, leads
across the park and beyond.
Hitler staged several massive military marches along this strip,
which was chosen to become the
east-west axis in Hitler's grand
post-victory capital, Germania. In
recent years the avenue has been
better known for gatherings of
another kind. The annual summer Love Parade, which since the
mid-1990s had attracted up to a
million ravers to a hedonistic,
hip-hopping, music parade
extravaganza, once filled the
boulevard. In 2005 it was canceled for lack of funds for the
subsequent cleanup operation,

but sponsors have been able to resurrect it for 2006, at least, and perhaps beyond.

The Love Parade ends at the Grosser Stern (Great Star) circle at the western end of the park. At the center of this traffic circle rises the **Siegessäule** (Victory Column), originally set up in front of the Reichstag to fete Prussia's military successes. Hitler had it moved here and placed on a higher column, taking the golden statue of the goddess of victory, known to Berliners simply as Goldene Else (Golden Else), to a height of 220 feet (67 m). There is a viewing platform 164 feet (50 m) up the column. Berlin's gay community was always at the forefront of the Love Parade and the Siegessäule has become a potent symbol, lending its name to a prominent gay magazine.

Prussia's Iron Chancellor, Otto von Bismarck, would doubtless not have approved of these goings-on. Perhaps that's why the bronze **statue** to him lies half hidden in the greenery off the northern side of Grosser Stern, near the Bundespräsidialamt.

Other monuments in the park commemorate a moment of political violence that set the tone for the following years. In 1919, Communists **Karl Liebknecht** and **Rosa Luxemburg** were assassinated by right-wing paramilitary troops in the Tiergarten. The spot where Liebknecht was shot is marked along Grosser Weg by the Neuer See lake, southwest of Grosser Stern, while the easily missed memorial to Luxemburg lies south of Landwehrkanal next to the Lichtensteinallee bridge, where her body was dumped.

A Soviet tank becomes a resting place in the Tiergarten.

Behind the Luxemburg memorial are the fences that restrain animals in Germany's oldest zoo. The **Zoologischer Garten** was founded in 1844 by Alexander von Humboldt. Today it houses 19,000 animals in an 84-acre (34 ha) space. There is also a fascinating aquarium. ∎

Siegessäule

www.monument-tales.de

 Map p. 117

 Strasse des 17. Juni, Grosser Stern

$ $

Bus: 100

Zoologischer Garten

www.zoo-berlin.de

Map p. 116

 Hardenbergplatz 8

 030 25 40 10

Zoo & aquarium $$$$

 U-Bahn & S-Bahn: Zoologischer Garten

The Iron Chancellor

When the *Junker* (landed noble) Otto von Bismarck became chancellor of Prussia in 1862, even he probably didn't imagine that in less than ten years he would succeed in uniting all Germany under Prussia's control. He thus became the first chancellor of Germany. Known as the Iron Chancellor for his toughness, he was also dubbed *Der Schmied*

des Reichs (the man who forged the empire) and was thus often depicted in blacksmith's clothes, sleeves rolled up and hammer in hand. Nothing could have made Berlin's working class laugh harder. Bismarck once declared in parliament: "I am a Junker and I insist on having the advantages that gives me!" Manual labor wasn't one of them. ∎

The shock of the new

In the first half of 2006, workers raced against time to finish building a central railway station for Berlin in time for the summer football (soccer) World Cup. The former Lehrter Bahnhof, now known as Hauptbahnhof (Central Station) is touted as Europe's biggest rail junction, where local, regional, and international trains crisscross at four levels beneath an elegantly vaulted steel-and-glass roof. The average Berliner, by now used to huge new public works, barely raised an eyebrow at the news.

Berlin has been one of the world's biggest playgrounds for an international phalanx of name architects since the city came together again in 1990. The scars left by the war and Berlin Wall provided unique opportunities to create a new cityscape. The prudent city council imposed a raft of building regulations, but still left room for imagination and creative playfulness.

Potsdamer Platz (see pp. 74–76) attracted enormous attention. From no-man's-land in 1990, it has become a thriving

commercial center, graced by a variety of extraordinary and unique buildings, from the domed Sony Center and adjacent Bahntower to the kaleidoscopic mix making up the DaimlerChrysler complex.

Equally surprising is the new Regierungsviertel complex (see pp. 118–119) around the new Reichstag, whose glass dome by Sir Norman Foster has become a symbol of the city.

Between Potsdamer Platz and the Reichstag, the challenging field of ominous gray pillars that forms the Denkmal für die ermordeten Juden Europas (Holocaust Monument; see pp. 60–61) is a controversial but daring addition to the cityscape.

The city has been peppered with extraordinary buildings that inevitably divide opinion. The zigzag Jüdisches Museum (see p. 179), which in its form seems to evoke the tortured history of German Jewry, has found a place in Kreuzberg, just as the strangely terraced and circular facade of the Ku'damm-Eck is now an accepted if odd part of the legendary Ku'damm. Not far away, the Ludwig-Erhard-Haus (see p. 139), home to the stock exchange, has been nicknamed the "armadillo" for its ranks of steel girders.

Several nations have awarded themselves new embassies. Among the eye-catchers are the Mexican, Nordic, and Austrian representations in the diplomatic district south of Tiergarten. Even the conservative CDU party got in on the act with its angular corner office building on Cornelius Strasse, near Tiergarten. Inside a glass structure floats the lentil-shaped main building.

The pace of (re)construction in Berlin has doubtless slowed since the 1990s, and public money is harder to come by. But various projects are still on the boil. Around Alexanderplatz (see pp. 102–04), the city has plans to build ten 492-foot (150 m) skyscrapers to create an alternative downtown to the Ku'damm area. Sonae Imobiliária, a Portuguese developer planning a four-building complex on Alexanderstrasse, is building one of them. Whether any of the others will see the light of day is debatable, as interest in renting so much space seems scarce.

Around the Hauptbahnhof, a new office and apartment complex is planned for 2010. More ambitious is the Media Spree project along the river in Friedrichshain and Kreuzberg. This complex would be a concentrated media and services district, interspersed with new housing and leisure facilities. ∎

Potsdamer Platz was a wasteland when the wall came down in 1989—some of the world's top architects have since let their imaginations run riot.

Kulturforum

Matthäuskirche

🄰 Map p. 117

✉ Sigismundstrasse

☎ 030 262 12 02

🕐 Closed Mon.

🚇 U-Bahn & S-Bahn: Potsdamer Platz

WHEN THE NAZIS CAME TO POWER IN 1933, IT SPELLED THE beginning of the end of peace and quiet for what had once been a well-to-do district on the south flank of the Tiergarten. Hitler's architect, Albert Speer, began tearing down houses and wiping whole streets off the map to make way for the grand project of the new capital, Germania. He didn't get past demolition; Allied bombs took care of what he had not destroyed. By 1945, the area between Potsdamer Platz and Stauffenbergstrasse had been razed to the ground. Yet after the war, this void became one of the main cultural centers of the city.

An orchestra of harpsichords takes center stage in the Musik-instrumenten-Museum.

All that remains of the once peaceful community here is the **Matthäuskirche.** Built by Friedrich August Stüler in 1844–46, this Evangelical church survived Speer's wrecking ball but succumbed to Allied bombs. It was patiently rebuilt in 1956–60, although the interior is a bland shadow of its former self. You can climb its bell tower for the views

and drop by for an organ recital from 12:30 to 12:50 p.m. *(Tues.–Sat.)*

First off the mark in the postwar construction was the **Philharmonie,** completed in 1963 (with a golden aluminum facade added in 1981) as the new home for the esteemed Berlin Philharmoniker (Berlin Philharmonic Orchestra). Designed by Hans Scharoun (1893–1972), it enjoys extraordinary acoustics. To join the 1 p.m. tours of the Philharmonie and adjacent **Kammermusiksaal** (Chamber Music Hall), which was opened in 1987 to another Sharoun design, wait at the artists' entrance (signposted).

In the following years, the other museums that make up the Kulturforum were completed, making this an extraordinary concentration of culture, difficult to tackle in less than two days.

Music lovers will not pass up a chance to visit the **Musikinstrumenten-Museum** *(Tiergartenstrasse 1, tel 030 25 48 11 78, www.mim-berlin.den, closed Mon., adm. fee),* next door to the Philharmonie. The collection was established in 1888 and then greatly expanded. Just about every kind of classical European instrument is represented. The sheer number of harpsichords (or cembalos), clavichords, and pianos is

impressive. Among them is the piano on which Carl Maria von Weber composed *Der Freischütz* in 1821. Next to it is a glass harmonica invented by Benjamin Franklin.

The biggest instrument on display is a giant Wurlitzer organ, cranked up at midday on Saturdays. Wurlitzers of this ilk were made for silent film showings; this one is the largest working model of its kind in Europe.

A short walk west is the **Kunstgewerbemuseum** (Museum of Decorative Art), with an exhaustive collection (on four floors) of European decorative arts and crafts from the Middle Ages to the art deco period of the early 20th century.

The exposition starts with the Middle Ages on the ground floor (the floor below the ticket desk). The riches are composed primarily of church treasures, along with tapestries and furniture. Delicately carved ivory and chunky precious-stone-encrusted jewelry abound. The following two rooms are dedicated to the Renaissance. Exquisite ceramics from Italy and Spain take pride of place. A separate corner is set aside for a collection of porcelain from Limoges.

The collection continues, oddly, two floors up with the baroque. Early Berlin porcelain is on show, along with French pewter and central European glassware. The next room, which extends from baroque to rococo, is home to the museum's extensive collections of fine 18th-century porcelain from Meissen.

Thereafter comes the 19th century, with brightly polished Empire furniture, still more porcelain, and sinuous art nouveau furniture. The top floor displays end with art deco furniture and household items.

The contemporary design section, roughly from the 1920s to the 1960s, is lodged in the basement. Look for furniture by Ludwig Mies van der Rohe.

Note that entry to the Kulturforum museums and many other Berlin museums is free the last four hours on Thursdays. ∎

Berlin Philharmoniker concerts regularly draw up to 2,500 fans to the Philharmonie.

Philharmonie & Kammermusiksaal

www.berliner-philharmoniker.de

🅰 Map p. 117

✉ Herbert-von-Karajan-Strasse 1

☎ 030 25 48 81 56

🕐 Guided tours 1 p.m. (reservations required for ten or more)

💲 $

🚇 U-Bahn & S-Bahn: Potsdamer Platz

Kunstgewerbemuseum

www.smb.museum

🅰 Map p. 117

✉ Matthäikirchplatz

☎ 030 266 29 51

🕐 Closed Mon.

💲 $$

🚇 U-Bahn & S-Bahn: Potsdamer Platz

The halls of the Gemäldegalerie are filled with priceless works of the old masters.

Gemäldegalerie & Kupferstichkabinett

ONE OF THE GREATEST COLLECTIONS OF OLD MASTERS IN Europe, the Gemäldegalerie warrants several hours per visit. The two strongest elements are Dutch and Flemish painting (from the Middle Ages to Rubens and Rembrandt) and the Venetian Renaissance. There is a smattering of German artists, stronger on the late medieval period, a splash of the Florentine Renaissance, and some teasers from Britain and France.

Gemäldegalerie
www.smb.museum
- Map p. 117
- Matthäikirchplatz
- 030 266 29 51
- Closed Mon.
- $$
- U-Bahn & S-Bahn: Potsdamer Platz

A word of warning: By the time you read this, some of the collection may have been transferred to the Bode-Museum (see pp. 96–97). The city plans eventually to concentrate Berlin's collections of antiquities and art up to the 19th century in the Museumsinsel. This process, if it ever happens, will take years. Eventually, the 20th-century collection of the Neue Nationalgalerie (see pp. 129–130) would hang in this gallery.

Of the gallery's 3,000 works, about half are on display. The **central hall** is graced with a parade of statues ranging from a delicate Renaissance bronze

figure of "Putti mit Tamburin" ("Cherubs with Drum," 1429) by Florentine sculptor Donatello (ca 1386–1466) to a series of statues of Greek gods by Andreas Schlüter. Around the hall spreads a number of rooms containing paintings, arranged more or less chronologically and by geographical area. The numbering is odd, switching between Roman and Arabic numerals. The following are some highlights.

The first rooms on the right contain principally German medieval religious images from the 13th century on. In **Room 2,** Nuremberg-born Albrecht Dürer

(1471–1528) is represented with a couple of works. Of the two, the "Bildnis einer Jungen Venezianerin" ("Image of a Young Venetian," 1506) is more interesting. Dürer made several trips to Venice, then a cultural epicenter. The light and color in this portrait of a young Venetian woman betray the influences of the north Italian city-state.

In **Room 3**, Lucas Cranach the Elder (1472–1553) has several works. Paintings by Hans Holbein the Elder (1465–1524) and the Younger (1497–1543)—the latter represented by a series of portraits—grace **Room 4.**

Cranach the Elder turns up again in **Room III** with "Flügelaltar mit dem Jüngsten Gericht" ("Side Altar with the Last Judgment," 1524). A close look at this painting is enough to make the most stubborn sinners repent. Bizarre monsters torture recent arrivals in hell, bodiless heads wander around, sinners are impaled on trees and boiled in huge pots. Who is responsible for all this woe? Take a look at Adam and Eve having a bite of an apple in the left flap of the triptych. Less distressing but equally bizarre is his "Der Jungbrunnen" ("The Fountain of Youth," 1546), in which old hags arrive at the left, enter a pool, and exit to the right in the flower of youth.

Room IV is a key stop, with two grand altar tableaux by the Flemish Rogier van der Weyden (1399–1464). The fine lines and detail in the background images of towns are striking in "Der Middelburger Altar" (ca 1445), which depicts Christ's birth and the Three Wise Men, and "Der

Losing oneself in the big picture: The Gemäldegalerie deserves at least a couple of hours for a visit.

Kupferstich-kabinett

www.smb.museum

✉ Matthäikirchplatz

☎ 030 266 29 51

🕐 Closed Mon.

💲 $$, Studiensaal free

🚇 U-Bahn & S-Bahn: Potsdamer Platz

Marienaltar" (1435), with the Virgin Mary at its center.

Just as absorbing is "Die Niederländischen Sprichwörter" ("Dutch Sayings," 1559) by the Flemish Pieter Breugel the Elder (ca 1525–1569) in **Room 7**. In what looks like a manic medieval village scene, each character or scene is the incarnation of one of 126 old sayings. On the lower left, for instance, is a man who embraces and bites a pillar. The Dutch called religious bigots "pillar biters."

Rooms 9 and **VIII** contain a wealth of works by Peter Paul Rubens (1577–1640), the Flemish baroque master. These grand paintings display an unusual verve of brushstroke and movement, evident in "Thronende Maria mit dem Kind und Heiliger" ("Mary Enthroned with the Christ Child and Saints," ca 1627).

After traversing a series of rooms filled mainly with land-scapes, portraits, and still-life images from Dutch artists, you stumble across a selection by the great Rembrandt (1606–1669). The most important are the six tableaux in **Room X,** including "Der Mennoiterprediger und seine Frau" ("The Mennonite Preacher and His Wife," 1642), next to which is a small self-portrait of the master.

Rooms 20–22 form a brief interlude between the Dutch masters and the brilliance of Renaissance Italy to come. England's Thomas Gainsborough (1727–1788) dominates Room 20 with several portraits, while France's Jean-Antoine Watteau (1684–1721) is the key figure in Room 21. Antoine Pesne, the French court painter brought to Berlin by King Friedrich I, has a few works in Room 22.

The next 23 rooms are a festi-val of Italian mastery, with partic-ular emphasis on Venetian Renaissance, baroque, rococo, and landscape art. The order is not chronological. You will glide by works from Giambattista Tiepolo (1696–1770, **Room 24**), Titian (Tiziano Vecellio, ca 1490–1576, **Room XVI**), Tintoretto (Jacopo Robusti, 1518–1594, **Room XVI**), and the master of Venetian scenes, Canaletto (Giovanni Antonio Canal, 1697–1768, **Room 12**).

The roll call of Florentine masters includes Andrea del Sarto (1486–1530, **Room 29**), Giorgio Vasari (1511–1574, **Room 30**), Fra Angelico (ca 1395–1455, **Room 39**), Fra Filippo Lippi (ca 1406–1469, **Room 39**), and Botticelli (1445–1510, **Room XVIII**). Urbino-born High Renaissance genius Raphael (1483–1520, **Room 29**) is repre-sented with five works including "Maria mit dem Kind, Johannes dem Täufer und einem Heiligen Knaben" ("The Virgin Mary with the Christ Child, John the Baptist, and a Holy Boy"), a circular por-trait that emanates a joyous, Mediterranean light.

Opposite the Gemäldegalerie in the same building and up one floor is the **Kupferstichkabi-nett,** a unique treasure of hun-dreds of thousands of sketches, drawings, pastels, and watercolors dating from the Middle Ages to the 19th century. Visitors may visit the **Studiensaal** (bring iden-tification) and ask to see some of the works (which include draw-ings by Albrecht Dürer and Rembrandt). The Studiensaal closes at 2 p.m.

Temporary exhibitions are held in the Kupferstichkabinett and the **Kunstbibliothek** (art library) downstairs. ■

Neue Nationalgalerie

THE EXISTENCE OF LUDWIG MIES VAN DER ROHE'S NEUE (New) Nationalgalerie, a work of art in which to house works of art, is due to the Cold War that split Berlin and its art collections. The bulk of the city's 19th-century art remained in East Berlin in what would later be known as the Alte (Old) Nationalgalerie. Most of the 20th-century collection, especially German works from the first half of the century, was stored in the West.

In 1968, this wealth of 20th-century art found a new home in Mies van der Rohe's building, a low-lying, glassed-in structure with a broad roof hanging over the surrounding piazza. Even so, only the cream of the collection can be shown. In addition to the treasures of its permanent exhibition, the Neue Nationalgalerie hosts rotating shows of international modern and contemporary artists.

Various sculptures grace the building and its **sculpture garden.** Among them are "The Archer" by Britain's Henry Moore (1898–1986)—a bronze created in 1964–65—and American Alexander Calder's (1898–1976) 1965 "Heads and Tail," the most striking of the exhibits in this outdoor gallery. It is a lively looking piece whose elements communicate the idea of a confused

Neue Nationalgalerie
www.smb.museum
🅰 Map p. 117
✉ Potsdamer Strasse 50
☎ 030 266 29 51
🕐 Closed Mon.
💲 $$
🚇 U-Bahn & S-Bahn: Potsdamer Platz

crowd of people. Spain's Eduardo Chillida (1924–2002) contributed "Gudari," a work that, with its branchlike elements, suggests the search for place and identity.

The heart of the art collection is made up of the German expressionists and their successors. Leading the way is Ernst Ludwig Kirchner. One of his better-known Berlin paintings is "Potsdamer Platz" (1914), in which two ladies of the night seem to rise out of a vortex at the heart of the painting, surrounded by furtive striding males and a distorted reduction of the buildings on the square.

Norway's Edvard Munch, another European pre–World War I expressionist, exhibited several times in Berlin. Some of his works, including the light-colored, twilit figures of "Paar am Strand" ("Couple on the Beach," 1907), appear here.

Other pre–World War I works on show include a mixed bag of the best. Pablo Picasso (1881–1973) and Juan Gris (1887–1927) contribute with some classics of cubism. Paul Gauguin (1848– 1903) and Emil Nolde (1867– 1956) add an exotic touch with their warm images from the Pacific.

Later work by Vienna's Oskar Kokoscka (1886–1980) is often infused with a nightmarish tone, and even his prewar works betray a taught nerviness, apparent in the fatigue in his portrait of Adolf Loos (1909).

The horrors of World War I had a telling effect on art and its makers. Otto Dix had served in the trenches and could hardly avoid reflecting this in his gruesome messages. As cruel as the war are paintings such as "Die Skatspieler" ("The Card-Players," 1920), depicting three mutilated war veterans who are missing limbs and other body parts. Meanwhile, Max Beckmann's late 1930s paintings seem to reflect the gathering darkness as Hitler moves closer to plunging Europe into war.

The feverish interwar period produced a wave of artistic movements and attracted all sorts of artists to Berlin. Among the exponents of Bauhaus were Switzerland's Paul Klee, Russia's Wassily Kandinsky, Oscar Schlemmer, and Lyonel Feininger, all of them represented here. Works by the doyen of the Berlin art world in the Weimar years, Max Liebermann, can also be seen. They include a melancholy self-portrait from 1925.

An early dada star who went on to lead the Neue Sachlichkeit (New Objectivity) group was Georg Grosz, whose "Stützen der Gesellschaft" ("Society's Props," 1926) is a fierce satire on German society: Its figures are equipped with props ranging from priestly robes and sabers to beer steins and socialist flags. Outside, the country burns.

Max Ernst (1891–1976), meanwhile, joined ranks with the surrealists, as is eminently clear from the hallucinatory lines in "Die Auserwählte des Bösen" ("The Evil One's Chosen One," 1928).

A smattering of greatly varied international works lends the collection an eclectic flavor. Salvador Dalí (1904–89), Joan Miró (1893–1983), Giorgio de Chirico (1888–1978), Alexander Calder, Constantin Brancusi (1876–1957), Robert Delaunay (1885–1941), Fernand Léger (1881–1955), and Alberto Giacometti (1901–1966) are among those who stand out in the wide-ranging collection. ■

The wavy facade of the Shell-Haus is a monument to pre–World War II architecture.

More places to visit in Tiergarten & around

BAUHAUS ARCHIV

Originally intended for the city of Darmstadt in the 1960s, this temple to Bauhaus design was created by the movement's father, Walter Gropius. It was finally erected in Berlin after Gropius's death. Gropius founded the original Bauhaus school, dedicated to avant-garde design, in Weimar; among his colleagues was architect Ludwig Mies van der Rohe. Local authorities forced Gropius to move, to Dessau in 1925 and then to Berlin in 1932, where the Nazis shut him down for good in 1933. This central archive building, itself late Bauhaus in design, has a permanent exhibition on the ground floor embracing household and furniture items made by Bauhaus teachers and students, including a couple by Mies van der Rohe and quite a few by Hungarian-born Marcel Breur (1902–1981). It also holds posters and art by Klee, Kandinsky, and Schlemmer, as well as models of some key Bauhaus constructions.

Map p. 117 Klingelhöferstrasse 14 030 254 00 20, www.bauhaus.de $$ Bus: M29; U-Bahn: Nollendorfplatz

DIPLOMATENVIERTEL

A stroll past some of the embassies in the Diplomatenviertel, the Diplomatic District, gives a visitor a tour of interesting Tiergarten architecture. This district, just south of Tiergarten and north of Landwehrkanal, was the idea of Hitler's chief architect, Albert Speer, and remnants of his era include the rather fascist-looking embassies of Hitler's World War II allies, Italy and Japan, which face each other across Hiroshimastrasse (Nos. 1 and 6, respectively) on the corner of Tiergartenstrasse. More modern are the combined Nordic (Denmark, Finland, Iceland, Norway, and Sweden) compound to the west at Rauchstrasse 1. The curious curving main facade appears to be made up of a coating of sea green ailerons that rise and fall as those inside require more or less light and privacy. Just south, the Mexican Embassy at Klingelhöferstrasse 3 is just as intriguing. The graceful vertical columns of its main facade seem to open out like a fan when seen from the side.

Map p. 117 Bus: M29 or 200; S-Bahn or U-Bahn: Potsdamer Platz

More places to visit in Tiergarten & around

GEDENKSTÄTTE DEUTSCHER WIDERSTAND (BENDLERBLOCK)

Enter the Federal Building and Town-Planning Office and you step back into the grim final year of World War II. Deep in the night of July 20, 1944, shots rang out across the courtyard as senior officer Claus von Stauffenberg and three others were summarily executed after they failed in their attempt to assassinate Adolf Hitler. The building, then part of the *Wehrmacht* (army) headquarters and known as the Bendlerblock—after the name of the street at the time—has seen little change since then. In January 1933, high officers discussed here whether they could prevent Hitler from becoming chancellor. One month later Hitler dropped in to let the generals know his plans: a war of conquest in Eastern Europe. And it was in these offices that the plot to kill Hitler was hatched in 1944. Those same offices on the second floor today house this memorial to German resistance. The extensive display of photos and documents highlights the sources of resistance to Nazism in Germany, ranging from the military staff and politicians to opponents within the Catholic and Evangelical churches, youth circles, or oppressed minorities such as Jews and Gypsies. They came from all walks of life, and many died for their convictions. An English-language audio device is available, which is indispensable, as the exhibition is all in German.

🅰 Map p. 117 ✉ Stauffenbergstrasse 13–14
☎ 030 26 99 50 00, www.gdw-berlin.de
🚌 Bus: M29

SHELL-HAUS

Virtually across the road from the Bendlerblock and still known as the Shell Building—although Berlin's GASAG gas company has been the owner for some time—this is a place with a much happier tale. Built for a subsidiary of the Shell Oil Company in 1930–32, its smooth, rippling facade, like stylized waves tipped on their side, is commonly classed as modernist. The number of floors rises gradually from six to ten from east to west. During the war the building was partly taken over by the German navy. Designed by Emil Fahrenkamp (1885–1966) and built with a steel frame dressed in a skin of travertine, it was one of the most innovative buildings constructed in interwar Berlin.

🅰 Map p. 117 ✉ Reichpietschufer 60
🚌 Bus: M29 ■

The plot to kill Hitler

Claus Schenk Graf von Stauffenberg (1907–1944), a career soldier, had risen through the officer class to become chief of staff of the Replacement Army in June 1944. As early as the late 1930s, discreet groups of officers and civilians had formed conspiratorial circles, especially the so-called Kreisauer Kreis (Kreisau Circle), with the aim of overthrowing Hitler. Several assassination attempts failed and by the time Stauffenberg decided to try in July 1944, the group's hopes were limited to ending the war quickly and with some dignity. As a senior officer, von Stauffenberg had access to meetings with Hitler and top staff at the Eastern Front headquarters near Rastenburg in East Prussia (today part of Poland). When he arrived on July 20, he placed a bomb in a briefcase beside Hitler and shortly thereafter walked out of the room. As he left, someone moved the briefcase; the explosion left Hitler wounded but alive. Stauffenberg flew back to Berlin, convinced of Hitler's demise, and his co-conspirators tried to set their coup, which envisaged the occupation of key points across the city, in motion. Reports that Hitler was alive stayed the hand of most of the wavering military and it quickly became clear the coup had failed. Stauffenberg and three others were shot that night (another committed suicide). In the coming months more than 7,000 conspiracy suspects would be arrested and over 100 tortured, tried, and in most cases, executed in the Plötzensee prison. Hitler had the trials and executions filmed for his personal entertainment. ■

oyal elegance and elegant shopping attract visitors to two focal points in this sprawling central-western district: Berlin's Versailles, Schloss Charlottenburg, and the legendary Ku'damm chic strip, capped by the city's most powerful war monument, the Kaiser-Wilhelm-Gedächtniskirche.

Charlottenburg

Contemporary flair in Ludwig-Erhard-Haus

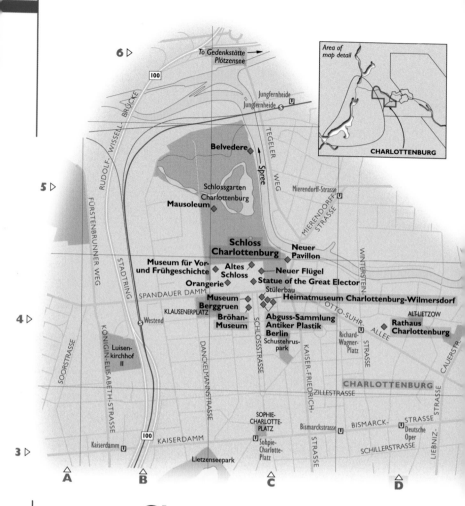

6 ▷

To Gedenkstätte
Plötzensee

100

Area of map detail

CHARLOTTENBURG

Jungfernheide
Jungfernheide U

Belvedere

Spree

TEGELER WEG

RUDOLF-WISSELL-BRÜCKE

5 ▷

Schlossgarten
Charlottenburg
Mausoleum

Mierendorff-Strasse
MIERENDORFF-STRASSE U

FÜRSTENBRUNNER WEG

STADTRING

Schloss
Charlottenburg

Neuer
Pavillon

WINTERSTEIN-ALLEE

Museum für Vor-
und Frühgeschichte

Altes
Schloss

Neuer Flügel

Orangerie

Statue of the Great Elector

SPANDAUER DAMM

Stülerbau

Heimatmuseum Charlottenburg-Wilmersdorf

OTTO-SUHR-ALLEE

ALT-LIETZOW

Museum
Berggruen

KLAUSENERPLATZ

Westend

4 ▷

Bröhan-
Museum

Abguss-Sammlung
Antiker Plastik
Berlin

Rathaus
Charlottenburg

SOORSTRASSE

KÖNIGIN-ELISABETH-STRASSE

Luisen-
kirchhof
II

DANCKELMANNSTRASSE

SCHLOSSSTRASSE

Schustehrus-
park

KAISER-FRIEDRICH-STRASSE

Richard-
Wagner-
Platz

STRASSE

CAUERSTR.

CHARLOTTENBURG

ZILLESTRASSE

STRASSE

100

KAISERDAMM

Kaiserdamm U

SOPHIE-
CHARLOTTE-
PLATZ

Sophie-
Charlotte-
Platz U

Bismarckstrasse U

BISMARCK-STRASSE U

Deutsche
Oper

LIEBNIZ-STRASSE

3 ▷

Lietzenseepark

SCHILLERSTRASSE

△ A

△ B

△ C

△ D

Charlottenburg

A SEPARATE CITY UNTIL ABSORBED BY BERLIN IN 1920, CHARLOTTENBURG has traditionally been home to much of Berlin's upper middle class. The onetime village of Lietzow (or Lützow) took its present name after the palace built for Queen Sophie Charlotte by King Friedrich I, renamed Charlottenburg after his wife's death. The present-day municipality stretches from the quiet residential district around the palace south to the equally tranquil Wilmersdorf and southeast to the racier Kurfürstendamm. The palace and the "Ku'damm" are the area's counterparts.

Charlottenburg celebrated its 300th anniversary in 2005. King Friedrich I had granted the title of town to a huddle of houses along the Schlossstrasse south of Schloss Charlottenburg in 1705. But things didn't take off until the mid-19th century. Industry set up along the Spree River and housing spread. The population rocketed from 10,000 in 1850 to 182,000 by 1900, at which time Charlottenburg was the richest city in Prussia.

The laying of the Kurfürstendamm boulevard in the late 19th century created a new attraction to rival Unter den Linden and Friedrichstrasse in the city center. In the 1920s, the boulevard was the focal point of much of the city's shopping, café hopping, and nightlife. The area became known to many as Charlottengrad, as most of Berlin's several hundred thousand Russian émigrés, who had fled the nascent, war-torn Soviet Union, chose to settle here.

Today the Kurfürstendamm is largely a label-slaves' shopping strip—but not exclusively. Among the fashion houses and mansions glitter several jewels of interest. At its eastern end rises the silhouette of one of Berlin's best known monuments, the Kaiser-Wilhelm-Gedächtniskirche.

A short stroll in any direction leads to something of interest for all possible tastes. Shoppers, especially with a weakness for gourmet products, will want to head east to one of Europe's greatest department stores, KaDeWe.

Bahnhof Zoologischer Garten (Bahnhof Zoo for short) has long had an edgy flavor; the sex shops and video stores around it remain in action despite a clean-up. Indulge a little erotic fantasy at the Erotikmuseum or admire the best in provocative fashion photography at Helmut Newton's nearby Museum für Fotografie.

Rather less playful is the art on show at the Käthe-Kollwitz-Museum, just south off the Ku'damm. Those wanting a quick multimedia introduction to the city could pop into "The Story of Berlin," which includes a fascinating visit to a 1970s subterranean nuclear shelter, still ready for the worst.

Another world altogether lies west around the Schloss Charlottenburg. The long low palace and its gardens are a magnet for tourists and local strollers alike. A couple of fine museums stand across the road from the palace. One of them (Museum Berggruen) is dedicated to Pablo Picasso (1881–1973) and three other modern artists, the other (Bröhan-Museum) to applied arts, especially from the art nouveau period around the turn of the 20th century. ∎

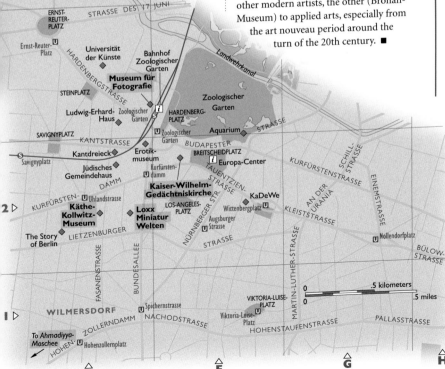

Kaiser-Wilhelm-Gedächtniskirche

Kaiser-Wilhelm-Gedächtniskirche

🅰 p. 135 F2

✉ Breitscheidplatz

☎ 030 218 50 23

🕐 Entrance hall closed Sun.

🚇 U-Bahn & S-Bahn: Zoologischer Garten

A STRANGER DESTINY COULD NOT HAVE BEFALLEN SUCH a public building. Erected by a warlike emperor to the memory of his grandfather, the Kaiser-Wilhelm-Gedächtniskirche almost fell victim to the ravages of another war unleashed by the successors to the emperor's fallen empire. After coming within an ace of demolition, the shattered church stands today not as a memorial to emperors past, but to the folly of war. Lit up at night, it is an especially powerful sight and a symbol of modern Berlin.

The eerily lit ruins of the Gedächtniskirche are a reminder of the futility and suffering of war.

Kaiser Wilhelm II ordered the neo-Romanesque church to be built in honor of his grandfather, Kaiser Wilhelm I. The central part of the church was rich in mosaics and stained glass; the memorial hall was decorated with reliefs depicting the history of the Hohenzollern dynasty. For all that, the church was not considered a monument of great importance in the pre–World War II cityscape of Berlin.

Allied bombs destroyed the church in 1943, leaving little more than the truncated bell tower. In the 1950s, plans to pull down these remnants, by then affectionately dubbed the "Rotten Tooth" by Berliners, called forth such an outcry that it was decided instead to create a memorial.

The exterior remains partly blackened and pockmarked, while parts of the interior mosaics in the entrance hall have been restored. They include a series showing the German emperors, including Wilhelm I and Wilhelm II.

In front of the entrance is a modern chapel. Just to the right as you enter is a charcoal drawing known as the Stalingrad Madonna. Dr. Kurt Reuber, chief field doctor with the German army trapped in Stalingrad in 1942 to 1943, drew it on the back of a Russian map and wrote: "Christmas 1942 in the Stalingrad Pocket. Light, Life, Love." Dr. Reuber died in a Siberian POW camp.

Behind the ruin rises a 1960s octagonal bell tower with blue stained-glass windows. Known to Berliners as the "Lipstick," it houses a shop selling gifts from developing nations. ∎

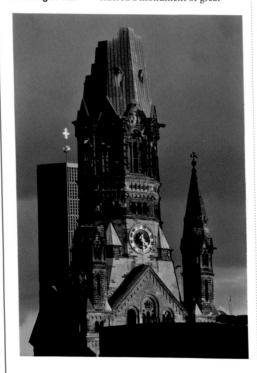

Käthe-Kollwitz-Museum

HOUSED IN A LATE 19TH-CENTURY BOURGEOIS HOME OFF the Ku'damm, this museum is the most complete collection of the works of one of Germany's finest expressionist artists. Käthe Kollwitz's art, mostly drawings, etchings, and woodcuts, always had an intensely socially conscious message.

Kollwitz depicted human suffering, such as that of the Silesian weavers in her 1897 series of lithographs, "A Weavers' Revolt."

Married to a doctor, Kollwitz lived most of her life in Prenzlauer Berg (on what is today Kollwitzstrasse). She first captured the public's attention with her series "Ein Weberaufstand" ("A Weavers' Revolt") in 1897.

The exhibition begins on the first floor. One room is dedicated to post–World War I antiwar posters and others appealing for aid for starving children and POWs. Kollwitz had been hit hard by the death of one her sons, Peter, on the Western Front in 1914. This is reflected in a series of sketches depicting a woman pursued by Death.

The complete series of "Ein Weberaufstand" is on the second floor; the six pieces portray the abject misery in which cottage-industry weavers lived in late

19th-century Germany. Another series, "Bauernkrieg" ("Peasant War"), includes such chilling scenes as "Vergewaltigt" ("Raped"), showing a woman lying unconscious in a field. One room is dedicated to self-portraits from 1888 to 1938.

Death dominates the fourth floor, especially in its relationship with mothers. For instance, Death stretches out his hand to mother with cowering children in "Frau Vertraut Sich dem Tod an" ("Woman Entrusts Herself to Death"). In the attic are three bronzes made from her plaster statues, in which the mother is the central theme.

In 1936, the Nazis banned Kollwitz's art. She died on April 22, 1945, about two weeks before World War II ended. ∎

Käthe-Kollwitz-Museum
www.kaethe-kollwitz.de
🅰 p. 135 E2
✉ Fasanenstrasse 24
☎ 030 882 52 10
🕐 Closed Tues.
💲 $$
Ⓤ U-Bahn: Uhlandstrasse

Shoppers in Europe's biggest department store, KaDeWe, enjoy one of its gourmet bars.

Strolling around the Ku'damm

Long before Berlin was divided in two, the broad Kurfürstendamm exerted a magnetic charm with its boutiques and cafés. During the Cold War, the Ku'damm, as it is better known, became West Berlin's central artery. It suffered after reunification, as everyone's interest in the city shifted to the scarred but reunited center. Since the dawn of the new century, the Ku'damm has again taken its place in Berlin's sun.

When West Berlin was a separate city, all mainline trains terminated at **Bahnhof Zoologischer Garten** ❶. In the 1970s and 1980s the station and its surroundings developed a grim reputation as a junkies' gathering point and prostitution strip. The station has been cleaned up since then, but its glory days are past, as most mainline trains pour into the new Hauptbahnhof to the northeast.

A phalanx of cheap porno-film joints still ekes out a living around the station, and it is hard to imagine a more appropriate spot for the **Erotikmuseum** ❷, a few steps down Joachimstaler Strasse *(Joachimstaler Strasse 4, tel 030 886 06 66, $)*. Created by Germany's late sex-shop queen, Beate Uhse, the collection of 5,000 sex-related objects and art spreads over two floors.

A brisk walk east along Kantstrasse takes you to the **Kaiser-Wilhelm-Gedächtniskirche** ❸ (see p. 136). Past it

stretches the busy Breitscheidplatz, dominated by the Europa-Center, a shopping and office center. About 1,150 feet (350 m) down Tauentzienstrasse on Wittenbergplatz is the **Kaufhaus des Westens** ❹ (Department Store of the West), better known as KaDeWe and one of the world's great department stores. It claims to be continental Europe's biggest such store, with 80,000 customers a day. The fine foods department is also Europe's biggest.

Walk back to Breitscheidplatz, where Ku'damm begins, stretching west. Lined on either side by elegant (mostly restored) late 19th- and early 20th-century buildings, it is rich in international name stores and frequented by people who can afford the labels.

A short way west of Breitscheidplatz, take a detour left down Meinekestrasse to **Loxx MiniaturWelten** ❺ (see p. 154), an impressively detailed model of Berlin, and back up Fasanenstrasse past the **Käthe-Kollwitz-Museum** ❻ (see p. 137). Taking a left back on Ku'damm, you reach **"The Story of Berlin"** ❼ *(Kurfürstendamm 207–208, tel 030 88 72 01 00, www.story-of-berlin.de, $$$).* This multimedia tour of eight centuries of Berlin history is not a bad introduction to the city, although a trifle cheesy. You can also tour the 1970s nuclear fallout shelter below ground: It can hold 3,600 people in cramped conditions for two weeks in case of nuclear assault. What they are supposed to do after that is anyone's guess.

Back on the surface, return to Kantstrasse via Knesebeckstrasse and elegant, restaurant-lined Savignyplatz. From Kantstrasse, a quick nip south down Fasanenstrasse is the **Jüdisches Gemeindehaus** ❽, *(Fasanenstrasse 79–80),* the Jewish community center. It stands on the site of a synagogue damaged in the 1938 *Kristallnacht,* then again by Allied bombing, and finally demolished in 1958. A few remainders of the old facade have been erected in front of the modern building.

Back north on the corner of Kantstrasse is one of Berlin's odd new buildings, **Kantdreieck** ❾. Holding offices of the city's gas company, Vattenfall, it is topped by what looks like a cross between a sail and an aircraft wing. North across Kantstrasse, **Ludwig-Erhard-Haus** ❿ *(Fasanenstrasse 85)* houses Berlin's stock exchange. Its curious mix of arches and straight glass lines has won it the nickname "armadillo." On your way back to the train station, the **Museum für Fotografie** ⓫ (see p. 151), on Jebensstrasse, is a worthwhile detour. ∎

⬛ See area map p. 135
▶ Bahnhof Zoologischer Garten
↔ 3 miles (4.8 km)
🕑 2.5 hours
▶ Museum für Fotografie

NOT TO BE MISSED
- Käthe-Kollwitz-Museum
- The Story of Berlin
- Museum für Fotografie

Schloss Charlottenburg

ONE OF THE MOST POPULAR SIGHTS IN BERLIN, THE Charlottenburg palace and its gardens could easily occupy a day of your time. If you want to see everything, get here in the morning, and try to avoid weekends and summer holidays as the crowds are enough to make you claustrophobic.

The original, sober baroque summer palace was built for Sophie Charlotte, second wife of Friedrich III, who would become Prussian king in 1701. It went up in 1695–99 under the direction of architect Johann Arnold Nering. Relatively close to the central Hohenzollern winter palace—the now vanished Berliner Schloss in Mitte—it was surrounded by thick woodland. The riverside location on the Spree appealed to the Hohenzollerns, who liked nothing better than parading from residence to residence by river.

Sophie Charlotte turned the palace, which she dubbed Lietzenburg after the nearby hamlet of Lietzow, into an intellectual salon, surrounding herself with musicians, poets, and philosophers. Having crowned himself Prussia's King Friedrich I, the monarch wanted grander residences to match those of other European monarchs. The new court architect, Johann Friedrich Eosander von Göthe, set to work in 1702, lengthening the palace on either side and adding two south wings to create a grand courtyard. Then came the majestic dome atop the core of the palace and the western Orangerie, a low-slung addition that was supposed to be mirrored on the east side. Queen Sophie Charlotte did not live to see the work finished. After her death in 1705, the palace and the surrounding district became known as Charlottenburg.

Friedrich Wilhelm I's arrival on the throne in 1713 put an end to work on what he considered frivolous projects. Only when Friedrich II (Frederick the Great) replaced him in 1740 was the Neuer Flügel (New Wing) added in place of the eastern Orangerie that had been canceled by his

father. Later would come the theater at the west (now a museum), the Neuer Pavillon (New Pavilion, a separate house at the east end), and the buildings erected in the palace gardens.

A good deal of the palace was destroyed in British Royal Air Force night-bombing raids in 1943. The decision to restore the palace was partly political. After the Berliner Schloss was demolished in East Berlin in 1950, the West Berlin administration decided to demonstrate its greater sensibility to German heritage by giving the nod to restoration (after having seriously considered demolition). Ironically, the palace was in the British occupation sector. The people who had bombed it to smithereens now encouraged its reconstruction. Although largely complete, detail work still continues today.

Start a visit in the **Altes Schloss** (Old Palace), the original Nering-designed core, most of which can only be seen by a guided tour. You approach the domed palace building through the main courtyard, presided over by Andreas Schlüter's equestrian **statue of the Great Elector Friedrich Wilhelm** (completed in 1708). This originally stood in

Altes Schloss
www.spsg.de

🅰 p. 134 C4

✉ Spandauer Damm 20–24

☎ 030 32 08 14 40

🕐 Closed Mon.

💲 $, guided visit to first and top floor $$$

🚇 U-Bahn: Richard-Wagner-Platz; Bus: 109, 145, or 309

Schloss Charlottenburg was restored after World War II.

All in one
You can save a few
euros on entry prices by
buying the all-in-one
Kombinationskarte
Charlottenburg ($$ adult
for one day or $$$ for
two days). This does not
include the lower floor in
the Altes Schloss. Another
collective ticket groups the
Museum für Vor- und
Frühgeschichte, Museum
Berggruen, and Museum für
Fotografie ($$ adult).

the center of Berlin and was placed here after World War II.

After an introductory chat in a room with models of the palace, groups are led through three rooms that mostly survived the bombing. From here you pass to the garden side of the palace, where the newness of most of the woodwork indicates where complete rebuilding has taken place. You are then led east into the **Ahnengalerie** (Ancestral Gallery), lined with portraits of the Prussian royal family—note how unflatteringly realistic many of them are)—and then on to a banquet hall.

Retracing your steps westward, you cross some of Sophie Charlotte's apartments (various items of furniture were saved from the Berliner Schloss) before entering the **Ovaler Saal** (Oval Hall), at the center of the palace

beneath the dome, looking on to the garden. The series of queenly apartments continues. The ceiling paintings you see in the **Rote Tresenkammer** (Red Room) are original. You may have noticed in many restored rooms that only the stucco has been renewed in the ceilings and no frescoes painted. Frequently this is because none had ever been painted; in others no hint remained as to what they had looked like. In the Rote Tresenkammer the paintings were laid on canvas and could thus be removed to safety during the war.

You wind up in the gaudy **Porzellankabinett,** which contains a wall-to-wall display of some 2,700 pieces of porcelain of limited artistic, but great showoff, value. The point of the chamber was to provide an impressive talking point for visiting dignitaries. It is followed by the palace **chapel,** now used for concerts.

The guided visit ends on the first floor. You may freely wander the second floor, formerly the apartments of King Friedrich Wilhelm IV and his family. Harder hit by the bombs, the floor has simply been rebuilt as exhibition space. The main attractions here are the **Kronprinenzsilber** (Crown Prince's Silver) and the **Kronkabinett.** The first is a dazzling collection of early 20th-century Prussian silverware presented to Crown Prince Wilhelm, son of Kaiser Wilhelm II, on his wedding day in 1904. The latter is a modest but intriguing collection of Hohenzollern crowns.

If you like, take some refreshment in the café-restaurant in the Kleine Orangerie nearby. Then it is time to tackle the **Neuer Flügel** (New Wing). Pick up the informative audio tour for this self-guided stroll. Climb the stairs and turn left into the **Weisser Saal** (White Room), a magnificent dining hall which Friedrich II rarely used. The still more impressive **Goldene Galerie** (Golden Gallery), a 138-foot-long (42 m) ballroom, follows. Its aquamarine walls and ceiling are liberally festooned with gold-painted floral stucco motifs. The king used the four modest rooms that follow as his private chambers. In among the paintings is the "Einschiffung nach Cythera" ("Boarding for Cythera," 1718–19) by Antoine Watteau (1684–1721).

You then return to the stairway and walk through the rooms that stretch to the west. The first six, among Friedrich II's private rooms on the south side, were renovated as winter quarters by King Friedrich Wilhelm II in late 18th-century neoclassicist style. He died before seeing them finished, and his daughter-in-law, Queen Luise (1776–1810), wife of King Friedrich Wilhelm III, moved in. In the sixth room is the bed she slept in. Destroyed in 1943, the rooms were restored in 1983 through 1995.

More of Friedrich's private rooms lie along the garden side. The most interesting is the **Bibliothek** (Library). Six original cedar cabinets contain a collection of the king's favorite reading (these books came mostly from Potsdam). The king liked to read in French rather than German, and kept copies of the same books in all his residences, so that he could consult them wherever he was.

Downstairs you enter a vestibule with a model and photos of the Berliner Schloss, the former principal royal palace in central Berlin. The bulk of the remaining rooms constituted the apartments of King Friedrich Wilhelm III. Worth seeing in **Room 317,** an antechamber, is Jacques-Louis David's (1748–1825) stirring portrait of Napoleon as first consul leading the French army across the St. Bernard Pass from Switzerland into Italy in 1798. It was brought to Berlin from Paris as war booty after Napoleon's defeat at Waterloo in 1815.

Just beyond the Neuer Flügel stands the Italian-style **Neuer Pavillon,** built as a separate summerhouse by Karl Friedrich Schinkel in 1824–25 for King Friedrich Wilhelm III and his morganatic wife, Auguste, Princess of Liegnitz and Countess of Hohenzollern. It was rebuilt in 1970 as it appeared originally.

Neuer Flügel
www.spsg.de
- p. 134 C4
- Spandauerdamm 20–24
- 030 32 08 14 40
- Closed Mon.
- $$ (including audio guide)
- U-Bahn: Richard-Wagner-Platz; Bus: 109, 145, or 309

Neuer Pavillon
www.spsg.de
- p. 134 C4
- Spandauerdamm 20–24
- 030 32 08 14 40
- Closed Mon.
- $
- U-Bahn: Richard-Wagner-Platz; Bus: 109, 145, or 309

the king's bedroom.

Back outside, a walk west past the Neuer Flügel and Altes Schloss leads to the slender west wing of the palace. This is the **Orangerie,** now used for cultural events. It is capped by the theater added to the building by Carl Gotthard Langhans (1732–1808; designer of the Brandenburger Tor) in 1788–91. This looks rather like the afterthought it was, out of proportion with the main building and showing signs of the neoclassicism that would inform much early 19th-century building in Berlin. Used for storage from 1902, most of its original decoration, art, and furnishings were lost.

Since 1991 the onetime theater has housed the **Museum für Vor- und Frühgeschichte,** (Museum for Pre- and Early History), with artifacts from prehistoric times to around the 12th century A.D. The collection (which is not administered by Schloss Charlottenburg) was established in 1839 and has since been enriched. Russian forces made off with some of the most precious objects as war booty in the wake of World War II.

The display starts on the first floor with a handful of prehistoric artifacts and exhibits showing how people lived as long as two million years ago. Technical displays illustrate how various objects were made from those times into the Middle Ages.

The **Schliemannsaal** room is named after the German archaeologist Heinrich Schliemann who, in the late 19th century, carried out digs at the Turkish coastal site of Hisarlik, thought to be ancient Troy. Among the ceramics and bronze implements are some reproductions of the gold treasure that he wrongly

Inside the 18th-century Belvedere, deep in the Schloss grounds, is an extensive porcelain collection.

The building has been filled with period furniture and a modest collection of art, porcelain, and other objects. In the **Chamois Zimmer** (Chamois Room) and various other rooms you can see images of Berlin and landscapes, in particular by Eduard Gärtner. His 1839 panorama of the Kremlin in Moscow is a highlight of an upstairs passage on the building's west flank. Two more views of Berlin by the same artist are on show in the king's study on the same floor. Some modest landscapes by Schinkel hang in attributed to the mythical Trojan leader Priam. Also on display are weapons, helmets, and other implements from around the Caucasus, Iran, China, Siberia, and Cyprus. The second floor continues on a similar theme, with displays ranging from Celtic-Iberian tribes from the sixth century B.C., through Roman-occupied provinces in Europe and on to the Vikings and other medieval peoples.

The **Schlossgarten Charlottenburg** is a mixed garden reflecting different periods of the palace's history. An imitation of the French royal Palace of Versailles, the garden was originally a rigidly geometrical affair. In the 19th century it was completely reworked in the English style, which sought to replicate the randomness of nature. Peter Joseph Lenné (1789–1866), Berlin's top landscape architect, was behind this change. Having been used as a potato field in the immediate postwar years, it is today a compromise: The part behind the Altes Schloss follows the French model, while most of the rest is primarily in the English manner. A couple of buildings lurk amid its greenery.

The neoclassical **Mausoleum** *(closed Nov.–March & Mon. April–Oct.)* is half hidden in the greenery between the Museum für Vor- und Frühgeschichte and the northern rim of the garden. Built in 1810 to house the tomb of Queen Luise, it was later expanded for her husband, King Friedrich Wilhelm III, and, much later, Kaiser Wilhelm I and his second wife, Augusta.

Sitting alone in the garden's northern reaches is the **Belvedere** *(closed Mon., $)*, a dainty three-story tower conceived as a teahouse in 1788 by

Langhans. Rebuilt after World War II, it houses a collection of Berlin porcelain. Porcelain manufacture, mainly by two producers, the Wegely and Gotzkowsky houses, began in Berlin in 1751. From 1763 all production was brought together under the Königliche Porzellan-Manufaktur (KPM, Royal Porcelain Factory). The second floor is mainly given over to decorative porcelain (wall fittings, vases, and statuettes), the third floor to dinner service sets of various Prussian kings, and the fourth floor to delicate tea sets. ∎

Priam's gold

One of Berlin's most precious treasures lies in storage at Moscow's Pushkin Museum. The legendary gold of Troy, found by German archaeologist Heinrich Schliemann (1822–1890) in Turkey in 1873, was stolen from underground vaults by the Red Army in 1945 and kept under lock and key until it went on display in 1993. In spite of German demands that Russia return this and other museum collections stolen in World War II, the Russians appear to feel entitled to hang on to them as compensation for losses suffered in Germany's war of aggression. A 2000 law in Russia distinguishes between those goods removed under military orders and those simply stolen. Schliemann was convinced that the treasure, known also as Priam's gold, belonged to the legendary king of Troy mentioned in Homer's *Iliad*. Experts later deduced that the gold dated to 2500 B.C., long before the events described in Homer's tale. A few copies can be seen in the Museum für Vor- und Frühgeschichte. ∎

Museum für Vor- und Frühgeschichte
www.smb.museum
🅰 p. 134 C4
✉ Spandauerdamm 20–24
☎ 030 32 67 48 11
🕐 Closed Mon.
💲 $
🚇 U-Bahn: Richard-Wagner-Platz; Bus: 109, 145, or 210

Berlin's brightest Christmas lights

For some, the onset of the northern winter is like a long icy ride down a dark tunnel until the following spring. In Berlin there's no need for that sort of gloom. The German tradition of the *Weihnachtsmarkt* (Christmas market) fills the city with concentrated cheer. Across Berlin, better and lesser known markets set up in the squares, some with amusement-park attractions, others with all sorts of stands selling plenty of Christmas gifts. All are laden with food and drink stops. Standard traditional elements include sausages, *Glühwein* (mulled wine), *Zuckerwatte* (cotton candy), and *kandierte Äpfel* (candied apples).

The action usually starts around November 23; most markets finish a few days before Christmas Day. Although most Christmas markets open up around 11 a.m. and continue until about 9 or 10 p.m., they are at their most atmospheric when lit up at night (which means beginning around 4:30 p.m., when it is already pitch dark).

As many as 60 markets set up across Berlin. Some of the tried and true remain the best. Easily the best known and biggest Weihnachtsmarkt in Berlin is held in the old town of **Spandau** in the northwest suburbs. It is worth the trip. The village setting lends it more of a cozy feel than some of the big city center markets. More than 150 stands open, and gourmands can cruise the international food and drink specialty stands. Brass bands perform on most nights; on Fridays there are Christmas concerts. In addition to Glühwein, you'll definitely find *Feuerzangenbowle,* a red-wine-and-rum punch with kick.

Those with kids may head for **Schlossplatz** in Mitte, where a giant Ferris wheel and other amusement park rides are set to get you screaming for dear life. After some of these, a Glühwein is definitely in order. Central and popular with families, Schlossplatz tends to get crowded at night.

Another of the big markets takes place over on the west side of town at

Breitscheidplatz by the Ku'damm. Rides are usually limited to a few merry-go-rounds for young children. The place is jammed with stands selling all sorts of (mostly useless) trinkets. Even so, the atmosphere is fun, although again it can become very crowded.

Perhaps the classiest of the city's Christmas markets is the one held at **Gendarmenmarkt.** The setting is the

prettiest in central Berlin. There are no rides, but there are lots of attractive stands selling all manner of goods, from crafts to gourmet food. The entry price *($)* and relatively high prices for your Glühwein help to keep crowds down to manageable levels. Similarly genteel are the markets that spread around **Bebelplatz** in the southwest of the city and the park between the Staatsoper and Opernpalais off Unter den Linden.

Less atmospheric is the **Potsdamer Platz** market, but they do set up an artificial snow slope so that you can try out your sledding technique with a toboggan or inflated tire. The market also has a free ice-skating rink.

For more information on the present year's markets in Berlin and elsewhere, take a look at www.weihnachtsmarkt-deutschland.de.

Berlin's streets light up for Christmas, too. The best are along and around the Ku'damm. Close behind come those on Friedrichstrasse and Unter den Linden. ∎

Berlin prides itself on its Christmas street decorations, such as these lights near KaDeWe along Tauentzienstrasse.

Bröhan-Museum
www.broehan-museum.de

⬛ p. 134 C4
✉ Schlossstrasse 1a
☎ 030 32 69 06 00
🕐 Closed Mon.
$ $$
🚇 U-Bahn: Richard-
   Wagner-Platz; Bus:
   109, 145, or 309

Bröhan-Museum

AFTER DECADES OF NEGLECT, THE WHIMSICAL STYLE OF decorative arts known as art nouveau is again attracting attention in Europe. Known in Germany as *Jugendstil* (youth style) and closely associated with the arts and crafts movement in Britain, it swept Europe in art, architecture, and design in a wave of youthful creativity in the first decades of the 20th century. This period, along with later movements of art deco and functionalism, is the subject of this original museum.

Art nouveau treasures of the Bröhan-Museum range from designer furniture of the period to lovingly crafted vases.

A room is dedicated to porcelain and cutlery by Hamburg-born Peter Behrens (1868–1940). Originally a painter, he moved to architecture and design. His was a sober, geometrical approach to design, with clean lines, gentle curves, and restrained decorative motifs. Better known for his architecture (two of his buildings still stand on Alexanderplatz), Behrens counted among his apprentices Walter Gropius, Ludwig Mies van der Rohe, and Le Corbusier (1887–1965).

Equally striking is the dining room furnished by Eugène Gaillard (1862–1933). The designs were originally done around 1900 for the Galeries de l'Art Nouveau in Paris, run by the art dealer Siegfried Bing (1838–1905). Some consider Bing to be the father of art nouveau, a term he concocted to describe the fresh new style, which was influenced heavily by Japanese art and the imitation of natural forms.

This desire to reflect the sinewy forms of nature could not be clearer than in the furniture of Hector Guimard (1867–1942). His buffet cabinet is a unique piece. Above the main cabinet, a smaller cabinet is raised as if on exposed tree roots. What look like vines rise up and culminate in pods in which lamps could be set.

Office furniture designed by the Paris group Atelier

Although paintings from the late 19th century to World War II are scattered throughout the collection, the weight is on applied arts from porcelain to furniture.

The first floor holds a collection of glassware and vases produced in the French city of Nancy, a leader in the art nouveau movement. Glass factories there produced wonderfully original pieces, some of which have found their way here.

Dominique in 1922 was considerably more sober. Softly curved and with slender legs, the lady's writing desk is an example of restrained elegance.

Art deco lines tended to be more decisive, as is evidenced in the hefty dining table on lyre-shaped legs by Jacques-Emile Ruhlmann (1879–1933).

Some of the porcelain and glassware scattered around the exhibition reflects the taste for Japanese art, decorated with Oriental motifs. Other pieces predate art nouveau, including items from Berlin's Königliche Porzellan-Manufaktur (KPM, Royal Porcelain Factories), Meissen, and Sèvres in France.

Most of the museum's art collection is displayed on the third floor. Paintings, drawings, and pastels are gathered here, including works by Berlin turn-of-the-20th-century Secession artists like Karl Hagemeister (1848–1933) and Hans Baluschek (1870–1935).

The permanent exhibition continues on the fourth floor.

One room is devoted to the Belgian exponent of art nouveau Henry van de Velde (1863–1957). He drifted from his calling as a painter to design and even architecture. In 1895 he designed a house, the Bloemenwerf, outside Brussels for himself and his wife. His designs included all the interior and even the objects that were to go into it. On display here are samples of his work. Above a clean-lined, simple dining table and chairs hangs a striking ceiling lamp whose arms dangle like loose tropical branches ending in voluptuous flower bulbs. Porcelain dinner sets and silver plated bronze candlesticks complete this room.

Another room is given over to material by the Vienna Secession designer Josef Hoffmann (1870–1956). Most striking is his 1905 wooden "Sitzmaschine" ("Sitting Machine"), really just an elaborate, tall-backed chair. This floor also contains an extensive collection of porcelain from the 1920s and 1930s. ■

The art and artful household objects making up the Bröhan collection span three floors.

Alberto Giacometti's lithe figures adorn several rooms of the Museum Berggruen.

Museum Berggruen

SET OVER THREE FLOORS IN AN ELEGANT BUILDING WHOSE empty, circular core culminates in a dome, the Berggruen collection (named after collector Heinz Berggruen, born 1914) is devoted to four giants of 20th-century art: Spaniard Pablo Picasso, Frenchman Henri Matisse (1869–1954), and Switzerland's Paul Klee and Alberto Giacometti (1901–1966). The biggest part of the collection is dedicated to Picasso, with more than 80 of his works.

Museum Berggruen
www.smb.museum
🅜 p. 134 C4
✉ Schlossstrasse 1
☎ 030 326 95 80
🕐 Closed Mon.
💲 $$
🚇 U-Bahn: Richard-Wagner-Platz;
Bus: 109, 145, or 309

Center stage beneath the dome is occupied by a typically spindly Giacometti bronze, "Stehende Frau" ("Standing Woman"). The first two rooms are filled with an eclectic collection of works by Matisse, from an early portrait of Lorette, done in 1917, to some of his later, more abstract pieces, including "Die Seilspringerin" ("Woman Skipping Rope"), a 1952 blue-on-white work in strips of gouache.

Matisse gives way to early Picasso in the third room. Works include a page from a sketchpad in which he practiced quick drawings, including a pensive one of his art-teacher father. In the same rooms are portraits from his so-called blue and pink periods of the early 1900s.

The first three rooms on the second floor are devoted mostly to Picasso's cubist period, with a couple of works by his cubist contemporary, Georges Braque (1882–1963). The following four rooms concentrate on Picasso's paintings from the 1920s to the 1940s, mostly in his characteristic distorted style. Compare "Die Weinende Frau" ("The Crying Woman," 1937), whose very distortion reflects her sorrow, with the utterly peaceful "Schlafender" ("Sleeping Man," 1942). The last room contains rather explicit sketches of female nudes from the 1960s and 1970s.

On the top floor, Klee's art, interspersed with some of Giacometti's bronzes, takes a different tack. Klee's work ranges from elegant, geometrical pieces to satirical sketches, such as "Der Grosse Kaiser Reitet in den Krieg" ("The Great Kaiser Rides off to War," 1920). ■

Museum für Fotografie/ Helmut Newton Stiftung

A MAN OBSESSED WITH PHOTOGRAPHY AND WOMEN, fashion photographer Helmut Newton (1920–2004) was born in Berlin and picked up his first camera at the age of 12. Forced into exile as a Jew in 1938, he lived abroad most of his life. In 2003 he gave this gallery of his work to the city that turned its back on him. It shares its premises with the Museum für Fotografie (Museum for Photography), part of the Kunstbibliothek (Art Library).

Museum für Fotografie/ Helmut Newton Stiftung
www.smb.museum
🗺 p. 135 E3
✉ Jebensstrasse 2
☎ 030 31 86 48 56
🕐 Closed Mon.
💲 $$
🚇 U-Bahn & S-Bahn: Zoologischer Garten

The Helmut Newton collections span two floors. "Private Property," the exposition on the first floor, is the most personal, with pictures from Newton's young Berlin years and his later years in Australia.

for his many exhibitions across the years.

A separate theme, entitled "A Gun for Hire," leads you through a selection of his most stunning fashion photography, produced

His wife, June Newton, is also an accomplished photographer who uses the name Alice Springs. You can view a series of her shots of him as well as some fascinating video footage of Newton on shoots with the likes of Pierre Cardin and Vanessa Redgrave.

Photos from his books and magazine articles appear, along with an extensive series of posters

for names like Chanel, Yves St. Laurent, and Versace. Some of his more erotic photography is also on display, along with landscapes.

The Museum for Photography, under the same roof, is being rebuilt in stages. It will eventually become a combined exhibition, research, and documentation center for the study of the photographic arts. ■

The female form in various states of undress dominates Helmut Newton's photography and his museum.

Gedenkstätte Plötzensee

**Gedenkstätte
Plötzensee**
www.gedenkstaette-
ploetzensee.de
 p. 134 C6
✉ Hüttigpfad
🚌 Bus: TXL

HITLER HAD THEIR FINAL AGONY FILMED IN PLÖTZENSEE prison, north of central Berlin. On August 8, 1944, a group of 89 people who were condemned to death in connection with the July plot to kill the Führer (see p. 132) were killed in Plötzensee: Eight were hanged on butcher's hooks in Hitler's perverted justice system.

**Policemen lead
Peter Graf Yorck
von Wartenburg,
one of the 1944
conspirators, to
court. He died at
Plötzensee.**

Prisoners on death row were held in Haus III, most of which was destroyed in World War II. Part of the execution shed survived and has been turned into a memorial to the victims of Nazi rough justice. Around it, a modern prison still operates today, but the ruins of Haus III were torn down.

The prison, which Berliners soon dubbed "the Plötz," opened its doors to inmates in 1879. It was built under Kaiser Wilhelm I with a view to holding large numbers of rebels (its capacity was around 1,200) should Berliners ever rise against the government and kaiser. In the end, it was used mainly for common criminals.

From 1890 to 1932, almost 40 inmates were executed by beheading. In the 12 years of Nazi dictatorship, 2,891 people met their end in Plötzensee. Most were political prisoners who in some cases had spent months here

being interrogated under torture before they were convicted in rigged trials. At first, prisoners were beheaded by the executioner's axe, but Hitler ordered a switch to the guillotine in 1936.

Prisoners condemned to death in cells in Haus III would spend their last hours in special cells on the first floor, known to inmates as the *Totenhaus* (house of the dead). What you see today is a simple execution room, with five butcher's hooks hanging from a steel beam. Instead of being beheaded, many prisoners convicted of treason, including the July 1944 conspirators, were hanged from these hooks. Today you will probably find fresh wreaths there dedicated to the memory of the dead. Next door, the story of the prison is told in a series of panels. Finally, you can check the names of the executed on a computer. ■

More places to visit in Charlottenburg

ABGUSS-SAMMLUNG ANTIKER PLASTIK BERLIN

This curious collection of plaster casts of ancient statuary is aimed at students and professors, but grabs quite a few passing visitors, too. Copies of statues and reliefs dating back as far as the third millennium B.C. and reaching about A.D. 500, form the bulk of the display. The focus is on Greek, Roman, and, to a lesser extent, Byzantine work. The place looks like a frenetic sculptor's workshop. Shelves are lined with plaster heads, cabinets are stuffed with figurines, and phalanxes of classical statues in all manner of poses seem to have a problem with breaking ranks. In this one higgledy-piggledy spot, you can dive into (copies of) treasures of antiquity held in museums around the world, including Athens, Rome, London, Paris, and Vienna. In all, about 1,850 items are on show. Among them are a gold-painted statue of a discus thrower by Myron (ca 450 B.C.), one of the greatest sculptors of classical Greece; the original is in Rome. The "Apoll vom Belvedere" ("Belvedere

Apollo") is a particularly gracious statue of the god. The original was unearthed in the 15th century in Rome and was itself an ancient Roman copy of a Greek bronze originally in Athens' Temple of Apollo. The gilt copy of a Roman statue of winged Victoria, made to celebrate the military successes of caesars Marcus Aurelius and Lucius Verus in the second century A.D., has an interesting story. The original was part of Berlin's collection of antiquities. It went missing after World War II, then resurfaced in Moscow in early 2006, and is now awaiting an unknown fate in the Pushkin Museum.

🔼 Map p. 134 C4 ✉ Schlossstrasse 69b ☎ 030 342 40 54, www.abguss-sammlung-berlin.de 🕐 Closed Mon.–Wed. 🚇 U-Bahn: Richard-Wagner-Platz; Bus: 309 or 145

AHMADIYYA-MOSCHEE

A wholly unexpected sight in leafy, suburban southwest Berlin is this grand mosque, built in 1924 to 1928 in Indian Mogul style by German architects on commission for the Ahmadiyya

The fascinating Loxx scale-model railway system re-creates parts of Berlin, including an airport.

More places to visit in Charlottenburg

Anjuman religious association, based in Pakistan. The association was founded in the 19th century to propagate the Muslim faith. The bright white mosque is surmounted by a series of slender towers and a bulbous metallic dome topped by the crescent of Islam. It is the oldest mosque in Germany and, like so much of the city, nearly met its end in the dying days of World War II. Used by German soldiers as a machine-gun post to snipe at advancing Russian soldiers, much of the building was destroyed. It was partly restored by British and Indian military after the war and since 1993 has been catalogued as a monument. One minaret has been rebuilt and the mosque serves as a local information center. It is generally open from around 1 p.m. for Friday prayers.
🅰 p. 135 E1 ✉ Brienner Strasse 7–8 ☎ 030 873 57 03, www.muslim.org 🚇 U-Bahn: Fehrbelliner-Platz

HEIMATMUSEUM CHARLOTTENBURG-WILMERSDORF

Set in just a couple of rooms on the first floor, next door to the Abguss-Sammlung Antiker Plastik (see p. 153), this modest museum tells the story of Charlottenburg since its birth in 1705. With photos, newspaper clippings, first-day stamp collections, models, and documents, you can get to know aspects of this district's past—if you read German. One of the most interesting sections is a collection of official letters received by Albert Levy, one of the 27,000 Jews who lived in the area in 1933. The letters mainly deal with the confiscation of most of Mr. Levy's valuables by the Nazi authorities. It makes painful reading. Mr. Levy, kept in hiding by friends, was one of the few Berlin Jews to survive the war. Next door in the Stülerbau (*Schlossstrasse 70*), the Sammlung Scharf collection of surrealist art will be housed beginning in 2006.
🅰 p. 134 C4 ✉ Schlossstrasse 69 ☎ 030 902 913 201, www.heimatmuseum-charlottenburg-wilmersdorf.de 🕐 Closed Mon. 🚇 U-Bahn: Richard-Wagner-Platz; Bus: 309 or 145

LOXX MINIATURWELTEN

This will have the kids (and some grown-ups) oohing and aahing. Buried in a basement deep inside a shopping mall is a vast composite model of Berlin. Around it tootle highly detailed model trains, from local S-Bahn commuter trains to high-speed, long-distance ICE models. Famous parts of the city are reconstructed in admirable detail, among them Alexanderplatz (complete with soaring Fernsehturm), the Reichstag (with a rock concert taking place before it), and Bahnhof Zoologischer Garten. The sound effects range from traffic noise to amusement park rides near Alexanderplatz. The closer you look, the more details you see: A handful of street trams skids about, as do some of the tiny model road vehicles. A separate display presents an airport, complete with the planes landing and taking off. Take a look at the bank of closed-circuit TV screens near where the engineers sit. You could swear they are real scenes from various train stations around Berlin. Look closer and you realize they are from the grand diorama behind you. Even some of the trains themselves have microscopic cameras installed in their noses as they trundle around.
🅰 p. 135 E2 ✉ Meinekestrasse 24 ☎ 030 44 72 30 40, www.loxx-berlin.de 💲 $$$ 🚇 U-Bahn: Kurfürstendamm

RATHAUS CHARLOTTENBURG

With its 287-foot (87.5 m) tower and mix of Gothic and art nouveau ornament, this imperious building seems oversize for a seat of local government. When it was opened in 1905, Charlottenburg was still a separate and rather proud city. Designed by local architects Heinrich Reinhardt (1868–1947) and Georg Süssenguth (1862–1947) and expanded in 1911 to 1916, it was mostly destroyed in World War II. It was then patiently rebuilt by 1958. The colossal statuary on the facade represents trade guilds and various allegories. Through the wrought-iron main doors is a majestic stairway that leads you into the labyrinth inside.
🅰 p. 134 D4 ✉ Otto-Suhr-Allee 96–102 🕐 Closed Sat. and Sun. 🚇 U-Bahn: Richard-Wagner-Platz ■

Beyond Mitte spread the districts of what was East Berlin. They bristle with curious corners, from café-crammed Prenzlauer Berg to the chilling central Stasi prison, and from a sprawling zoo to Köpenick's country palace.

Prenzlauer Berg, Friedrichshain, & the east

Lenin's image was ubiquitous in the days of communist East Berlin.

Schloss
Schönhausen
Schlosspark
BLANKENBURG

0   1 kilometer
0   1 mile

114

Pankow-
Heinersdorf

TSCHAIKOWSKI-
STRASSE

OSSIETZKY-
STRASSE

BLANKEN-
BURGER
STRASSE

Schönholz

6

Panke

PANKOW

Pankow

Pankow

HEINERSDORF

Wollankstrasse

RENNBAHNSTR

BERLINER ALLEE

Vinetastrasse

109

WEISSENSEE

HANSASTRASSE

Bornholmer
Strasse

Der Weisse See

HERBERT-
BAUM-
STRASSE

ALBERTINEN-
STRASSE

HOHENSCHÖN-
HAUSEN

BORNHOLMERSTR.

Pankstrasse

WEDDING

PRENZLAUER
ALLEE

Zeiss-
Gross-
planetarium

Gesundbrunnen

Schönhauser Allee

Gethsemanekirche

Prenzlauer
Allee

96a

Humboldthain

Voltastrasse

Eisdieler

Eberswalder
Strasse

Ernst-
Thälmann
Park

Greifswalder
Strasse

Jüdischer
Friedhof
Weissensee

Gedenkstätte Berlin-
Hohenschönhausen

5

Hartbo & L'wig
Thatchers

KASTANIEN-
ALLEE

DANZIGER

GREIFSWALDER STR.

RHINSTRASSE

GENSLER-
STRASSE

Bernauer
Strasse

KOLLWITZPLATZ

PRENZLAUER
BERG

Nordbahnhof

Rosenthaler
Platz

Senefelderplatz

Volkspark
Prenzlauer
Berg

LANDSBERGER   ALLEE

Weinmeisterstr.

Rosa-Luxemburg-
Platz

Märchenbrunnen

Kleiner
Bunkerberg

2

Landsberger
Allee

Hackescher
Markt

Alexander-
platz

Volkspark
Friedrichshain

96a

Storkower
Strasse

Zentralfriedhof
Friedrichsfeld

LICHTENBERG

2

KARL-MARX-

Grosser
Bunkerberg

Friedhof der
Märzgefallenen

MITTE

STRAUSBERGER
PLATZ

ALLEE

FRIEDRICHSHAIN

Weberwiese

Frankfurter Tor

1

Straus-
berger
Platz

Café
Sibylle

FRANKFURTER ALLEE

Frankfurter
Tor

Frankfurter
Allee

Gedenkstätte
Normannenstr.

4

Jannowitz-
brücke

Samariter-
strasse

ALLEE

Lichtenberg

1   5

Heinrich-Heine-
Strasse

Ostbahnhof

Berlinomat

Magdalene-
strasse

Friedrichsfeld

Prenzlauer
Berg,
Friedrichshain,
& the east

KREUZBERG

Spree

Warschauer
Strasse

BOXHAGENER
PLATZ

Nöldnerplatz

FRIEDRICHS-
FELDE

Schlesisches
Tor

Ostkreuz

Rummelsburg

Betriebsbahnhof
Rummelsburg

96a

Treptower
Park

Rummelsburger See

3

Treptower
Park

TREPTOW

Plänter-
wald

Plänterwald

KÖPENICKER LANDSTR.

Spree

KIEFHOLZ

Baumschulenweg

STRASSE

96a

2

Schöneweide

BERLIN'S EAST IS A FASCINATING MIX. WHILE
much of it seems to have changed relatively little since the
days of the German Democratic Republic, some areas are
hopping. Prenzlauer Berg, once a relatively poor district, has
become gentrified and hip. Friedrichshain to the south is winning a
name for itself with a busy nightlife scene. Farther out, quiet, working-class suburbs hide keys to the city's rough-and-tumble 20th century.

Little more than countryside until the mid-
19th century, Prenzlauer Berg became a dense-
ly populated working-class district by the 20th
century. While 50 percent of the city center
and even 40 percent of neighboring
Friedrichshain was destroyed in World War II,
less than 20 percent of this area succumbed to
fire storms. Neglected and crumbling in GDR
days, it attracted East Berlin's intellectuals and

artists. This ambience (and cheap
rent) brought in West Berlin's
Bohemians when the wall came down.

Since then, much has been renovat-
ed, prices have soared, and the penniless
Bohemians have scattered, leaving behind
a young population of go-ahead folk.
Catering to their needs, especially around
Kastanienallee and Kollwitzplatz, is a

rainbow spectrum of restaurants, bars, and shops. One of Berlin's biggest synagogues managed to survive here, a couple of 19th-century breweries have been imaginatively recycled, and the area is one of the best preserved in the city. While specific sights are thin on the ground, it is a delightful area in which to wander and take the pulse of the city.

Nearby Friedrichshain is bisected by a curious experiment in 1950s Soviet-style town planning and architecture, the somehow captivating Karl-Marx-Allee. Nearby Boxhagener Platz has become a focal point of frenetic nightlife for the many students and other restless young people who bailed out of Prenzlauer Berg.

Pankow, Hohenschönhausen, Lichtenberg, and Karlshorst line up in a broad arc from north to south like an outer ring beyond these districts. For the most part residential, each has one or two rough-edged gems. Pankow, once the suburb of choice for Communist Party bosses, hides among its gentle streets a somewhat neglected palace and park, while Weissensee, near Pankow, hosts the city's biggest Jewish cemetery.

Not much goes on in the high-rise housing districts of Hohenschönhausen and Lichtenberg, but they are home respectively to the GDR's security police prison and headquarters, each of them offering sobering insights into the police state that was dismantled in 1990. Among the pleasant villas of Karlshorst, once the nerve center for the Soviet military in East Germany, you can find a curious war museum dedicated to the fighting on the Eastern Front during World War II.

Southeast, on the city limits, are peaceful Köpenick with its restored palace and a bucolic string of lakes. ■

A Prenzlauer promenade

More than many other of Berlin's inner suburbs, Prenzlauer Berg oozes atmosphere and invites a gentle stroll. There are few major sights, but you can visit several lesser sources of curiosity and find plenty of opportunities for refreshment along the way.

Visitors find plenty of charming stores and cafés in Prenzlauer Berg.

Start at the Rosenthaler Platz U-Bahn station, through which the city's defensive wall once ran. A slightly uphill stroll (a rare experience in determinedly flat Berlin) along Weinbergsweg (Vineyard Way) takes you past the Volkspark am Weinbergsweg, which was a vineyard in the 18th century. Turn left on Fehrbelliner Strasse and then right to towering **Zionskirche** ❶ on the square of the same name.

The grand brick church was built under Kaiser Wilhelm I and opened in 1873. Designed by August Orth (1828–1901) in a mix of neo-Romanesque and neo-Gothic styles, it stands with a 220-foot (67 m) tower on central Berlin's highest natural point. Its restoration was completed only in 2002. Evangelical theologian Dietrich Bonhoeffer (1906–1945) was once Zionskirche's parish priest. This opponent of the Nazis, who was active in the German underground from 1940 on, was arrested in 1943 and later died in Flossenbürg concentration camp in April 1945.

Zionskirchstrasse leads east past pleasant Teutoburger Platz to Christinenstrasse and the back of the onetime **Pfefferberg brewery** ❷ that houses the Vitra Design Museum (see p. 172), scheduled to open in early 2007. A walk around its north flank leads to Schönhauser Allee, north of which spreads out the historic, leafy **Jüdischer Friedhof** ❸. Established in 1827, this Jewish cemetery was in use until 1976 and holds the remains of composer Giacomo Meyerbeer and painter Max Liebermann. Across Schönhauser Allee stands the red-brick neo-Gothic **Segenskirche** ❹, a 1908 church with a north Italian flavor. A short walk farther north on Schönhauser Allee brings you to the massive **Kulturbrauerei** ❺. Built in 1889, this dazzling complex of 20 red-and-yellow brick buildings was doubtless Berlin's most attractive brewery and only stopped bottling in 1967. Today it is an entertainment center, with clubs, bars, cinema, theater, and stores.

One of the city's great old beer gardens, the **Berliner Prater** **6**, is around the corner on Kastanienallee. They have been serving summer ambers since 1852.

Walk east along Danziger Strasse and then south (right) down Husemannstrasse, lined with shops, restaurants, and bars. Husemannstrasse leads into charming **Kollwitzplatz** **7**, named after artist Käthe Kollwitz (who lived nearby on what is now the elegant, cobbled Kollwitzstrasse), the scene of a bustling Saturday market.

A block east on Knaackstrasse stands the **Synagoge Rykestrasse** **8**, one of only two to survive Nazis savagery and war damage. A redbrick building from 1904, it can seat 2,000. The interior was restored after the war. Straight ahead in the small green park on the right rises what locals refer to as Dicker Hermann (Fat Hermann), a former **Wasserturm** **9**, or water tower, that

Hitler's SA (Stormtrooper Department) turned into a prison for local Jews. It is now a highly original apartment block.

Around the corner, on Prenzlauer Allee, you can learn a little more about local history in the **Prenzlauer Berg Museum** **10** *(Prenzlauer Allee 227–228, tel 030 902 953 916, closed Sat.–Sun.).* ■

⚐ See area map p. 156 A5
▶ Rosenthaler Platz
↔ 2.4 miles (3.8 km)
🕐 1.5 hours
▶ Prenzlauer Berg Museum

NOT TO BE MISSED
- Zionskirche
- Kulturbrauerei
- Synagoge Rykestrasse
- Prenzlauer Berg Museum

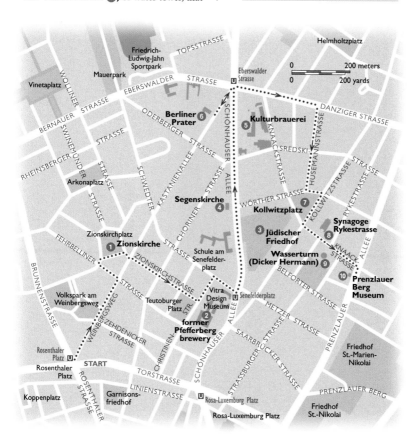

Volkspark Friedrichshain

Volkspark Friedrichshain
p. 156 B4

CENTRAL BERLIN'S PRETTIEST PARK AFTER THE TIERGARTEN, and one of the city's more interesting green spaces, the Friedrichshain People's Park straddles the municipal frontier between hip Prenzlauer Berg and frumpier, working class Friedrichshain. It is filled with historic symbolism, although for locals it is simply a lovely spot for a Sunday stroll or jog.

The beautiful green space of the Volkspark Friedrichshain offers respite to local high-rise residents.

Located less than a mile from Alexanderplatz, the park owes its form to World War II. It was Berlin's first communal park, laid out in the late 19th century to give a little relief to the working-class masses living in miserably cramped conditions in the surrounding area. During World War II, air-raid shelters were built here. After 1945, creative builders used the masses of rubble left over from Allied air raids to create two hills over the shelters. The result was the 256-foot-high (78 m) **Grosser Bunkerberg** (Big Bunker Hill) in the heart of the park and the smaller 157-foot (48 m) **Kleiner Bunkerberg** (Little Bunker Hill) to the east. Between them lies a pleasant lake.

One thing that remained unchanged after 1945 was the 1913 **Märchenbrunnen** (Fairytale Fountain), fronted by a gracious colonnade, in the park's northwestern corner.

Memorials to violent events of the past abound. The **Friedhof der Märzgefallenen,** the original burial place of 183 Berliners killed by royal troops in the March 1848 uprisings, lies at the southern end of the park (*off Landsberger Allee*). Few gravestones remain; the cemetery is now also a memorial to rebels killed in a mutiny that accelerated Germany's capitulation in 1918.

Only 18 years later, civil war broke out in Spain and Hitler sent the Condor Legion to back Gen. Francisco Franco's military coup. Some Germans volunteered to join the International Brigades that aided the left-wing government forces. A monument to them stands on the western Friedenstrasse side of the park.

At the east end of the park is another memorial—this time to Polish soldiers and resistance fighters of World War II as well as to members of the German resistance. The monument was raised in 1972 in an act of socialist brotherhood between the Warsaw Pact allies. ∎

Lichtenberg

A VISIT TO THE EASTERN SUBURBS OF LICHTENBERG AND around is a voyage into the dark side of Berlin's more recent past. Here stand the former Ministerium für Staatssicherheit (Ministry for State Security, or Stasi for short), the headquarters of an incredibly tight web of state control, and the former Stasi prison of Hohenschönhausen. The communist ideal was not meant to degenerate like this. Many of the German Left's greatest historical figures (along with a good swath of less reputable GDR chiefs) lie buried in the nearby Friedrichsfelde cemetery. For a little relief, make for Berlin's second zoo.

See inside the minds that ran East Germany's security apparatus at the Gedenkstätte Normannenstrasse.

Gedenkstätte Normannen-strasse

www.stasi-museum.de

🅰 p. 156 C4
✉ Ruschestrasse 103
☎ 030 553 68 54
💲 $
🚇 U-Bahn: Magdalenenstrasse

Housed in the anonymous, sprawling complex that was the Stasi ministry is the **Gedenkstätte Normannenstrasse,** also known as the Stasi Museum. Many of the buildings here today have other tenants, above all the Deutsche Bahn (German Railways). The one-time nerve center of the ministry now hosts a documentation center and permanent exhibition on the ministry's misdeeds. Thousands of East Berliners stormed the buildings in mid-1990 as the GDR ceased to exist.

Head for Haus 1. In the foyer stands a model of the typical vehicle used to transport Stasi prisoners. It is a harmless-looking thing with five tiny, windowless and airless cells. The first floor is given over to displays on bugging devices and other elements of the surveillance trade. As the internal propaganda in Rooms 3 and 3b makes clear, the Stasi aimed to "be everywhere." The bugging devices are curious, but more so the assorted hidden cameras. Everything from tree trunks to cigarette cases and from watering cans to handbags could be used.

On the next floor are the central offices of Erich Mielke, state security minister from 1957 to 1989, and his staff. The austere

Zentralfriedhof Friedrichsfelde

🗺 p. 156 C4

✉ Gudrunstrasse

🚉 S-Bahn: Friedrichsfelde-Ost

A tiger presides over the Tierpark, Berlin's second zoo, in Friedrichshain.

offices have been left as they were. In a lounge area, order a cup of coffee and take in one of a couple of videos on the Stasi (one in English and presented by Roger Moore, of James Bond fame). Only some of the labeling is in English, but visitors can borrow a printed guide in English.

About 1 mile (1.5 km) east of Stasi headquarters is the **Zentralfriedhof Friedrichsfelde.** It was primarily a poor people's cemetery in the 19th century, but gradually became

From the cemetery, the easiest route to Berlin's former central Stasi prison, the **Gedenkstätte Berlin Hohenschönhausen** (Berlin Hohenschönhausen Memorial), is by tram. Take any northbound tram along Rhinstrasse from outside the Friedrichsfelde-Ost S-Bahn station and change for westbound trams 6 and 7 at Landesberger Allee. Get off at Genslerstrasse. Only guided tours are possible; these take up to two hours and are intermittently in English. For

the burial place for important Socialists and Communists. One of the earliest great Socialists in Germany, Paul Singer (1844–1911), was given a hero's burial here. Singer lies with other Socialists of the era, like Wilhelm Liebknecht (1826–1900) and Friedrich Ebert. In the inner circle, gathered around a monument to socialism, are Rosa Luxemburg and Karl Liebknecht, alongside GDR leaders such as the detested Walter Ulbricht.

those who understand German, this tour is a chilling and moving experience, as many of the volunteer guides are former inmates. The prison (with more than 200 cells and interrogation rooms) was set up in 1951 in what had been a Soviet prison camp since 1945. The tour starts with a half-hour film on the prison's history. Visitors are then taken to the cellar prison (known as the U-Boot), a series of unspeakable, dank, lightless cells where Soviet intelligence interrogators and then their Stasi successors tortured political prisoners. In water cells, some prisoners were shut in with water up to their ankles for five months at a time. In the newer 1960s prison buildings, cells are not quite as awful, but treatment was brutal and arbitrary for the flimsiest of political "crimes." Being suspected of planning to flee the GDR was enough to get you a couple of years in here. The cells were in use until the end of 1989.

Berlin's post–World War II past has also resulted in a pleasant alternative to all this weighty history. The city's division in two left East Berlin without a zoo, and so the **Tierpark Berlin** was created from scratch and opened in 1955. The biggest animal park in Europe, it has some 10,000 occupants. The generous layout is the zoo's strong point, leaving plenty of open space for herds of camels, deer, and many others, caged in only by moats. The pink flamingo island is a high point. Others include the bear enclosures, the Dickhäuterhaus (where you'll find elephants and rhinos), and the snake farm.

At the northwest end of the park stands **Schloss Friedrichsfelde**, a palace that lay far from Berlin in the countryside when it was first built in 1695. It was given its present appearance in 1719 by Martin Böhme, Berlin's official palace architect at the time. It changed hands frequently, winding up in the von Treskow family from 1816 to 1945. After World War II it slowly decayed, until restored in 1981. The palace can be visited only by guided tours, which take place four times a day. On show is a cornucopia of 18th-century arts and crafts, from Berlin porcelain and silverware to paintings by artists such as Eduard Gärtner.

On either side of the palace stretch elegant manicured gardens. The Tierpark was once a private park belonging to the palace. In 1821, Peter Joseph Lenné converted it into carefully planned gardens, subsequently supplanted by the zoo. ∎

The rise & fall of Erich Mielke

After three decades at the top, Erich Mielke (1907–2000) must have seen the collapse of the GDR and its aftermath as a nightmare. Born into a working-class family in Berlin's northern suburb of Wedding, Mielke was a militant in the German Communist Party by the late 1920s. In street fighting in 1931 he shot two policemen dead (a crime for which he received a prison sentence in 1993) and fled to Moscow. After fighting in the Spanish Civil War (1936–39) and hiding in France during World War II, he returned to Berlin in 1945. A protégé of East German president Walter Ulbricht, Mielke was named minister for state security in 1957. His spy network had files on virtually the entire East German population. Feared rather than liked, this "hero of the working class" was quickly dropped by the ruling SED party after the Berlin Wall came down in November 1989. In mid-1990 he went on trial several times on murder and fraud charges. After a few years in jail, he was freed in 1995 and all further cases against him were dropped in 1998 on health grounds. ∎

Gedenkstätte Berlin Hohenschönhausen
www.stiftung-hsh.de
🅰 p. 156 C5
✉ Gensler Strasse 66
☎ 030 98 60 82 30
🕐 Guided tours Mon.–Fri 11 a.m. & 1 p.m., Sat.–Sun. 10 a.m.–4 p.m.
💲 $, free Wed.
🚃 M5 tram: Oberseestrasse; S-Bahn: Landsberger Allee & M5

Tierpark Berlin
www.tierpark-berlin.de
🅰 p. 157 D4
✉ Am Tierpark 125
☎ 030 51 53 10
💲 $$$
🚇 U-Bahn: Tierpark

Schloss Friedrichsfelde
www.stadtmuseum.de
🅰 p. 157 D4
✉ Am Tierpark 125
☎ 030 66 63 50 37
🕐 Closed Mon., guided tours hourly 1–4 p.m.
💲 $, with entry to Tierpark $$$
🚇 U-Bahn: Tierpark or Friedrichsfelde

Berlin design

Paris, Milan, London … Berlin? Germany's capital is home to no fewer than seven fashion schools. Ever since the first Bread & Butter fashion show was held in Spandau in 2000, the city has elbowed its way into the European fashion fair business.

Bread & Butter includes hundreds of established and emerging local designers of urban streetwear. Its philosophy of steering clear of government aid and pooling with more high-end fashion shows has given it an identity that reflects the unfettered, quirky Berlin milieu in which it blossomed.

In 2005 its organizers took a leap of faith and presented in Barcelona, Spain. The show was such a success that B&B decided to put on a winter *(Jan.)* and summer *(July)* show there annually until 2008, just as it does in Berlin. And in January 2006 the same people staged Milk & Honey, concentrating on out-there women's fashion.

Berlin's rise and rise as a threads capital has spawned more fashion shows. In 2005, three new shows premiered: Femme Plus (chic women's clothing), To Shoe (footwear and accessories), and B-IN-Berlin (since January 2005), which carries young men's and women's fashion. Another show to watch is Premium *(Jan. & July)*, which leans toward haute couture.

How did it all happen? West Berlin had long been the stage for Germany's most pulsating counterculture scene, and the fall of the wall in 1989 opened up new opportunities for young creators in need of low rents. They poured into the then-burgeoning artists' quarter of Prenzlauer Berg (initially on Kastanienallee) and have since spread farther afield.

Among the designers who gave Kastanienallee its fame for fashion flair are Eisdieler *(Kastanienallee 12, www.eisdieler.de)* and Thatchers *(Kastanienallee 21, www.thatchers.de)*. Thatchers designs mainly women's fashion using fine materials and unusual lines. Several more cheeky Berlin labels can be found on Kastanienallee and around the corner on Oderberger Strasse. Among the city's sassiest designers, Sarah Elbo and Andrea Hartwig form Hartbo & L'wig *(Oderberger Strasse 20, www.hartbol wig.de)*, specializing in clothes for young women.

Put off by rising rents in rapidly gentrifying Prenzlauer Berg, some designers have shifted to the new "in" district, Friedrichshain. Berlinomat *(Frankfurter Allee 89, www.berlinomat.com)* is a showroom for local designers, featuring not only clothing but anything from cookware to gadgets.

For lists of fashion stores divided up by district, check out Modedesign-Berlin's website *(www.modedesign-berlin.de)*. ∎

The Walk of Fashion extravaganza (left) is one of several shows that have put Berlin on the fashion map. Shoppers find some of the goods in stores like KaDeWe (below).

Among the Jews buried at the Weissensee cemetery are many who fought in World War I.

Pankow & Weissensee

PANKOW IS A QUIET NORTHERN SUBURB. LONG A working-class district and relatively undamaged at the end of World War II, it became home for most of the GDR's party *Bonzen* (bigwigs) until the East German state's demise in 1990. Along with Weissensee to the southeast, it remains essentially residential, with plenty of generous green spaces and a couple of attractions.

Schloss Schönhausen

- p. 156 A6
- Ossietzkystrasse
- Garden closed Oct.–March, palace closed for renovation until 2009
- U-Bahn & S-Bahn: Pankow & M1 tram to Tschaikowskistrasse

Jüdischer Friedhof Weissensee

- p. 156 B5
- Herbert-Baum-Strasse 45
- Closed Sat.
- M4 tram: Albertinenstrasse

Schloss Schönhausen and its 40-acre (16 ha) garden lie at the heart of Pankow. A mansion and some kind of green space have been here since the 17th century, but what you see today is largely the result of gardens laid out in 1829–1831 by Peter Joseph Lenné. Broad, leafy alleys crisscross the park, a favorite with summer picnickers. The palace—given its present form for Queen Elisabeth Christine, wife of Friedrich II, in 1764—is currently closed to the public. Restoration work due to begin in 2006 should finish in 2009.

A few miles southeast of Pankow is Weissensee, another suburban area mostly made up of GDR-era housing blocks. In the middle of it all is Europe's largest Jewish cemetery, the **Jüdischer Friedhof Weissensee.** Laid out in 1880, the cemetery suffered some wartime bombing damage but, remarkably, was left largely untouched by the Nazis. A memorial near the entrance honors the six million Jews who perished in the Holocaust.

A panel at the entrance points out the graves of outstanding individuals. To visit the cemetery, you need some kind of headwear. The flower shop at the entrance can lend you a head covering. Of particular interest, toward the southern end of the cemetery behind the UI and UII plots, is a burial ground for German Jewish soldiers who fell at the front in World War I. ∎

Karlshorst

IN THE FOUR YEARS BEFORE THE FINAL SOVIET PULLOUT from Berlin in September 1994, this area was one of the strangest parts of town. The recently reunited city may not have had a wall any more, but its citizens still lived in parallel worlds. In another dimension altogether, however, were the Soviet officers and soldiers who had made Karlshorst their headquarters in Berlin since the end of World War II.

Deutsch-Russisches-Museum
www.museum-karlshorst.de
🅰 p. 157 D3
✉ Zwieselerstrasse 4
☎ 030 50 15 08 10
🕐 Closed Mon.
🚇 S-Bahn: Karlshorst & Bus: 396

Westerners on day-trips to East Berlin were not allowed to visit, but after 1990 anyone could wander into what seemed like a Cold War spy movie set. By early 1993, soldiers could be seen loading Soviet military trucks with everything they could find for the return home to an uncertain future.

All that remains of the Soviet presence is the **Deutsch-Russisches-Museum** (German-

In 1995 the current museum opened as a joint Russo-German effort commemorating the events of the war on the Eastern Front. It is a difficult balancing act. Prewar relations, war planning on both sides, and the course of hostilities on the Eastern Front is presented with a mixture of German and Soviet texts, photos, audio and video streams, and some military gear (such as uniforms, medals,

The final act of German surrender was signed in 1945 in what would become the Soviet headquarters in East Germany.

Russian Museum). In this building, a German officers' school and club built in 1936, Germany signed its final, unconditional surrender to Allied forces on May 8, 1945. From that spring on, it was the headquarters of the Soviet Fifth Army. In 1967, the building was converted into the elaborately titled "Museum of Fascist Germany's Unconditional Surrender in the Great Patriotic War of 1941–1945."

and weaponry) from both sides.

Most interesting of all is the hall in which the capitulation was signed. The Germans sat at a separate, low table to the right of the main table, which seated representatives of the victorious Allied forces. After the formalities, the Germans were ushered out and the victory banquet started. The scene has been set up as it was back in 1945. A silent video shows the events of that day. ∎

Köpenick

Schloss Köpenick sits tranquilly on an island (above), a short stroll from the pretty old center of Alt-Köpenick (right).

SOUTHEAST OF CENTRAL BERLIN, KÖPENICK WAS ONCE a separate fishing village huddled on an island at the junction of the Spree and Dahme rivers. Bronze Age families, Slavic tribes, and, from the 12th century, German colonists all built forts here. Surrounded by riverways and villas, the compact old town oozes charm. At its center stands the baroque Schloss Köpenick, which alone merits the trip from downtown Berlin.

From the S-Bahn station you can walk about 20 minutes south along Bahnhofstrasse or catch the 68 tram to Alt-Köpenick, the old center. On the way you may notice a statue in the middle of a park called **Platz des 23. April.** The square's name commemorates the arrival of the Soviet army in Köpenick in 1945; the statue honors the 91 people shot here by the Nazis in a round-up of opponents in June 1933. A display in the nearby old **court cells** (*Puchanstrasse 12, open Thurs.*) describes this incident.

At the park, turn left and follow the tramlines over a bridge into the old town center. On the corner of Alt-Köpenick rises the bombastic, neo-Gothic *Rathaus* (city hall). The onetime mayor thought it a grand idea to tear down the building's medieval pre-decessor in 1904 and replace it with this edifice. The site became famous two years later when it was stormed by the "captain of Köpenick" (see below). A statue of this enterprising man stands at the foot of the entrance stairs.

A few minutes' walk south leads to **Schloss Köpenick,** the 17th-century royal palace that today holds part of the collection of the **Kunstgewerbemuseum** (Museum of Decorative Arts)— the main collection is in the Kulturforum (see p. 125). Rutger van Langerfeld built the palace over its Renaissance predecessor in 1685 for Prince Friedrich, later King Friedrich I.

Over four floors, a collection of fine furniture, marquetry, Berlin porcelain, pewter, and other 16th- to 19th-century objects graces the beautifully stuccoed palace rooms. The highlight is the second-floor collection of decorative gold-plated silverware; it has been set out as it was in the Rittersaal (Knights' Hall) of the Berliner Schloss (see p. 99) in central Berlin. At the other end of the same floor is the **Wappensaal** (Coats-of-Arms Hall), holding a banquet table set with delicate porcelain and crystal.

A look in the attic is worthwhile just to admire the enormous beams holding up the roof.

The palace looks onto a calm body of water, the Frauentog. Fishermen used to spread their nets from the **Kietz** on the east bank. This pleasant, cobbled street is lined by charming cottages where fishing families once lived. To the northeast stands a 17th-century house that today is home to the **Heimatmuseum.** Its display of photos, documents, and artifacts recounts the long history of Köpenick. ∎

Schloss Köpenick
www.smb.museum
🅰 p. 157 D2
✉ Schlossinsel
☎ 30 266 36 66
🕐 Closed Mon.
💲 $$
🚊 S-Bahn: Köpenick & tram: 68

Heimatmuseum
www.heimatmuseum koepenick.de
🅰 p. 157 E2
✉ Alter Markt 1
☎ 030 61 72 33 51
🕐 Closed Mon. & Fri.–Sun. p.m.
🚊 S-Bahn: Köpenick & tram: 68

The captain of Köpenick

Köpenick owes its fame to the startling escapade of a 60-year-old cobbler and part-time con man in October 1906. Out of work and in need of cash, Friedrich Wilhelm Voigt had an idea. Betting on the famed obedience of Prussian soldiers, Voigt bought a second-hand captain's uniform, commandeered a ten-man squad of troops he found passing by, and ordered the occupation of Köpenick City Hall. While local police maintained order outside, he arrested the mayor and had him sent to central Berlin. Then he impounded the cash box, taking 4,000 Marks. Voigt was later arrested and sentenced to four years in prison (he served two). They say Kaiser Wilhelm was rather pleased by the incident, as it confirmed the perfect subordination of his troops to officers! The story of *Der Hauptmann von Köpenick (The Captain of Köpenick)* was turned into a play by Carl Zuckmayer (1896–1977) in 1931. In 1956 director Helmut Käutner (1908–1980) brought the story to the silver screen. ∎

Boat tours cruise
the Müggelsee
lakes in the
warmer months.

Grosser Müggelsee & Grünau

Rahnsdorf
🔺 p. 157 F2
🚉 S-Bahn: Rahnsdorf

Grünau
🔺 p. 157 D1
🚉 S-Bahn: Grünau or
tram 68 from
Köpenick

**Grünauer
Wassersport-
museum**
🔺 p. 157 E1
✉ Regattastrasse 191
☎ 030 674 40 02
🕐 Open Sat. p.m.
🚉 S-Bahn: Grünau

BERLIN'S BIGGEST LAKE, THE GROSSER MÜGGELSEE, OPENS up about 1.2 miles (2 km) east of central Köpenick. Stressed Berlin urbanites take the 3-square-mile (7.7 square km) lake by storm on summer weekends for boat tours, swims, and lakeside walks. Several boat companies crisscross the lake, and swimmers can find a handful of limited beaches (some of them for nude bathing). In colder winters the lake freezes over and becomes a popular natural ice-skating rink.

A walk along the wooded south bank is a pleasant way to pass an hour or two. The 377-foot (115-m) mound just to the south of the lake is the **Müggelberge**, one of the city's highest points. Of the villages that face the lake, eastern **Rahnsdorf** is the most pleasant. Villas and shady gardens surround the original core, once a fishing settlement. To soak up the atmosphere, walk along cobbled Dorfstrasse and follow the signs to the Altes Fischerdorf (Old Fishermen's Village).

Just over a mile (2 km) southwest of Köpenick lies the quiet settlement of Grünau, founded in 1749. It's a pleasant spot for a stroll on the Dahme River, which widens into the Langer See (Long Lake). As watersports gained in popularity in the late 19th century, Berliners with a penchant for the great outdoors built themselves lakeside residences. The spot was also chosen for the 1936 Olympic rowing events. To learn more, see the **Grünauer Wassersportmuseum** on the edge of Langer See. What started as a private collection in 1980 has developed into an oddly specialized museum dedicated to local watersports, with special emphasis on the 1936 Olympic Games. Boats, photos, newspaper cuttings, medals, and other such paraphernalia make up the bulk of the collection.

Grünau and Rahnsdorf are on the Berlin city limits, but the chain of streams and small lakes spreads out to the east and south. You can rent canoes and kayaks to explore this area. ∎

More places to visit in Prenzlauer Berg, Friedrichshain, & the east

ERNST-THÄLMANN-PARK

This modest suburban park in Prenzlauer Berg bears one of the names dearest to German communists. The park was created in the 1980s as part of a high-density GDR housing project. Its high-rise apartments, designed to accommodate 4,000 people, tower above the park, which was designed to provide them with a little green space. Facing Greifswalder Strasse is an enormous, 43-foot-high (13 m) bronze bust to the memory of Ernst Thälmann (1886–1944), his fist clenched in communist salute. Behind him flutters a revolutionary flag. Thälmann was born in Hamburg and by the age of 20 was active in the city's trade union movement. As a dockworker, warehouse employee, and member of the German Socialist Party, he was politically active until sent to the Western Front in World War I.

In the 1920s, Thälmann rose in the ranks of the German Communist Party (KPD) and led the Roter Frontkämpferbund (Red Front Fighters' Association), which spearheaded street battles with the Nazis' Sturmabteilung (SA) paramilitary units in the mid-1920s. The KPD was tightly linked to the Soviet Union; Thälmann became party president with Josef Stalin's explicit backing and stood for president of the Weimar Republic in 1932. Shortly after Adolf Hitler's arrival in power in 1933, Thälmann was arrested and accused of high treason. He was shunted from prison to prison and eventually wound up in Buchenwald concentration camp in August 1944, where he was shot dead on Hitler's orders.

On the northwest side of the housing project is the Zeiss Grossplanetarium (*Prenzlauer Allee 80, tel 030 42 18 45 12, www.astw.de*), a planetarium added in 1987 and popular with local children.

🅰 p. 156 B5 ✉ Greifswalder Strasse
🚈 S-Bahn: Greifswalder Strasse

GETHSEMANEKIRCHE

Prenzlauer Berg's brick Gethsemanekirche was one of an extraordinary 53 churches built on the orders of Kaiser Wilhelm II between 1890 and 1905. The kaiser hoped thus to draw the working classes away from the dangers of socialism. The building was designed by August Orth in a mixed style combining Romanesque and neo-Gothic elements and finished in 1893. The church community, far from becoming an instrument of established power, developed a reputation for dissent, especially under the Nazis and then during the 40 years of the GDR. In October 1989, shortly before the GDR edifice began to collapse, a peaceful protest in front of the church was violently broken up by Stasi agents.

🅰 p. 156 A5 ✉ Stargarder Strasse 77
🚈 S-Bahn: Schönhauser Allee

International Cinema, Karl-Marx-Allee

KARL-MARX-ALLEE

Of the myriad problems assailing postwar Berlin, the housing shortage was the most pressing. In 1952, East Germany launched a *Nationales Aufbauprogramm* (national rebuilding program). The jewels in the crown were to be the grand blocks of residential, office, and shopping space along Karl-Marx-Allee (at the time called Stalinallee), between Strausberger Platz and Frankfurter Tor, in East Berlin. Built in the Soviet-inspired *Zuckerbäckerstil* (wedding-cake style), these buildings exude a certain grandeur, much derided in the West but now making this strip worthy of national heritage protection. The buildings are multitiered, some with fluted columns and/or clad in Meissen tiles. At **No. 84** on the south side, on the site of what was

Communist hero Ernst Thälmann is commemorated in the East Berlin park bearing his name.

More places to visit around Prenzlauer Berg, Friedrichshain, & the east

from 1906 to 1945 the Rose Theater, the building has reliefs depicting working-class heroes. Drop in to **Café Sibylle** (*Karl-Marx-Allee 72, tel 030 29 35 22 03*) to see a small display on the boulevard's development—or just to eat some cake. The café will organize a quick trip (*$$$*) to an observation deck on the roof of their Zuckerbäcker building for views up and down this broad thoroughfare.

Strausberger Platz and Frankfurter Tor have a monumental appearance. East of Frankfurter Tor, the style continues in rather more dilapidated-looking buildings a short way along Frankfurter Allee (as far as Niederbarnimstrasse). Whatever you make of the style, the apartments themselves, with par-quet floors and central heating, represented unprecedented luxury for Berliners in the tough postwar period.

🅰 p. 156 A4–B4 ✉ Karl-Marx-Allee
🚇 U-Bahn: Alexanderplatz

VITRA DESIGN MUSEUM

Due to reopen in the former Pfefferberg brewery in Prenzlauer Berg in early 2007, this modern and contemporary design gallery will bring a further dynamic touch to the city. The brewery was in business from 1841 to 1920 and the complex is considered one of the most outstanding examples of Berlin industrial architecture still extant. Later used as anything from a chocolate factory to a printing press, since the fall of the wall the buildings have been host to a cultural center, with exhibition space, a theater, cinema, and beer garden. The design museum occupies the rear part of the complex, with a stark, white exterior protruding from the brickwork of the original brewery buildings. Over two floors in the part of the industrial complex given over to the museum, ever changing exhibitions are the order of the day. In the cellar, items on display will come from the design museum's own collections of modern furniture, regularly rotated and, where possible, complementing the temporary exhibitions on the main floor. Collections range from the early 19th century to the present day. Emphasis is on the creative period of the 1920s and early 1930s as well as Scandinavian design from the 1930s to the 1960s.

🅰 p. 159 ✉ Christinenstrasse 18–19, www.design-museum.de 🕐 Closed Mon.
💲 $$ 🚇 U-Bahn Senefelder Platz ∎

Must-see museums combine with a string of minor pearls of historical interest to make this broad swath of southern Berlin a path of discovery. A couple of hot spots attract flocks of Berlin night owls, too.

Schöneberg to Kreuzberg

Painter Thierry Noir stands in front of his artwork at the Berlin Wall.

Schöneberg to Kreuzberg

THE EASTWARD SWEEP FROM SLEEPY RESIDENTIAL WILMERSDORF ACROSS trendy Schöneberg and into the predominantly Turkish quarters of eastern Kreuzberg presents a cross-section of modern Berlin. Concentrated in western Kreuzberg are three major museums with completely different themes: The Berlinische Galerie presents a cornucopia of contemporary art, the Jüdisches Museum a provocative panorama of German-Jewish history, and the Deutsches Technikmuseum a panoply of human invention and ingenuity.

Historic figures from Marlene Dietrich to U.S. President John F. Kennedy have left an impression on this part of town. One of the sultriest actresses ever to grace the silver screen, Dietrich was born and buried in Schöneberg. Not far from where she rests in peace, a rather different star put in a memorable appearance in 1963. President Kennedy made his unforgettable *Ich bin ein Berliner* speech at the Rathaus Schöneberg in West Berlin.

Nearby Tempelhof airport, once the biggest in Europe, was made famous by the

Kreuzberg hops each May with its *Karneval der Kulturen* (carnival of cultures).

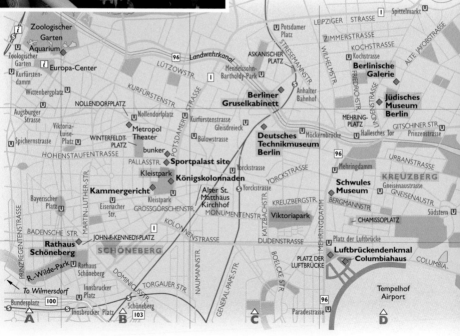

Berlin Airlift in 1948–49. A memorial commemorates the airlift; the buildings themselves are a fascinating example of Nazi-era architecture.

Scratch the surface and other traces of Berlin's troubled 20th-century history emerge. On Kleistpark stands the building where the Nazis held show trials in the so-called People's Court. An enormous and indestructible wartime flak tower and bunker looms nearby.

Heading east out of Kreuzberg and into Treptow, one crosses a border that no longer exists, once marked by the Berlin Wall. A watchtower stands a lonely vigil and, just beyond it, inside what was East Berlin, is a massive Soviet war memorial. The single longest stretch of the wall left standing runs across the Spree River over the city's most beautiful bridge.

Key points across Schöneberg and Kreuzberg lend themselves to meandering strolls by day and night. In Kreuzberg, head for Little Istanbul around Kottbusser Tor. A few minutes' walk south of Kottbusser Tor, a huge Turkish market takes place on Tuesdays and Fridays on the Maybach Ufer

of the Landwehrkanal. They still call this area SO36, the old postal code for what was once an alternative urban scene in Berlin. It has calmed down a lot since the fall of the wall, but the area retains an edgy feel and pulsates with life once the sun goes down. Görlitzer Park, Wiener Strasse, Oranienstrasse, and Maybach Ufer are lined with bars and eateries.

The heart of the action in Schöneberg was and remains Nollendorfplatz. Famous in the 1920s as the busiest gay quarter in Europe, it was a cauldron of intellectual life as well. The revolutionary stage director Erwin Piscator opened up a theater at the 1920s art deco Metropol Theater on Nollendorfplatz in 1927 with the premiere of a sold-out production, *Hoppla, Wir Leben! (Whoops, We're Alive!).* Nearby, one of the city's most attractive produce markets takes place on Saturdays in Winterfeldplatz. Most of the interesting sights in Schöneberg remain within walking distance of Nollendorfplatz. Although not nearly as outrageous as in the 1920s, the area retains plenty of nightlife, gay and otherwise. ■

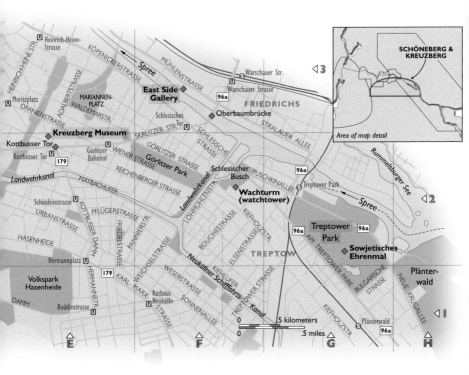

Kleistpark

TIDY LITTLE KLEISTPARK, BERLIN'S BOTANICAL GARDEN from 1679 to 1903, is surrounded by history. On the west side of the park, the neobaroque Kammergericht court building, which now houses the Berlin branch of the national constitutional court, was the scene of show trials in Hitler's Volksgerichtshof (People's Court).

From 1942 to 1945, Roland Freisler (1893–1945), the most feared judge in Germany, headed the court. After the July 1944 attempt on Hitler's life (see p. 132), Freisler's court went into full gear. About 140 people were executed in the ensuing months. Freisler was killed by a bomb here on February 3, 1945.

On the Potsdamer Strasse side of the park stretch the baroque **Königskolonnaden** (King's Colonnades), built by Carl von Gontard (1731–1791) in 1780. They were moved here from a spot near Alexanderplatz in 1910.

A brief walk north and a left turn into Pallasstrasse brings you face to face with a postwar apartment complex that bridges the road. It engulfs an enormous concrete antiaircraft gun tower and bunker that resisted demolition attempts after World War II.

Opposite it stood the Nazi-era **Sportpalast** (now vanished), a popular location for rousing harangues. On February 18, 1943, Propaganda Minister Joseph Goebbels (1897–1945) gave the speech of his life: "I ask you: do you believe, with the Führer and us, in the final and total victory of the German people? … I ask you: Do you want total war?" His broadcast voice was drowned out by applause. He was later heard to mutter: "What idiocy! If I'd asked them to jump from the third floor of the Columbiahaus [a Gestapo prison at Tempelhof airport], they'd have done it."

About a ten-minute wander east of Kleistpark lies the **Alter St. Matthäus Kirchhof,** a cemetery founded in 1856. The brothers Grimm, known for their collections of fairy tales, are buried here. The cemetery also contains a memorial to Claus Schenk Graf von Stauffenberg, the officer who tried to assassinate Hitler in July 1944. ■

Berlinische Galerie

BERLIN'S FEVERISH CULTURAL ACTIVITY SEEMS TO KNOW no bounds. In 2004, this airy museum (formally known as Berlinische Galerie—Landesmuseum für Moderne Kunst, Fotografie und Architectur, or the Berlin Gallery—State Museum for Modern Art, Photography and Architecture) opened up in northern Kreuzberg. Its substantial permanent collections include modern paintings, photography, and architectural models and designs.

Berlinische Galerie
www.berlinischegalerie.de
🅰 p. 174 D3
✉ Alte Jakobstrasse 124–128
☎ 030 78 90 26 00
💲 $$
🚉 U-Bahn: Hallesches Tor

How many of these attractions you get to see depends on the extent of the museum's temporary exhibitions.

Otto Dix is a prime representatives the Realists of the 1920s. A striking work is his 1926 portrait of the poet Iwar von Lücken, a gaunt man in an ill-fitting suit in a Berlin apartment.

Austrian Oskar Kokoschka (1886–1980) makes an appearance with paintings such as "Bildnis von Nell Walden" ("Portrait of Nell Walden," 1916), in which the essence of the woman in question seems to leap from the canvas through his vigorous expressionism.

The onetime star of Dada in Berlin, George Grosz, who became a leading figure of the Neue Sachlichkeit (New Objectivity) movement, also has works here. Among them is the blue-gray "Selbstbildnis mit Hut" ("Self-portrait with Hat," 1928).

Hannah Höch (1889–1978) was another engaging painter of the Neue Sachlichkeit period. Her paintings have a provocative zest about them. "Roma" (1925) turns

You never know what you might see in the Berlinische Galerie, a highlight on the city's art circuit.

The Berlinische Galerie's eclectic collection ranges from German expressionists to architectural plans and models.

sunny Roman scenes on their head and focuses them on the image of a woman in a bathing suit, but with the face of Italian Fascist dictator Benito Mussolini in a bowler hat. "Die Braut, oder Pandorra" ("The Bride, or Pandora," 1927) converts the traditionally happy image of a wedding couple into a nightmare. The dour-looking groom fades into gray insignificance as a giant baby's head grows out of the bride's shoulders.

An important slot is occupied by the somber realism of Karl Hofer. Most of his earlier works were destroyed in a fire toward the end of World War II, but a disturbing exception made it into this collection. "Die Gefangenen" ("The Prisoners," 1933), created as Hitler came to power, is a disturbingly prophetic look into the future. Hopeless, starving, hairless prisoners look out from a bleak background at the observer.

"Alarm" (1945) is disturbing almost for its matter-of-factness.

A couple looks from a window as an air raid is launched. Tension, rather than fear, emanates from them. Gloomier is "Totentanz" ("Dance of Death," 1946), in which a simple postwar dance-hall scene is perverted by the skull-like faces of those dancing.

Aside from painting, the collections include drawings, photomontages, watercolors, and more by these and other artists of the same periods. Christian Schad (1894–1982), Max Beckmann, and Otto Dix are among them.

Another Berlin accent is applied with works from the Novembergruppe (November Group), which included the likes of Ludwig Mies van der Rohe (better known as an architect).

The architecture collection is enormous; only a tiny portion is likely ever to be on display. It includes 300,000 plans and drawings and about 2,500 models reflecting 20th-century city planning in and around Berlin. Models include that of the Bundespräsidialamt (see p. 119) and the fascinating Sternkirche, a sci-fi-looking church design by Otto Bartning (1883–1959) that never got past the drawing board.

The photographic collections could constitute several separate exhibitions. Archives range from late 19th-century images taken in and around Berlin to intriguing shots from the former East Germany. Some fascinating early photos come from Heinrich Zille (1859–1928), including "Handstand machende Jungen an einem Sandhang" ("Youths Doing Handstands on a Sandbank," 1898). The Berlin of another age is reflected in Michael Schmidt's (born 1945) series from the 1980s, "Waffenruhe" ("Cease-fire"), photos of West Berlin at the height of Cold War saber rattling. ■

Jüdisches Museum Berlin

ITS CREATOR CALLED THE DESIGN "BETWEEN THE LINES."
Architect Daniel Libeskind (born 1946), faced with the delicate task
of creating a modern museum on the often-tragic history of Jews in
Germany, came up with a powerful statement. Inside, an absorbing
exhibition on German-Jewish culture awaits.

**Jüdisches
Museum Berlin**
www.juedisches-museum-
berlin.de
🔲 p. 174 D3
✉ Lindenstrasse 9–14
☎ 030 25 99 33 00
💲 $$
🚇 U-Bahn: Hallesches Tor

Libeskind created a gleaming, low-slung, zinc-clad edifice to house the museum. Its angular and seemingly erratic ground plan reflects the complex twists and turns that life took for Germany's Jews through the centuries.

The remarkable building is attached like a metallic scribble to a stately baroque building (formerly a Prussian court and then city museum) that serves as the entrance. An intentionally disorienting subterranean corridor connects the two. This "Axis of Continuity" is intersected by two others, the "Axis of Exile," with names of the cities to which Jews fled from Nazi Germany, and the "Axis of the Holocaust," with the names of concentration camps. The latter ends in an empty tower for quiet contemplation.

The permanent exhibition starts on the top floor of the new building with the arrival of Jews in medieval Germany. It continues with images, audiovisual displays, household objects, and engaging texts in 13 sections spread over two floors.

Treated as second-class citizens, German Jews were at the forefront of German Enlightenment thinking and, later, 19th-century literature. Their contributions are illustrated by displays on the life of philosopher Moses Mendelssohn. Other displays take you inside German-Jewish homes at the turn of the 20th century.

The final rooms deal with the emigration, deportations, and massacre of German Jews in the Nazi period with honesty but restraint. They finish by describing the slow re-creation of a small Jewish community in Germany since the war. ■

**The "Shalechet"
(Fallen Leaves)
art installation
contains 10,000
iron faces.**

Marvelous Marlene

Berlin-born Marlene Dietrich was one of the great seductresses of the silver screen, both on the set and off.

The ice-cool siren of stage and screen, Marlene Dietrich was the icon of a generation. Born into an upright, bourgeois family in suburban Berlin, she plunged into the twilight whirlwind of liberal 1920s Berlin, became the queen of Hollywood and sweetheart of GIs across Europe, only to finish the last decades of her life in quiet seclusion in a central Paris apartment.

Born Marie Magdalene Dietrich von Losch in Berlin's Schöneberg District on December 27, 1901, she grew up the daughter of a Prussian police officer. In her youth she saw Berlin go from grand imperial capital to depressed postwar city after Germany's defeat in World War I.

Dietrich finished school in 1919. By 1922 she had made her first stage appearance, studying under director Max Reinhardt. Fame came in 1930, when she starred in Josef von Sternberg's *Der Blaue Engel (The Blue Angel)*.

Five years earlier she had married Rudolf Sieber, a production assistant with whom she had her only child, Maria, but their open marriage soon flagged (although they never divorced and Dietrich always traveled as Mrs. Sieber). Von Sternberg became her lover and convinced her to move to Hollywood, where together they churned out movies to great acclaim, including *Morocco* (1930) and *Shanghai* (1932). They split in 1935 and her film career began to falter, although she remained for a while the highest-paid actress in Hollywood.

Dietrich's tumultuous life gave the lie to her apparent on-screen control and distance. Her string of Hollywood lovers included Douglas Fairbanks, Jr. (who wrote to her from London: "The bed is lonely, my heart is lonely and I love you so much"), John Wayne ("The most intriguing woman I have ever known"), Gary Cooper, and James Stewart. The number of women lovers, including American billionaire Jo Castairs, was just as long.

More important in Dietrich's life were the exiled German writer Erich Maria Remarque and, from 1941, the tough-guy French actor Jean Gabin. Their wartime romance did not survive the peace. Filmmaker Jean Cocteau later mused: "Whoever knows her ... has experienced perfection itself." Gabin clearly did not think so.

Back in 1937, Nazi Germany's propaganda minister, Joseph Goebbels, had tried to lure Dietrich back to the *Reich*. She became a U.S. citizen instead. She once told reporters: "I don't hate the Germans, I hate the Nazis." During the war she threw herself into the Allied cause, performing for GIs from the Pacific to France.

Her postwar film career was unspectacular. One of the better efforts was a starring role in Billy Wilder's *A Foreign Affair*, set in postwar Berlin. From then on, she dedicated herself to singing and cabaret until the 1960s. Burt Bacharach was then her musical arranger and the one who, she later said, definitively broke her heart. She had been no slouch in the heart-breaking department herself, but Ernest Hemingway once remarked: "It makes no difference how she breaks your heart if she is there to mend it."

Dietrich returned briefly to Berlin after

the death of her mother in November 1945. She would not set foot in her hometown for another 15 years, when she appeared in May on part of a European tour. Some of the locals were less than enthusiastic, considering her a traitor and picketing her show with posters demanding "Marlene go home."

Not everyone felt that way. The Americans awarded her the Medal of Freedom in 1947 and the French made her a chevalier (knight) of the Légion d'Honneur in 1950. In 1971, President Georges Pompidou elevated her to officier. Not to be outdone, President François Mitterand promoted her again in 1989, to commandeur.

But by the early 1970s Dietrich had largely withdrawn from the world to her Paris apartment. In 1978, she came out of retirement for two days (and $250,000) to play the manager of a ring of Berlin gigolos in *Just a Gigolo*. In 1992 she passed away quietly in Paris. She was buried beside her mother in Berlin's 19th-century Friedhof Stubenrauchstrasse, in Schöneberg. Ten years later the city of Berlin declared her an honorary citizen. ∎

Dietrich's film career included westerns like *Destry Rides Again* with Brian Donlevy (bottom). Later, she donned boots and fatigues (below) to set off for the front lines to entertain GIs in Europe and Asia.

The cast-iron memorial dominating Viktoriapark gave the area its name.

Kreuzberg & Viktoriapark

THE SUBURB OF KREUZBERG TAKES ITS NAME FROM THE neoclassic cast-iron monument, topped by a cross, that was erected here by Karl Friedrich Schinkel in 1817 through 1821. The memorial commemorates Napoleon's demise in 1815.

Viktoriapark
📷 p. 174 C2

Schwules Museum
www.schwulesmuseum.de
📷 p. 174 D2
✉ Mehringdamm 61
☎ 030 69 59 90 50
🕐 Closed Tues.
💲 $$
🚇 U-Bahn: Mehringdamm

In those days, the area was largely rural and the monument, mounted on a hill (hence Kreuzberg, or Cross Hill), could be seen for miles around. As suburban and industrial sprawl invaded the area in the second half of the 19th century, the monument was raised higher and placed above an octagonal stone structure with a neo-Gothic, fortress-like appearance. In 1888, the Viktoriapark was established around it.

The monument was erected both to the memory of the fallen and in thanks to the survivors of the Napoleonic wars. The fighting spanned the time from 1806, when Prussia was invaded, until 1815, when Napoleon was definitively beaten at the battle of Waterloo. Around the monument's base are inscribed the names of various conflicts.

The Iron Cross atop the monument would, in miniature, become the most coveted of military decorations. It was the first in Prussia that could be awarded to anyone for courage, regardless of rank or class. Previously, most awards and medals had been the preserve of officers.

The other attraction in the park is an artificial waterfall, along with what is claimed to be the northernmost vineyard in Germany.

A short walk east from the park is the **Schwules Museum,** which sponsors temporary exhibitions (on the first floor) as well as a permanent display on gay life in Germany. Most interesting are the sections on the busy gay scene in 1920s Berlin and repression under Hitler. Along with photos of prominent gay men, newspaper clippings and documents enrich the exhibition. The display continues with the reawakening of gay bars in 1950s Berlin, repression in the German Democratic Republic, and on to the 1980s, when AIDS reared its ugly head.

There is little on the lesbian scene; labeling is in German (some information in English is available at the counter). ■

Deutsches Technikmuseum Berlin

One of Europe's biggest rail shunting yards is now a museum of the wonders of human invention, from planes to trains.

UNTIL 1945, ANHALTER BAHNHOF WAS BERLIN'S BIGGEST train station, the gateway to southern Germany and Europe. All that remains after World War II and demolition is the ruined facade on Askanischer Platz and, a long block south, the locomotive sheds now at the heart of this German Museum of Technology.

The new building at the front of the complex can't be missed, as outside dangles an American Douglas C-47 transport plane of the kind used during the Berlin Airlift (see sidebar p. 184).

You could spend hours in here. Upstairs from the ticket desk are displays on textile production and telecommunications. The latter includes Siemens's first telephone (1878) and German-made TV sets from the 1950s. Displays on paper production (with demonstrations), printing, and typesetting are on the third floor.

In the new building are four floors on shipping and air travel. The sea travel section contains a massive engine room and a 1901 steam tugboat, along with fleets of models that come with interactive touch screens.

The flight section holds World War II wrecks, including a Junkers Ju-87 Stuka dive-bomber and part of a British RAF Lancaster bomber. Trainspotters will love the train shunting yards, jammed with locomotives from early mid-19th-century steam jobs on. Visitors can inspect the bottom of a couple of trains, including a 1938 locomotive that still bears a Nazi insignia. Also remembered is the railways' role in the deportation of Jews.

You can visit a brewery, mills, and a depot full of classic cars outside the main buildings. ■

Deutsches Technikmuseum Berlin
www.dtmb.de
🅰 p. 174 C2
✉ Trebbiner Strasse 9
☎ 030 90 25 40
🕐 Closed Mon.
💲 $$
🚇 U-Bahn: Gleisdreieck

Tempelhof
p. 174 D1

Tempelhof airport is at once a relic of Nazi architecture and a symbol of West Berlin's resistance to the Soviet Union.

Tempelhof

THE TEMPELHOF AERODROME WAS ONE OF GERMANY'S oldest when, in 1935, Hitler decided to rebuild it in monumental style. Architect Ernst Sagebiel (1892–1970) created an airport with 30 times the required capacity. Thirteen years later the airport became a symbol of West Berlin's struggle to remain free during a Soviet blockade as the United States and Britain mounted an airlift to ferry in supplies.

What was once Europe's biggest airport now serves a handful of domestic flights. Approaching the airport, which may be closed to commercial traffic in the coming years, you reach the Platz der Luftbrücke (Airlift Square), at whose center rises the **Luftbrückendenkmal,** a monument to the Allied airlift. It bears the names of servicemen who died during the operation. The front ranks of airport buildings stretch back like an open fan from the square, revealing the main entry building in the background.

Columbiahaus, on the north side of Platz der Luftbrücke, is built in the same style. The Gestapo ran a prison here from 1933 on. More than 8,000 people passed through its gates, including Erich Honecker, later the East German president. ■

Look upon this city!

When the Soviet Union cut off road access to West Berlin in the summer of 1948, the Allies decided to bust the blockade by air. From June 26, 1948, to May 12, 1949, U.S. and British aircraft flew 200,000 sorties, mostly into Tempelhof. At the height of the effort, an aircraft was landing every 90 seconds. They flew in 1.5 million tons of material; 71 Allied servicemen and 8 Germans died in accidents. On September 9, 1948, West Berlin's soon-to-be mayor, Ernst Reuter, held a rousing speech before the Reichstag ruins: "We will live to see the day of freedom! ... Peoples of the world, look upon this city, look upon Berlin!" In the end, the threat of a U.S. nuclear strike on Moscow forced the Soviets to back down. ■

East Side Gallery & Treptower Park

HARD THOUGH IT MAY BE TO BELIEVE, BERLIN HAS MORE bridges than Venice. Of the 1,700 bridges scattered throughout the greater Berlin area, easily the loveliest is the 19th-century Oberbaumbrücke, which was once one of eight crossover points between West and East Berlin.

"Molecule Man," by Jonathan Borofsky, rises from the Spree River near the Oberbaumbrücke.

Across the bridge, a surviving stretch of the Berlin Wall (the longest, at just under a mile) runs parallel to the Spree along Mühlenstrasse. Now covered by a kaleidoscope of murals, it is known as the **East Side Gallery.** The art is rather less impressive than expected. Much has faded away and been replaced with graffiti. There is talk of restoration.

More rewarding is a longish walk (or bus ride on the No. 265) south of the Oberbaumbrücke along Schlesische Strasse. Where the street changes name to Puschkinallee, you cross into what was East Berlin. A solitary leftover **Wachturm** (watchtower) stands guard in the park, Am Schlesischen Busch, which was created from the death strip around the wall.

A brisk march along Puschkinallee takes you into **Treptower Park,** at whose heart looms the **Sowjetisches Ehrenmal** (Soviet Memorial). This immense mausoleum/monument celebrates the Soviet victory over "fascist Germany" in the Great Patriotic War of 1941 to 1945 (for the Soviets, World War II didn't get started until the U.S.S.R. was invaded). Of the more than 20,000 Soviet casualties in the 1945 Battle of Berlin, 5,000 are buried here.

A stone triumphal arch on the right as you head southeast along Puschkinallee signals arrival. You reach a statue of weeping Mother Russia and then, to your left, behold the monument. Two triangular structures adorned with the hammer and sickle of the U.S.S.R. and encased in rose marble—purportedly recycled from the ruins of Hitler's chancellery—serve as a symbolic entrance. What look like 16 giant sarcophagi, representing the ex-Soviet republics, are laid out before you. They are decorated with reliefs of wartime heroism. The monument culminates in a hilltop hero's grave, topped by a 38-foot-high (11.5 m) bronze of a Soviet solder crushing a swastika underfoot, sword in one hand and a German child he has saved in the other. (This touch was inspired by a real incident during fighting around here.) ∎

East Side Gallery
www.eastsidegallery.com
🅜 p. 175 F3
✉ Mühlenstrasse
🚇 U-Bahn: Schlesisches Tor to walk; S-Bahn & U-Bahn: Warschauer Strasse to go directly to gallery

Treptower Park
🅜 p. 175 G2
✉ Am Treptower Park
🚇 S-Bahn: Treptower Park

More places to visit in Schöneberg & Kreuzberg

The elegant area around Chamissoplatz was largely untouched by wartime bombing.

BERGMANNSTRASSE & CHAMISSOPLATZ

This is the chic end of Kreuzberg. A lazy wander along Bergmannstrasse and in the cobbled side streets around Chamissoplatz is a pleasure for the senses. Mostly refurbished late 19th-century apartment buildings, all decked out in different colors, lend uncommon grace to the area. Thoroughly gentrified now, it is hard to believe that this was a largely working-class area when the buildings were raised. At ground level, a feast of restaurants, bars, and shops lends constant and infectious animation.

🗺 p. 174 D2 🚇 U-Bahn: Mehringdamm

BERLINER GRUSELKABINETT

The most interesting part of this otherwise cheesy chamber of horrors is the setting, a massive World War II air-raid bunker. Head for the basement, where the walls are more than 6.5 feet (2 m) thick. On display are bomb fragments, contemporary newspaper clippings, and Allied aerial photos of the bunker. On the ground floor you may be horrified by the scenes from operations of centuries gone by, while the scary special effects on the top floor are designed to make your heart skip a beat.

🗺 p. 174 C3 ✉ Schöneberger Strasse 23a ☎ 030 26 55 55 46, www.gruselkabinett-berlin.de ⊕ Closed Wed. 💲 $$$
🚇 U-Bahn: Mendelssohn-Bartholdy-Park

KREUZBERG MUSEUM

Since late 2005, this museum has presented the history of Kreuzberg in documents, images, and artifacts over three floors. The first floor covers industrialization in the 19th century and the Golden Mile, Ritterstrasse, which until 1945 was one of the city's busiest export areas. The second floor deals with the protest movements of the 1960s and squatting in the 1970s and 1980s; the third is devoted to immigration in Kreuzberg and Friedrichshain. From the 1960s, Turkish and southern European *Gastarbeiter* (guest workers) began to migrate to West Berlin and wound up living in this neglected area. In East Berlin, *Vertragsarbeiter* (treaty workers) from communist states, in particular Vietnam, settled in Friedrichshain.

🗺 p. 175 E2 ✉ Adalbertstrasse 95a ☎ 030 50 58 52 33, www.kreuzbergmuseum.de ⊕ Open Wed.–Sun. 12 p.m.–6 p.m. 🚇 U-Bahn: Kottbusser Tor

RATHAUS SCHÖNEBERG

The huge, rather pompous-looking Schöneberg city hall, finished shortly before World War I, was part of the citywide tendency to equip each district with centers of local government. From the 1940s until reunification, it served as West Berlin's city hall. Crowds gathered here on June 26, 1963, to hear U.S. President John F. Kennedy's famous Cold War speech: "All free men, wherever they may live, are citizens of Berlin and … I take pride in the words *Ich bin ein Berliner.*" (A slight grammatical hitch meant that these words sounded like he was claiming to be a jelly donut.) The crowds returned on November 22 on hearing of Kennedy's assassination. A plaque commemorates his speech and death. Inside is an exhibition about German chancellor and Berlin mayor Willy Brandt.

🗺 p. 174 B1 ✉ John-F.-Kennedy-Platz ☎ 030 7 56 00 🚇 U-Bahn: Rathaus Schöneberg ∎

In Berlin's quiet western suburbs lurk many surprises. They range from Spandau's splendid Renaissance citadel and Hitler's monumental Olympic Stadium to an extraordinary ethnological museum complex and lakeside beaches. Take a woodland walk or inspect classic warplanes.

Spandau, Dahlem, & the west

The Final Solution was born at the Wannsee Conference in this villa.

Spandau, Dahlem, & the west

TO CITY DWELLERS WITH A RURAL HEART, MUCH OF THE WESTERN
extremity of Berlin is a summer getaway or a residential neighborhood of choice. Spandau,
Dahlem, and Wannsee still seem more like country towns than parts of a European
metropolis. Among the spacious houses and gardens is scattered an array of sights so varied that few visitors will resist the temptation and a longer-than-usual U-Bahn or
S-Bahn trip to seek them out.

As is commonly the case in Berlin, paradoxes
are not lacking and reminders of the past
abound. The Nazi Olympic stadium, stage
of one of Adolf Hitler's early propaganda tri-
umphs, survived the war to play a double role
today as a protected monument—a symbol of
the Nazi misuse of sports—and as Berlin's
modern-day football (soccer) temple. Its
origins make it a unique stop for both sports
and history buffs.

To Berlin's west, Spandau remains to all
intents and purposes the satellite village it
always was, notwithstanding the 1920 law
that incorporated it into suburban Berlin.
The compact town center makes for a pleasant stroll, but the main sight is the *Zitadelle,*
an enormous Renaissance fortress that saw
action during the Napoleonic wars.
Miraculously, it was left mostly untouched
in the final days of World War II.

South of the Olympic stadium stretches
the forest paradise of Grunewald (Green
Forest). At its northern end is the
Teufelsberg, a 377-foot (115 m) "mountain"
made entirely of rubble left behind by the
bombing of Berlin and the final months'
fighting. Nature lovers can follow a path
from near the stadium south along the east
bank of the broad Havel River to Wannsee
and even on to Potsdam.

On the eastern flank of the forest, in
another onetime village, Dahlem, is a center
of culture. The Museen Dahlem constitute
some of the world's most extensive and
impressive ethnological collections. From
South America's pre-Columbian gold and
statuary to South Sea outrigger boats, from
Indian Buddhist statuary to Japanese graphic art, the combined museums would take
days to inspect in any detail.

Dahlem also holds the art gem of the
Brücke Museum and the nearby Alliierten-
Museum, dedicated to the history of the
three western Allied powers in occupied
West Berlin. A pleasant stroll west into the
forest brings one to the Grunewaldsee, a
sausage-shaped lake. Locals can be seen
walking their dogs on the lake when it
freezes over in winter. Overlooking it is a
charming onetime royal hunting lodge, the
Jagdschloss Grunewald.

The Havel swings slowly southwest to
Potsdam, passing Wannsee, Berlin's extreme
southwest corner, along the way. A favorite
location with Berlin and Potsdam yachties,
Wannsee is a bucolic retreat and a delight
to discover. From the summertime
beach activity at Strandbad Wannsee
to the princely Schloss Glienicke,
the walker will come across traditional eateries, the pleasant
Pfaueninsel and, unhappily,
another reminder of Nazi
evil: the villa where the
Wannsee Conference
on the Final
Solution was
held. ∎

Luftwaffen-
museum

KLADOW

Meierei

Pfaueninsel
(Peacock
Island)

Schlösschen

PFAUENINSEL-
CHAUSSEE

Volkspark
Klein-Glienicke
Schloss
Glienicke

To Potsdam

DÜPPEL
FOREST

KÖNIGSTRASSE

WANNSEE

Pohlesee

Griebnitzsee

Stölpchensee

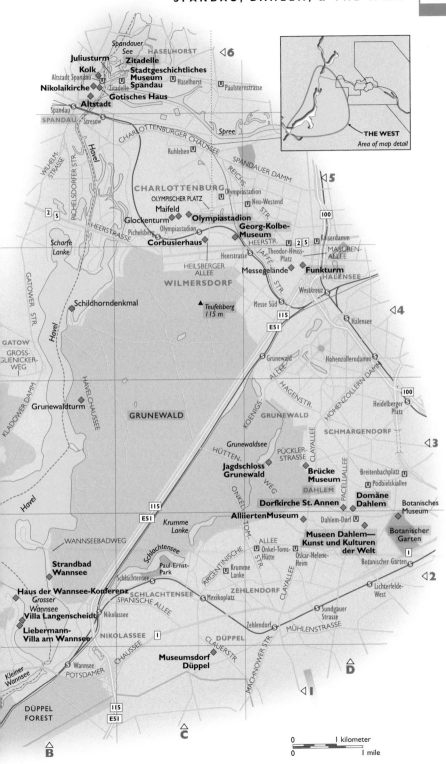

THE WEST
Area of map detail

Spandauer See
HASELHORST
Juliusturm
Zitadelle
Kolk
Stadtgeschichtliches
Altstadt Spandau
Museum
Nikolaikirche
Spandau
Haselhorst
Paulsternstrasse
Gotisches Haus
Zitadelle
Altstadt
Spandau
SPANDAU
Stresow
Spree
CHARLOTTENBURGER CHAUSSEE
Ruhleben
SPANDAUER DAMM
WILHELM-STRASSE
PICHELSDORFER STR.
Havel
CHARLOTTENBURG
OLYMPISCHER PLATZ
Olympiastadion
Neu-Westend
REICHS-STR.
100
HEERSTRASSE
Maifeld
Glockenturm
Olympiastadion
Olympiastadion
Georg-Kolbe-Museum
Scharfe
Lanke
Corbusierhaus
Pichelsberg
HEERSTR.
Kaiserdamm
2
5
Heerstrasse
JAFFÉ-STR.
Theodor-Heuss-Platz
2
5
MASUREN-ALLEE
HEILSBERGER
ALLEE
Messegelände
Funkturm
GATOWER STR.
Havel
Schildhorndenkmal
WILMERSDORF
Teufelsberg
115 m
HALENSEE
Messe Süd
115
E51
Westkreuz
Halensee
GATOW
GROSS-GLIENICKER-WEG
Grunewald
ALLEE
Hohenzollerndamm
100
KLADOWER DAMM
Grunewaldturm
HAVELCHAUSSEE
GRUNEWALD
HAGENSTR.
HOHENZOLLERN DAMM
Heidelberger
Platz
KOENIGS-ALLEE
GRUNEWALD
SCHMARGENDORF
Grunewaldsee
PÜCKLER-STRASSE
CLAYALLEE
PACELLIALLEE
HÜTTEN-WEG
Jagdschloss
Grunewald
Brücke
Museum
Breitenbachplatz
Podbielskiallee
DAHLEM
ONKEL-TOM-STR.
Dorfkirche St. Annen
Domäne
Dahlem
Botanisches
Museum
Havel
Krumme
Lanke
AlliiertenMuseum
Dahlem-Dorf
Museen Dahlem—
Kunst und Kulturen
der Welt
Botanischer
Garten
WANNSEEBADWEG
Schlachtensee
Paul-Ernst-Park
Onkel-Toms-Hütte
Oskar-Helene-Heim
Botanischer Garten
Strandbad
Wannsee
Schlachtensee
ARGENTINISCHE ALLEE
Krumme
Lanke
ZEHLENDORF
Lichterfelde-West
Haus der Wannsee-Konferenz
Grosser
Wannsee
SCHLACHTENSEE
SPANISCHE ALLEE
Mexikoplatz
CLAYALLEE
Villa Langenscheidt
Nikolassee
Sundgauer
Strasse
Liebermann-Villa am Wannsee
NIKOLASSEE
Zehlendorf
MÜHLENSTRASSE
I
DÜPPEL
CLAUERSTR.
D
Kleiner
Wannsee
Wannsee
POTSDAMER CHAUSSEE
Museumsdorf
Düppel
MACHNOWER STR.
I
DÜPPEL
FOREST
115
E51
C
B
0   1 kilometer
0   1 mile

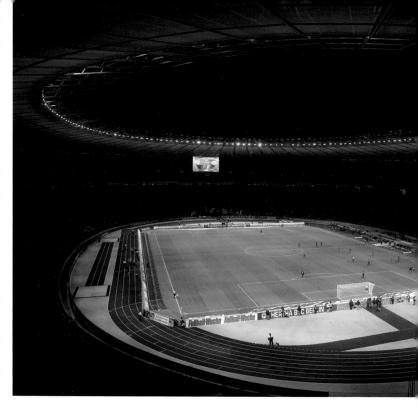

Olympiastadion
www.olympiastadion-berlin.de

p. 189 C5

✉ Olympischer Platz 3

☎ 030 25 00 23 22

🕐 Tours April–Oct.
11 a.m., 1 p.m.,
3 p.m.; Nov.–March
1 p.m.

💲 $, plus fee for
audio guide. Guided
tour $$

🚇 U-Bahn:
Olympiastadion

The recent renovation of the Olympiastadion cost nearly 30 times more than the cost to build the entire original structure in the 1930s.

Olympiastadion

HITLER'S 1936 OLYMPIC STADIUM HAD TO WAIT 70 YEARS for international redemption. Recently modernized, the stadium was selected for the finals (including the final match) of the 2006 FIFA World Cup football (soccer) fest. Amid the football fever, one wonders how many onlookers had flashbacks to 1936.

Built in 1934 to 1936 by Werner March (1894–1976) in monumental Nazi style (due in part to Hitler's meddling), the stadium today presents a curious mix. The solid lines and powerful stonework remain those of Hitler's day; the stadium is catalogued as a national monument. The old stonework is combined with the latest in stadium technology, most evident in the partial roof that protects nearly all the seats from inclement weather. The roof was set in place during renovation work in 2000 through 2004 (at a cost of nearly €240 million). The stadium is thus at once an homage to modern sports and a quiet reminder of the past.

The original was quite an achievement for its day, holding up to 100,000 people (today reduced to 74,400, largely because of fire safety requirements). Every element had a message. The reinforced concrete structure was partially coated in hand-cut Bavarian limestone, in a typically Nazi tribute to traditional values. The two towers of the East Gate

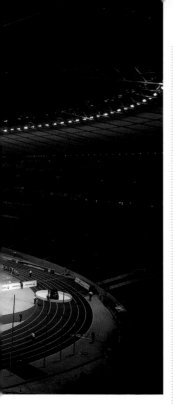

The Nazi Olympics

Although World War I prevented Germany from hosting the 1916 Olympic Games, the country did manage to win the 1936 games for Berlin. By the time they were held, Hitler had been in power for three years. He used the games masterfully as a propaganda vehicle. These were the first televised games and the first in which telex was used to transmit results. Some 4,000 athletes from 49 countries attended. To divert international media attention from the unpleasant realities of Nazi rule, all posters and other signs of anti-Semitic policy were removed for the duration. The '36 games were an unqualified success for Nazi Germany, which took 89 medals, leaving the United States in second place with 56. ∎

represent Prussia and Bavaria linked by the five Olympic rings. (The two regions historically loathe one another, but not according to Hitler.) The opposite end of the stadium was dubbed the Marathon Gate. Here the Olympic flame burned; in fact, the Germans came up with the idea of the relay that brings the Olympic flame from Greece to the current stadium.

The names of the 1936 Olympic gold-medal winners are engraved on the walls here, led by African-American athlete Jesse Owens, who took four. Protocol dictated that the head of state give all champion athletes a handshake. "Do you really think I will allow myself to be photographed shaking hands with a Negro?" the Führer frothed when Owens's turn came. And so he ducked out on an affair of state.

Beyond the stadium to the west is the Maifeld (May Field), designed for massive Nazi May Day parades. The rather ominous Glockenturm (Bell Tower), rebuilt in the 1960s, was another Nazi Olympic touch. A giant bell inside it tolled to open the games. The bell, with the inscription "I Call the Youth of the World," has been placed on the south flank of the stadium.

Nowadays, the stadium is the home field to Berlin's top first-division football team, Hertha BSC. Since 1985, the German national football league cup final has been held here.

You are free to visit the stadium alone, but joining a 75-minute tour *(1–3 times a day, but not held during events)* has the advantage of taking you into nooks and crannies otherwise off-limits. ∎

Spandau Altstadt & the Zitadelle

Zitadelle
www.zitadelle-berlin.de

🅰 p. 189 C6
✉ Am Juliusturm
☎ 030 354 944 200
🕐 Closed Mon.
Courtyard open 7
a.m.–midnight
💲 $. Courtyard free
🚇 U-Bahn: Zitadelle

The weapons of another age are lined up in the Renaissance-era Zitadelle in Spandau.

THE HISTORY OF THE MEDIEVAL VILLAGE OF SPANDAU, about 9 miles (15 km) west of central Berlin, reaches back to the eighth century. Declared a city in 1232, the market and fortress town on the confluence of the Havel and Spree rivers was swallowed up by greater Berlin in 1920. For centuries Spandau was one of Berlin's main defensive bastions; its 16th-century fortress, or Zitadelle, is a gem of Renaissance military architecture.

Spandau was also a major arms-production center by the late 19th century. The 1919 Versailles peace treaty was a disaster for the town, as it forbade weapons manufacture and cost Spandau 44,000 jobs. After World War II (during which it was again an important arms center), the area was assigned to the British sector of divided Berlin. In 1947, a 19th-century military prison a few miles from the town center (*on Wilhelmstrasse*) was turned into a high-security compound for just seven top Nazis condemned for war crimes. The prison was demolished after its last inmate, Hitler's unrepentant right-hand man, Rudolf Hess, committed suicide in 1987 (see pp. 194–195).

Spandau's fortress, the Zitadelle, was overrun during the Thirty Years' War in the 17th century and taken by the French

without a shot being fired in 1806. (The Prussians had more difficulty dislodging Napoleon's men in 1813.) The fort miraculously survived the Allied bombings that heavily damaged the nearby Altstadt (Old Town) in World War II. Nor was it harmed by the last days of street fighting between German and Soviet troops.

The fortress was built from 1560 to 1594 in the style of complex Renaissance Italian forts, its walls designed to deflect artillery shot. The square-based citadel replaced an earlier medieval castle, of which the 13th-century crenellated **Juliusturm** is about the only reminder. You can climb this tower for views over all Spandau. The local history museum, the **Stadtgeschichtliches Museum Spandau,** is housed in the armory (Zeughaus), but for history of the fortress itself you need to wander over to the **Kommandantenhaus** building, where a modest display explains all. Other rooms are given over to exhibition space, galleries, and a luxurious, medieval-style restaurant. The courtyard is used for various events. The citadel's tunnels and other darker corners also attract up to 10,000 wintering bats every year.

Today, the tiny Altstadt has recovered some of its medieval appeal, with cobbled lanes leading into the main square, the Reformationsplatz. At its center rises the 14th-century **Nikolaikirche** (Church of St. Nicholas), a late-Gothic brick church inside which you see a medieval bronze baptismal font and a late 16th-century Renaissance altar. It is possible to climb the doughty fortified west tower. The name of the square is no coincidence. The first

Protestant service was held here in 1539 after Elector Joachim II (1505–1571) adopted the new faith.

Nearby, Spandau's tourist office has taken refuge in what is thought to be Berlin's oldest house, the mid-15th-century brick **Gotisches Haus** (Gothic House), which frequently holds temporary art and history exhibitions beneath its vaulted roof.

The oldest part of the Altstadt, known as the **Kolk,** lies north of Am Juliusturm street. Its endearing, wood-framed houses are called *Fachwerkhäuser* (timbered houses).

Spandau's old town is particularly worth a visit in the run-up to Christmas, as its lanes and squares host one of Europe's most popular Christmas markets (see pp. 146–147). You can pick up arts and crafts, sip *Glühwein* (mulled wine), and listen to concerts on market evenings.

About 6 miles (10 km) south of the old center of Spandau is an air force buff's dream destination, the **Luftwaffenmuseum,** once the Gatow aerodrome. Built for the Luftwaffe (Air Force) in 1935, it was home to one of four air force officer schools under the Third Reich. From 1945 until 1994 it was a British Royal Air Force base and, along with Tempelhof airport, was used to fly supplies into West Berlin during the 1948 Soviet blockade of the city. The German Luftwaffe moved in again in 1995 and turned the place into a grand museum. More than a hundred military aircraft are displayed in hangars and around the base, including many World War II classics, such as the Messerschmidt Bf109 and the Heinkel He-111 (both gifts of the Spanish air force). ■

Nikolaikirche
- p. 189 B6
- ✉ Reformationsplatz
- ☎ 030 333 56 39
- 🕐 Museum closed Mon.–Tues.; church closed Fri.; tower open for tours Sat. noon, Sun. 2 p.m. April–Oct.
- 💲 Tower: $
- 🚇 U-Bahn: Altstadt Spandau

Gotisches Haus
- p. 189 B6
- ✉ Breite Strasse 32
- ☎ 030 333 93 88
- 🕐 Closed Sun.
- 🚇 U-Bahn: Altstadt Spandau

Luftwaffen-museum
www.luftwaffenmuseum.de
- p. 188 A3
- ✉ Berlin-Gatow Aerodrome, Ritterfelddamm/Am Flugplatz Gatow
- ☎ 030 36 87 26 04
- 🕐 Closed Mon.
- 🚇 U-Bahn: Rathaus Spandau & Bus 135 to Kurpromenade. Follow Am Flugplatz Gatow east to museum

The strange story of Rudolf Hess

A t the 1946 Nuremberg war crimes trials after World War II, Adolf Hitler's one-time right-hand man, Rudolf Hess (1894–1987), was asked if he was guilty. His reply was a simple *Nein.*

Earlier in the trial, Hess had asserted that, given the choice, he would have done it all again, "even in the knowledge that I would end up burning at the stake!" In spite of doubts about his sanity, Hess was found guilty of planning a war of aggression and of being part of a conspiracy against world peace. He was not found guilty of war crimes or crimes against humanity. He was one of seven top-ranking Nazis to receive long jail sentences.

Hess, the son of a salesman, fought in the infantry and air force in World War I. An economics and history student in Munich, he joined Hitler's Nazi Party as member No. 16 in 1920. The two spent much of 1924 in prison after Hitler's failed Munich coup attempt in 1923. To while away the hours, Hitler dictated *Mein Kampf* to Hess. After their release, Hess became Hitler's personal secretary. Although from 1933 he was made the "Führer's Deputy," he gradually lost influence. Hess remained blindly loyal to Hitler to the end (in prison he often said: "I

rue nothing"), but the Führer had increasingly little time for a hypochondriac who believed in astrology and the occult (as well as Nazism).

Perhaps that loss of influence prompted him, on May 10, 1941, to make a secret flight to Britain. Hess piloted the Messerschmidt 110 himself on the same night that hundreds of Luftwaffe bombers launched one of the heaviest air raids of the war on London. He parachuted into Scotland and was sent as a POW to London, where he claimed to be bringing a peace offer. Perhaps his thinking was: If I can convince the British to exit the war, Hitler will be free to concentrate on the coming invasion of Russia and I shall be back among the big boys in the Nazi hierarchy.

The British thought he might be unbalanced and subjected him to psychiatric examination. As if to confirm their suspicions, on May 11 Hitler disavowed his former pal and declared him a psychopath. The whole affair is so odd that historians still speculate on Hess's motives. Was it as Hess told it? Alternative theories abound. One suggests Hess fell into a trap set by the British secret service, while another claims the man was a double (but why, and what happened to the real Hess?). British documents on the case will enter the public domain only in 2018.

Hess and his companions were incarcerated not in Spandau's citadel, but in a prison built for the purpose west of Spandau's old town center and jointly run by the four Allied powers. All prisoners but Hess were set free by 1966. Repeated appeals for his release were stubbornly vetoed by the Soviet Union and he finally committed suicide in 1987. The building was demolished shortly thereafter. ∎

After sharing jail time with Hitler, Rudolf Hess (right, and on the right in photo top left) became the Führer's right-hand man. A fervid Nazi, he lost influence after 1933.

Museen Dahlem—Kunst und Kulturen der Welt

Museen Dahlem—Kunst und Kulturen der Welt

www.smb.museum

🅰 p. 189 D2

✉ Lansstrasse 8

☎ 030 830 14 38

🕐 Closed Mon.

💲 $$

🚇 U-Bahn: Dahlem-Dorf

THIS MUSEUM COMPLEX SET IN PEACEFUL DAHLEM IN southwest Berlin is a treasure chest of artifacts. They come primarily from non-European cultures, ranging from the Arctic to the South Seas and from Japan to Africa. You would need a full day to give the collections—divided into four museums spread over three floors—even a fraction of the attention they deserve. The itinerary suggested below is just one option. Pick and choose the elements that most attract you.

Ticket in hand, head toward the museum café and turn left into the **Museum für Indische Kunst** (Museum of Indian Art), a multi-faceted excursion into the world of Indian art, with some detours into neighboring countries.

The collection starts with a tiny terra-cotta statuette of a female figure from about 3300 B.C., but rapidly moves to more recent times. A curious early piece is a standing Bodhisattva with tight curly hair and a friendly smile. This statue was found in Afghanistan and dates to at least the third century B.C. Take time to examine the series of small, intricate reliefs set in the middle of the first room. Carved mostly from schist, they recount various Buddhist scenes, such as the veneration of a stupa (a Buddhist monument) or Buddha and his miracles. The green soapstone bust of the four-headed god Harihara, made in the ninth century in Kashmir, is a beautiful piece.

Brief sections on Islam and the Jain faith in India follow. The former includes beautifully carved wooden doors and colorful, glazed ceramics with geometrical patterns. The 19th-century Jain household shrine is especially admirable. Nearby is a huge temple wall hanging of the Krishna cult from Rajastan and a room full of mural fragments from all over the country.

Objects from Southeast Asia, especially Thailand and Cambodia, occupy the mezzanine level. Among them are pottery, jewelry, and bronze statues. A beautiful illustrated manuscript from Thonburi, Thailand, dates to 1776. The display rounds off with Nepalese painted-cloth images of Vishnu.

Walk back past the café to the beginning of the **Ethnologisches Museum** (Ethnology Museum), the backbone of the Dahlem collections. It starts with a long hall crammed with an extraordinary array of statuary, ceramics, figurines, and jewelry from across pre-Columbian South America. Giant steles lead the way. Found in a Maya temple complex near Santa Lucía Cozumalhuapa in Guatemala in the 1860s, they date from the Preclassic period, roughly 1500 B.C. to A.D. 200. There follows a varied collection of artifacts from Preclassic Maya culture, mostly in ancient Mexico. A particularly rich collection of artifacts comes from La Venta, a temple site in southern Mexico that thrived from about 900 to 400 B.C. Curious human figurines in jade, basalt, and other hard stones are among the more intriguing objects.

The door at the end of this hall leads into what is for most visitors a still more fascinating world, the **South Seas collections.** Objects from across the South Pacific present an utterly unexpected diversity. Among the first items you see on entering are enormous, prettily decorated wooden carvings of fish, examples of Malanggan ceremonial burial art in New Ireland. Near them are more than a century ago, these wooden vessels used in the Pacific fire the imagination. Most impressive is the one at extreme left, a deep-hulled Micronesian affair powered by sail and paddles and used for war and trade. It could carry up to 50 people.

Facing the boat collection are more masks, representing the recently dead who, in this form, were said to visit the living. Made

some fairly scary masks used in ceremonies in New Britain and a pair of towering New Guinean ancestral poles, which depict men sitting or standing on each other's shoulders. Other New Guinean art includes a ceremonial lectern adorned with an angry-looking Rasta-like male figure.

It is difficult to resist the temptation to skip all of this and head straight for the island boat collection. Brought to Berlin of wood, leaves, woven textiles, and other materials, they are all quite different from one another and uniformly unnerving. Items from the Sepik River area in deepest New Guinea include decorated skulls. Farther on is a limited collection of Australian Aboriginal art and objects. In the center of the hall stands a reconstructed thatched-roof men's clubhouse from the Pacific island of Palau.

The priceless statuary in the Museum für Indische Kunst represents just a fraction of the anthropological collections in the Museen Dahlem.

Pre-Columbian art from Latin America in the Ethnologisches Museum is one of the most important such collections in the world.

The South Seas collection continues upstairs, with furniture, jewelry, and dresses from Palau and the Marianas island group. The armor and helmets used by warriors in Kiribati are impressive. They were made of tightly woven coconut fiber and complemented with wooden swordlike weapons serrated with shark's teeth. Other interesting items include Maori wood carvings—particularly the complex decorative boat prows and sterns—Easter Island wooden statuary, and bark cloth from Tahiti.

From here, return downstairs to the South American collection and follow the signs to the **North American Indian collection.** You start with the Eskimos. Among the predictable items of clothing (caribou-skin coats, snowshoes, and fur boots) is an interesting piece: a canoeist's raincoat made of a seal's intestinal lining. The collection soon takes you to the United States, with displays on the proud past and difficult present of various

Indian tribes. Examples of animal-hide clothes and a chieftain's exuberant feather headdress are gathered in glass cabinets around a tepee. The history of the Indians' struggles against white conquest and their situation today brings this collection to an end.

From the spot where the North American Indian collection begins, follow a side hall up a few stairs into the **Goldkammer** (Gold Chamber), a collection of gold jewelry, figurines, bottles, and the like from pre-Columbian Colombia, Mexico, and Peru.

The succeeding rooms are dedicated to **South American archaeology** and are dominated by ceramics, busts, and textiles from the Inca Empire. They were found in an area around the Andes mountains stretching from Ecuador in the north via Peru to Chile in the south.

The remaining rooms on this floor are occupied by the **Museum Europäischer Kulturen** (Museum of European Cultures), which presents rotating exhibitions

of everything from artwork to videos. The final room contains the **Juniormuseum,** an interactive journey from Berlin to the four corners of the world, aimed at young children (at least, those who read German).

Apart from the already mentioned extension of the South Seas collection, the next floor hosts a display of **African art,** notably wooden statuary (often representative of ancestors or magicians), weapons, and the like from the Congo region, Cameroon, and Benin. The collection, one of the most important of its kind in the world, covers five centuries of African history, although most of the objects date from between the late 19th century and 1945.

The other star attraction on this floor is the **Museum für Ostasiatische Kunst** (Museum of East Asian Art). Pick up the handy room plan as you enter. The collections are evenly divided between Chinese items—bronzes, porcelain,

religious objects, paintings, and graphic arts—and a similar array of Japanese material. In one of the central rooms is a 17th-century Qing dynasty rosewood imperial throne with mother-of-pearl lacquer and a huge Qing dynasty vase. Ming dynasty objects are also spread through the rooms dedicated to Chinese crafts. Among the Japanese crafts is a series of masks used in traditional Noh theater. A separate room displays Korean ceramics, and a central room is devoted to Japanese and Chinese religious art, including statues dating as far back as the sixth century and Ming-dynasty wall paintings.

The displays rather peter out on the top floor, which houses a small collection of **musical instruments** from Southeast Asia (including a gamelan ensemble from Indonesia), the Middle East, and Africa. Also here is a section on daily life in East Asia, with a mixed bag of art and religious and household items from Japan and China. ■

Displays about European culture in the Museen Dahlem range from Krakow nativity scenes (above) to items from postwar German society.

Grunewald

AlliiertenMuseum
www.alliiertenmuseum.de
⚠ p. 189 D2
✉ Clayallee 135
☎ 030 818 19 90
🕐 Closed Wed.
🚇 U-Bahn: Oskar-
Helene-Heim

IF YOU WALK OR CYCLE THROUGH THE GRUNEWALD woods now, you'll find it hard to believe that two-thirds of this forest was destroyed by the end of World War II. Since 1949 the woods have been reforested with more than 20 million conifers and broad-leaved trees. Always popular with Berliners in need of fresh air away from urban chaos, the area took on special significance for West Berliners after the wall went up in 1961. This was the only bit of countryside they could enjoy, as everything else was in East Germany.

Brücke Museum
www.bruecke-museum.de
⚠ p. 189 D3
✉ Bussardsteig 9
☎ 030 831 20 29
🕐 Closed Tues.
💲 $$
🚇 U-Bahn: Oskar-
Helene-Heim & Bus:
115 to Pücklerstrasse

Even in this bucolic corner of town, one is reminded of those Cold War days at the **Alliierten-Museum** (Allied Museum). The museum tells the story of the western Allied occupying forces—the United States, Britain, and France—in Berlin in the Cold War years. (The Allies' wartime partner, the Soviet Union, had by the late 1940s exchanged the role of ally for that of bogeyman in the West.)

A British Hastings transport plane of the kind used in the 1948 to 1949 Berlin Airlift stands in the yard between the museum's two buildings. Behind it is a French military train wagon and the last of the U.S. Checkpoint Charlie buildings (in use from 1986–1990), moved here from central Berlin after reunification. The permanent exhibition contains Allied uniforms, medals, and equipment, complemented by a wealth of documents, letters, newspaper clippings, and a huge store of photos, only a fraction of which is ever shown. The display is split between the **Outpost Theater,** which covers the period from 1945 to 1950 (with particular coverage of the airlift), and the **Nicholson Memorial Library,** which runs from 1951 to 1994, the year all foreign troops withdrew from Berlin. Among the items are the front of the first Checkpoint Charlie,

erected in 1961, a re-creation of a spy tunnel built by the Allies under East Berlin to tap Soviet communications, and an array of Cold War–era signs and newspaper front pages.

The **Brücke Museum** is just a quick bus ride north of the AlliiertenMuseum inside the Grunewald woods. It holds an impressive collection of paintings, sketches, watercolors, and

other works by a singular group of pre–World War I artists. Works on display include material by the group's main protagonists, Ernst Ludwig Kirchner, Erich Heckel (1883–1970), Otto Müller (1874–1930), and Karl Schmidt-Rottluff (1884–1976). They were joined briefly by Emil Nolde (1867–1956) and Max Pechstein (1881–1955).

Young and rebellious, the artists founded their group in Dresden in 1905 and swore never to abandon one another. They drifted to Berlin in 1911, where big-city distractions, rivalry, and the increasing desire of each to win art gallery success and recognition led to the formal dissolution of the group in 1913.

In that brief period, these young artists turned out a prolific collective oeuvre, which repre-

sents the dawn of German expressionism. The museum, whose creation was largely promoted by Schmidt-Rottluff, contains the single most extensive collection of the artists' graphic works (lithographs, woodcuts, and crayon and pencil drawings).

The Alliierten-Museum recounts the tale of occupied West Germany.

The peaceful Schlachtensee is just one of several lakes around the woods of Grunewald.

**Jagdschloss
Grunewald**
www.spsg.de
p. 189 D3
Hüttenweg 10
030 813 35 97
Closed Mon. mid-
May—mid-Oct.; open
Sun. only rest of year
$
U-Bahn Oskar-
Helene-Heim & Bus
115 to Pücklerstrasse

Given his key role in the creation of the museum, it is not surprising that many of Schmidt-Rottluff's primary-colored later works are also held in the museum's archives. From 1946 until his death, Schmidt-Rottluff was based in Berlin and his themes remained mostly constant, with landscapes (especially from the Ticino region of Switzerland in the 1950s), still lifes, and occasional nudes.

**For centuries,
Jagdschloss
Grunewald was
used as a princely
and royal hunting
lodge.**

**Museumsdorf
Düppel**
www.dueppel.de
p. 189 C1
Clauerstrasse 11
030 802 66 71
Open Sun. only
and holidays
Easter—early Oct.
$
S-Bahn: Zehlendorf &
Bus: 115 to
Ludwigsfelder Strasse

The best known of the Brücke artists was, however, Kirchner. To him we owe a rich collection of Berlin street scenes and not a few nudes. His human figures are often long and angular, with a resemblance to African art, and the colors strong but dark.

He and his pals spent a fair amount of time in Berlin's bordellos and cabarets and with their models. Kirchner's "Erich Heckel und Otto Müller beim Schach" ("Erich Heckel and Otto Müller Play Chess," 1913) shows his two colleagues playing chess, taking no notice of a nude woman draped on a sofa like a coat. Heckel was prolific; many of his paintings and sketches are on display, such as his nude "Sich Waschende" ("Woman Washing,"

1912) and "Akt im Raum" ("Nude in the Room," 1912). Pechstein is also known for his nudes, in particular those in seaside locations.

Stroll for about 15 minutes west from the Brücke Museum down Pücklerstrasse and follow a forest path through quiet woods to the enchanting **Jagdschloss Grunewald,** a lordly hunting lodge on the edge of a pretty lake, Grunewaldsee. Elector Joachim II of Brandenburg had this three-story Renaissance-era mansion built in the "Green Woods" in 1542. Baroque alterations and lower outbuildings that form a courtyard around the mansion were added in the 18th century. The hunt was a popular activity with the rulers of Brandenburg and Prussia, and the Jagdschloss was in use until World War I. The long, low building that faces the mansion stored hunting material and is lined with the antlers of felled beasts. Inside there is a museum on the business of the hunt, with weapons and other equipment, as well as explanations of how the princely activity was practiced. The most impressive part of the *Schloss* itself is the main hall on the first floor. The building now has a mixed collection of 15th- to 18th-century art, including works by Lucas Cranach the Elder (1472–1553) and the Younger (1515–1586).

The **Museumsdorf Düppel,** a self-proclaimed center for "experimental archaeology," is a 15-minute bus ride south from Pücklerstrasse. A medieval village has been re-created on the site of a 12th-century settlement. At the village's core is a huddle of thatched houses, where volunteers make crafts, breed near-extinct species of sheep and pigs, and grow varieties of long-forgotten plants. ■

Wannsee

TUCKED AWAY IN THE EXTREME SOUTHWEST OF BERLIN, Wannsee is a peaceful, wooded outpost of grand villas and boat clubs on the south shore of the Havel River. One of the grandest villas was the location for the 1942 Nazi conference that formally decided on the extermination of European Jews. A few villas away is Berlin artist Max Liebermann's former summer house, now a museum. Longish walks in the woods lead to Pfaueninsel, an island in the Havel and site of a onetime royal country palace.

Coming from central Berlin, your first stop can be the lakeside beaches of **Strandbad Wannsee,** although it might be more logical to finish a day of sightseeing by flopping on the beach last of all. The southern end is about a ten-minute walk from the Nikolassee S-Bahn stop. The sandy beach, with snack stands, beach basketball, and a kids' playground, is a popular summer draw. The beach's supporting buildings are a century old.

Southwest of the beach across the Grosser Wannsee lake stands the **Liebermann-Villa am Wannsee,** which Max Liebermann built in 1910 as a summer retreat. In early 2006 it reopened as a museum dedicated to the Berlin impressionist's life and works. Liebermann, born into a wealthy Jewish family, became head of the Prussian Art Academy after World War I. He later resigned in disgust at the Nazi's anti-Semitic policies. On the first floor of the two-story villa is a collection of memorabilia, while the top floor, which has his restored studio, displays some of his paintings.

Across the street is the striking wood-framed caprice known as the **Villa Langenscheidt,** which still belongs to the famous

In summer, swans and Berliners alike flock to lake beaches.

Strandbad Wannsee
- p. 189 B2
- Wannseebadweg
- Closed Oct.–March
- $
- S-Bahn: Nikolassee

Liebermann-Villa am Wannsee
www.max-liebermann.de
- p. 189 B2
- Colomierstrasse 3, Am Grossen Wannsee
- 030 80 58 38 30
- Open Fri. p.m. & Sat.–Sun.; Closed mid-Dec.–Feb.
- $
- S-Bahn: Wannsee & Bus: 114 to Colomierstrasse

**Haus der
Wannsee-
Konferenz**
www.ghwk.de
🅰 p. 189 B2
✉ Am Grossen
Wannsee 56–58
☎ 030 805 00 10
🚆 S-Bahn: Wannsee &
Bus: 114 to Haus
der Wannsee-
Konferenz

Pfaueninsel
www.spsg.de
🅰 p. 188 A2
☎ 030 80 58 68 30
(Schlösschen)
🚆 S-Bahn: Wannsee &
Bus: 218 & ferry

**Schloss
Glienicke**
www.spsg.de
🅰 p. 188 A1
✉ Königstrasse 36
☎ 030 805 30 41
🕐 Closed Mon.–Fri.
💲 $
🚆 S-Bahn: Wannsee &
Bus: 316

The Final Solution

The "solution of the Jewish question" was discussed at Wannsee like any other bureaucratic matter. That the topic was how to destroy 11 million European Jews (from neutral Portugal and unconquered Great Britain to the Soviet Union) seems to have fazed no one. From a policy of forced emigration, halted in 1941, the Nazis had moved to deportation of Jews (mostly to Polish work and death camps). The ultimate aim was genocide. The matter-of-factness of the 15 pages of minutes from the 1942 meeting, which can be downloaded from the museum website, is hard to believe. ∎

gathered here to discuss the *Endlösung* (Final Solution), i.e., the extermination of European Jewry. Displays cover the history of Jewish persecution in Nazi Germany and occupied Europe from 1933 to 1945.

After this sobering visit, you may need a long walk. Follow the riverbank walkway west for just over a mile (1.5 km) and you reach a ferry *(fee)* to **Pfaueninsel** (Peacock Island), named for its resident birds. A stroll around the 185-acre (75 ha) island is a delight. Apart from the sculpted gardens, you can visit the late 18th-century white **Schlösschen** (Little Castle) near the ferry landing from late April to October *(closed Mon., $)*, and the **Meierei** *(weekends only, Nov.–March, $)*, a farm also created by Prussia's

In the Haus der Wannsee-Konferenz, the cold-blooded planning of the Final Solution is set against the human suffering it unleashed.

German dictionary dynasty that had it built.

A short walk farther north is the **Haus der Wannsee-Konferenz.** The sprawling gardens and magnate's villa were acquired by the SS paramilitary security organization in 1941. On January 20, 1942, a group of 15 high-ranking Nazi Party officials

royals in the 18th century, at the island's northeast end. Check times for the last ferry back.

Hardy walkers can go another 2 miles (3 km) west along the Havel's banks to reach the rear entrance to **Schloss Glienicke.** This neoclassic palace built by Karl Friedrich Schinkel in 1824 is the scene of regular concerts. ∎

More places to visit in Spandau, Dahlem, & the west

BOTANISCHER GARTEN

A great way to get warm on a winter's day in Berlin is to visit the *Schauhäuser* (hothouses) of this extensive suburban botanical garden. The central house is by far the biggest, a sweaty haven with soaring palms and bamboo trees. Giant rulers next to some of the latter mark the amazing rapidity of their growth. Another house is filled with the perfume of rhododendrons and camellias. Other structures are dedicated to Australian, South African, or Mediterranean plants; everything from cactuses to orchids is on display. All manner of trees and plants spread out in the surrounding gardens—it is definitely best to visit in summer to enjoy them. Those wanting to understand the flora in the garden a little better can pop into the **Botanisches Museum,** where models and other displays reveal the inner workings of plant life. There are sections on everything from poisonous mushrooms to the many uses of plants.

🗺 p. 189 D2 ✉ Königin-Luise-Strasse 6–8 ☎ 030 83 85 01 00, www.bgbm.de 💲 $$ 🚆 S-Bahn: Botanischer Garten

DOMÄNE DAHLEM

Dahlem retains much of the air of the village it once was, which makes it a logical location for this urban agricultural oasis. Kids especially will enjoy this 30-acre (12 ha) open-air agricultural museum, the latest incarnation of a centuries-old Prussian farm. The stately master's home contains a museum with temporary exhibitions about farming and food. In the surrounding outbuildings you can see various activities, from pottery to printing. In warmer weather, a view of the farm animals will delight children. Wander around the fields (where several crops are grown) and sample the products in the shop or a drink in the beer garden. It makes for a bucolic, child-friendly antidote to the cultural concentration of the nearby Dahlem museums (see p. 196–199).

🗺 p. 189 D3 ✉ Königin-Luise-Strasse 49 ☎ 030 666 30 00, www.domaene-dahlem.de 🕐 Closed Tues. 💲 Museum: $ 🚆 U-Bahn: Dahlem Dorf

DORFKIRCHE ST. ANNEN

Just across Pacelliallee from the Domäne Dahlem is the village church of St. Anne, a charming little stone, brick, and *Fachwerk* (timbered) place of worship set amid a crowded cemetery. A church has stood here since the 13th century, but what you see was built in the 17th century. The late-Renaissance-style wooden pulpit was inserted in 1679. The carved altar dates to around 1500, while the crucifix on the altar, from 1490, was in the Klosterkirche in central Berlin, a church destroyed in World War II.

🗺 p. 189 D3 ✉ Königin-Luise-Strasse 55 🕐 Sat.–Sun. 11 a.m.–1 p.m. 🚆 U-Bahn: Dahlem Dorf

FUNKTURM

One of the symbols of the city, this radio-transmitter tower set amid the Messegelände (Trade Fair Grounds) was built in 1926. Nicknamed *der lange Lulatsch* (lanky lad) by the quick-witted Berliners, it looks a little like a simplified version of Paris's Eiffel Tower. In 1935 the world's first regular TV transmission took place from this tower, but since 1962 it has been used only as a relay station for amateur and police radio. Nowadays tourists and trade fair visitors stop by to take an elevator to the top for views around Berlin. Some stop off a third of the way up for a meal and view of the surroundings in the Funkturm Restaurant *(tel 030 30 38 29 00, www .funkturmrestaurant.de)*. Marlene Dietrich ate here shortly after it was opened. To get to the tower, enter the fairgrounds from Masuren Allee.

🗺 p. 189 D4 ✉ Hammarskjöldplatz ☎ 030 30 38 29 96 🕐 Closed Mon. 💲 $ 🚆 U-Bahn: Kaiserdamm

GEORG-KOLBE-MUSEUM

One of Germany's leading 20th-century sculptors, Georg Kolbe (1877–1947) was a controversial figure, an artist on the edge who managed to garner Nazi approval. The museum is located in the brick studio he had built in 1928 after the sudden death of

The Corbusierhaus apartment building rises like a monolith on a rise in suburban Berlin.

More places to visit in Spandau, Dahlem, & the west

his wife, Benjamine. Next door, constructed in the same stark, cubical style, was his house (now home to a café). Kolbe's statues are scattered about the gardens and in the main first-floor room. His figures rarely strike heroic poses, but rather exude a pensive, fragile quality. An example is "Der Einsame" ("The Lonely Man," 1927). Among other curios are 1941 clippings on the artist in French and German from the propaganda magazine *Signal* and expressionist paintings by Ernst Ludwig Kirchner and Karl Schmidt-Rottluff. Other rooms host temporary exhibitions. The museum makes little mention of the sculptor's Nazi-era work. From 1933 to 1943 he produced a long line of grand statues, which often took pride of place in the Nazi's Haus der Deutschen Kunst (House of German Art) in Munich.

If you think Kolbe's house and studio are harsh in their design, continue down Sensburger Allee to Heilsberger Allee. Atop the wooded rise before you stands a stark housing complex concocted by the Swiss architect Le Corbusier (1887–1965) in 1957. The **Corbusierhaus** was the precursor to

the wave of characterless high-rise apartments that swept the West from the 1960s on. Werner March, who built the nearby Olympiastadion (see pp. 190–191), was so incensed by this building he went to court to have it torn down. Mindful of Berlin's postwar housing shortage, the judges threw his plea out of court.
🅰 p. 189 C5 ✉ Sensburger Allee 25 ☎ 030 304 21 44, www.georg-kolbe-museum.de 🕐 Closed Mon. 💲 $$ 🚆 S-Bahn: Heerstrasse

TEUFELSBERG

About a third of a mile (0.5 km) south of the Georg-Kolbe-Museum stretches a peaceful wooded hill, one of the highest in Berlin at 377 feet (115 m). Known as the Teufelsberg (Devil's Mountain), it is entirely artificial, made from about 882 million cubic feet (25 million cubic m) of rubble carted here in the wake of World War II. The hill and surrounding woods are laced with walking tracks, and the hill is a good spot for tobogganing in winter.
🅰 p. 189 C4 ✉ Teufelsee Strasse 🚆 S-Bahn: Heerstrasse ∎

Just beyond Berlin's city limits is the royal pleasure dome of Potsdam as well as a somber symbol of suffering at Sachsenhausen. The Reformation was born in pretty Lutherstadt Wittenberg; the Saxon cities of Dresden and Leipzig beckon farther south.

Excursions

A bust of Johann Sebastian Bach honors the man who was choirmaster of Leipzig's Thomaskirche for 27 years.

Dresden is booming after the horrors of World War II and long years of GDR stagnation.

Excursions

BERLIN IS THE NOT THE ONLY EXCITING DESTINATION IN NORTHEASTERN Germany. The capital is ringed by significant sites: Some are cultural, while others offer wonderful ways to lose yourself in the countryside.

It was Friedrich II (Frederick the Great) who pushed the satellite town of Potsdam, southwest of Berlin, into the limelight; he preferred Schloss Sanssouci to his Berlin palaces. Nowadays the city is the capital of Brandenburg state. The old town was devastated by World War II bombings, but the sprawling parade of palaces and parks to its west and north was left intact, presenting a fairy-tale escape hatch for Berliners.

An altogether different trip leads to Sachsenhausen. An hour-long S-Bahn ride through the northern suburbs of Berlin brings the visitor to this former concentration camp, one of the first established by the Nazis in the 1930s. Hundreds of thousands of Jews, homosexuals, Communists, and others considered dangerous to Hitler's regime suffered and, in many cases, died here. It is a potently moving place to visit.

Farther from the capital, a wealth of possibilities opens up. The two main cities of the onetime kingdom of Saxony, Dresden and Leipzig, are magnets to the south. Both have worked miracles to put themselves back on the German map since the German Democratic Republic collapsed in 1990.

Dresden is perhaps best remembered for the horrific Allied bombings in 1945 that wiped out much of its old center. Its greatest symbol, the baroque Frauenkirche (Church of Our Lady) is only the latest of its historic monuments to rise from the ashes. Leipzig, 44 miles (115 km) to the west, is an equally attractive town, once home to the likes of Bach and Mendelssohn. Its compact historic center holds churches, art collections, and history museums.

Between Leipzig and Berlin lies one of the most important towns in the history of modern Christianity. For it was in pretty Lutherstadt Wittenberg that the Reformation, which would split Europe into Catholic and Protestant camps, was born. The churches and other buildings associated with Martin Luther and his contemporaries are a UNESCO World Heritage site.

Escapes into the countryside can be launched in the Spreewald, southeast of Berlin, or among the lakes of southern Mecklenburg, north of the capital. A host of other small towns, typically not much more than an hour by train from Berlin, complete the options for exploration. ∎

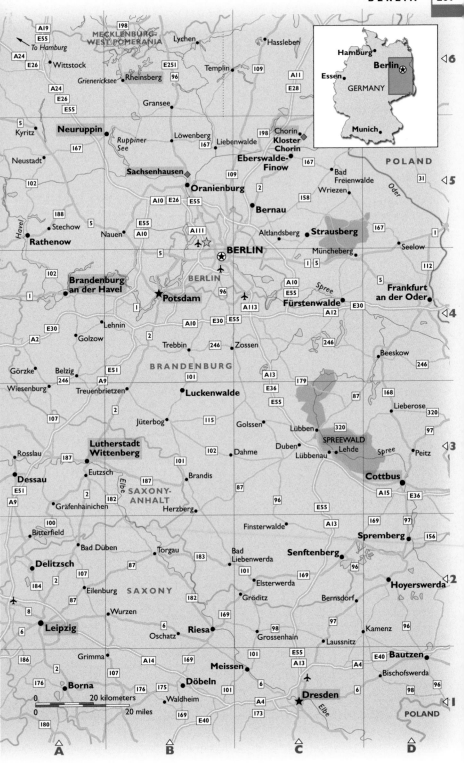

A19
E55
To Hamburg
A24
E26

198
MECKLENBURG-
WEST POMERANIA
Lychen
Hassleben

Wittstock

E251
Templin
109
A11
E28

Grienericksee
Rheinsberg
96

Kyritz
5

Neuruppin
167
Ruppiner
See
Löwenberg
167
Liebenwalde
198
Chorin
Kloster
Chorin

Neustadt
102

Gransee

POLAND

Eberswalde-
Finow
167
Bad
Freienwalde
31

Sachsenhausen
109
Oranienburg
2
158
Wriezen

Oder

188
Stechow
5
A10 E26 E55
Bernau

Rathenow
E55
A10
Nauen
A111

Altlandsberg
Strausberg
167
1
Seelow

BERLIN
Müncheberg
112

BERLIN
5
5

102
Brandenburg
an der Havel
96
Potsdam
A10
E55
A113
Fürstenwalde
Spree
A12
E30
Frankfurt
an der Oder

1
Havel
1

E30
A2
Lehnin
Golzow
2
A10 E30 E55
Trebbin
246
Zossen
246
Beeskow
246

Görzke
Belzig
246
E51
A9

BRANDENBURG
101
Luckenwalde
A13
E36
E55
179
87
168
Lieberose
320

Wiesenburg
Treuenbrietzen
2
Jüterbog
115
Golssen
Lübben
320
97

107
Rosslau
187
Lutherstadt
Wittenberg
101
102
Dahme
Duben
Lübbenau
SPREEWALD
Lehde
Spree
Peitz

Dessau
Eutzsch
187
Brandis
87
Cottbus

E51
A9
2
182
SAXONY-
ANHALT
Gräfenhainichen
Herzberg
96
E55
A15
E36

100
Bitterfield
Bad Düben
Torgau
183
Bad
Liebenwerda
Finsterwalde
A13
169
97
Spremberg
156

Delitzsch
87
101
Elsterwerda
169
96
Hoyerswerda

184
2
107
Eilenburg
182
Gröditz
Bernsdorf
97
Kamenz
96

8
87
Wurzen
169
Grossenhain
98
Laussnitz
Bautzen
E40

Leipzig
6
6
Oschatz
Riesa
101
E55
A13
A4
E40
Bischofswerda

186
2
Grimma
A14
169
Meissen
98
96

176
Borna
107
176
175
Döbeln
101
6
Dresden
98

0 20 kilometers
Waldheim
A4
Elbe
POLAND

0 20 miles
180
169
E40
173

Potsdam

Potsdam

⚑ p. 209 B4

Visitor information
www.potsdamtourismus.de

✉ Brandenburger
Strasse 3

☎ 0331 27 55 80

🚗 Car: A115 from
Charlottenburg to
the Babelsberg exit.
Follow Nuthestrasse
W to Potsdam.
S-Bahn: Potsdam
Hauptbahnhof

NOT OVERLY ENAMORED OF BERLIN, FRIEDRICH II CREATED for himself a majestic bucolic getaway in the nearby town of Potsdam (15 miles/24 km southwest of the city), complete with gardens and a pair of palaces. His successors took up where he left off. By the end of World War I the town boasted three parks, dotted by palaces, mansions, and other whimsical buildings, along with the pleasantly planned baroque quarters gathered around the Old Town core.

On the night of April 15, 1945, a hail of British bombs rained down on this royal vacation spot, wreaking havoc on the old center but leaving the surrounding parks and palaces largely untouched. Easily reached from central Berlin,

Potsdam today is a relatively well-to-do residential satellite of Berlin. It offers more than enough to fill a couple of days.

If you come by S-Bahn from Berlin, your first impressions may prompt you to turn around and

catch the first train back. Don't! Having crossed the Lange Brücke (Long Bridge), you have before you a strange mix. The dome and neoclassic facade of the Karl Friedrich Schinkel–designed **Nikolaikirche** fronts a somewhat desolate square, still known as the Alter Markt (Old Market). Facing the square are the **Altes Rathaus** (Old City Hall) and some awful GDR-era buildings (most earmarked for eventual demolition). This is the core of old Potsdam and it bore the brunt of the bombing.

The church and former city hall (the latter now a cultural

center) were mostly rebuilt after the war, but something is missing: the **Stadtschloss** (City Palace). The 17th-century royal residence was damaged and subsequently demolished by the GDR as a hated symbol of Germany's imperial past. In 2005 the state government decided to build a new state parliament, whose exterior will be a duplicate of the Stadtschloss, on this spot. The first step has been taken with the re-creation of the **Fortunaportal,** a ceremonial gateway topped by a gold-leaf statue of Fortune.

The nearby **Marstall** is a long, low, fire-red 18th-century orangerie designed by Georg Wenzeslaus von Knobelsdorff. It was turned into stables under Friedrich Wilhelm I and restored in the 1960s. Today it houses the **Filmmuseum Potsdam,** a look at the history of cinema.

A block north, the Neuer Markt (New Market) square boasts pretty renovated houses and the rather pompous facade of the Kutschstall (Coach Stable), which houses the **Haus der Brandenburgisch-Preussischen Geschichte** (House of Brandenburg-Prussian History) that has displays on 900 years of Brandenburg history.

The aptly named Breite Strasse (Broad Street) is lined by mostly GDR-period buildings, but in coming years another key Potsdam building will reappear. The 18th-century baroque **Garnisonkirche** was heavily damaged in 1945, but its 1735 bell tower survived. The ideologues of the GDR, however, decided it was representative of nasty imperial German tendencies and demolished it in 1968. With private funding, it is being rebuilt from scratch.

Nikolaikirche
✉ Alter Markt

Altes Rathaus
✉ Alter Markt
🕐 Closed Mon.

Filmmuseum Potsdam
www.filmmuseum-potsdam.de
✉ Marstall am Lustgarten, Breite Strasse 1a
☎ 0331 271 810
💲 $

Haus der Brandenburgisch-Preussischen Geschichte
www.hbpg.de
✉ Kutschstall, Am Neuen Markt 9
☎ 0331 620 85 50
🕐 Closed Mon.
💲 $

Gedenkstätte Lindenstrasse 54
✉ Lindenstrasse 54
☎ 0331 289 68 03
🕐 Closed Sun.–Mon., Wed., Fri. & every 2nd & 4th Sat.
💲 $

Park Sanssouci
🚌 Bus: 695 or X15 from Potsdam Hauptbahnhof

The elaborate Neues Palais was built by Friedrich II in 1770.

**Schloss
Sanssouci**

www.spsg.de

✉ Maulbeerallee

☎ 0331 96 94 190

🕐 By guided tour only;
closed Mon.

💲 $

A few blocks north, the streets around Brandenburger Strasse make up Potsdam's baroque district, consisting mostly of pedestrian-only streets with two-story houses. Friedrich Wilhelm I ordered the district built from 1732 to 1742. Its prettiest part, just north of Bassinplatz, is the **Holländisches Viertel** (Dutch Quarter), with more than 130 gabled houses that Dutch workers called home. The core of it lies between Kurfürstenstrasse

and Gutenberg Strasse.

A sobering excursion into Potsdam's darker history can be made at the **Gedenkstätte Lindenstrasse 54,** used by the Nazis as an *Erbgesundheitsgericht* (hereditary health court). Decisions on compulsory sterilization were made here; later it was used as a prison. Under the GDR, the Stasi (Secret Police) expanded it as a jail for political prisoners. The cells have been left as they were when the building

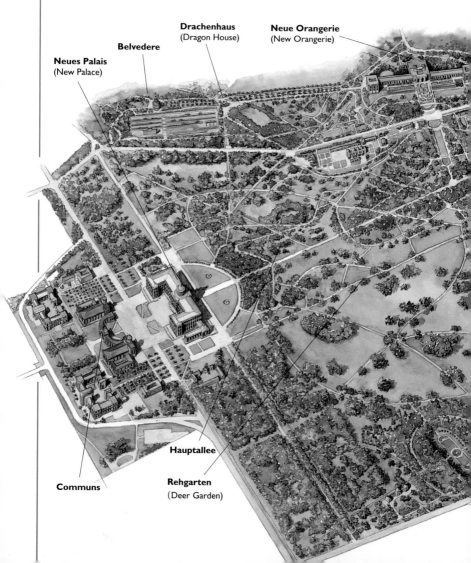

Neues Palais
(New Palace)

Belvedere

Drachenhaus
(Dragon House)

Neue Orangerie
(New Orangerie)

Communs

Hauptallee

Rehgarten
(Deer Garden)

was opened to the public in 1989.

The Nauener Tor (Nauen Gate) and Jägertor (Hunter's Gate) mark the northern boundary of the baroque quarter. A brisk walk a few hundred yards north of either gate leads to the **Alexandrowka,** also known as the Russian Colony, a group of Siberian-style chalets built in 1826 in memory of the Prusso-Russian alliance that helped defeat Napoleon in 1813 to 1815. A delightful Orthodox church tops a nearby hill.

To the west is **Park Sanssouci,** Friedrich II's fairy-tale creation, given its present appearance by the great 19th-century landscape artist Peter Joseph Lenné. From Schopenhauerstrasse, entry to

Bildergalerie
www.spsg.de
- ✉ Im Park Sanssouci 4
- ☎ 0331 969 41 81
- ⏱ Closed Mon. & mid-Oct.–mid-May
- 💲 $

Neue Kammern
www.spsg.de
- ✉ Im Park Sanssouci
- ☎ 0331 96 94 206
- ⏱ Closed Mon. & mid-Oct.–mid-May
- 💲 $

Historische Windmühle
www.spsg.de
- ✉ Maulbeerallee 5
- ☎ 0331 550 68 51
- ⏱ Closed Dec. & Mon.–Fri. Nov. & Jan.–March
- 💲 $

Neue Orangerie
www.spsg.de
- ✉ An der Orangerie 3–5
- ☎ 0331 969 42 80
- ⏱ Closed Mon.
- 💲 $

Neues Palais
www.spsg.de
- ✉ Am Neuen Palais
- ☎ 0331 969 43 61
- ⏱ By guided tour only; closed Fri.
- 💲 $$

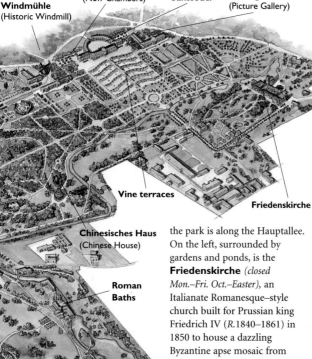

Historische Windmühle (Historic Windmill)

Neue Kammern (New Chambers)

Schloss Sanssouci

Bildergalerie (Picture Gallery)

Vine terraces

Friedenskirche

Chinesisches Haus (Chinese House)

Roman Baths

Schloss Charlottenhof

the park is along the Hauptallee. On the left, surrounded by gardens and ponds, is the **Friedenskirche** (closed Mon.–Fri. Oct.–Easter), an Italianate Romanesque–style church built for Prussian king Friedrich IV (R.1840–1861) in 1850 to house a dazzling Byzantine apse mosaic from Murano, Venice. The king and his wife are buried here.

At the **Grosse Fontäne** (Big Fountain) turn right for **Schloss Sanssouci,** Friedrich II's favorite summer residence. A sweeping stairway leads past vine terraces to this prime example of Prussian rococo. The king appointed von Knobelsdorff to build the palace but had the last word on all details. He wanted a place where

Chinesisches Haus

www.spsg.de

✉ Am Grünen Gitter

☎ 0331 969 42 22

🕐 Closed Mon. & mid-Oct.–mid-May

💲 $

Vine terraces bisected by sweeping stairs lead to Frederick the Great's favorite retreat, Schloss Sanssouci.

he could be "without care" (sans souci), to play music, talk philosophy with friends, and relax. The guided tour inside starts on the north flank in the vestibule, which features a statue of Mars, the god of war, at rest (as Friedrich wanted to be here). The king's private rooms follow. In the **Kleine Galerie,** the twisting, floral motifs of rococo decor are in full evidence. Among the paintings are some by Antoine Watteau, underlining the king's preference for all things French. His library, next up, contains many of his original collection of books, all in French. He read even German literature in translation, and the language of this palace was strictly that of Molière.

Friedrich Wilhelm II, who loathed the rococo giddiness, later changed the decoration in

Friedrich's study and bedroom. After the Seven Years' War, the gout-plagued king retired to Sanssouci and died of old age in a pale green armchair that remains in his study. He wanted to be buried on the top wine terrace outside, but this wish was carried out only in 1991.

The **Konzertzimmer** (Music Room) is where Friedrich II would regale guests with flute performances of his own composition. Then comes the **Marmorsaal** (Marble Room), an oval room made largely of Carrara marble shipped from Italy. Here the king and his friends (including French philosopher Voltaire, who lived at Sanssouci from 1750 to 1753) conducted round-table chats late into the night.

A series of guest rooms follows, of which the last is the most curious. Painted in yellow Chinese lacquer, its walls drip with reliefs of flora and fauna. It is said the king had this special decoration made for Voltaire, but that it was finished only after the fiery French thinker had left Prussia in a huff, never to return.

Just east of the palace, the sober baroque **Bildergalerie** (Picture Gallery) was built to house the king's art collection. Much of the original collection was lost after World War II. On the other side of the palace is a similar building, the **Neue Kammern** (New Chambers), which houses more guest rooms. The **Historische Windmühle** (Historic Windmill) stands just behind it. This windmill was originally built in the late 18th century to mill wheat and was one of the few structures in the park destroyed in World War II. Rebuilt in 2003, it is a functioning museum-mill. Perhaps the

most self-indulgent structure of all is the **Ruinenberg** (Ruin Mountain), set on a rise directly north of the palace. A series of classical "ruins" hide a complex pumping system for fountains in the park that, sadly, did not work.

The **Neue Orangerie** (New Orangerie), west of Schloss Sanssouci, is an enormous Italianate building with paintings in the style of Italian Renaissance artist Raphael (1483–1520). Beyond it are the pagodalike **Drachenhaus** (Dragon House), now a restaurant, and the **Belvedere,** which has views across the park.

The **Neues Palais** (New Palace) stretches to the south. It was built by Friedrich II in 1770 to reflect Prussia's growing self-confidence as a great power after the king's victory in the Seven Years' War. Kaiser Wilhelm II (whose taste in architecture was notoriously poor) loved the place and stayed in a suite of rooms on the first floor. The most striking room is the **Grottensaal** (Grotto Room) on the first floor, with an over-the-top decoration of mineral fragments, shells, and semiprecious stones. Above it, on the second floor, are two enormous ballrooms, the most stunning of them the **Marmorsaal** (Marble Room). Behind the palace stand more ostentatious buildings, the **Communs.** Now used by the Potsdam university, they served as servants' quarters and kitchens.

The **Rehgarten** (Deer Garden), once hunting grounds, rolls east of the Neues Palais. At its eastern end stands the **Chinesisches Haus** (Chinese House), a fantasy pavilion that expresses perfectly the fad for Chinese art that swept European courts in the late 18th century.

Spy swap

The iron Glienicker Bridge that links Berlin and Potsdam over the Havel River was rebuilt by the East Germans and named the Brücke der Einheit (Unity Bridge), in what must have been a moment of black humor, in the 1950s. From 1961 only authorized military personnel of the four occupying powers could cross this bridge. On three occasions between 1962 and 1986, it was the stage for international spy swaps, starting on February 10, 1962, with U.S. Capt. Gary Powers (1929–1977), who had been shot down in his U2 spy plane over the Soviet Union two years earlier. The last swap took place on February 11, 1986, when Russian dissident Anatoli Sharansky (born 1948), accompanied by three Allied spies, was exchanged for two busloads of Eastern-bloc spooks. (See www.glienicker-bruecke.de.) ■

The modest **Schloss Charlottenhof** (tel 0331 969 42 28, closed Mon., $), southwest in the park, is a palace in neoclassic style backed by a rose garden. The building was planned in the 1820s by Schinkel and Lenné for Friedrich Wilhelm IV when he was still crown prince.

Pilot Gary Powers crossed the Glienicker Bridge when exchanged for a Russian spy in 1962.

Schloss Cecilienhof
www.spsps.de
✉ Im Neuen Garten
☎ 0331 969 42 44
🕐 Closed Mon.
💲 $$
🚋 Tram: 92 from Potsdam Hauptbahnhof & Bus: 692

Marmorpalais
www.spsg.de
✉ Im Neuen Garten
☎ 0331 969 42 46
🕐 Closed Mon. April–Oct. & Mon.–Fri. Nov.–March
💲 $
🚋 Tram: 92 from Potsdam Hauptbahnhof & Bus: 692

Kaiser Wilhelm II could never have envisioned his Schloss Cecilienhof as the site for an Allied conference.

Flatowturm
www.spsg.de
✉ Park Babelsberg 12
☎ 0331 969 42 49
🕐 Closed Nov.–Mar., Mon. April–June, Mon.–Fri. July–Oct.
💲 $
🚇 S-Bahn: Babelsberg & Bus: 694

Filmpark Babelsberg
www.filmpark.de
✉ Grossbeerenstrasse
☎ 0331 721 27 50
🕐 Closed Nov.–Feb. (sometimes closed Mon. & Fri. Call ahead to check.)
💲 $$$$
🚇 S-Bahn: Griebnitzsee

You can find another Lenné park, the **Neuer Garten** (New Garden), northeast of central Potsdam. Within sight of the Jungerfernsee, a lake that branches off the Havel River, is the enchanting **Schloss Cecilienhof.** Kaiser Wilhelm II had this fantasy palace built from 1913 to 1917 for his son, the Crown Prince Wilhelm, who didn't get to enjoy it for long, as the royal family fled to Holland in 1918. The palace is best known as the location of the Potsdam Conference, held by the Allies from July 17 to August 2, 1945. Fateful decisions, such as the shifting of the German-Polish border and the division of Berlin into four occupation sectors (as had been agreed at the Yalta Conference in February 1945) were made here. Much of this historic palace has been a hotel since 1960 (see p. 265).

Built over a series of inner courtyards, the place has the air of a rustic country mansion, all wooden framing and brick vaguely in the style of an (admittedly enormous) English "cottage." Its modest layout belies the fact that it has 176 rooms. The palace—including the conference rooms where Allied delegations met—can generally be visited only with a guided tour.

The **Marmorpalais** overlooks another lake, the Heiliger See, on the east edge of the park. Originally built in 1787 to 1799 from designs by Carl Gotthard Langhans (1732–1808) and Carl von Gontard (1731–1791) under the command of Friedrich Wilhelm II, the palace did not have a complete interior until 1845. Damaged in World War II, the building wound up as the GDR's Army Museum. It is now being restored.

Potsdam extends east across the Havel into the Babelsberg District. Its northwestern corner holds the Lenné-designed **Park Babelsberg,** dotted by several 19th-century caprices including **Schloss Babelsberg**—built in 1833 as a summer residence for Kaiser Wilhelm I and currently closed for restoration—and the rather odd-looking neo-Gothic **Flatowturm** (Flatow Tower) built in the 1850s. To the east of the district lies the **Filmpark Babelsberg,** a U.S.-style movie theme park on the grounds of the Babelsberg film studios. The studios are still in action, although the pre–World War II glory days are vanished. ∎

Sachsenhausen

THE SACHSENHAUSEN CONCENTRATION CAMP (21 MILES/ 34 km northwest of Berlin) was built by prison labor in 1936. From then until 1945, more than 200,000 people (Jews, Communists, opponents of the regime, and later foreign prisoners) were incarcerated and tormented here, and tens of thousands died. Today, with some of its barracks restored and the watchtowers in place, it is a chilling place.

After picking up a map *(fee)* or audio guide *(fee)*, go down the street to the camp entrance. You pass a museum on the history of the camp as a memorial site and then through the main gate, adorned with the taunting phrase: *Arbeit Macht Frei* (Freedom through Work).

Inside is the Appellplatz, where prisoners would be called for daily muster and often left to stand for hours, no matter what the weather. Stone markers indicate the position of the former barracks.

To the right of the Appellplatz, two of the barracks have been reconstructed, mostly with original materials. The crowded triple bunks and common toilet and shower areas are on display. Wardens regularly tortured and drowned inmates in the toilets and footbaths. Exhibitions in the two barracks explore Nazi persecution of the Jews and the horrors of daily life (and death) in the concentration camp.

Nearby is a remaining wing of the former cellblock. On the camp's west flank are factories where prisoners toiled, along with mass-execution ditches and the remains of crematoriums. Here the visitor will find an exhibition on murder in Sachsenhausen. The southwest corner holds the hospital barracks, where prisoners were subjected to vile medical experiments.

Sachsenhausen was transformed into a Soviet prison from 1945 to 1950. Some 60,000 people were held in those years, and thousands of them died. ■

Gedenkstätte Sachsenhausen
www.gedenkstaette-sachsenhausen.de
🅰 p. 209 B5
✉ Strasse der Nationen 22, Oranienburg
☎ 03301 20 01
🚗 Car: A111 (toward Hamburg), then A10 (Berlin ring road) at Oranienburger Kreuz toward Prenzlau. Exit at Birkenwerder, take the B96 to Oranienburg and follow signs for Sachsenhausen. S-Bahn: (line 1) from Berlin to Oranienburg, then Bus 804 (heading for Malz) or 20-minute walk.

An empty watchtower stands guard over Sachsenhausen's bleak grounds.

Güstrow's Renaissance-era castle, set in magnificent gardens, is a lake district highlight.

Mecklenburg Lake District drive

Glorious Müritzsee, Germany's second biggest lake, lies at the heart of a national park encompassing countless lakes and waterways about 80 miles (130 km) northwest of Berlin in the state of Mecklenburg-Vorpommern (Mecklenburg-West Pomerania). In summer especially, the Mecklenburg Lake District (known in German as the Mecklenburgische Seenplatte) is a watery paradise beloved of yachting folk, paddlers, and cyclists. Adding some miles, you can carve out a two-day route taking in intriguing towns and finishing up in Schwerin, the region's beautiful capital.

Head north out of Berlin along the A111 toward Oranienburg, continuing for another 35 miles/57 km (west on 167 at Löwenberg and north on L19 after Herzberg) for **Rheinsberg** ❶, where you can find a lakeside palace (see p. 232). The road north leads past a string of lakes to Wesenberg and on to Neustrelitz. Skip this town to proceed north along the Tollensesee lake on E251/96 to **Neubrandenburg** ❷. Although much of the old town was devastated in the final days of World War II, its 1.5-mile-long (2.5 km) medieval defensive wall was left intact. Punctuated by four city gates, the wall is 24.5 feet (7.5 m) high and dotted by restored *Wiekhäuser,* fortlets that were manned by armed citizens in case of attack.

From Neubrandenburg, the 192 road leads west via Penzlin to **Waren** ❸, a pretty town on the north flank of **Müritzsee** and a pleas-

ant spot to spend the night. Those with more time might prolong their stay and take advantage of the lake, which is 18 miles (29 km) long and covers an area of 45 square miles (117 sq km). Yachts and canoes are available for rent. The latter are a great way to discover the waterways of the **Müritz-Nationalpark** *(www.nationalpark-mueritz.de),* a patchwork of more than a hundred lakes created by receding glaciers at the end of the last ice age. Cycling is another option, with some 124 miles (200 km) of marked riding paths in the park. Animals, especially birds, abound in the area, including cranes, storks, and sea eagles.

From Waren take the 192 road south along the west side of the lake, and veer west via Malchow to the A19, which you follow north. Take the Güstrow exit and drive west on 104 to **Güstrow** ❹. In one of the most charming of the lake district towns, the compact Altstadt (Old Town) rewards a stroll. Its heart is the Marktplatz square, lined by tightly knit houses and a dazzling Rathaus (City Hall). Also worth visiting is the Renaissance-era Schloss *(Franz-Parr-Platz 1, tel 03843 75 38, closed Mon. Oct.–April, $).* The 16th-century palace set in beautiful gardens is a mix of French, German, and Italian models. The Gothic Dom (cathedral), a towering medieval structure, contains, among other things, the stout looking "Schwebende Engel" ("Hovering Angel"). This wood carving was created by Ernst Barlach (1870–1938), a major modern sculptor from Güstrow.

Although it is another 31 miles (50 km) west on 104, it would be a shame to miss out on **Schwerin** ⑤. Set on a hill amid seven lakes, the old town's narrow alleys are a joy to wander. The highlight is the Schloss *(Lennéstrasse 1, tel 0385 525 29 20,*

www.museum-schwerin.de, closed Mon. Oct.–April, $$), located on its own island. Rebuilt in the 19th century in the style of a Loire château, it is a lavish chocolate box. The old town is dominated by the 384-foot (117 m) 19th-century tower of the Gothic brick Dom. You can climb the tower for sweeping views. ∎

▲ See area map p. 209
➤ Berlin
↔ 197 miles (317 km)
🕐 2 days
➤ Schwerin

NOT TO BE MISSED
- Neubrandenburg
- Müritzsee
- Güstrow
- Schwerin

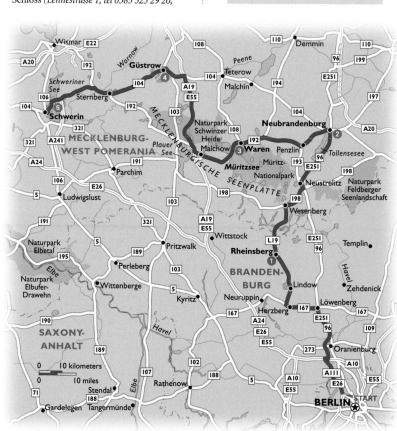

Dresden

Dresden
△ p. 209 CI

Visitor information
www.dresden.de
✉ Prager Strasse & Schinkelwache, & Theaterplatz
☎ 0351 49 19 21 00
🚗 Car: A113 to the A13, which runs to Dresden. Train: From Berlin Ostbahnhof (2–3 hours)

Zwinger
www.skd-dresden.de
✉ Sophienstrasse
☎ 0351 49 14 20 00
🕐 Closed Mon.

Rüstkamer
🕐 Closed Mon.
💲 $. With Gemäldegalerie Alter Meister $$

HAILED AS FLORENCE ON THE ELBE, THE CAPITAL OF SAXONY, 124 miles (200 km) south of Berlin, has doggedly rebuilt much of its glorious architecture since February 1945, when Allied bombs destroyed its historic center. A pinnacle, but by no means the finish line, was reached with the opening of the completely rebuilt baroque Frauenkirche in 2005. The city is richly stocked with world-class museums and galleries, and the nearby pretty Elbe Valley scenery is a draw for those with wheels. Dresden lies at the heart of Germany's northernmost wine area.

Dresden's partially rebuilt **Altstadt** (Old Town) lies on the left bank of the Elbe, but the silhouette is best viewed from the Neustadt (New Town) on the north side of the river. The skyline is dominated by the monumental dome of the Frauenkirche (Church of Our Lady), completed in 1743 as the city's surprisingly opulent central place of Protestant worship, destroyed in 1945, and rebuilt and opened again in 2005.

The magnificence of the new-old church is testimony to the stubborn determination of Dresden's population to resurrect at least part of the city's past charm. The process began shortly after World War II. In the last months of the war, refugees fleeing the advance of the Red Army had crowded into Dresden, where they and the local populace had thought they would be safe from Allied bombing. Dresden had no industry to speak of and was not a military target. Germans hoped also that the Western Allies would spare a city of such artistic and cultural importance. They were wrong. Massed bomber fleets unleashed a deadly firestorm in the heart of Dresden on the night of February 13, destroying three-quarters of the city and killing an unknown number of locals and refugees. Work continues today, and the city seems determined to

re-create the old town in as close to its entirety as possible.

Marking the western end of the Altstadt is the **Zwinger.** Intended as a magnificent backdrop for courtly ceremonies and festivals, the fabulous architectural fancy is now a museum complex. Architect Matthäus Daniel Pöppelmann (1662–1736) built it on the orders of the most colorful of Saxony's kings, August der Starke (Augustus the Strong, 1670–1733), who came to the throne in 1694. Consisting of a series of lavish, low-slung buildings arranged around a spacious, grassy courtyard with pools and fountains, the Zwinger is the supreme expression of German baroque architecture and the repository of Dresden's collection of old master paintings.

Approach the Zwinger through the gateway of the **Glockenspielpavillon,** with its carillon of bells made from Meissen porcelain. In the center of the left wing is the **Kronentor** (Crown Gate), topped by sculptures of eagles guarding the crown of Poland. (Augustus also ruled Saxony's eastern neighbor for a time.) To the right is the massive **Sempergalerie** (Semper Gallery), designed by Gottfried Semper (1803–1879) and added to the complex in 1855. The structure that commands the most attention,

Opposite:
The medieval splendor of Dresden, as seen in the Residenzschloss, is being lovingly restored.

**Mathematisch-
Physikalischer
Salon**
🕐 Closed Mon.
💲 $

**Porzellan-
sammlung**
🕐 Closed Mon.
💲 $$

though, is the **Wallpavillon,** on the far side of the courtyard. This is Pöppelmann's masterpiece, enhanced by the lively sculptures carved by his collaborator, Baltasar Permoser (1651–1732). Even greater exuberance appears in the adjoining **Nymphenbad,** a sunken grotto in which stone nymphs disport themselves.

Inside the Zwinger are varied treasures. The **Rüstkammer**

porcelain. By experimenting in the vitrification of clays with heat, his alchemist, Johann Friedrich Böttger (1682–1719), discovered how to make fine china, thereby laying the foundation of an industry that is inseparable from the names of Dresden and Meissen.

The main attraction in the Zwinger is the **Gemäldegalerie Alter Meister** (Old Masters

The Semperoper, built in the late 19th century, is one of the world's finest opera houses.

(Armory) contains one of the world's greatest collections of arms and armor (which will eventually be transferred to its original home in the Residenzschloss), while the **Mathematisch-Physikalischer Salon** (Mathematics-Physics Salon) displays an array of scientific instruments from the 16th century on. The extensive **Porzellansammlung** (Porcelain Collection) presents superb examples of porcelain from the royal collections. Augustus the Strong was fascinated by

Gallery), a collection assembled by Augustus the Strong and his successor, Augustus III (R.1734–1763). The gallery's most celebrated painting (in **Room 117** on the second floor) is the "Sixtinische Madonna" ("Sistine Madonna," 1512–13) by Raphael, admired not only for its exquisite representation of the Mother and Child, but also for the delightful pair of bored cherubs at the base of the picture. Another renowned painting from the Italian Renaissance is Giorgione's "Schlummernde Venus"

("Sleeping Venus"), which Titian (ca 1490–1576) completed after the artist died in 1510. Works by many of the great names of Western European art abound; Rembrandt, Vermeer, Claude Lorrain, Nicholas Poussin, El Greco, Velázquez, Lucas Cranach the Elder, and Dürer are among the stars. The gallery also contains a series of six paintings of Dresden (in **Room 102**) by Canaletto (Bernardo Bellotto, 1722–1780), nephew of the more famous painter of the same name.

The northeast facade of the Gemäldegalerie looks out over **Theaterplatz,** an imposing square bounded by some of Dresden's outstanding landmarks. Even the visitor information center is a neoclassic temple, a guardhouse (Schinkelwache) designed by Berlin's star 19th-century architect, Karl Friedrich Schinkel, in 1830 to 1832.

Also on Theaterplatz is the grandiose **Semperoper** (Semper Opera House), home to the Saxon State Opera and the State Orchestra. Named after the architects Gottfried Semper and his son, Manfred, the theater's sumptuous interior was the backdrop for premieres of operas by Richard Wagner and Richard Strauss (1864–1949). The building was reduced to a shell in 1945; the complex task of rebuilding it was completed on the 40th anniversary of its destruction. It is usually possible to join a guided 45-minute tour (in German) of the lavish interior at least once a day. Times are posted outside.

The nearby **Residenz-schloss** (Residential Palace) is where the rulers of Saxony lived for centuries until 1918. Construction of the palace began on the site of an earlier castle in 1530 and has constantly been

meddled with since. Heavily damaged in World War II, the building is still being restored. The steep-roofed **Georgenbau** serves as a dazzling entrance tower. Examine the extraordinary frieze on the long wall facing Augustusstrasse. Made of Meissen tiles, it depicts the *Fürstenzug* (princely procession), glorifying key figures from the dynasty's 800-year rule. That they appear on horseback is no coincidence, for within was the **Stallhof** (Royal Stables).

Inside the palace are the restored **Grünes Gewölbe** (Green Vaults), which house a dazzling treasure of jewelry and gold. Don't miss the wildly extravagant porcelain piece known as the "Hofstaat des Grossmoguls" ("The Court of Delhi on the Birthday of the Great Moghul"). Augustus the Strong's court jeweler, Johann Melchior Dinglinger (1664–1731), worked with his brothers for seven years to make this thinly veiled glorification of the Saxon king's own ostentatious court. Other collections include the **Kupferstichkabinett** (Engravings Cabinet) and the **Münzkabinett** (Coin Cabinet). You can climb the 328-foot-high (100 m) **Hausmannsturm** tower (closed Nov.–March).

Linked to the palace by a bridge, the Roman Catholic **Hofkirche** caused a stir in this ultra-Protestant city when Catholic convert Augustus the Strong ordered it built in 1738. The king's architect was Italian Gaetano Chiaveri (1689–1770), who brought in a team of his countrymen to carry out the work. They were housed on the Elbe embankment in what is still called the **Italienisches Dörfchen** (Little Italian Village), now home to several restaurants.

Gemäldegalerie Alter Meister
🕐 Closed Mon.
💲 $$

Semperoper
www.semperoper.de
✉ Theaterplatz
☎ 0351 49 11 705
💲 Guided tours $$

Residenzschloss
www.skd-dresden.de
✉ Taschenberg 2
☎ 0351 49 14 20 00
🕐 Closed Tues.
💲 $$

Hofkirche
www.bistum-dresden-meissen.de
✉ Schlossstrasse 24
☎ 0351 484 47 12

Frauenkirche
www.frauenkirche-dresden.de

✉ An der Frauenkirche

☎ 0351 49 81 10

🕐 Services closed to visitors

💲 Dome $$$

Sandstone statues of saints parade on the balustrade of Chiaveri's lovely church and the interior has fine baroque furnishings. The remains of Saxon rulers lie buried in the crypt.

The city's main church is, however, the **Frauenkirche.** The dome survived the hail of Allied bombs in 1945 only to collapse a few days later as the stonework cooled. For decades the heap of rubble remained as silent testimony to the wanton

The classic view of the mighty Elbe River is from the **Brühlsche Terrasse,** a promenade laid out over the riverside fortifications in the 18th century by Count Heinrich von Brühl (1700–1763). You reach the terrace by a magnificent flight of steps that begin near the Hofkirche and are decorated with sculptures representing the seasons. The stairs also lead to the **Albertinum,** which once served as the royal arsenal and now houses a number of

Augustus the Strong had the elaborately decorated Hofkirche (court church) built in 1738, after he had converted to Catholicism.

Albertinum

✉ Tzschirnerplatz-Neumarkt

🕐 Closed for restoration

destruction of war. In 1994, rebuilding began, aiming for the city's 800th anniversary in 2006. The work was financed mainly through private donations and the sale of souvenirs. How little of the original soaring, circular, baroque beauty survived is clear from the color of the stone. The sparse darker patches are original. (A chunk of the original dome now stands behind the church as a memorial.) Inside, soft roses, blues, and ochers dominate the color scheme. The altar bursts with decoration. Three galleries line the high walls. You can climb up inside the dome and then go to a viewing platform atop the church. Head for entrance G.

museums. It closed in late 2005 for restoration and will not open before 2009.

Its treasures include antique (mostly Roman) sculptures and the **Gemäldegalerie Neuer Meister** (New Masters Gallery), a major collection of German 19th- and 20th-century painting, with a few works by such foreigners as Gauguin, van Gogh, and Manet thrown in.

On the far bank of the river, reached via the Augustusbrücke of 1910, is the **Neustadt** (New Town), laid out in the 18th century. It was barely touched by the 1945 bombing and, with its shops and cafés on and around Königstrasse and Rähnitzgasse, makes for a pleasant wander. ■

Leipzig

SAXONY'S SECOND CITY (POPULATION 497,500) IS KNOWN for its musical and intellectual traditions and trade fairs. Since the overthrow of the GDR regime in 1990, in which Leipzig's citizens played a leading role—Leipzig came to be known as the City of Heroes for its anti-regime demonstrations in 1989—the city (100 miles/160 km southwest of Berlin) has moved swiftly to recover its place as one of Germany's stars. Its go-ahead spirit is expressed in a wealth of new and restored buildings and a busy nightlife.

Leipzig makes a grand first impression for travelers by train. The city's main station, the **Hauptbahnhof** (completed in 1915 and completely rebuilt after World War II), is one of Europe's great rail terminals, its vastness tempered by tasteful ornament.

Southwest across Willy-Brandt-Platz and the ring road, Leipzig's historic core, the **Innenstadt,** is compact and easily explored on foot.

Occupying much of wide-open Sachsenplatz is the **Museum der Bildenden Künste** (Fine Arts Museum). What looks like a giant glass-and-cement cube from the outside is an impressive new temple to the city's top art collections. Inside, interlocking planes of glass, cement, and wood paneling form the framework for a broad range of art, covering centuries of German painting from the Middle Ages to a swath of GDR artists. Thrown in are collections of mostly minor French, Italian, Spanish, and Dutch works from the 15th to the 18th centuries.

On the same square is the new building that houses temporary exhibitions of the **Stadtgeschichtliches Museum** (Municipal History Museum). Included in the ticket is a visit to the permanent display on the city's history in the **Altes Rathaus** (Old Town Hall), a

Locals treat themselves to some shopping in the elegant art nouveau Mädlerpassage.

Leipzig
🅰 p. 209 A2

Visitor information
www.leipzig.de
www.lts-leipzig.de
✉ Richard-Wagner-Strasse 1
☎ 0341 71 04 260
🚗 Car: A9 toward Nuremberg. Train: From Berlin Ostbahnhof (1.5–2.5 hours)

**Museum der
Bildenden
Künste**
www.mdbk.de
✉ Katharinenstrasse 10
☎ 0341 21 69 90
🕐 Closed Mon.
$ $$

**The centuries-old
Nikolaikirche was
a rallying point for
opponents of the
GDR regime in
1989.**

block south in the old city center. Built in 1556, it is one of the earliest and finest examples of Germany's Renaissance town halls, with a high roof, tall tower, stepped gables, and arcaded first floor facing the marketplace. Its imposing reception hall is hung with portraits of princes and city fathers.

In the adjacent **Naschmarkt** square stands a statue of Johann Wolfgang von Goethe (1749–1832), one of Germany's greatest poets and playwrights. The small baroque building, the **Alte Börse,** behind it was a produce exchange and now serves as a concert hall.

Germany's recent history is explored in the town's **Zeitgeschichtliches Forum Leipzig** (Contemporary History Forum), south across Grimmaische Strasse from Naschmarkt. Its displays, an engaging mix of audio, video, photos, documents, newspapers, and artifacts, start with the Allied occupation of Germany in 1945 and the country's subsequent division. The sections on life in the GDR and the events that led to its collapse in 1989 and 1990 are fascinating. Stretching south from Grimmaische Strasse is the **Mädlerpassage,** the most splendid of Leipzig's *Passagen*

(shopping arcades). It is three stories high and an attractive combination of art nouveau and neo-Renaissance. Its most famous establishment lurks, however, below ground. **Auerbachs Keller** *(tel 0341 21 61 00)* owes its reputation to Goethe's *Faust,* in which Faust and Mephistopheles descend into the cellar tavern to carouse with students. Most visitors to Leipzig follow in their footsteps, past bronze statues of the two characters, to enjoy a glass of Saxon wine or a substantial meal among the Faustian memorabilia.

Another early 20th-century arcade, the tastefully modernized

Specks Hof, can be found diagonally north of the Mädlerpassage. Opposite it stands the **Nikolaikirche** *(Nikolaikirchhof, tel 0341 960 52 70),* or St. Nicholas's Church. Regular Monday prayer meetings for peace began to be held here in 1982, and in 1989 the meetings were a rallying point for demonstrators against the East German government. The somber exterior of what was originally a Romanesque church belies the glittering 18th-century interior.

About 1,300 feet (400 m) west along Grimmaische Strasse and its continuation, Thomasgasse, is Leipzig's second great church, the **Thomaskirche** *(Thomaskirchhof 18, tel 0341 960 28 55).* Founded in 1212, St. Thomas's was rebuilt in Gothic style at the end of the 15th century. It is best known as the home of the Thomaner, a celebrated boys' choir that has been around since the church was founded.

From 1723 until his death in 1750, Johann Sebastian Bach (1685–1750) was cantor (choirmaster) of St. Thomas's and also Leipzig's director of music. He is now buried in the church and a statue of him stands outside. Bach had a big family and always seemed to be short of cash, which is why the left pocket in the statue is turned out. Opposite, the **Bachmuseum** *(Thomaskirchhof 16, tel 0341 9 13 72 00, www. bach-leipzig.de)* has documents on the composer's life and musical instruments. The best way to honor the musician and the choir he led, however, is to attend one of the regular services at which the Thomaner performs *(see www.thomaskirche.org for details).*

If the Thomaskirche represents one pole of Leipzig's musical life, the other is the vast

Stadtgeschicht-liches Museum
www.stadtgeschichtliches-museum-leipzig.de
✉ Altes Rathaus, Markt 1
☎ 0341 965 13 20
🕐 Closed Mon.
$ $

Zeitgeschicht-liches Forum Leipzig
www.hdg.de/zfl
✉ Grimmaische Strasse 6
☎ 0341 2 22 00
🕐 Closed Mon.

Grassi-Museum
www.grassimuseum.de

✉ Johannisplatz 5–11
☎ 0341 214 21 75
🕐 Closed Mon.
💲 Ethnology
museum $

Museum in der Runden Ecke
www.runde-ecke-leipzig.de/cms

✉ Dittrichring 24
☎ 0341 961 24 43
🕐 Closed Mon.

Augustusplatz, on the far east side of the Innenstadt. At the north end of the square is the **Opernhaus** (Opera House) of 1960, and on the south the **Neues Gewandhaus** (New Concert Hall), home to the city's orchestra, whose origins go back to the mid-18th century. Felix Mendelssohn was appointed its director in 1835 at the age of 26. The present building is a far cry from the clothmakers' guildhall *(Gewandhaus)* where a concert hall was initially improvised in 1781. One of the prestige projects of GDR times, this concert hall was built in 1981. Not so successful was the university building raised on the square's southwest flank to replace the Paulinerkirche (St. Paul's Church), blown up in GDR times because the government did not want a church on a socialist square. The city government will be tearing this down to make way for a new university campus.

A block east and built in the Bauhaus style in the late 1920s, the **Grassi-Museum** contains three separate areas: **Völkerkunde** (Ethnology), **Musikinstrumente** (Musical Instruments), and **Angewandte Kunst** (Applied Arts). Partially reopened in spring 2006 after extensive renovation, the building can accommodate only a fraction of these extensive collections at one time. They are being progressively opened in the course of 2006. The ethnology section has more than 100,000 objects from all over the world, ranging from Aboriginal Australian art to traditional North African jewelry. The musical instrument section is rich in instruments, mostly European, dating from the 14th century. The applied arts collection is equally diverse, spanning the continents

and a couple of millennia. Ceramics, glassware, furniture, woodwork, costumes, jewelry, and textiles are (or will be) on display.

Dominating the southwest edge of the Innenstadt is the **Neues Rathaus** (New City Hall), a monumental affair raised in 1905 and dominated by its stout 354-foot (108 m) tower. To its north along the ring road is the **Museum in der Runden Ecke** (Museum in the Round Corner), installed in the Stasi secret police's former local headquarters. Its permanent display, "Stasi—Macht und Banalität" ("Stasi—Power and Banality"), documents the lengths to which the GDR's rulers went in order to control their subjects.

In October 1813, Napoleon suffered a crushing defeat on the outskirts of Leipzig in a six-day battle at the hands of the allied armies of Prussia, Austria, and Russia. The clash, known in German as the *Völkerschlacht* (Battle of the Peoples), involved half a million troops and cost about 85,000 lives. On October 18, 1913, Kaiser Wilhelm II opened the enormous **Völkerschlachtdenkmal** memorial *(Prager Strasse, tel 0341 878 04 71, www.voelker-schlachtdenkmal.de, $$)* just south of Leipzig's city center. Inside the giant crypt, titanic statues look down upon you, their tiny visitors. Climb the steps (or take an elevator) to the viewing platforms at 223 feet (68 m) and 299 feet (91 m) for views over Leipzig.

Business people often head for the **Neue Messe,** the modern trade fair on the city's northern outskirts. The complex of five exhibition halls is the latest incarnation of Leipzig's 800-year-old trade-fair tradition. ■

Spreewald

A chauffeur-driven punt is the best way to get around the wooded waterways of the Spreewald.

ABOUT AN HOUR'S DRIVE SOUTHEAST OF BERLIN, THE Spree River splits into slow-moving channels, a strange kind of inland delta shaded by alder, poplar, and ash trees. This watery forest is the 111-square-mile (287 sq km) Spreewald. For centuries local people, mostly of the Sorbian minority, got around by flat-bottomed punt *(Kahn)*. Berliners started visiting in the 19th century.

Today more than two million visitors a year pour into the forest, declared a UNESCO biosphere in 1990. Apart from taking rides in a punt, there are endless options for walking, cycling, and canoeing.

The most popular gateway to the Spreewald is **Lübbenau** (Lubnjow in Sorbian). The **Spreewald-Museum** *(Topfmarkt 12, tel 03542 24 72, closed Mon. & Nov.–March, $)* is housed in the 1850 Torhaus, a three-story building that in GDR times was used as a prison. The museum is a curious mix, where displays on Sorbian culture rub shoulders with others on local GDR history.

The Sorbians (also known in German as Wenden) were the original Slavic inhabitants of much of the Mark Brandenburg before the Germans arrived in force in the Middle Ages. They have maintained their cultural identity (and refer to the Spreewald as Blota), but few Sorbians still speak the language. You can find more about them at the **Freilandmuseum** *(tel 03542 24 72, closed mid-Oct.–March, $),* where traditional farmsteads and other buildings have been reassembled. The museum is in **Lehde** (Ledy in Sorbian), a short punt trip or 1.2-mile (2 km) stroll from Lübbenau.

You will quickly become aware that one of the Spreewald's biggest claims to fame is the gherkin. In GDR times it was a popular local product and nowadays has become a slightly silly regional symbol. It is the subject of guided tours in Lübbenau.

Just 8 miles (13 km) from Lübbenau is the smaller, 12th-century **Lübben** (Lubin), with a castle and beautiful gardens by the Spree River. It is accessible by bus or train. ∎

Spreewald

🅐 p. 209 C3

✉ 50 miles (80 km) SE of Berlin

🚗 Car: A113 to the A13 and exit at Duben. Train: From Berlin Ostbahnhof to Lübben and Lübbenau

Visitor information Spreewald
www.spreewald-online.de

✉ Ehm-Welk-Strasse 15, Lübbenau

☎ 03542 36 68

Visitor information Lübben
www.luebben.com

✉ Ernst-von-Houwald-Damm 15, Lübben

☎ 03546 2 25 00

Lutherstadt Wittenberg

Statues of Martin Luther and Melanchthon on Holzmarkt are unperturbed by the cold.

ONE OF THE GREATEST UPHEAVALS IN WESTERN SOCIETY began in this attractive Saxon town 1.5 hours by train (62 miles/100 km) southwest of Berlin. On October 31, 1517, Catholic scholar Martin Luther (1483–1546) hammered his 95 theses against abuses in the Church to the main door of the Schlosskirche at the edge of town—or so the legend goes. What is indisputable is that he launched the Reformation that split the Christian Church in Western Europe.

Lutherstadt Wittenberg

🔼 p. 209 A3

Visitor information

www.wittenberg.de

✉ Schlossplatz 2

☎ 03491 49 86 10

🚗 Car: A9 toward Leipzig. Train: From Berlin Ostbahnhof (1–1.5 hours)

Today a bronze door with the theses inscribed in it, a monument to Luther erected by Prussian king Friedrich Wilhelm IV, stands in place of the original wooden door, which was destroyed with much of the church in a fire in 1760.

Four years after Luther attracted the wrath of Rome for his 95 impertinent theses, the world's first Protestant service took place in the **Stadtkirche St. Marien** in the center of the compact old town. Luther gave lectures here and later married an ex-nun in the church. His friend, artist Lucas Cranach the Elder (1472–1553), who once lived in Wittenberg, painted the altar.

To gain a perspective on all this upheaval, visit the whitewashed **Lutherhaus** *(Collegienstrasse 54, tel 03491 4 20 30, www.martinluther.de, closed Mon. & Nov.–March, $$)*. This museum in the house where Luther lived from 1508 contains artifacts, furniture, and multimedia displays. There is an extensive collection of portraits of Luther, not all of them particularly flattering. Another section, the Schatzkammer (treasury), holds religious relics.

A brisk walk from the Lutherhaus toward the town center takes you to the restored Renaissance **Melanchthon Haus** *(Collegienstrasse 60, tel 03491 4 20 30, www.martinluther.de, closed Mon. & Nov.–March, $$)*, where Luther's supporter Philipp Melanchthon (1497–1560) lived. It now contains a museum on his life and times. Not far off is the house where Luther was born, **Luthers Geburtshaus** *(Lutherstrasse 15, tel 03491 4 20 30, www.martinluther.de, closed Mon. & Nov.–March, $)*. The monuments relating to Luther's life were together declared a UNESCO World Heritage site in 1996. ∎

Schloss Branitz in Cottbus is as remarkable for its gardens as for the building itself.

More excursions from Berlin

BRANDENBURG AN DER HAVEL

This ancient town, whose historic center is split into three parts intersected by the Havel River, Beetzsee lake, and canals, has gone through some ups and downs. Mostly destroyed in the Thirty Years' War and badly damaged in World War II, it remained neglected in GDR times, too. Today it makes a pretty excursion about one hour southwest of Berlin. The oldest building is the **Dom St. Peter und Paul** *(Burghof, tel 03381 211 22 21, museum $)* on the Dominsel (cathedral island) in the heart of the old town. The original 12th-century cathedral was expanded in Gothic style in the following two centuries and renovated several times thereafter. In spite of work to stabilize the bog-ridden foundations in the 20th century, it is still in danger of keeling over (13 million euros are to be spent on this and general restoration). Inside are some precious medieval altars, the pretty **Bunte Kapelle** (Colorful Chapel), and a museum. From here, a stroll around the Dominsel, across to **Neustadt** and then **Altstadt** is a pleasant way to spend a few hours. Of the half dozen other churches, the most engaging is the early 15th-century brick **St. Katharinenkirche**
(Katharinenkirchplatz 2, tel 03381 52 11 62) in Neustadt, dedicated to St. Catherine. On the Neustadt side of the Havel River, when approaching from Dominsel, is the medieval **Mühlenturm** (Mill Tower), which acted as a customs checkpoint and prison when Neustadt and Dominsel were still separate villages.

🅰 p. 209 A4 **Visitor information**
✉ Steinstrasse 66–67 ☎ 03381 58 58 58, www.stadt-brandenburg.de

CHORIN

The village of Chorin is dominated by its redbrick *Kloster,* or monastery, and for once it is not yet another example of the late 19th-century north German predilection for neo-Gothic building, but the real McCoy. Cistercian monks started building the monastery in 1273. Although it fell into disuse in the 16th century and was half-heartedly meddled with in subsequent centuries, the monastery is surprisingly intact. At its heart is the early Gothic *Klosterkirche,* which was much restored in the 19th century. Also well preserved are the central cloister and ambulatory, which you reach through the imposing western facade. Just to the south of the monastery you can

More excursions from Berlin

climb a hill for a nice view over the monastery and surrounding area. The monastery is the setting for the **Choriner Musiksommer** series of concerts on most weekends from June to August.

🅰 p. 209 C5 ✉ Amt Chorin 11 ☎ 033366 7 03 77, www.kloster-chorin.com 🆂 $

COTTBUS

The main reason for heading southeast to Cottbus (population 105,000), which lies by the Spree River, is the magnificent **Schloss Branitz** *(Robinienweg 5, tel 0355 7 51 50, www.pueckler-museum.de, closed Mon. Nov.–April, $$).* In the von Pückler family since 1696, the property became subject to the gardening craze of Hermann von Pückler-Muskau (1785–1871) when he moved here in 1845. The 1,483 acres (600 ha) of planned gardens that he created offer delightful walks. The Schloss, a dignified mansion, is home to a museum on the gardener-prince's life and times as well as local art. The town is also proud of its art nouveau theater, for the architecture as well as the productions. Cottbus considers itself a bicultural town, with its German and Sorbian history woven together (see p. 229). Find out more about this ancient minority at the **Wendisches Museum** *(Mühlenstrasse 12, tel 0355 79 49 30, www.wendisches-museum.de, closed Mon., $).*

🅰 p. 209 D3 **Visitor information** ✉ Berliner Platz 6 ☎ 0355 7 54 20, www.cottbus.de/tourismus

NEURUPPIN

Almost completely enclosed by its 15th-century walls, the old town core of Neuruppin, about an hour by train northwest from Berlin's Charlottenburg station, makes for a pleasant stroll. Located on the 9-mile-long (14 km) **Ruppiner See** (Ruppiner Lake), it is best known as the birthplace of Theodor Fontane (1819–1898), one of Germany's greatest 19th-century novelists. The grand, late 18th-century **Gymnasium** *(Schulplatz),* or high school, hosts exhibitions and a Fontane research center. Not far away is

Fontane's 18th-century **birthplace** *(Karl-Marx-Strasse 84, closed to the public),* where his father ran a pharmacy. The **Klosterkirche St. Trinitatis** *(Niemöllerplatz)* was begun in the 13th century but most of what you see today was redesigned by Karl Friedrich Schinkel (who was born in Neuruppin) in the mid-19th century. Around the lake are bathing spots and small beaches.

🅰 p. 209 B5 **Visitor information** ✉ Rheinsberger Tor, Karl-Marx-Strasse 1 ☎ 03391 4 54 60, www.neuruppin.de

RHEINSBERG

The future Friedrich II, tired of the thrashings and martial treatment meted out by his soldier-king father, Friedrich Wilhelm I, may well have considered the four years he spent as a young man in Rheinsberg the happiest of his life. His father bought the Renaissance residence, which itself had replaced an earlier medieval moated castle, in 1734. Young Friedrich oversaw much of its transformation into a baroque palace overlooking **Grienericksee,** a pretty lake. He later passed the castle on to his brother Heinrich. From 1802 until after World War II, it could not be visited. Today you can see the sparsely furnished but impressive **Schloss Rheinsberg** *(Mühlenstrasse 1, tel 033931 72 60, closed Mon.)* and wander through its romantic gardens. Inside, you will observe some ceiling frescoes by Antoine Pesne (1683–1757), for instance those depicting Apollo and the goddesses of dawn and night in the broad **Spiegelsaal** (Hall of Mirrors), one of the most attractive rooms in the palace, although today bereft of mirrors. The **Muschelsaal** (Shell Room) is one of the oddest spaces, its ceiling festooned with mussel and snail shells. Long after young Friedrich's time, the cheeky satirical essayist of 1920s Berlin, Kurt Tucholsky, came here with his sweetheart. He published a book on the experience in 1912: *Rheinsberg—A Picture Book for Lovers.*

🅰 p. 209 B6 **Visitor information** ✉ Rhinpassage, Rinstrasse 19 ☎ 033931 3 95 10, www.rheinsberg-tourismus.de ■

Travelwise

Trams, trains, and buses will get you anywhere you need to go in Berlin.

TRAVELWISE INFORMATION.

PLANNING YOUR TRIP

WHEN TO GO

All seasons in Berlin have their charms, but by and large, the spring, summer, and early fall are the best times to explore the city. The big exception is arguably December, when the Christmas markets scattered around the area have a certain magic. Some people say you haven't lived until you've popped the bubbly on New Year's Eve at the Brandenburger Tor.

Holidays—notably Easter, Christmas, and New Year's—tend to attract more visitors. To avoid the crowds, enjoy a festival or two, and have a shot at good weather, try visiting either in April through early June, or in late September to early November. There are fewer visitors then and lines at the museums are shorter. Berlin crawls with vacationers in July and August, but on the upside, the weather is more reliable and the city hums with outdoor events.

CLIMATE

Berlin has a relatively cool, humid climate that has more in common with Moscow than Paris. All told, the seasons are more extreme than the German average, with hotter summers and harsher winters. Cold fronts roll in regularly from central Russia, bringing freezing temperatures and moderate, but usually not paralyzing, amounts of snow.

In summer, from June to late August, the mercury can soar into the low 90s°F (low 30s°C). That's when Berliners make the most of life by eating, drinking, and making merry outdoors. Indian summer can also be delightful, with blue skies, fluffy clouds, and trees turning to gold.

AVERAGE DAYTIME TEMPERATURES:

Spring: mid-March to mid-May 50°F (10°C)
Summer: mid-May to the end of August 65°F (18°C)
Fall: September to mid-November 52°F (11°C)
Winter: mid-November to mid-March 35°F (2°C)

FESTIVALS & EVENTS

Berlin's status as capital, political and cultural—as well as its admirable trade-fair facilities—means the annual calendar is packed with a wealth of cultural events, festivals, and fairs. The main ones are listed here.

JANUARY
Grüne Woche
The venerable "Green Week" is a consumer fair for food, agriculture, and gardening held at the trade-fair grounds. If nothing else, it's worth visiting to sample a zillion cuisines and catch the horse shows. Tel 030 30 38 20 28, www .gruenewoche.de

FEBRUARY
International Film Festival (Berlinale)
The stars come out, both Hollywood and German, as hundreds of movies are shown at cinemas around town. Many performances sell out fast, so check the schedules in the Berlin entertainment magazines *Zitty* or *TIP*. Tickets are available at cinemas and ticket offices. 2nd–3rd week of Feb. Tel 030 25 92 00, www.berlinale.de

MARCH
International Tourism Fair
This fair is the world's largest travel show, with exhibitors from all over the planet. Held at the trade-fair grounds, it's open to the public on weekends. Expect to tote bags of brochures. Tel 030 30 38 55 55, www.itb-berlin.com

APRIL
Festival Days (Festtage)
This ten-day festival of gala concerts and operas assembles some of the world's finest conductors, soloists, and orchestras. Concerts are held at the Berliner Philharmonie, operas at the Staatsoper. Tel 030 20 35 45 55, www.staatsoper berlin.org

MAY
Carnival of Cultures
Held in Kreuzberg, this vibrant weeklong carnival features a street parade of costumed characters posing on floats and playing music. Tel 030 60 97 70 22, www.karneval-berlin.de

JUNE
Potsdam Music Festival
Thousands of music fans flock to nearby Potsdam for classical concerts and plays, held on summer evenings in the Sanssouci gardens or the palace theater. The undisputed highlight is the final concert with fireworks. Two weeks in early June. Tel 0331 288 8828, www.musikfestspiele potsdam.de

Christopher Street Day
The city's biggest gay parade draws several hundred thousand fans. Late June. Tel 030 23 62 86 32, www.csd-berlin.de

JULY
Classic Open Air
A series of classical concerts held on Gendarmenmarkt. A big social occasion with heavyweight talent like Montserrat Caballé or Ute Lemper. Early July. Tel 030 315 75 40, www.classicopenair.de

Love Parade
Back from the dead, this legendary techno-parade draws about a million ravers who treat sexuality not as a right but as a creed. The Tiergarten and clubs vibrate at full decibels, nonstop. Mid-July. Tel 030 308 81 20, www.loveparade.net

Berlin Fashion Week
International trade shows for professionals are held at several venues, but the public can attend some events. A catwalk is usually set up in the Sony Center, and the Walk of Fashion shows off the models on a stroll through Mitte. Late July. Tel 030 30 38 21 93, www.fashion-week.de

AUGUST
International Consumer Electronics Fair
The largest event of its kind worldwide, and one of the oldest, this mammoth fair hosts a thousand-plus exhibitors airing the latest gadgets and technical advancements. Tel 030 30 38 21 47, www.ifa-berlin.de

SEPTEMBER
Musikfest Berlin
A two-week blowout of classical music, including lesser-known and new works performed by renowned orchestras, ensembles, and soloists in the Berliner Philharmonie. Tel 030 25 48 91 00, www.berlinerfestspiele.de

Berlin Marathon
Come rain or shine, tens of thousands of runners and about a million spectators turn up, sooner or later, at the Brandenburger Tor. Late Sept. www.berlin-marathon.com

OCTOBER
Art Forum Berlin
An international fair of contemporary art hosted by Berlin's top galleries. From video and photography to paintings, sculptures, and whizbang multimedia installations, it's all here. Tel 030 69 6969, www.art-forum-berlin.com

NOVEMBER
JazzFest Berlin
A blue-ribbon jazz festival with performances held at venues throughout Berlin. The off-festival scene thrives as well, offering free concerts. Three days in early Nov. Tel 030 25 48 92 79, www.jazzfest-berlin.de

DECEMBER
Christmas markets
Berlin's many *Weihnachts-märkte*—as many as 60 in total—are definitely something special, with stalls selling handicrafts, *Glühwein*, spiced cookies, and much more. The biggest ones include Alexanderplatz (stalls and a decent fun fair), Opernplatz (upscale stalls), and Breitscheidplatz (at the Gedächtniskirche, with still more stalls). Late Nov.–around Dec. 21. (See pp. 146–147)

WHAT TO TAKE
If you're coming to Berlin to enjoy the city's architecture and historic monuments, bring comfortable footwear. The weather can be unpredictable, so even in summer bring along a waterproof jacket and layers of clothing. The sun can be intense, so make sure you pack hats and sunscreen, especially if you're going to be outdoors for long periods.

Don't forget any prescription drugs you might need and a second pair of glasses if you wear them. Everything else is readily available. Pharmacies (*Apotheke*, recognizable by the red "A" sign) are open during normal business hours, and in each Berlin district, one is open evenings and Sundays for emergencies. Drugstores (*Drogerien*) sell a limited range of nonprescription medicines, but for anything stronger than toothpaste, you'll have to hit the pharmacy.

Lastly, don't forget the essentials: passport, driver's license, ATM card (or traveler's checks), and insurance documents.

INSURANCE
It pays to take out a travel insurance policy. Make sure you have adequate coverage for medical treatment and expenses, including repatriation, and also for baggage and money loss. It's also a good idea to take photocopies of important documents and keep them separate from the originals, in case the latter are stolen.

ENTRY FORMALITIES
Visitors from the United States, Canada, Australia, New Zealand, Israel, Hong Kong, Japan, South Korea, the European Union, and most non-E.U. European countries can visit Germany for three months without a visa. People visiting from other countries need to apply for a visa in advance from the German embassy in their own country. To stay more than three months, you should apply to the German embassy in your own country for a residence permit. This transaction is usually no problem if you can prove you have the means of supporting yourself and a legitimate reason for living in the country.

FURTHER READING
Aimée & Jaguar by Erica Fischer. A tender wartime memoir of two women, one the wife of a German soldier and the other a Jew, who pick the wrong time to fall in love. A pageturner and literary award winner, the book was made into a movie in 1999.

Berlin: The Downfall 1945 by Antony Beevor. An excellent account of the last days of World War II, seen from the contrasting viewpoints of city dwellers and of advancing Russian and American troops. The book abounds with personal vignettes of those trapped in the city.

Berlin Rising: The Biography of a City by Anthony Read and David Fisher. An excellent social history told through a range of extraordinary personalities, from colorful people on the street to the often bizarre Hohenzollern princes who ruled the city before 1918.

Berlin, Then and Now by Tony Le Tissier. Charts the city's history since the Weimar Republic in brilliant black-and-white photographs and somewhat stodgy text. The author was a warden of Spandau Prison when arch-Nazi Rudolf Hess committed suicide.

A Dance between Flames: Berlin between the Wars by Anton Gill. An evocative description of Berlin's creative frenzy between the world wars. Includes a wealth of material on the city's grand café society, criminals, theater arts, and regimented system of education.

Goodbye to Berlin by Christopher Isherwood. A hilarious, semi-autobiographical tale of a young man lost in the Berlin of the 1920s. The book later formed the basis of the classic film *Cabaret.*

Man without a Face by Markus Wolf and Anne McElvoy. The autobiography of Wolf, the wily chief of East Germany's much feared secret police, the Stasi. A fascinating look into the Stasi's bag of tricks and Wolf's own devious mind.

The Rise and Fall of the Third Reich by William L. Shirer. Written by CBS's wartime correspondent in Berlin, this vivid, very readable history of Adolf Hitler's "Thousand Year" empire is widely regarded as the seminal work on the topic. After publication, it was reprinted 20 times in the first year alone.

Spies beneath Berlin by David Stafford. A gripping true-life account of how MI6 and the CIA tunneled under the Soviet sector of Cold War Berlin and tapped into the Red Army's secret communications. A section of the tunnel can be viewed in Berlin's Allied Museum.

The Wall: The People's Story by Christopher Hilton. Based on experiences of those whose lives were profoundly affected by the wall on both sides: leading politicians, Allied and East German military, and ordinary people.

HOW TO GET TO BERLIN

BY PLANE
There are few direct flights to Berlin from overseas. At the time of writing, only Continental and Delta among the U.S. major carriers were offering direct links from the States. Often you'll be routed through a larger hub such as London, Amsterdam, or Frankfurt, where you'll have to catch a connecting flight.

Berlin has not one but three airports, all within the city limits. To the northwest, Tegel Airport serves mainly destinations within Germany and Western Europe, while in the south, Schönefeld Airport links the city with much of the rest of the globe. The third airport is tiny Tempelhof airport, which handles only domestic flights. By 2010 all air traffic will be shifted to the new Berlin-Brandenburg Airport being built at Schönefeld, while Tegel and Tempelhof will be closed. The airports have a single flight information desk (tel 0180 500 01 86) and a website at www.berlin-airport.de.

All airports can be reached by train, bus, or taxi in roughly 30 minutes from downtown. (A taxi fare into Berlin will cost €15–20.) Tegel is linked to the Mitte District by the TXL ExpressBus and to Charlottenburg by Bus X9 or 109. Schönefeld airport is an easy train ride away via the AirportExpress to and from the main Lehrter Bahnhof and other central train stations. From the station you can connect by bus, U-Bahn, or S-Bahn to anywhere in the city. Tempelhof is served by the U6 (station: Platz der Luftbrücke).

AIRLINES SERVING BERLIN

Air Berlin tel 0180 57 37 800
American Airlines tel 01803 24 23 24
British Airways tel 01805 26 65 22
Continental tel 01803 2126 10
Delta tel 01803 33 78 80
EasyJet tel 01803 65 43 21
Germanwings tel 0900 19 19 100
Lufthansa tel 01803 80 38 03

BY TRAIN
The German train system is frighteningly efficient, making it a snap to reach Berlin from the rest of Germany and other European countries. Many long-distance trains (including the bulletlike ICEs) stop at both the main Hauptbahnhof-Lehrter Bahnhof and Ostbahnhof stations. If you have a Deutsche Bahn Bahncard discount card, you can travel on any S-Bahn (but not U-Bahn) for free.

Deutsche Bahn offers reduced rates that are in constant flux, and even Germans are confused from time to time. For ticket and time information in English, call tel 11861 (from anywhere in Germany), or look it up on www.bahn.de.

BY BUS
Berlin is well connected to the rest of Europe by long-distance bus. Most buses arrive at and depart from the ZOB (Zentraler Omnibusbahnhof), the central bus station, in Charlottenburg opposite the stately Funkturm (radio tower).

BY CAR
If you've got wheels, the Autobahn A10 is a ring road around Berlin that links it with other German and foreign cities. Drivers from Britain can bring their car to Germany via ferry and hovercraft services to the Netherlands. P&O North Sea Ferries (www.ponsf.com), Stenaline (U.K. tel 08705 70 70

70, www.stenaline.com), and DFDS Scandinavian Seaways (U.K. tel 08705 33 30 00, www.dfdsseaways.co.uk) will all take vehicles. After crossing the Channel, plan on eight to ten hours' driving time to Berlin.

GETTING AROUND

BY SUBWAY, BUS, & TRAM

Throughout Berlin, a tightly woven network of buses, trams (Stassenbahn), subways (U-Bahn), and commuter rail (S-Bahn) will get you where you want to go. The U- and S-Bahns run from 4:30 a.m. till at least 12:30 a.m., with some lines still running until 1:30 a.m. Then the buses take over with a nighttime service.

Combined local transportation tickets are valid on buses, trams, and U-Bahns. Buy tickets from either ticket machines at U- or S-Bahn stops or, in the case of buses and trams, from either the conductor or ticket machine on board. Before you travel, you must validate your ticket in one of the time-stamping machines installed at the entrance of every bus and U-Bahn/S-Bahn station.

Berlin is divided into three travel zones: Zones A and B include the urban area, and zone C is farther away from the center of Berlin (including Potsdam). Most destinations can be reached with a single A + B ticket.

The WelcomeCard (available at ticket offices and many Berlin hotels) is a public transportation ticket valid for 72 hours on all buses, trams, and trains within the A, B, and C fare zones. In addition, WelcomeCard holders are entitled to free admissions, or up to 50 percent reductions, on guided tours or walks, boat trips, museums, theaters, and leisure facilities in Berlin and Potsdam. For a good rolling tour of the city, bus lines 100 and 200 take you past all the main sights.

BY TRAIN

For excursions farther afield such as Dresden or Leipzig, you'll need to take the train. Tickets are available from the counters of Deutsche Bahn, the German national railway, at the main Hauptbahnhof or the Ostbahnhof.

BY CAR

Germany has a huge network of toll-free expressways (Autobahnen). If you're not in a hurry, secondary roads (Landstrassen or Bundesstrassen) are usually more picturesque. Since reunification, the network in the east is rapidly being modernized, though you'll still encounter a number of charming but bumpy cobblestone roads.

BY TAXI

You'll find taxi stands at airports, train and subway stations, and throughout the city. You can also hail taxis in the street. Taxi drivers in Berlin operate on two tariffs: one for short journeys from taxi stands, and a second for trips ordered by telephone.

PRACTICAL ADVICE

COMMUNICATIONS

POST OFFICES

Berlin's main post office is located at Neues Kranzler Eck, Joachimstaler Strasse 7, 10623 Berlin near the Zoologischer Garten station. It's open 8 a.m. to midnight Monday to Saturday, and from 10 a.m. on Sundays and holidays. There are post office branches around town with shorter hours, and Sunday hours at those in airports and large railroad stations. Buy stamps at the post office counter or from automatic stamp machines. Mail sent to you general delivery (Postlagernde Sendungen) must include the zip code of the specific post office. Take your passport when picking up mail.

TELEPHONES

Public telephones run by Deutsche Telecom are located in U- and S-Bahn stations, post offices, restaurants, cafés and on street corners. The rate from telephone booths is about 15 cents a minute. Most public telephones are now card operated. Phone cards (Telefonkarten) can be bought at any post office or newspaper shop for €5, €10, and €20. Note that numbers prefixed with 0900, 0180 or 0190 are toll numbers.

Telephone rates are generally lower between 6 p.m. and 7 a.m. and on weekends. To call a German number from abroad, dial the international code (011 from the United States and Canada, 00 from the U.K.), then the code for Germany (49), followed by the number, omitting the first 0.

To make an international call from Germany, dial 00 followed by the country code and the rest of the number, deleting the initial 0 if there is one. Country codes include Australia 61, Canada 1, U.K. 44, United States 1.

USEFUL TELEPHONE NUMBERS

International information: 11834
National information: 11837 (in English)

CONVERSIONS

1 kilo = 2.2 lbs
1 liter = 0.2642 U.S gallons
1 kilometer = 0.62 mile

Women's clothing

U.S.	8	10	12	14	16	18
European	36	38	40	42	44	46

Men's clothing

U.S.	36	38	40	42	44	46
European	46	48	50	52	54	56

Women's shoes

U.S.	6/6.5	7/7.5	8/8.5	9/9.5
European	37	38	39	40

Men's shoes

U.S.	8	8.5	9.5	10.5	11.5	12
European	41	42	43	44	45	46

ELECTRICITY

German sockets are of the round, continental two-pin variety, so you'll need a converter to use equipment with U.S. or U.K. plugs. The voltage (220, 50 Hz) is fine for British gear, but you'll still need a plug adapter. Airport shops routinely carry this item.

ETIQUETTE & LOCAL CUSTOMS

Berlin serves as a useful corrective to Germany's reputation for formality. The capital city hasn't forgotten the Roaring '20s and is, in short, a very casual, elbow-rubbing kind of place. Except for hoity-toity dining rooms or opera nights, you needn't dress up most of the time. Some nightclubs may have dress codes, though, that are enforced by choosy bouncers. Business attire tends to be stylish casual.

Shaking hands is common among both men and women, at least at first meeting. Friends and acquaintances, and especially the younger set, will exchange a hug and peck on both cheeks. Do not use first names or the informal *Du* unless invited to do so, but this being Berlin, younger people will dispense with the formal *Sie* more or less immediately. In formal situations, people might introduce themselves as *Herr* or *Frau* (perhaps even *Frau Doktor*), and if they do, that's how they want to be addressed.

If invited to someone's home, take along a little something like flowers or a bottle of wine. A polite thank-you card or call the next day is much appreciated.

Berliners are renowned for their *Schnauze* (big mouth) and won't hesitate to express themselves on any imaginable topic. To contradict John Cleese's character in *Fawlty Towers*, it is quite all right to mention The War as long as you do it with tact and to the point. More than

six decades on, the debate continues and many Berliners feel a responsibility to join in. What doesn't go down well is a victor's mentality laden with gloating. Remember that most living Germans were born after the war in a thoroughly democratic regime set up in the postwar period by the Allies.

HOLIDAYS

All banks and post offices and many museums, galleries, and stores close in Berlin on the following holidays. Many stores and businesses are also shut on Christmas Eve and New Year's Eve.

January 1—New Year's Day
March/April—Good Friday
March/April—Easter Monday
May 1—Labor Day
May/June—Ascension Day
May/June—Pentecost (Whit) Monday
October 3—Day of German Unity
December 25 & 26—Christmas

MEDIA, NEWSPAPERS, & MAGAZINES

The main broadsheets are the left-leaning *Berliner Zeitung,* the center-right *Tagesspiegel,* and the more moderate *Berliner Morgenpost.* The sensationalist *BZ* has the largest circulation, roughly equivalent to the American *National Enquirer* or Britain's *Sun.* The *Berliner Kurier* is another saucy tabloid.
    Berlin doesn't have a heavyweight national daily, so serious readers resort to newspapers published elsewhere in Germany. These include the liberal *Sueddeutsche Zeitung (SZ),* the conservative *Frankfurter Allgemeine Zeitung (FAZ),* the leftish *Frankfurter Rundschau (FR),* and the conservative *Die Welt.* Popular national tabloids are *Bildzeitung* and *Express.*

Weekly periodicals also play an important role. On Monday the hard-hitting magazines *Der Spiegel* and *Focus* are published,

on Thursday the sophisticated *Die Zeit* and the more entertaining, gossipy magazines *Stern* and *Bunte.* American and British newspapers are available in airports, major railroad stations, and most large hotels.

ENTERTAINMENT LISTINGS

The twice-monthly *Zitty* and *TIP* are the best magazines for listings of entertainment and cultural events. The free event guides *Flyer* and *030* are available in many cafés and clubs. A thin monthly English-language magazine, *The Ex-Berliner,* provides somewhat useful listings. The tourist office hands out *New Berlin,* a free city guide with tips and recommendations for dining and nightlife. Local newspapers also carry weekly supplements with listings.

TELEVISION

German television relies heavily on the two national networks ARD and ZDF, which form the parent networks for a host of regional public channels. Among them, RBB and TVB are the regional broadcasters for Berlin-Brandenburg. Stiff competition comes from the private channels, above all RTL and SAT 1. The most authoritative news broadcasts are the ZDF evening news *Heute* at 7 p.m. and the ARD *Tagesschau* at 8 p.m. Channels available in English include CNN, NBC, MTV Europe, and BBC World.

RADIO

As you'll hear if you take a taxi, most people listen to *Radio Eins,* the commercial rock-and-pop channel. If you seek English-language programs, tune in to BBC World Service at 90.2 or Rock Star FM at 87.9, which carries American news bulletins.

MONEY MATTERS

In 2002 the euro (€) replaced the beloved Deutsche Mark as Germany's official currency. There are 100 cents to 1 euro.

Banknotes come in denominations of 5, 10, 20, 50, and 100, as well as the rarer 200 and 500 bills. Coins consist of €1 and €2 as well as 1, 2, 5, 10, 20, and 50 cents.

Most major banks have ATMs for bank cards and credit cards, with instructions in a number of languages. Cash and traveler's checks can be exchanged in banks and currency booths at railroad stations and airports.

OPENING TIMES
Banks
8 a.m to 4 p.m. (5:30 p.m. on Thurs.); some in outlying areas close for lunch between 1 p.m. and 2 p.m. All banks are closed Saturday and Sunday.

Museums
Generally 9 a.m. to 6 p.m. Many museums are closed on Monday but stay open later on Thursday evenings.

Pharmacies
Open during store hours and on a rotation schedule to cover nights and weekends.

Post Offices
Generally 8 a.m. to 6 p.m. weekdays and until noon on Saturday.

Stores
Weekdays 8:30 a.m. to 6:30 p.m. (till 8 p.m. for many department stores and on Thurs.). On Saturday, hours are 8:30 a.m. to 8 p.m., although many smaller shops close noon to 2 p.m. With a few exceptions, stores are closed on Sunday.

RELIGION
Berlin is a remarkably diverse place when it comes to religion, the product of waves of immigrants from around the world. The city has grown secular, however, and less than half of Berliners are regular churchgoers. Of this group, about one-third are of a Christian faith, with Protestants far outnumbering Roman Catholics. The Islamic

community makes up about 7 percent of the population. Berlin also has a tiny but growing Jewish community, bolstered by an influx of Russian Jews.

Regular services are held in English at the All Saints Catholic Church at Hüttenweg 46 in Dahlem and the Faith Christian Fellowship at Hauptstrasse 134 in Schöneberg-Tempelhof (both 10 a.m. Sun.), as well as the small egalitarian Jewish synagogue at Oranienburger Strasse 29 (6 p.m. Fri., 7 p.m. in summer).

RESTROOMS
Self-cleaning toilet cabins are usually located near big railroad and bus stations. Large department stores have public restrooms available for a small fee (usually 25 cents). Every bar or café has a restroom, signposted Toilette or WC and marked Herren (men) and Damen (women). Men can also slip into the Café Achteck, a euphemism for the old-fashioned public urinals still found in parts of Berlin.

TIME DIFFERENCES
Germany runs on Central European Time, one hour ahead of Greenwich Mean Time and six hours ahead of Eastern Standard Time. Noon in Germany is 6 a.m. in New York. Remember that Germany uses the 24-hour clock, so that 8 p.m. becomes "20 Uhr" in German.

TIPPING
By law, sales tax and a service charge are included in your restaurant bill. It's customary, though, to include a small tip of 5 to 10 percent if you're happy with the service. Tips in taxis vary widely—some people round up to the nearest euro, others pay 5 to 10 percent. Bellhops typically get €1 per bag in the top-end hotels.

TRAVELERS WITH DISABILITIES
Germany is fairly well set up for the needs of disabled travelers,

especially the wheelchair-bound. There are access ramps and elevators in many public buildings, including restrooms, train stations, museums, theaters, and cinemas. On public transportation, buses with a blue wheelchair symbol have special ramps, but quite a few S- and U-Bahn stations still don't have elevators.

For information and support, contact the Berlin Disabled Association at Jägerstrasse 63D (tel 030 204 38 47, www.bbv-ev.de). Tourist offices also have details of disabled facilities included in their brochures.

VISITOR INFORMATION
The city's tourist authority, Berlin Tourism and Marketing (BTM), is helpful and well organized. The main Infostore is on the ground floor of the Europa-Center at Budapester Strasse 45 near the Gedächtniskirche (open 10 a.m.–7 p.m. Mon.–Sat. and 10 a.m.–6 p.m. Sun.). There are other branches in the south wing of the Brandenburger Tor, the downstairs lobby of the Fernsehturm TV tower on Alexanderplatz, the Reichstag pavilion, and the new main Lehrter Bahnhof train station (all open 10 a.m.–6 p.m.). Smaller InfoPoints can be found around town, including the main hall of Tegel Airport. Their call center (for hotels, tickets, and general inquiries) is tel 030 25 00 25. The best all-around web resource, run by the BTM, is www.berlin-tourist-information.de.

EMERGENCIES
CRIME & POLICE
Dial the emergency number 110 to contact the police. If you have been robbed or need help for any reason, there are police stations all over Berlin, including ones at Jägerstrasse 48 near Gendarmenmarkt and Joachimstaler Strasse 14–19 just

EMERGENCIES

south of Zoologischer Garten station. The police will take a statement, cancel your credit cards, and provide telephone facilities and help with contacting your embassy if necessary. If in trouble on trains, you should contact the train police *(Bahnpolizei)*, with offices at all major stations.

The German police can be identified by their somber green-and-beige uniforms and green-and-silver police cruisers. (Autobahn police drive stylish new blue-and-silver vehicles, the future European standard.) Motorized police known as the *Verkehrspolizei* patrol the streets, roads, and motorways. Many German police officers speak English and are approachable and easy to find in busy areas.

EMBASSIES & CONSULATES

U.S. Embassy
Neustädtische Kirchstrasse 4–5,
10117 Berlin
Tel 030 238 51 74
Fax 030 238 62 90

U.S. Consulate
Clayallee 170,
14195 Berlin
Tel 030 832 92 33
Fax 030 830 51 215

Canadian Embassy
Leipziger Platz 17,
10117 Berlin
Tel 030 20 31 20
Fax 030 20 31 25 90

British Embassy
Wilhelmstrasse 70–71,
10117 Berlin
Tel 030 20 45 70
Fax 030 20 45 75 94

EMERGENCY PHONE NUMBERS

**Fire department &
    ambulance** *(Feuerwehr)* 112
Police *(Polizeinotruf)* 110
Medical emergency *(Notarzt,*
    for house calls) 030 31 00 31

Dental emergency 030 89 00
    43 33
Poison Control 030 192 40

WHAT TO DO IN A CAR ACCIDENT

If you have an accident or serious breakdown on the Autobahn, seek out one of the special orange telephones that are set at regular intervals along the shoulder of the highway. An operator will answer and inform emergency services. Otherwise, the emergency number 112 can be called on any telephone, including mobile phones, free of charge.

Be sure to move the damaged vehicle out of the flow of traffic, turn on the hazard blinker, and position a red warning triangle about 165 yards (150 m) behind the vehicle. Next, exchange names, addresses, telephone numbers, and registration numbers and ask to see the other party's driver's license to confirm these details. You should also make a note of the events leading to the collision, with drawings, which you may need as part of your insurance claim. The police must always be called, regardless of whether injuries occurred.

The German automobile club ADAC, which you can join on the spot, offers an emergency breakdown service (tel 0180 222 22 22). You may already have reciprocal membership if you belong to a similar organization in your home country.

HEALTH

Apart from party fatigue, there are few health risks involved in visiting Berlin. For minor ailments, qualified staff at pharmacies offer expert advice. Doctors' consulting hours are normally 9 to noon and 3 to 5 p.m., except weekends. For urgent attention outside consulting hours, go to a hospital *(Krankenhaus)*. German medical treatment and facilities are generally very good. The best-

known hospital in Berlin is the Charité (Schumann Strasse 20–21, tel 030 450 50), which has a 24-hour emergency ward.

LOST PROPERTY

Your travel insurance should cover the loss or theft of your property if you are not already covered by your home insurance. Theft must be reported to the police so you can obtain a certificate confirming that the crime has been reported. The national railroad run by Deutsche Bahn has its own lost property office (tel 01805 99 05 99), as does the Berlin urban transportation network BVG (tel 030 194 49). For items lost elsewhere, try asking at the Berlin lost property office (Zentrales Fundbüro, Platz der Luftbrücke 6, tel 030 69 95). It's south of the center in Tempelhof.

LOST OR STOLEN CREDIT CARDS

American Express (AE) tel
    069 97 97 10 00
Diners Club (DC) tel 0180 5
    33 66 95
MasterCard (MC) tel 069 79
    33 19 10
VISA (V) 0800 81 49 100

HOTELS & RESTAURANTS

Travelers who have wined, dined, and slumbered in other European cities will find their pocket money goes a long way in Berlin. After reunification the hotel and gastronomy sector expanded rapidly, and although the boom stuttered, the number of guest beds continues to rise: 84,000 at last count, more than in New York City. This is an investment in the future, and good news for visitors as the excess capacity means rates are well below those of, say, London or Paris. And you'll find affordable places to stay even during high-octane events such as the Berlinale film festival.

HOTELS
Charlottenburg and other districts of west Berlin still have the most options, but the east is catching up fast. Central Berlin is arguably the most inviting area, in terms of both culture and nightlife. Here you'll find the bulk of the museums, art galleries, and restaurants that capture the capital's newfound self-confidence. By contrast, the west can feel a bit staid, but there's a refined charm in the placid squares and boutique-lined streets that feed into the Kurfürstendamm (Ku'damm).

Many hotels are located in atmospheric surroundings ranging from historic villas and luxury palaces to industrial lofts. Smaller hotels may ooze charm and take up several floors of historic apartment blocks, while designer hotels can offer unforgettable combinations of art and accommodation. There's also a trend toward ecofriendly hotels, with anti-allergenic materials and organic breakfasts.

Some hotels include breakfast in their rates, and we've pointed out this feature where it applies. Breakfasts tend to be a substantial affair with all-you-can-eat buffets and a cornucopia of breads, cold cuts, cheese, jam, and fruits.

Older hotels usually offer a variety of rooms, with either private or communal bathrooms—it pays to check before you book. Ditto for elevators, air-conditioning, direct-dial phones in rooms, and facilities for the disabled. This is less of an issue at newer, more modern places. Also, check the location of your hotel. Many hotels overlook busy streets, and not all have decent soundproofing. Rooms at the rear may be preferable, even if you sacrifice a nicer view.

If you're driving, note that many central hotels do not have their own parking and may direct you to a paid lot or garage nearby. Street parking may be a little tricky in congested areas, although some establishments will provide guests with parking permits.

ONLINE RESOURCES
A good starting point is www.berlin-tourist-information.de, run by the city tourist authority, Berlin Tourismus Marketing (tel 030 25 00 25). It gives details of availability, special offers, location, features, and photos for over 400 of Berlin's hotels and guesthouses. Use www.stadtplandienst.de to check how close you are to the center and to public transportation.

RESTAURANTS
Once a culinary wasteland, Berlin can now hold its own on the world stage. There are thousands of options to choose from, ranging from the corner kebab stand to dinner with belly dancing to gourmet temples. Competition is fierce and prices are reasonable on a European scale.

Local German and Brandenburg specialties prepared with local ingredients are definitely worth exploring. In an expert chef's hands, even rib-sticking fare like traditional *Kassler Rippen* (smoked pork chops) can be terrific. Foreign influences on cuisine are led by the Mediterranean rim and top-notch Asian food can be ordered anywhere in town. Dishes from Eastern Europe, such as borscht or blini, are more common east of the Brandenburger Tor. Spicy kitchens (such as Mexican or Indian) are likely to be toned down to German tastes. Purely vegetarian eateries are few and far between, but most menus will have a list of meatless dishes.

Once you have a table, no one will hassle you to eat up and move on, as dinner (or coffee, or evening drinks) is seen as a social activity. You must remember to ask for the bill at the end of the meal; it is considered rude for the server to bring the bill before you're ready to go. The flip side of all this is that service can be slow.

Smoking is still popular in cafés and restaurants, although large nonsmoking areas are becoming more common. Germany is slowly moving into line with E.U. nonsmoking guidelines: By 2008, nine out of ten restaurants must make at least half of their seats available to nonsmokers.

Tips are usually included in the bill, but most patrons still round up by 5 to 10 percent. Give the server the tip upon payment, rather than leaving it on the table. If your bill is 14 euros, you might hand the server a 20 and say "15." Waiters are happy to split group bills for individuals.

■ UNTER DEN LINDEN & POTSDAMER PLATZ

HOTELS

🏨 GRAND HYATT
🍴 $$$$$
MARLENE-DIETRICH-PLATZ 2, 10785

HOTELS & RESTAURANTS

TEL 030 25 53 12 34
FAX 030 25 53 12 35
www.berlin.hyatt.com
A favorite haunt of movie stars during the Berlin film festival, this modern hotel embedded in Potsdamer Platz has a Euro-Japanese feel, with matte black surfaces and carved cedarwood. Rooms are generously sized and equipped with perks such as heated bathroom floors and Bauhaus art. Leisure options include a rooftop gym, pool, and beauty center.
[i] 342 suites [P] [S1, S2], U2 Potsdamer Platz [ ] [ ] [ ] [ ] [ ] All major cards

HOTEL ADLON KEMPINSKI
$$$$$
UNTER DEN LINDEN 77, 10117
TEL 030 22 61 11 11
FAX 030 22 61 22 22
www.hotel-adlon.de
British club meets art deco at this splendid portal of German history, where Marlene Dietrich was discovered and Joseph Göbbels chased his mistress down the corridor. Badly damaged in World War II, the structure has been restored to its former brilliance. Suites have a view of the Brandenburger Tor, and the elegant restaurant is a byword for exclusivity.
[i] 336 [S1, S2 Unter den Linden] [P] [ ] [ ] [ ] All major cards

RITZ-CARLTON BERLIN
$$$$$
POTSDAMER PLATZ 3, 10785
TEL 030 33 77 77
FAX 030 337 77 55 55
www.ritzcarlton.com
One of Berlin's premier luxury hotels, housed in a retro U.S.-style skyscraper near Potsdamer Platz. Inside, the Ritz-Carlton harks back to the Prussian Empire, with a hushed, elegant lobby and sweeping staircase. Rooms gleam with polished cherrywood, posh marble, and brass fittings—heaven.

[i] 341 [S1, S2, U2] Potsdamer Platz
[P] [ ] [ ] [ ] [ ] All major cards

DORINT SOFITEL AM GENDARMENMARKT
$$$$
CHARLOTTENSTRASSE 50–52, 10117
TEL 030 20 37 50
FAX 030 20 37 51 00
www.dorint.com
This ex-communist hotel on the corner of Gendarmenmarkt, a church-studded square, has benefited from a major facelift. Light floods into the atrium restaurant, the rooftop gym, and even the ballroom via translucent floor tiles. Rooms are on the snug side but comfortable, and the upper-floor balconies are a treat, being level with the stunning dome of the Französicher Dom.
[i] 114 [U2 Stadtmitte], U6 Französische Strasse
[P] [ ] [ ] [ ] [ ] All major cards

THE MANDALA SUITES
$$$–$$$$
FRIEDRICHSTRASSE 185–190, 10117
TEL 030 20 29 20
FAX 030 20 29 29 20
www.themandala.de
All kinds of sophisticates frequent this luxurious, ultra-discrete hideaway on Berlin's swanky Friedrichstrasse. If you want room service, bellboys, and concierges then try someplace else: On offer here are five types of spacious suites, ranging from 430 to 1,100 square feet (40–100 sq m), with a maximum of perks and a minimum of fuss. All have marble baths, walk-in closets, a kitchen, and a modern workspace with Internet and Wi-Fi.
[i] 82 suites [U2, U6] Stadtmitte [P] [ ] [ ] [ ] [ ] All major cards

HOTELS
The cost of a double room without breakfast:
$$$$$	Over $270
$$$$	$200–$270
$$$	$130–$200
$$	$80–$120
$	Under $80

RESTAURANTS
The cost of a three-course dinner without drinks:
$$$$$	Over $80
$$$$	$50–$80
$$$	$35–$50
$$	$20–$35
$	Under $20

Hotels and restaurants are listed alphabetically by price category within each district.
L = lunch; D = dinner

RESTAURANTS

MARGAUX
$$$$–$$$$$
UNTER DEN LINDEN 78
TEL 030 22 65 26 11
A stone's throw from the Brandenburger Tor, the vaunted kitchen of Michael Hoffmann has occupied the front ranks of Berlin's gourmet elite for years. Clad in a princely robe of black onyx, marble, and gold, the interior itself might be worthy of a Michelin rating. The changing five-course meals offer everything a connoisseur of French cuisine can desire, and the wine list is a classy blend of top European and New World vintages.
[ ] 74 [ ] Closed Sun. [S1, S2 Unter den Linden] [ ] All major cards

SOMETHING SPECIAL

VAU
Chef Kolja Kleeberg wanted to become an actor, and in a sense he is, in this movie set of a Michelin-starred restaurant near Gendarmenmarkt. The bright orange walls, wooden floors, and halogen spots are a fitting stage

for his dynamic creations. You might start with the chestnut soup before moving on to breast of pigeon with black root and a dusting of cocoa, polishing it off with braised pineapple and a lemongrass-chili sherbet. The courtyard is open for dining in summer. Reserve, as it's extremely popular.
$$$$–$$$$$
JÄGERSTRASSE 54–55
TEL 030 202 97 30
🍴 115 🕓 Closed Sun.
🚇 U6 Französische Strasse
💳 All major cards

🍴 GUY
$$$
JÄGERSTRASSE 59–60
TEL 030 20 94 26 00
The skillfully prepared Mediterranean cuisine makes this elegant four-level restaurant a top choice near Gendarmenmarkt. The venison with mushrooms and rosemary jus is a winner, and *Jakobsmuscheln* (scallops) on a bed of asparagus is a specialty. Service is snappy and waiters can advise on your choice of 150-odd wines to go with your meal. In summer, tables on the peaceful inner courtyard are sought after.
🍴 120 🕓 Closed Sat. L & Sun. 🚇 U6 Französische Strasse 💳 MC, V

🍴 DESBROSSES
$$–$$$
POTSDAMER PLATZ 3
TEL 030 337 77 64 00
This traditional brasserie from 1875 originally served as a ladies' hat boutique in Macon, Burgundy. It was transplanted, piece by historic piece, to Potsdamer Platz a few years ago to celebrate fine French cuisine with menus changing daily, an open kitchen, and a bakery where everything is freshly made. The lunch specials are a great value. For good luck, rub the snout of the porcelain pig on display.
🍴 220 🚇 U2, S1, S2 💳 All major cards

🍴 OPERNCAFÉ
$$
UNTER DEN LINDEN 5
TEL 030 20 26 83
One short look at the photos of celebrities and politicians by the entrance will tell you that anyone who's anybody has been seen in the Operncafé. White-aproned servers glide around the 19th-century tearoom delivering the café's to-die-for cream cakes and pies (reputed to be Berlin's largest selection). Classics such as Sachertorte or Black Forest gateau can be had along with house specialties like fig and poppyseed pie.
🍴 120 🚇 S5, S7, S9, U2, U5, U8 Alexanderplatz 💳 All major cards

🍴 GOSCH SYLT
$
ALTE POTSDAMER STRASSE 1
TEL 030 25 29 68 20
For a quick bite, forget the local food court and check out this stylish fish bistro, a copy of the original on the North Sea island of Sylt. The staff knows its marine creatures inside out, and the intimacy shows. Take the fish soup: Where others go thin and runny, the Gosch version is a hearty affair with chunks of tender filet.
🍴 180 🚇 S1, S2, U2 Potsdamer Platz 💳 No credit cards

🍴 METZKES DELI
$
BEHRENSTRASSE 72
TEL 030 206 28 80
Across the street from the Holocaust monument, this simple but movingly elegant deli sells Italian antipasti, bagel sandwiches, wraps, blueberry muffins, and more (we fell for the handmade Spanish chocolate). The inspiration is Harald Metzke, a Jewish artist whose painting "Poacher's Banquet" is on display. Shelves at the front stock deli and kosher items as well as choice

wines and champagne. Serves a mighty good breakfast, too.
🍴 120 🚇 SS1, S2 💳 No credit cards

🍴 SCHLOTZSKY'S DELI
$
FRIEDRICHSTRASSE 200
TEL 030 22 33 88 99
If you find your visit to Checkpoint Charlie awakens a familiar craving, seek out the local outpost of this famous American deli. They serve their mouth-stretching trademark sandwiches on sourdough bread, plus pizzas, wraps, and salads, and you can pore over the daily papers.
🍴 75 🚇 U6 Kochstrasse 💳 No credit cards

🍴 SUPPENBÖRSE
$
DOROTHEENSTRASSE 43
TEL 030 20 45 59 03
This tiny but accomplished soup bar is a welcome alternative to the fast-food joints around the corner on Friedrichstrasse. The health-conscious chef prides himself on a worldly menu that migrates weekly (no preservatives, thank you). Soup varieties might include creamed French celery with orange juice, honey, and cayenne pepper, or Thai chicken-peanut with coconut milk and rice.
🍴 25 🕓 L. only. Closed Sun. & (on very hot days in summer) Sat. 🚇 S1, S2, S5, S9, U6 Friedrichstrasse 💳 No credit cards

◼ CENTRAL BERLIN

HOTELS

🏨 ART'OTEL BERLIN 🍴 MITTE
$$$$
WALLSTRASSE 70–73, 10179
TEL 030 24 06 20
FAX 030 24 06 22 22
www.artotels.de
This rococo mansion, a one-time haunt of Berlin's cultural and intellectual elite, has been

HOTELS & RESTAURANTS

transformed into a plush hotel-cum-art gallery. Spread over its six trendy floors is a collection of works by modernist painter Georg Baselitz (a favorite of Prince Charles, for what it's worth). You can dine in the glass-roofed Factory restaurant or outside on the banks of the Spree.

🏨 105 🚇 U2 Märkisches Museum 🅿 ⬍ 🚭 🔖 🦽 All major cards

🏨 RADISSON SAS HOTEL
🍴 $$$–$$$$

KARL-LIEBKNECHT-STRASSE 3, 10178
TEL 030 23 82 80
FAX 030 238 28 10
www.radissonsas.com

The Radisson claims the world's largest cylindrical aquarium (82 feet/25 m high with 2,500 inhabitants), and most guests fall under its Jules Verne spell right away. Rooms face either the exotic tank in the atrium-style lobby or overlook the Spree River and majestic Berlin Cathedral. The sleek quarters have flat TVs and free high-speed Wi-Fi, and all guests get a free riverboat tour.

🏨 427 🚇 S5, S7, S9, U2, U8 Alexanderplatz 🅿 ⬍ 🚭 🔖 ⛱ 🖥 🦽 All major cards

🏨 ALEXANDER PLAZA
🍴 BERLIN
$$$

ROSENSTRASSE 1, 10178
TEL 030 240 010
FAX 030 240 01 777
www.hotel-alexander-plaza.de

Housed in a stolid but charming Bismarck-era building that was once a fur-designer studio, this protected building is brimming with period details such as vintage glazed tiles and a "floating" staircase apparently held up by stucco. Rooms wear an ergonomic look accented by soothing colors, with the best panoramas being over the historic quarter. Breakfast is

served in the glass-covered *Wintergarten.*

🏨 92 🚇 S5, S7, S9, U2, U8 Alexanderplatz 🅿 ⬍ 🚭 🖥 🦽 All major cards

🏨 ARCOTEL VELVET
🍴 $$$

ORANIENBURGER STRASSE 52, 10117
TEL 030 278 75 30
FAX 030 278 75 38 00
www.arcotel.at

This stylish member of the Arcotel chain occupies a plum spot in Mitte, close to the Neue Synagogue and Friedrichstrasse. All its light, airy rooms have a contemporary feel with floor-to-ceiling windows, gorgeous bathrooms, and time-destroying perks like flat-screen TVs. Rooms on the upper floors offer the best views. If you can tear yourself away, have breakfast at the fine Lutter & Wegner restaurant downstairs.

🏨 85 🚇 U6 Oranienburger Tor 🅿 ⬍ 🚭 🔖 🦽 All major cards

🏨 ARTIST HOTEL
🍴 RIVERSIDE CITY
CENTER
$$$

FRIEDRICHSTRASSE 106, 10117
TEL 030 284 900
FAX 030 284 90 49
www.great-hotel.de

Behind its bland communist-era facade lies a surprisingly quirky hotel with a nice combination of art nouveau and spa facilities. Rooms range from budget to the pleasure-filled spa suite with waterbed and a claw-footed tub. A highlight is the sauna and "flotarium," a shell-shaped saltwater tub. Many rooms, as well as the downstairs café and restaurant, have river views.

🏨 40 🚇 S5, S7, S9, U6 Friedrichstrasse 🅿 ⬍ 🚭 🖥 🦽 All major cards

🏨 HACKESCHER MARKT
$$$

GROSSE PRÄSIDENTENSTRASSE 8, 10178
TEL 030 28 00 30
FAX 030 28 31 11
www.look-hotels.com

This carefully renovated town house is just off fun-filled Hackescher Markt, so few guests linger indoors. The smallish rooms have country-style pinewood furniture and most face a tranquil courtyard; some have balconies. The friendly English-speaking staff will help you navigate the myriad bars and restaurants in the vicinity.

🏨 31 and 3 suites 🚇 S5, S7, S9 Hackescher Markt 🅿 ⬍ 🚭 🦽 All major cards

🏨 HONIGMOND GARDEN
$$$

INVALIDENSTRASSE 122, 10115
TEL 030 28 44 55 77
FAX 030 28 44 55 88
www.honigmond.de

This romantic, family-run hotel cheerily eschews the modern in lieu of the late 19th century, with original antiques, stucco ceilings, and polished wood floors. Front rooms are busy but the rear chambers face an idyllic, shady garden with a Japanese fishpond and century-old trees. The kitchen-equipped garden cottages are roomier. If all's full up, the Garden's sister hotel is just two blocks away at Tieckstrasse 12. Breakfast is included.

🏨 20 🚇 U6 Oranienburger Tor 🅿 🚭 🦽 No credit cards

🏨 HOTEL AUGUSTINEN
HOF
$$$

AUGUSTSTRASSE 82, 10117
TEL 030 30 88 60
FAX 030 30 88 67 00
www.hotel-augustinenhof.de

Considering it's run by a Christian charity, this small hotel dating from 1868 has a hedonistic location, in the bar-and-gallery-filled

Auguststrasse. Rooms and the small apartments have gleaming wooden floors, original art, and all the mod cons, with good facilities for the disabled. Rooms facing the two courtyards are the quietest. Breakfast is included.

ⓘ 63 & 3 apts. 🚇 S1, S2 Oranienburger Strasse 🅿 ⬌ 🚭 All major cards

SOMETHING SPECIAL

🏨 KÜNSTLERHEIM LUISE

To get a DNA profile of Berlin's creative juices, check into this wacky "art hotel" where each room is an installation dreamed up by a young European artist. Some play with your head ("Mammal's Dream" has a ridiculously huge four-poster bed), some draw on sci-fi (a Jetsons-era shower in "Future Comforts"), and others are simply tranquil ("Three Stages of Meditation" has Japanese screens and zenlike music). The location is convenient to the Reichstag, Unter den Linden, and the sights along Oranienburger Strasse.

$$$
LUISENSTRASSE 19, 10117
TEL 030 284 480
FAX 030 284 48 448
www.kuenstlerheim-luise.de
ⓘ 46 🚇 U6 Oranienburger Tor; GS1, S2, S5, S9, U6 Friedrichstrasse
⬌ 🚳 🚭 🌊 🚭 All major cards

🏨 LUX ELEVEN
🍴 $$$
ROSA LUXEMBURG STRASSE 9–13, 10178
TEL 030 936 28 00
FAX 030 93 62 80 80
www.lux-eleven.com
These spacious apartments done up in Far Eastern style would surely cost a fortune in Tokyo. Soft cuddly things abound—pillows, comfy chairs, piles of towels—to make spaces plush and inviting; rooms also feature high-tech stuff like Wi-Fi and

flat TVs. Guests here can plug into the gallery scene of Mitte or just retreat to their personal cocoons.

ⓘ 72 apts. 🚇 S5, S7, S9, U2, U8 Alexanderplatz
🅿 ⬌ 🚭 🌊 🚭 All major cards

🏨 ANDECHSER HOF
🍴 $$
ACKERSTRASSE 155, MITTE 10115
TEL 030 28 09 78 44
FAX 030 28 09 78 45
www.andechserhof.de
Not in the trendiest part of town, but within staggering distance of Prenzlauer Berg's buzzing café-bar scene. Rooms are large, quiet, and furnished in a diversity of styles, often all mixed together but always comfortable. Breakfast is served in the adjoining Austrian-style restaurant.
ⓘ 19 🚇 U8 Rosenthaler Platz ⬌ 🚭 🚭 MC, V

🏨 HOTEL PRINZALBERT
🍴 $$
VETERANENSTRASSE 10, 10119
TEL 030 590 02 94 20
FAX 030 590 02 94 29
www.prinzalbert-berlin.de
This stylish hotel has an enviable location overlooking the rolling Weinbergspark, in the twilight zone between Mitte and Prenzlauer Berg. Though on the snug side, the rooms all have huge windows, pleasing designs, and plenty of artistic flair thanks to abstract canvases by a London artist. Breakfast is served in the Mediterranean restaurant-bar downstairs.
ⓘ 7 🚇 U8 Rosenthaler Platz ⬌ 🚭 🚭 No credit cards

🏨 GREEN EGGS & HAM
🍴 CAFÉ & PENSION
$
NOVALISSTRASSE 2, 10117
TEL 030 49 85 39 58
FAX 030 29 37 57 77
www.greeneggsandham.de
The children's books of Dr.

Seuss inspired the name of this cuddly little café-hotel. With a total of seven rooms in what used to be two apartments above the café, this pension is perfect for meeting the neighbors. There are six doubles in various sizes and a good-size studio apartment (with the only private bathroom). Rooms are clean but basic, with cheery walls and high ceilings. Kitchen access.
ⓘ 6 & 1 apt. 🚇 U6 Oranienburger Tor 🚭 No credit cards

RESTAURANTS

🍴 MAXWELL
$$$$
BERGSTRASSE 22, PRENZLAUER BERG
TEL 030 280 71 21
Few locations could be more enticing than the pretty courtyard of the former Josty brewery, facing a beautiful neo-Gothic facade. The owners are buddies with enfant terrible artist Damien Hirst, and ironically it's his stomach-turning work (on display) that inspired the mouthwatering house dish, a crisp-fried duck confit with black pepper sauce. There are also vegetarian dishes such as celery gratin with shiitake mushrooms and dried apples.
🍴 220 🕐 Closed Sat. & Sun. L. 🚇 U2 Rosenthaler Platz 🚭 All major cards

🍴 AIGNER
$$$
FRANZÖSISCHE STRASSE 25
TEL 030 203 75 18 50
Perched on a corner of Berlin's prestigious Gendarmenmarkt, the Aigner was, in fact, a historic café in Vienna before it was dismantled and moved to the German capital. It's a prime spot for a business lunch or dinner, thanks to tasty Austro-German dishes such as braised shoulder of young bull with pureed olives or

HOTELS & RESTAURANTS

pan-fried Brandenburg duck. The desserts are divine, too: Try Aigner's warm chocolate-laced pear with vanilla ice cream.

⬛ 150 🚇 U6 Französische Strasse, Stadtmitte 🅰 All major cards

🍴 GANYMED
$$$
SCHIFFBAUER DAMM 5
TEL 030 28 59 90 46
This let-your-hair-down riverside brasserie exudes the spirit of la belle France on vacation. The forté of chef Vincent Garcia is seafood: mussels from Brittany, shrimp, crabs, and oysters prepared in a bewildering number of ways. In summer you can dine on the roomy terrace next to the Berliner Ensemble, but the candlelit dining room with checkered tablecloths and art deco globes is a treat after sunset.

⬛ 75 🚇 S1, S2, S5, S9, U6 Friedrichstrasse 🅰 All major cards

🍴 REMAKE
$$$
GROSSE HAMBURGER STRASSE 32
TEL 030 20 05 41 02
A blink and a world away from the trendy crowds of Mitte, this contemporary Spanish-Italian restaurant is an unexpected delight. Christiano Rienzner, a former chef of a three-star restaurant in Catalonia, puts a winning spin on anything he touches, from braised scallops with lychee mousse to breast of quail with a scoop of olive ice cream. The wine list is a tour de force of German and Mediterranean Rim vintages.

⬛ 75 🕐 Closed L & Sun. 🚇 S5, S7, S9 Hackescher Markt 🅰 AE, MC, V

🍴 WEINBAR RUTZ
$$$
CHAUSSEESTRASSE 8
TEL 030 24 62 87 60
An oenophile's dream that

lives up to its name, the Rutz has over a thousand different wines; you pay a mere €15 above the retail price to have one brought up from the shop and uncorked. You can nibble on tapas with wine at street level, or go straight to the elegant upstairs restaurant. The contemporary cuisine is terrific across the board, but the showstopper is the entrecote from milk-fed Kobe cattle served in truffle gravy.

⬛ 110 🕐 Closed L 🚇 U6 Oranienburger Tor 🅰 All major cards

🍴 LAS OLAS
$$
KARL-LIEBKNECHT-STRASSE 29
TEL 030 241 54 72
Berlin's best paella may be found in what's got to be the ugliest spot around Alexanderplatz. Jammed under a concrete building in a sea of socialist-era eyesores, this Spanish eatery turns out to be amazingly friendly, cozy, and a source of authentic Andalusian fare. Patrons who get over this shock usually don't get beyond the mind-boggling array of reasonably priced tapas, but there's a great selection of paellas (including a quirky one with noodles and duck).

⬛ 120 🕐 Closed L 🚇 S5, S7, S9, U2, U5, U8 Alexanderplatz 🅰 AE, MC, V

🍴 SCHWARZENRABEN
$$
NEUE SCHÖNHAUSER STRASSE 13
TEL 030 28 39 16 98
A charity soup kitchen a century ago, the rooms of this handsome building near Hackescher Markt are now a nexus of night owls. The chefs pull out all the stops with dishes such as cannelloni filled with ricotta, peach, and goat's cheese in a lavender-red wine sauce. Service here can be slow, but maybe that's the price

---

HOTELS
The cost of a double room without breakfast:

$$$$$	Over $270
$$$$	$200–$270
$$$	$130–$200
$$	$80–$120
$	Under $80

RESTAURANTS
The cost of a three-course dinner without drinks:

$$$$$	Over $80
$$$$	$50–$80
$$$	$35–$50
$$	$20–$35
$	Under $20

Hotels and restaurants are listed alphabetically by price category within each district.
L = lunch; D = dinner

---

you pay for hip.

⬛ 230 🕐 Closed Sun. L 🚇 U8 Weinmeisterstrasse 🅰 AE, MC, V

🍴 SCHWARZWALD-STUBEN
$$
TUCHOLSKYSTRASSE 48
TEL 030 28 09 80 84
This place is a tongue-in-cheek homage to all things Swabian (from Germany's southwest corner). The combination of living room furniture, brewing equipment, antlers, and hunting gear is refreshingly bizarre and puts a question mark over Hemingway's view that the Black Forest was too orderly. To get in the groove, order a Flammkuchen (thin-crusted pizza) with pear and gorgonzola topping and savor a tasty Tannenzäpfle pils, a beer rarity in Berlin.

⬛ 50 🚇 S1, S2 Oranienburger Strasse 🅰 No credit cards

🍴 PAN ASIA
$–$$
ROSENTHALER STRASSE 38
TEL 030 27 90 88 11
This favorite haunt of Schickies

(yuppies) is perfect for munching into the wee hours. The elegant lighting, long communal banquettes, and manga videos make it a fine place to chill after club-hopping. Whether it's unusual sushis (e.g., papaya) or spicy curries of dim sums, everything is fresh, flavorful, and on your table in an instant. It's tucked away in a rear courtyard—look for the red sign similar to the old PanAm logo.

🛏 180 🚇 S1, S7, S9 Hackescher Markt 🚫 No credit cards

🍽 DE NHAT
$
AUGUSTSTRASSE 2A
TEL 030 28 87 59 95
The orange spaceship interior of this small, friendly Thai restaurant gives a hint of things to come. Bright, well-defined aromas of herbs and spices waft up from delectable towers of chicken satay or spicy pork on rice. The Tiger beer is great; if your food is especially spicy, douse the fire with one of the smooth fruit shakes.

🛏 85 🕐 Closed Sun. 🚇 S1, S25 Oranienburger Strasse 🚫 No credit cards

🍽 KELLERRESTAURANT IM BRECHT-HAUS
$
CHAUSSEESTRASSE 125
TEL 030 282 38 43
Formerly the home of author Bertolt Brecht and next door to the cemetery where he was buried, this cellar eatery has heaps of atmosphere and Germanic specialties such as *Fleischlabberln* (spicy meat patties) and *Wiener schnitzel*. All dishes are from his wife Helene Weigel's handwritten cookbook, based on recipes from Bohemia. In summer, the lovely little garden is thrown open to diners.

🛏 65 🚇 U6 Oranienburger Tor 🚫 AE, MC, V

🍽 MUTTER HOPPE
$
RATHAUSSTRASSE 21
10178
TEL 030 24 72 06 03
This old-fashioned wood-paneled restaurant in the Nikolai quarter is named for Mother Hoppe, a formidable cook who used to whip up mountains of food for her family and friends. It's superbly atmospheric, with lots of photos and knickknacks from yesteryear. Sit down to a hearty serving of *Eisbein* (pork knuckle) or an oversize schnitzel and savor golden oldies from the '20s and '30s (live music on weekends).

🛏 90 🚇 U2, S3, S5, S9 Alexanderplatz 🚫 MC, V

▪ TIERGARTEN

RESTAURANTS

🍽 PARIS-MOSKAU
$$$$
ALT-MOABIT 141
The pretty wood-frame house wrested from a train signalman has long been renowned for its perfect service and excellent wine selection. The cuisine balances fine nuances with hearty flavors, such as fresh pike-perch in fried blood sausage with red wine and shallots. Reservations are not a bad idea, especially for the al fresco tables in summer.

🛏 60 🕐 Closed Sat. & Sun. L 🚇 S5, S7, S9 Lehrter Bahnhof-Hauptbahnhof 🚫 No credit cards

🍽 ANGKOR WAT
$$–$$$
PAULSTRASSE 22
TEL 030 393 39 22
Palms, bright flowers, and a beach-hut bar set the tone of this sprawling Cambodian fondue restaurant. The house specialty is served with beef, shrimp, chicken, octopus, or shark filet. The food arrives uncooked in earthy wire baskets, ready for dunking in a

bubbling cauldron right at your table. What sets it apart from European fondues are the spicy sauces, lemongrass, and bamboo sprouts. If you've still got room, try a sugar palm fruit with sweet rice and coconut milk.

🛏 220 🕐 Closed L Mon.–Fri. 🚇 S5, S7, S9 Bellevue 🚫 MC, V

▪ CHARLOTTENBURG

HOTELS

🏨 BRANDENBURGER 🍽 HOF
$$$$$
EISLEBENER STRASSE 14, WILMERSDORF
10789
TEL 030 21 40 50
FAX 030 21 40 51 00
www.brandenburger-hof.com
Bauhaus and modern design come together in this elegant villa dating from the early 1900s. It has a great location but is also very quiet, featuring stylish but livable rooms with a feeling of endless space (thanks to the incredible 13-foot ceilings). The house restaurant Die Quadriga is considered one of the city's finest and serves only elite German wines.

🛏 78 🚇 U1 Augsburger Strasse 🅿 🛗 🚫 🆎 📺 🚫 All major cards

🏨 HOTEL Q!
🍽 $$$–$$$$
KNESEBECKSTRASSE 67 10623
TEL 030 810 06 60
FAX 030 810 066 666
www.loock-hotels.com
A cool gray facade signals your arrival at the Q, an ultrachic retreat named for the nearby Ku'damm. Corners are a rarity: Hardwood floors curve up the walls in the rooms, where you can literally slide from the tub into bed. The spa has its own self-contained "beach" with heated sand, aromatherapy,

and calming sound and light effects.

ℹ 77 🚇 S5, S7, S9 Savignyplatz 🅿 🚭 📺 ♿ All major cards

🏨 SAVOY HOTEL
🍴 $$$–$$$$
FASANENSTRASSE 9–10 10623
TEL 030 31 10 30
FAX 030 31 10 33 33
www.hotel-savoy.com
This Berlin institution oozes the kind of Old World charm that brings to mind bowler hats and rustling petticoats. Standard rooms are a little generic, but suites named after regular guests—like the "Henry Miller" or "Greta Garbo" on the 6th floor (the only level with air-conditioning)—have tons of character. Stogie lovers will enjoy the Savoy's walk-in humidor.

ℹ 125 🚇 S5, S7, S9, U2 Zoologischer Garten 🚭 🚫 💱 ♿ All major cards

🏨 BLEIBTREU
🍴 $$$
BLEIBTREUSTRASSE 31, 10707
TEL 030 88 47 40
FAX 030 88 47 44 44
www.bleibtreu.com
The cheery, ecofriendly materials and minimal Italian furniture of this boutique hotel are completely in step with the fancy apparel shops along Bleibtreustrasse. Some rooms are on the tight side, but the in-house bar and Restaurant 31 are quite elegant.

ℹ 60 🚇 S5, S7, S9 Savignyplatz, U1 Uhlandstrasse 🚭 🚫 📺 ♿ All major cards

🏨 CASA HOTEL
$$$
SCHLÜTERSTRASSE 40, 10707
TEL 030 280 30 00
FAX 030 28 03 00 50
www.hotel-casa.de
This new Charlottenburg hotel caters to travel-savvy

urbanites who value chic but practical decor. The color schemes tread a fine line between designer cool and welcoming hospitality, with sleek Philippe Starck furniture offset by warm Mediterranean hues. Breakfast is served till noon.

ℹ 29 🚇 S5, S7, S9 Savignyplatz, U1 Uhlandstrasse 🚭 🚫 ♿ All major cards

🏨 HECKER'S HOTEL
🍴 $$$
GROLMANSTRASSE 35, 10623
TEL: 030 889 00
FAX 030 88 90 260
www.heckers-hotel.de
Just a few steps off busy Ku'damm, this famous boutique hotel prides itself on the personal service it has heaped on celebrities such as Michael Douglas, Valéry Giscard d'Estaing, and German crooner Udo Jürgens. Rooms are enormous, elegant, and styled to please, ranging from Bauhaus to Italo-chic with tasteful stops in between. The lobby has a striking ice blue backlit bar.

ℹ 72 🚇 U1 Uhlandstrasse 🅿 🚭 🚫 🚫 ♿ All major cards

🏨 KU'DAMM 101
🍴 $$$
KURFÜRSTENDAMM 101, 10711
TEL 030 520 05 50
FAX 030 520 05 55 55
www.kudamm101.com
It's a bit removed from the action, but this hotel is fascinating viewing for anyone with an eye for minimalist design. The lobby manages to combine '60s shapes with a New Age feel thanks to its column lamps, curvy banquettes, and recessed ceilings. In the rooms a clever blend of light and shadow has a soothing effect. There's high-speed Internet as well as retro gear like the wood-grain console that hides the TV.

ℹ 170 🚇 S41, S42, S47 Halensee 🅿 🚭 🚫 ♿ All major cards

🏨 ASKANISCHER HOF
$$–$$$
KURFÜRSTENDAMM 53, 10707
TEL 030 8 81 80 33
FAX 030 8 81 72 06
www.askanischer-hof.de
For a dose of Berlin history, stay at this delightful private hotel on the city's most famous shopping avenue. The Askanischer Hof was built in the early 1900s and furnished in Roaring '20s style. The rooms are all individually designed, with plenty of high-tech features. Rock star David Bowie was a regular guest here in the 1970s.

ℹ 16 🚇 S5, S7, S9 Savignyplatz 🅿 📺 ♿ All major cards

🏨 HOTEL PENSION DITTBERNER
$$–$$$
WIELANDSTRASSE 26, 10707
TEL 030 884 69 50
FAX 030 885 40 46
www.hotel-dittberner.de
This friendly third-floor pension has been in the Lange family for generations. This is old Berlin in spades: rooms with soaring ceilings, adorned with stucco and old lithographs, and an airy breakfast room with an antique sideboard. However, they provide direct-dial phones and free Wi-Fi. Breakfast included.

ℹ 22 🚇 S5, S7, S9 Savignyplatz 🅿 🚭 🚫 ♿ No credit cards

SOMETHING SPECIAL

🏨 PROPELLER ISLAND CITY LODGE
Prepare to be surprised— nothing about this place is ordinary. Once a 19th-century apartment building south of Kurfürstendamm, the Propeller has been rewired as an eccentric hotel where every room is an inhabitable work of art. Most

draw on fantasies: the "Flying Bed" seems to hover in the air, while in the "Castle Room" you snooze atop a wooden fortress. For something wilder try the "Crypt," with spine-tingling coffin beds, or the "Two Lions," with a pair of caged mattresses 5 feet (1.5 m) above the ground. Every piece of furniture was designed and crafted by the owner-artist Lars Stroschen himself.

$$–$$$
ALBRECHT-ACHILLES-STRASSE 58, 10709
TEL 030 891 90 16
FAX 030 892 87 21
www.propeller-island.com
🛈 42 🚇 U7 Adenauerplatz
🏨 All major cards

🏨 KORFU II
$
RANKESTRASSE 35, 10789
TEL 030 212 47 90
FAX 030 21 24 79 60
www.hp-korfu.de
A typical Berlin guesthouse cobbled out of several apartments, the Korfu offers simple but comfortable rooms with and without private bath. The location is right in the thick of things, with the famous Gedächtniskirche across the road. Free Web access.
🛈 39 🚇 U1, U9 Kurfürstenstrasse 🅿 🔄
🏨 MC, V

RESTAURANTS

🍽 FLORIAN
$$$
GROLMANSTRASSE 52
TEL 030 313 91 84
A haunt of actors, gallery owners, and the glitterati who meet here to munch and tipple during the Berlinale film festival. The menu hovers between down-home German and refined international dishes, served in elegant bistro-style surroundings. Vegetarian fare is available. A long-standing ritual is the Nuremberg

bratwurst with sauerkraut, served only after 11 p.m.
🍽 70 🚇 S5, S7, S9 Savignyplatz 🏨 MC, V

🍽 KADEWE
$$–$$$
TAUENTZIENSTRASSE 21
TEL 030 212 10
Berlin's most famous department store has a legendary food hall on the sixth floor, a must-see for galloping gourmets. It's known locally as the *Fress-Etage* (glutton's floor). You can wander goggle-eyed past counters selling roast bison, fresh octopus quiche, gooey French cheeses, and more filled chocolates than Willy Wonka ever dreamed of. If you find the choice paralyzing, try the atrium cafeteria on the seventh floor.
🕐 Closed Sun. 🚇 U1, U2, U3 Wittenbergplatz 🏨 AE, MC, V

🍽 BORRIQUITO
$$
WIELANDSTRASSE 6
TEL 030 312 99 29
After dark, things really get rolling in the "little donkey," fueled by the night owls and artists of Savignyplatz. Around midnight, the chefs and waiters converge on this place for Rioja and classic Spanish cuisine. The paella and seafood are particularly good. Someone's always singing or playing the guitar.
🍽 125 🕐 Closed L 🚇 S5, S7, S9 Savignyplatz 🏨 No credit cards

🍽 BREL
$$
SAVIGNYPLATZ 1
TEL 030 31 80 00 20
If the chic, glass-fronted locales on Savignyplatz are for seeing and being seen, Brel is the latest master of the art. The menu is Belgian and at lunch offers light classics such as onion soup and monster salads (you can order half portions as an appetizer).

Later on the kitchen gets down to business: rump steak with *frites* (fries), roast beef with remoulade, and mussels worthy of Jacques Brel, the Belgian chanson singer.
🍽 95 🚇 S5, S7, S9 Savignyplatz 🏨 AE, MC, V

SOMETHING SPECIAL

🍽 CAFE IM LITERATURHAUS
This café/restaurant in an old villa a heartbeat from the Kurfürstendamm provides a well-stocked bookshop in the basement, plus food from breakfast to supper in the first-floor salon. Supper dishes— perhaps roast lamb with rosemary or trout with new potatoes—are strictly seasonal. The regulars exude the kind of worldly sophistication that comes from a lifetime of intellectual debate over coffee. Free tables are a scarce commodity on weekends.
$$
FASANENSTRASSE 23
TEL 030 882 54 14
🍽 100 🚇 U15 Uhlandstrasse 🏨 No credit cards

🍽 JULEP'S
$$
GIESEBRECHTSTRASSE 3
TEL 030 881 88 23
In a quiet side street off the Ku'damm, Julep's is a latter-day clone of a New York speakeasy, a friendly place that's popular with locals and expats alike. The menu is a toothsome trip across the North American continent: Juicy steaks, quarter-pound burgers, and Manhattan clam chowder rub shoulders with Tex-Mex and the Pacific Rim. Some patrons come to cheer the big-screen sports (including American football) or to linger over a mint julep, one of 120 cocktails on offer.
🍽 100 🚇 U7 Adenauerplatz 🏨 AE, MC

HOTELS & RESTAURANTS

🍴 **SACHIKO SUSHI BAR**
$$
GROLMANSTRASSE 47
TEL 030 313 22 82
Tucked into an alleyway
by the railway line on
Savignyplatz, this intimate little
sushi bar could hardly find a
better hiding place. The food
is always fresh and excellent,
however, and dining becomes
a journey as the sushi floats to
you on little boats in a river
built right into the oval bar.
🪑 25 🚉 S5, S7, S9
Savignyplatz 💳 AE, MC, V

🍴 **SCARABEO**
$$
LUDWIGKIRCHSTRASSE 6
TEL 030 885 06 16
Arguably not the best name
for a restaurant, the scarabeo
is a dung beetle celebrated in
ancient Egypt as a symbol of
life. You'll find it hard to
resist the 27 different mezes
(starters) in this Egyptian
eatery, or main dishes such as
sayadia (a Mediterranean fish)
served with lemon and salad
on a bed of perfumed pine
rice, or the belly dancers on
Saturday night.
🪑 90 🕐 Closed L
🚉 U1 Uhlandstrasse, U3
Hohenzollernplatz 💳 No
credit cards

🍴 **ZWÖLF APOSTEL**
$$
BLEIBTREUSTRASSE 49
TEL 030 312 14 33
Party animals take note: The
tireless staff of the 12
Apostles serves stone-oven
pizza virtually round the clock,
in an ambience that makes
even the most exhausted
clubber look great. It attracts a
broad crowd of patrons,
however, thanks to its
attractive pseudo-Roman
dining rooms, mouthwatering
pastas, and homemade
breads. Reservations are
recommended.
🪑 200 💳 No credit cards
🚉 S5, S7, S9 Savignyplatz

🍴 **ASHOKA**
$
GROLMANSTRASSE 51
TEL 030 313 20 66
A hole-in-the-wall with a
restaurant's ambition, this
rustic Indian snack bar makes
its delectable meat and
vegetarian dishes an arm's
length from your well-worn
table. On nice evenings, you
may prefer to sit at the
sidewalk tables.
🪑 25 🚉 S7, S9 Savignyplatz
💳 No credit cards

■ **PRENZLAUER
BERG,
FRIEDRICHSHAIN,
& THE EAST**

HOTELS

🏨 **HOTEL ADELE**
🍴 **$$$**
GREIFSWALDER STRASSE 227,
10504
TEL 030 4432 4350
FAX 030 4432 4351
www.adele-hotel.de
From the street this cool
"lounge hotel" is nearly
invisible, fading into a row of
stylish businesses, including
separate coffee and wine
shops as well as a fine Med-
inspired restaurant. Rooms
look like something out of
Wallpaper magazine, with dark
hardwoods and leathers
against cream and pastel hues.
🛏 14 🚉 U2 Senefelder Platz
🅿 🔁 🚭 💳 All major cards

🏨 **HOTEL KASTANIEN-
HOF**
$$$
KASTANIENALLEE 65, 10119
TEL 030 443 050
FAX 030 4430 5111
www.kastanienhof.biz
This guesthouse enjoys an
enviable spot on the
Kastanienallee, one of
Prenzlauer Berg's hippest
strips. The historic building
served as a butcher shop, a
Russian military post, and
socialist tenements before
being turned into one of East

HOTELS
The cost of a double room
without breakfast:
$$$$$ Over $270
$$$$ $200–$270
$$$ $130–$200
$$ $80–$120
$ Under $80

RESTAURANTS
The cost of a three-course
dinner without drinks:
$$$$$ Over $80
$$$$ $50–$80
$$$ $35–$50
$$ $20–$35
$ Under $20

Hotels and restaurants are
listed alphabetically by price
category within each district.
L = lunch; D = dinner

Berlin's first hotels after
reunification. The furnishings
are simple, but the real
atmosphere comes from
the historic maps and
photos in the halls and
guest rooms.
🛏 35 🚉 U8 Rosenthaler
Platz 🅿 🔁 🚭 💳 All major
cards

🏨 **EAST SIDE HOTEL**
🍴 **$$**
MÜHLENSTRASSE 6,
10243
TEL 030 29 38 34 00
FAX 030 29 38 35 55
www.eastsidehotel.de
A stone's throw from the East
Side Gallery—the longest
remaining section of the
Berlin Wall—this friendly,
super-modern hotel has a
minimalist decor that focuses
attention on art and photos
devoted to the Wall. Front
rooms have views of the
former barrier and the river
but are noisier than those to
the rear. Breakfast is included
(and served around the clock).
🛏 36 🚉 S5, S7, S9, U1
Warschauer Strasse
🅿 🔁 💳 All major cards

HOTEL 26 BERLIN
$$
GRÜNBERGER STRASSE 26,
10245
TEL 030 29 77 78 70
FAX 030 29 77 78 79
www.hotel26-berlin.de
For no-nonsense digs a cut above a hostel, try this eco-friendly, smoke-free hotel in the young, café-filled Friedrichshain District. Breakfast consists only of organic foods, from the cheeses and fresh-pressed juices to cold cuts from farm-raised animals. You can chill with a newspaper in the café or, when it's warm, flake out on the lounge chairs in the rear garden.
🅘 19 suites 🚇 S5, S7, S9, U1 Warschauer Strasse
🅿 🚫 🅢 All major cards

JUNCKER'S HOTEL
$$
GRÜNBERGER STRASSE 21,
10243
TEL 030 293 35 50
FAX 030 29 33 55 55
www.junckers-hotel.de
This welcoming, family-run hotel is one of Berlin's best deals. The kind owner, Herr Juncker, is a font of local knowledge—in fluent English. Rooms aren't huge and a bit modular in flavor, but everything is clean and in great shape. All rooms face away from the street, but things can get a bit rowdy at the hostel next door.
🅘 30 🚇 S5, S7, S9, U1 Warschauer Strasse
🅿 🛗 🅢 MC, V

UPSTALSBOOM
HOTEL
$$
GUBENER STRASSE 42, 10243
TEL 030 293 750
FAX 030 29 37 57 77
www.upstalsboom-berlin.de
This perky hotel flies the blue-and-white colors of a North Sea village because it's part of a small chain of German seaside resorts. Rooms have a streamlined look and come in four sizes, some with kitchens. As you'd expect, the cozy restaurant is great for fish, and there's a rooftop garden with sweeping views of Berlin. Rates include bicycle rentals and gym use.
🅘 169 🚇 S5, S7, S9, U1 Warschauer Strasse
🅿 🛗 🚫 🏋 🅢 All major cards

HOTEL GREIFSWALD
$–$$
GREIFSWALDER STRASSE 211,
10405
TEL 030 442 78 88
FAX 030 442 78 98
www.hotel-greifswald.de
Tucked into a historic building, this little hotel is something of a rock shrine. Members of Steppenwolf have stopped by and guitarist Albert Lee has signed the guest book. Dozens of autographed photos adorn the reception area and breakfast room. The comfy, albeit generic rooms and small apartments (with kitchen access) are as popular with families as groupies.
🅘 30 🚇 Tram M4 or Bus 200 🅿 🚫 🅢 All major cards

EASTERN COMFORT
$
MÜHLENSTRASSE 73–77, 10243
TEL 030 66 76 38 06
FAX 030 66 76 38 05
www.eastern-comfort.com
Berlin's first floating hotel is moored on the Spree within spitting distance of the East Side Gallery (a large remnant of the Berlin Wall). Cap'n Edgar and his crew put you up in cabins (all smoke-free) with plush red carpets, mahogany, and lots of brass fittings. The top deck has a pert little café and there are nice bikes for hire.
🅘 24 🚇 S5, S7, S9, U1 Warschauer Strasse
🅿 🚫 🅢 No credit cards

RESTAURANTS

🍴 GUGELHOF
$$$
KNAACKSTRASSE 37
TEL 030 442 92 29
Ever since President Clinton dropped in for dinner with Chancellor Schröder, this lively Franco-German eatery has been on every Berliner's radar. Serving Alsatian delights such as *Flammkuchen* (a thin-crusted pizza) and *choucroute* (meats and sausages on a bed of sauerkraut), the staff will also advise on the proper wine (try a crisp Riesling). In summer you can dine outside with a view of pretty Kollwitzplatz.
🍽 90 🚇 U2 Senefelder Platz 🅢 All major cards

🍴 NOCTI VAGUS
$$$
SAARBRÜCKER STRASSE 36–38,
TEL 030 74 74 91 23
If you've never had the pleasure, a visit to Berlin's first "dark restaurant" will open up new sensory worlds. Past reception, you're led to your table in utter blackness by blind waiters. For many it's a disconcerting but enriching experience as the senses of taste, smell, and hearing are heightened. You'll also discover people that say different things under cover of darkness. Reservations, for set meals only, are required.
🍽 52 🕐 Closed L 🚇 U2 Senefelder Platz 🅢 MC, V

🍴 BABEL
$$
GABRIEL MAX STRASSE 16
TEL 030 29 36 87 84
The Babel sells Middle Eastern flair. Diners squat on padded poufs for cozy conversation in soft red lighting. Enjoy tasty Lebanese specialties like *kafta* (grilled lamb sausages), hummus (spicy pureed chickpeas), or the bulging Babel Platter for two to three people, paired with a Lebanese wine. Some patrons

come for the potent cocktails or water pipes stoked with fruity tobaccos.

🍴 85 🕐 Closed L 🚇 U5 Frankfurter Tor 💳 No credit cards

🍴 GORKI PARK
$$
WEINBERGSWEG 25,
TEL 030 448 72 86

For a former outpost of the former Soviet empire, Berlin has surprisingly few Russian restaurants. So it's all the more rewarding to discover Gorki Park, just off busy Rosenthaler Platz. Past the small bar serving glasses of Riussian beer, you can choose from several dining areas with a vague feel of Soviet decline. Specialties include lightly peppered *pelmeni* (dumplings) with sour cream, a hearty borscht, and big fresh salads. The Sunday brunch is legendary.

🍴 40 🚇 U8 Rosenthaler Platz 💳 No credit cards

🍴 MIRO
$$
RAUMER STRASSE 28–29
TEL 44 73 30 13

Miro means "hero" in Kurdish, but it takes no courage to sample the exotic dishes of this delightful Anatolian restaurant. The grilled meats are infused with mysterious spices and garlic, and there are plenty of vegetarian dishes. Romantically lit, with fashionable bare brick walls and a wooden floor, this dining area has two parts, a front section with small tables and bar and a back room furnished with traditional cushions and waterpipes.

🍴 100 🚇 S8, S41, S42 Prenzlauer Allee 💳 MC, V

🍴 NOLA'S AM WEINBERG
$$
VETERANENSTRASSE 9
TEL 030 44 04 07 66

Just north of the bar scene in Mitte, this Swiss-style restaurant in a postwar pavilion is an oasis of calm overlooking the sweet little Weinbergspark. The ambience draws the occasional Hollywood star—Brad Pitt and Angelina Jolie were spotted here—but the outdoor terrace sees a cross section of humanity in summer. The menu is a patchwork of Swiss cuisine, from fondue to river trout.

🍴 100 🚇 U8 Rosenthaler Platz 💳 All major cards

🍴 UMSPANNWERK OST
$$
PALISADENSTRASSE 48
TEL 030 42 80 94 97

Housed in the transformer hall of a 19th-century power plant, this is Friedrichshain's largest restaurant and one of its most atmospheric. Right inside the entrance you'll spot the open kitchen preparing its German-international dishes. Tasty starters include razor-thin beef carpaccio and orange-carrot soup. Main dishes like thyme-crusted lamb don't skimp on quality or quantity. It's tough to decide where to sit—on the spacious terrace, in the enormous dining hall, or right at the bar.

🍴 160 🚇 U5 Weberwiese 💳 MC, V

🍴 WEINSTEIN
$$
LYCHENER STRASSE 33
TEL 030 441 18 42

Roy Metzger and his brother Marc built up this wine bar–restaurant from humble beginnings, and the result is impressive. A cross between tapas bar and beerhouse, Weinstein serves up an eclectic mix of cuisines prepared with fine and often local ingredients. Mixed salad with Brandenburg veal, potato dumplings stuffed with goat cheese, tuna marinated Japanese style—the menu is impossible to predict and changes every two weeks.

Roy is also a wine dealer, so there are bottles to go.

🍴 65 🕐 Closed Sun. L 🚇 U2 Eberswalder Strasse 💳 MC, V

🍴 I DUE FORNI
$–$$
SCHÖNHAUSER ALLEE 12
TEL 030 44 01 73 33

Where else but Berlin would you find punk-rock pizza? The waiters in this popular Italian eatery don grunge garb but are happy to serve great thin-crust creations to anyone and everyone—young couples, families, and students—who crowds the communal tables in an atmosphere of barely contained chaos. Try to reserve ahead as the cavernous hall gets packed even before the bands start playing.

🍴 150 🚇 U2 Senefelder Platz 💳 No credit cards

🍴 CONMUX
$
SIMON DACH STRASSE 35
TEL 291 38 63

Located in the thick of the café-filled district of Friedrichshain, Conmux is renowned for its industrial decor, gargantuan breakfasts, and dishes made exclusively with organic ingredients. The food is frighteningly fresh, but arguably the greatest pleasure is sitting on the shady terrace and watching the ebb and flow of trendy urbanites along Simon Dach Strasse.

🍴 85 🚇 S3, S5, S7, S9, U1 Warschauer Strasse, U5 Frankfurter Tor 💳 No credit cards

🍴 KONNOPKE
$
SCHÖNHAUSER ALLEE 440

This legendary stand-up snack bar under the U-Bahn tracks at Danziger Strasse/Schön-hauser Allee claims to be the birthplace of Berlin's famous *Currywurst* (curried sausage), which has been served here since 1930. Lines are typically

long; the owners say the secret's in the ketchup.
🚫 Closes 8 p.m. 🚇 U2 Eberswalder Strasse 🚭 No credit cards

▮ SCHÖNEBERG & KREUZBERG

HOTELS

🏨 HOTEL RIEHMERS ▯ HOFGARTEN
$$$
YORCKSTRASSE 83, 10965
TEL 030 78 09 88 00
FAX 030 78 09 88 08
www.riehmers-hofgarten.de
This romantic small hotel near Viktoriapark was the brainchild of Wilhelm Riehmers, a renowned 19th-century architect. French double doors open into spacious rooms with high ceilings, tasteful contemporary decor, and dynamic colors. The in-house restaurant, named after writer E. T. A. Hoffmann, serves meals in a cobblestone courtyard.
🛏 22 🚇 U6, U7 Mehring-damm 🅿 ⬆ 🚭 All major cards

🏨 MÖVENPICK HOTEL ▯ BERLIN
$$$
SCHÖNEBERGER STRASSE 3, 10963
TEL 030 23 00 60
FAX 030 23 00 61 99
www. moevenpick-hotels.com
Housed in the former headquarters of electronics giant Siemens, this hotel south of Potsdamer Platz offers funky design in a historic shell. Industrial items serve as works of art, from the lounge bar made of high-voltage equipment to the glass-encased turbines in the halls. Other highlights are the glass-bricked bathrooms, furnishings made of seductive olivewood, and perky colors recalling Mövenpick ice cream.
🛏 243 🚇 S1, S2 Anhalter Bahnhof 🅿 ⬆ 🚭
🗗 🎮 🚭 All major cards

RESTAURANTS

▯ ALTES ZOLLHAUS
$$$
CARL-HERZ-UFER 30
TEL 030 692 33 00
Enjoy fine dining in this picturesque half-timbered house, a former customs post with a superb location on the banks of a Kreuzberg canal. The food is German-international: Try the roast rabbit and venison with chanterelles, or the house specialty, roast duck on Savoy cabbage. It's best visited in summer, when you can dine in the idyllic garden at the water's edge.
🪑 180 🚫 Closed Sun.–Mon. 🚇 U1 Prinzenstrasse 🅿 🚭 DC, MC, V

▯ LE COCHON BOURGEOIS
$$$
FICHTESTRASSE 24
TEL 030 693 01 01
The "bourgeois pig" is one of the best French restaurants in Berlin. Chef and owner Hannes Behrmann not only has a close relationshiip with all things pork—the jugged wild boar on candied liquorice gets rave reviews—but he also puts his *je ne sais quoi* into game and seafood (such as monkfish in bacon sauce on green lentils). Every night at 8 p.m. a pianist tickles the ivories in the stylish interior, the former showroom of a colonial-goods dealer.
🪑 55 🚇 U7 Südstern 🚫 Closed Mon. 🚭 No credit cards

▯ AROMA
$$–$$$
HOCHKIRCHSTRASSE 8
TEL 030 782 58 21
A little off the beaten track, in a quiet side street east of Kleistpark, Aroma is so good you'd suspect the locals want to keep it to themselves. The Italian menu, created by a duo of talented chefs from Lombardy and south Tyrol,

features seasonal ingredients from the Brandenburg countryside. A hunter from the Spreewald, for instance, provides the wild boar and venison. The dining area doubles as a gallery, concert hall, and de facto Italian cultural center.
🪑 60 🚫 Closed Mon.–Fri. L 🚇 U7, S1, S2 Yorckstrasse 🚭 No credit cards

▯ AMRIT
$$
ORANIENSTRASSE 202–203
TEL 030 612 55 50
Everything about Amrit is big: the lurid wall mirrors, the ringed chandeliers, the servings, and (deservedly) the reputation. The Indian dishes prepared in the tandoori ovens are sublime, e.g., spiced shrimp fried in basmati rice, nuts, vegetables and raisins, or the spicy marinated duck in honey sauce. The name means "holy water of paradise," but best wash it all down with a mango lassi or yogi tea.
🪑 110 🚇 U1 Görlitzer Bahnhof 🚭 All major cards

SOMETHING SPECIAL

▯ DER GOLDENE HAHN
This gem of an Italian restaurant is done up in Tuscan country style, with old farm utensils on the walls and an apothecary's cabinet behind the bar. Handwritten on a chalk slate, the daily menu is classic trattoria at its best. Stuffed pearl hen with anise sauce, giant grilled calamares, or pumpkin gnocchi in Parma butter are a few of the stunners that the owner is happy to pair with an excellent Italian wine. Special requests are prepared with no fuss, and they'll even spin a disc of your choice.
$$
PÜCKLERSTRASSE 20
TEL 030 618 80 98
🪑 110 🚫 Closed L 🚇 U1 Görlitzer Bahnhof 🚭 MC, V

🚭 Nonsmoking ⬆ Elevator 🔆 Air-conditioning 🏊 Indoor/🏊 Outdoor pool 🎮 Gym 🚭 Credit cards   **KEY**

HOTELS & RESTAURANTS (side vertical text)

OUSIES
$$
GRUNEWALDSTRASSE 16
TEL 030 216 79 57
In Greece, many tavernas used to serve hot and cold appetizers instead of main dishes, a custom well suited to the hearty consumption of wine and ouzo. Ousies happily picks up this tradition with its barrage of tasty Greek tapas: hamburger balls filled with spinach and cheese, mussels baked in lemon-oregano juice, or morsels of *tsatsiki* chicken. The interior walks a fine line between kitsch (note the glued-on faux eaves) and bacchanalia. Reserve ahead.
🪑 65 🕐 Closed L 🚇 U7 Eisenacher Strasse 💳 MC, V

CAFE EINSTEIN
$–$$
KURFÜRSTENSTRASSE 58
TEL 030 261 50 96
Red leather banquettes, Thonnet furniture, parquet flooring, and wooden chairs re-create old Vienna in this opulent villa from 1878. The Einstein has it all, from coffee and cake to Austrian nouvelle cuisine, where even the schnitzels give you a frisson of culinary excitement. Or try the *Sylt* breakfast—a large plate of smoked fish. Patrons include both celebrities and workaholics who spite Viennese etiquette by continuing to toil over Apfelstrudel.
🪑 300 🚇 U2 Kurfürstenstrasse 💳 DC, MC, V

PRANZO E CENA
$–$$
GOLTZSTRASSE 32
TEL 030 216 35 14
This cute little Italian eatery could write the book on authentic. The stone-oven-cooked pizza is the hottest item, but the lasagnas and spaghettis (all fresh pasta) are just as tempting. The friendly staff will even fill requests for

off-menu items. This is a great spot for a bargain lunch or dinner before hitting the bars and clubs around Winterfeld-platz just to the north.
🪑 70 🚇 U2, U3, U4 Nollendorfplatz 💳 AE, MC, V

YELLOW SUNSHINE
$
WIENERSTRASSE 19
TEL 030 69 59 87 20
This vegetarian fast-food cafe in Kreuzberg sells dozens of types of veggie burgers, country-style fries, and salads, plus soy-milk ice cream and a potpourri of other vegan delights, topped off with organic juices or beer. It's enough to convert the most stubborn of carnivores to the other side. The staff speaks English fluently.
🪑 40 🚇 U1 Görlitzer Bahnhof 💳 No credit cards

ZUR HENNE
$
LEUSCHNERDAMM 25
TEL 030 614 77 30
Just off Kreuzberg's vibrant Oranienstrasse, this earthy bar-cafe is where dyed-in-the-wool Berliners meet to eat, drink, and trade gossip. Back in '63, the Henne sent John F. Kennedy an invitation to stop by. JFK couldn't make it, but sent a letter of apology which is still framed over the bar. The menu is easy to get your head around: roast chicken, sauerkraut, and bread. But the roast birds are so juicy you'll want nothing else. Reserve ahead.
🪑 80 🕐 Closed L & Mon. 🚇 U1, U8 Kottbusser Tor 💳 No credit cards

SPANDAU, DAHLEM, & THE WEST

RESTAURANTS

ZITADELLENSCHÄNKE
$$$
AM JULIUSTURM
TEL 030 334 21 06

HOTELS
The cost of a double room without breakfast is indicated by $ signs.
$$$$$ Over $270
$$$$ $200–$270
$$$ $130–$200
$$ $80–$120
$ Under $80

RESTAURANTS
The cost of a three-course dinner without drinks is indicated by $ signs.
$$$$$ Over $80
$$$$ $50–$80
$$$ $35–$50
$$ $20–$35
$ Under $20
Hotels and restaurants are listed alphabetically by price category within each district.

Located in Spandau's 16th-century fortress, this is the place to live out your medieval fantasy—if it involves consuming a leg of boar to the strains of authentic minstrel song. Try to book ahead as the vaulted, candlelit banquet hall is popular with groups.
🪑 220 🕐 Closed Mon. & L Tues.–Fri. 🚇 U7 Rathaus Spandau 💳 DC, MC, V

ALTER KRUG
$$
KÖNIGIN LUISE STRASSE 52
TEL 030 84 31 95 40
This half-timbered eatery just south of the Botanical Gardens retains a village feel, going back to an era before Berlin's tram lines reached Dahlem. It's known for hearty standards like *boulette* (spicy hamburger patties) and Swabian fare such as *Maultaschen* (ravioli). There's a lovely beer garden that's inevitably packed in summer.
🪑 125 🚇 U1 Dahlem Dorf 💳 No credit cards

■ EXCURSIONS

POTSDAM

🏨 SCHLOSSHOTEL
🍴 CECILIENHOF
$$$
NEUER GARTEN, 14469
TEL 0331 370 50
FAX 0331 29 24 98
www.relexa-hotel.de
Situated in a park on the shore of the Wannsee, this grand mansion was the setting for the Potsdam Conference, where Truman, Churchill, and Stalin met in 1945 to discuss the fate of a defeated Germany. Furnished in classic Tudor style, the hotel is close to Potsdam but has a tranquil country atmosphere.
🛏 41 � S1, S7 Wannsee or Potsdam, then taxi 🅿 🆂 All major cards

🍴 SPECKERS
GASTSTÄTTE ZUR
RATSWAAGE
$$$
AM NEUEN MARKT 10
TEL 0331 280 43 11
Enjoy country food such as hearty eel soup or roast rabbit filled with black pudding at this elegant restaurant in historic surroundings. Much of the produce is from local farmers. The old well in the romantic courtyard is a much-loved feature.
🍴 70 🕐 Closed Sun. D
� S1 Potsdam 🆂 AE, MC, V

🍴 BLOCKHAUS
NIKOLSKOE
$$-$$$
NIKOLSKOER WEG 15
TEL 030 805 29 14
About 2.5 miles (4 km) east of Potsdam, and boasting a fine view of the Wannsee lake, this sprawling wooden lodge was built by Prussian king Frederick Wilhelm III for his daughter and her husband, Czar Nicholas I. Game dishes are the menu's strength, but the selection runs the gamut, as do the prices. In good weather, dining is popular on the riverside terrace.
🍴 260 � S1, S7 Wannsee
🆂 All major cards

DRESDEN

🏨 ART'OTEL DRESDEN
🍴 $$-$$$
OSTRAALLEE 33, 01067
TEL 0351 492 20
FAX 0351 492 27 77
www.artotels.de
Situated a ten-minute walk from the Semperoper and the historic Old Town. Expect a voguish allure in these large, snazzy rooms where form scores highly over function. The stylish interior is the product of a Milan designer; the in-house gallery features some challenging works by Dresden artist A. R. Penck. The staff speaks English.
🛏 183 🅿 🛗 🆂 🆂
🍴 🆂 All major cards

🍴 FOUR RESTAURANTS
& OPERNRESTAURANT
$$
THEATERPLATZ 2
TEL 0351 4 91 15 21
In a posh modern building behind the Semperoper, this sophisticated place offers cuisine from Italian to German. Opera lovers flock here before and after performances. Guests can enjoy the terrace in fine weather.
🍴 80 🕐 Closed Mon.–Sat. L
🆂 All major cards

🍴 KUPPEL RESTAURANT
$$
WEISSERITZSTRASSE 3
TEL 0351 490 59 90
Located in the former Yenidze cigarette factory, this restaurant serves Middle Eastern and Saxon specialties under a terrific stained-glass dome. The building is fairly surreal, styled after an oriental mosque with a smokestack disguised as a minaret. In warm weather you can dine on the rooftop terrace and admire the twinkling lights of Dresden.
🍴 130 🆂 MC, V

LEIPZIG

🏨 LEIPZIGER HOF
🍴 $$
HEDWIGSTRASSE 1–3, 04315
TEL 0341 697 40
FAX 0341 697 41 50
www.leipziger-hof.de
This protected building may have been built in Bismarck's day, but rooms are equipped with the latest technology. Paintings of historic Leipzig adorn the walls, giving the place a documentary feel. Breakfast is included and there's a beer garden that teems with socialites after local art shows.
🛏 68 & 4 apts. 🅿 🆂 🆂
🍴 🆂 All major cards

🍴 AUERBACHS KELLER
$$
MÄDLER-PASSAGE,
GRIMMAISCHE STRASSE 2–4
TEL 0341 21 61 00
One of Germany's classic restaurants, founded in 1525, Auerbachs Keller has earned plenty of acclaim for its contempory European cuisine. Whatever you do, sneak a peek at the historical section, which depicts a scene from Goethe's *Faust*. In it, Mephistopheles and Faust carouse with students before riding off on a barrel—a scene often reenacted at night.
🍴 250 🆂 All major cards

🍴 BARTHELS HOF
$$
HAINSTRASSE 1
TEL 0341 141 31 13
This sprawling, historic eatery—Leipzig's oldest—has a bar, wine cellar, and restaurant serving Saxon dishes such as *Heubraten* (marinated lamb roasted on hay). Waitresses wear traditional costume, but the rooms are quite contemporary. The courtyard of the same name is nestled among Leipzig's oldest Renaissance buildings.
🍴 180 🆂 All major cards

SHOPPING

Berlin's shopping scene is scattered but comprehensive. You'll find flashy temples of consumption, flea and antique markets, makers of quality jewelry and handicrafts—but what sets the city apart are its wacky fashion boutiques. Before World War II, Berlin was an international center of fashion, and in recent years, its designers have set about reclaiming that title. Their output is generally not haute couture but rather edgy, young, off-the-wall creations.

The eastern districts of Berlin are a petri dish of the latest streetwear. To see what's sizzling, try the upscale fashion shops around Hackescher Markt and up to Prenzlauer Berg, where the Kastanienallee is filled with pocket-size boutiques selling retro gear. To test your credit card limits, try the Galeries Lafayette department store and the swank shopping passages of Quartier 206, both on Friedrichstrasse, or the excellent Potsdamer Platz Arkaden, a four-story American-style mall. In western Berlin, the Kurfürstendamm (Ku'damm) is the shopping street for Versace, Gucci, and Jil Sander as well as chain boutiques catering to young fashionistas. Side streets like Bleibtreustrasse and Fasanenstrasse feature upscale garments. Berlin's legendary department store, KaDeWe (Kaufhaus des Westens), is also here. For ethnic and specialty items, hit the alternative strips of Kreuzberg along Oranienstrasse and Bergmannstrasse for bookshops, esoterica, clothing, and outdoor and household gear.

OPENING HOURS

Under German law, stores can open no earlier than 6 a.m. and close no later than 8 p.m. Many smaller ones start business at 10 or 11 a.m. and close at 6:30 p.m. On Sunday everything is closed with a few exceptions, such as bakeries, souvenir shops on Unter den Linden, and shops in train stations, airports, and filling stations. Some stores, especially in the east, flout the Sunday closing law with little reprisal.

PAYMENT & TAXES

Cash is still king in Germany. Department stores will take credit cards, but smaller shops often do not; check the door stickers. Most Germans pay either by cash or EC direct-debit cards.

Except for E.U. citizens, visitors to Germany are entitled to a refund on value-added (sales) tax for all nonedible goods bought in German stores. The usual minimum is €50 in a single store. Ask for a special form at stores displaying the tax-free sign. When you leave Germany, the form must be stamped by customs and you'll have to present goods in their original packaging. The tax can be refunded on the spot or sent on, which requires patience.

BOOKS
Bücherbogen
Stadtbahnbogen, Savignyplatz 593, Charlottenburg, tel 030 31 86 95 11. This wonderfully cramped bookshop underneath the S-Bahn is strong on painting, sculpture, design, photography, and architecture. The staff knows its stuff and can advise on whatever you're seeking.

Bücherstube Marga Schöller
Knesebeckstrasse 33, Charlottenburg, tel 030 881 11 12. This venerable literary bookshop has been going for over 70 years. Once focused on theater, today its rooms are crammed with books on every subject under the sun and include an impressive English-language section. This is the place to spend time poring over literary treasures, as Bertolt Brecht and Canetti used to do. There's recorded music, too.

Dussmann
Friedrichstrasse 90, Mitte, tel 030 20 25 24 40. Billed as a "cultural department store," the greatest part of this store's selection is books, spread over three spacious floors. It's an attractive place, with an atrium spilling light into the center and padded armchairs inviting you to sit and read. The offerings include a CD section on two floors, a stationery shop and a slew of cut-rate books ready for offloading. The "cultural" part refers to the restaurant, regular concerts, readings, and even live talk shows.

DEPARTMENT STORES
Aus Berlin
Karl Liebknecht Strasse 17, Mitte, tel 030 41 99 78 96. This mini-department store has taken it upon itself to gather, promote, and market what it sees as Berlin's top products. It gives you a snapshot of Berlin's creative output—apparel from top Berlin designers like Andrea van Reimerdahl or Eastberlin but also local schnapps, cosmetics, furniture, books and CDs, board games, and fine comestibles.

Galeries Lafayette
Französische Strasse 23, Mitte, tel 030 20 94 80. This branch of the upscale French department-store chain is known best for its central atrium, a stunning funnel-shaped core made of translucent glass. Apart from that there's French designer apparel, cosmetics, and accessories, but little that really stands out.

KaDeWe
Tauentzienstrasse 21–24, Schöneberg, tel 030 21 22 0. "If we don't have it, it probably doesn't exist" is the motto of the Kaufhaus des Westens, the largest department store in Germany. A major tourist attraction in its own right, the lavish sixth-floor food hall stocks delicacies from around the globe.

Manufactum
Hardenbergstrasse 4–5,
Charlottenburg, tel 030 24 03 38
44. They're still around, those
good old products that your
grandparents grew up with.
This fascinating store specializes
in timeless design classics made
with quality materials and mostly
by hand. Straight razors crafted
in Solingen, a 1924 Desny desk
lamp, and mechanical scales from
Italy are but a few items in the
extensive catalogue.

Stilwerk
Kantstrasse 17, Charlottenburg,
tel 030 31 51 150. A gorgeous
monument to design, with 60
stores selling sleek top-end
items for house and home over
five floors. This is the place to
pick up a stylish Rolf Benz
couch, Artimide lamp, or
Bechstein grand piano without
breaking a sweat. Design-related
exhibitions are a regular feature.

Wertheim
Kurfürstendamm 231,
Charlottenburg, tel 030 88 00
30. Second only to the KaDeWe
in size, this mainstream
department store is a bit
disorganized but a good stop for
souvenirs. You can snack in the
basement food court or rooftop
café and savor the views of
the Gedächtniskirche.

FASHION
Whisper "Berlin" among fashion
mavens in London, Milan, or
New York, and you'll be treated
with respect. Since the wall
came down in 1989, legions of
apparel gurus have flocked to
the German capital to present
an ever expanding gala of shows.
The Fashion Week trade shows
in January and July (see pp.
234–35) are a must-see for
professional buyers.

Barfuss oder Lackschuh
Oranienburger Strasse 89, Mitte,
tel 030 28 39 19 91. Sneakers,
fine pumps: All the latest shoe
designs act like a magnet to
the visitors thronging
Oranienburger Strasse.

Berlinomat
Frankfurter Allee 89,
Friedrichshain, tel 030 42 08 14
45. This is a mini-department
store for designer duds, fed by
the work of 125-odd local
designers. You might pick up a
wooden sushi roller, Milkberlin
designer bag, or groovy Ic!berlin
sunglasses, against a background
of techno-beats.

Bless
Mulackstrasse 38, Mitte, tel 030
44 01 01 00. The Franco-
German design team of Ines
Kaag and Desirée Heiss
specializes in intelligent, avant-
garde items—clothing, jewelry,
shoes, bags, and furniture, some
of which double as art objects.

Bramigk
Savignypassage Bogen 598,
Charlottenburg, tel 030 313 51
25. Form-fitting, timeless
feminine garb, dresses, skirts,
and pants made of fine Italian
fabrics. The accessories are just
as tasteful—hand-painted
scarves, wraps, and felt slippers.
They also do a nice merino-
wool collection of children's
sweaters.

Budapester Schuhe
Kurfürstendamm 43 & 199,
Charlottenburg, tel 030 88 62 42
06. Ladies' shoes from Prada,
Miu Miu, Jimmy Choo.
Gentlemen can choose from
classic English brogues,
handcrafted shoes from
Budapest, or Gucci loafers.

Crème Fresh
Kastanienallee 221, Mitte, tel 030
48 62 58 27. No "sour cream" to
be found in this well-stocked
boutique, but instead European
cult labels like Fornaria, maphaia
Revolution, or Gsus, at
reasonable prices.

Eisdieler
Kastanienallee 12, Prenzlauer
Berg, tel 030 285 73 51. This
former ice-cream parlor is the
place to buy T-shirts, baggy
pants, sweaters, and accessories.
The five designers of this small

cooperative are known well
beyond the confines of Berlin.

Fiona Bennett
Grosse Hamburgerstrasse 25,
Mitte, tel 030 28 09 63 30. You'd
never guess that these exquisite
hats, mostly made from felt or
straw, are the result of the
owner's training at an old
Berlin millinery. The products
lead Berlin's cutting edge.
Vivienne Westwood, the British
design queen, can be spotted
wearing them.

Hut ab
Heckmann Höfe, Oranienburger
Strasse 32, Mitte, tel 030 28 38
61 05. Hats, clothes, and home
accessories made from felt and
combined with organza or
chiffon. It's the pick of the bunch
in the restored courtyards of
the Heckmann Höfe, home to
many fascinating boutiques.

Killerbeast
Schlesische Strasse 31,
Kreuzberg, tel 030 99 26 03 19.
Recyclable materials provide the
fodder for the clothing creations
rolled out under kooky themes
almost every week. For cool,
urban streetwear and
kiddiewear, this is a sure bet for
killing uniformity.

NIX
Heckmann Höfe, Oranienburger
Strasse 32, Mitte, tel 030 281 80
44. This name stands for New
Individual X-tras, aimed at men,
women, and children who want
garb for any occasion. Regular
markdowns are offered.

Sterling Gold
Heckmann Höfe, Oranienburger
Strasse 32, Mitte, tel 030 28 09
65 00. Glamour gals and their
mates will love the sleek taffeta
gowns and cocktail dresses of
this upscale boutique. Styles are
from the '50s to '80s but
virtually timeless. Price is of little
concern for most patrons.

Thatchers
Hackesche Höfe, Rosenthaler
Strasse 40–41, Mitte, tel 030 27

58 22 10. For over a decade Thatchers has produced three trendy lines a year for both men and women, inspired by music, digital art, and architecture, Bauhaus in particular. Their clothes are playfully tongue-in-cheek—try on a translucent "heartache" blouse, a snazzy airline-themed dress called Take Off, or their Alien boxer shorts with snakeskin pattern. A second outlet is found at Kastanienallee 21, Prenzlauer Berg.

Trippen Shoes
Hackesche Höfe, Rosenthaler Strasse 40–41, Mitte, tel 030 28 39 13 37. These shapely, award-winning shoes crafted in top-flight leather and wood turn heads in Tokyo and New York. If your wallet goes on strike, try the factory outlet at Chausseestrasse 35.

FLEA MARKETS
Berlin's many flea markets are a treasure trove of antiques, bric-a-brac, and weird clothing. With a little perseverance you can find some real bargains.

Berliner Kunst & Nostalgiemarkt
Am Kupfergraben, Mitte. Close to the Bode-Museum entrance, this "art and nostalgia" market is a gold mine of collectibles, books, ethnic crafts, and GDR memorabilia. A little touristy but fun. Open 11 a.m. to 5 p.m. Saturday and Sunday.

Boxhagener Platz
Friedrichshain. This street market is always buzzing with students and crunchy locals who find attic treasures to sell every single week. Plenty of junk, but gems can be found, such as unusual GDR memorabilia. Open Sunday.

Strasse des 17. Juni
Tiergarten. Just west of the S-Bahn stop Tiergarten, this sprawling market is a favorite tourist haunt, but has some nice art and Berlin mementos. Open Saturday and Sunday.

FOOD MARKETS
Kollwitzplatz
Prenzlauer Berg. In the heart of the Prenzlauer Berg District, this market is where yuppies come to buy crusty breads, flowers, French cheeses, exquisite Wurst, spices, and more from organic farmers. Kollwitzplatz's central square has a playground where customers leave their offspring while browsing the many stalls. There are plenty of handicrafts and great wooden toys, too. Open Saturday 8 a.m. to 4 p.m.

Turkish Market
Maybachufer, Neukölln. Just across the canal from Kreuzberg, this lively, crowded market caters to the large Turkish neighborhood. Colorful is the word, with vendors crying out prices over heaps of fruits and vegetables, delicious feta cheeses, teas, fresh breads, a variety of olives, and of course, Turkish carpets. Prices are about the lowest in town and the vendors are friendly and helpful. It's great for stocking a picnic lunch and an eyeful just for browsing. Open noon to 6:30 p.m. Tuesday and Friday.

Winterfeldt Markt
Winterfeldtplatz, Schöneberg. Perusing this finest of Berlin's open-air markets is a pleasure, because the selection is so large and the quality particularly high. Produce stands are set up like works of art, and there are premium cheeses, sausages, flowers, and handmade designer clothes to lighten your pocketbook. Come on Saturday around noon to see the market at its peak. After browsing, treat yourself to a coffee or late breakfast at one of the cafés lining the square. Open 8 a.m. to 2 p.m. Wednesday and Saturday

GALLERIES
Berlin has 300-plus private galleries that present their wares in a variety of venues—stately villas, pocket-size showrooms, and converted factories. The main drags are in Charlottenburg, in the vicinity of Knesebeckstrasse, Mommsenstrasse, and Pestalozzistrasse, and in Mitte along Auguststrasse and Linienstrasse. To see what's happening where, pick up the bi-monthly German-English *Kunstführer* (art guide), available from newsstands and galleries.

Camera Work
Kantstrasse 149, Charlottenburg, tel 030 31 50 47 83. A gallery displaying high-caliber photography in wonderfully airy rooms behind a renovated courtyard. Prints from the likes of Helmut Newton, Irving Penn, and Robert Lebeck are available starting at a few hundred euros.

C/O Berlin
Linienstrasse 144, Mitte, tel 030 28 09 19 25, open Wednesday to Sunday 11 a.m. to 7 p.m. Probably the best showcase of photography in the former east, this trendy art space is happy to promote emerging talent as well as works of icons like Henri Cartier-Bresson and Annie Leibovitz. Entrance fees cover several floors but anyone can peruse the library of glossy photo books for free.

Jarmuschek & Partner
Sophienstrasse 18, Mitte, tel 030 28 50 10 07, closed Monday. In the hotbed of art-hungry Mitte, a stone's throw from the Hackesche Höfe, this intimate courtyard gallery has a quick-moving collection of edgy but accessible works in paint, photography, and experimental media.

GIFTS
Absinth Depot
Weinmeisterstrasse 4, Mitte, tel 030 281 67 89. Absinthe was de rigeur in 19th-century bohemian Paris, so it's fitting that Berlin, another den of decadence, should host Germany's only shop devoted to the anise-based drink. Apart from fine absinthes, you'll find liqueurs, wines, and Bavarian beers.

Ampelmann Galerie Shop
Hackesche Höfe, Mitte, tel 030 44 04 88 01. An unabashed product of "Ostalgie," the crosswalk man (see sidebar p. 99) appears on everything in this shop—T-shirts, fridge magnets, fruit gums, beach thongs, you name it. Further outlets include the basement shop of the Potsdamer Platz Arkaden, Alte Potsdamer Strasse 7.

Berlin Bonbonmacherei
Heckmann Höfe, Oranienburger Strasse 32, Mitte, tel 030 44 05 52 43. The making of old-fashioned candies is something of a lost art, and this little basement store has tapped into that vein of nostalgia. The owners use antique equipment to turn out tangy sour drops and green leaf-shaped "may leaves," a local specialty, right before your eyes.

Blindenanstalt Berlin
Oranienstrasse 26, Kreuzberg, tel 030 902 98 66 21. The Berlin Institute for the Blind has been producing brushes, brooms, and wicker goods for over 120 years, and their experience shows. Their sightless craftspeople have an imagination that elevates these everyday items to the status of design objects.

Erzgebirgische Volkskunst
Dircksenstrasse 50, Mitte, tel 030 28 38 80 10. Traditional wooden handicrafts from the Ore Mountains of eastern Germany—incense-puffing "smoking men," Christmas pyramids, nutcrackers, and more. Ask for a "year-end figure with wings," a euphemism once used for a yuletide angel in the godless GDR.

Gipsformerei
Sophie-Charlotten-Strasse 17–18, Charlottenburg, tel 030 321 70 11. The museum shop at Schloss Charlottenburg stocks over 7,000 plaster casts of museum exhibits. The number-one best seller is the bust of Egyptian Queen Nefertiti.

Hanfhaus
Oranienstrasse 192, Kreuzberg, tel 030 614 81 02. This proudly alternative store carries only products made from hemp, which can be grown legally in Germany. Besides a wide selection of cosmetics, organic foods, and clothing you'll discover the weed's lesser known qualities (fabrics are anti-static, dirt repellent, and UV proof).

Hase Weiss
Windscheidstrasse 25, Charlottenburg, tel 030 31 99 67 37. This clever workshop makes wooden toys, dolls, and children's furniture that mutate as the little ones grow up; a highchair, for instance, converts to a set of shelves. Bring the kids if you have an hour to spare.

Königsberger Marzipan Wald
Pestalozzistrasse 54A, Charlottenburg, tel 030 323 82 54. Owner Irmgard Wald sells marzipan made from the original recipe from the former German province of Königsberg, now a part of Russia. She has been running this Old World Berlin institution since 1947. Pricey but oh, so good.

Leysieffer
Kurfürstendamm 218, Charlottenberg, tel 030 885 74 80. A century-old expert in the dark art of chocolate making, Leysieffer is renowned in Germany for its champagne truffles, nougats, milk chocolates, and other heavenly delights. This flagship store wraps gifts, too. There's another branch at Friedrichstrasse 68 in Mitte.

Meissener Porzellan
Unter den Linden 39, Mitte, tel 030 22 67 90 28. This shop sells fine plates, sculptures, and chandeliers from the famous Saxon porcelain make. Items range from everyday crockery to elaborate works of art costing scads of euros. The only place with a better selection is in Meissen itself.

Museum Shop at Checkpoint Charlie House
Friedrichstrasse 43-45, Kreuzberg, tel 030 253 72 50. Tiny chunks of the Berlin Wall, T-shirts stating "You are Leaving the American Sector," and posters of Brezhnev and Honecker kissing are some of the best-selling souvenirs.

Steiff
Kurfürstendamm 220, Charlottenburg, tel 030 88 72 19 19. Richard Steiff claimed to have made the first-ever teddy bear in 1902. The firm now rolls out the entire animal kingdom from furry little bees to life-size lions and elephants, woven with mohair and bearing Steiff's trademark button in the ear. Vintage Steiff teddy bears fetch a pretty penny at collectors' fairs.

Whiskey & Cigars
Sophienstrasse 23, Mitte, tel 030 282 03 76. Choose from a thousand-strong cache of whiskeys from Scotland (of course!) but also from Ireland, Japan, and far-flung corners of North America. Stogies are kept in a walk-in humidor. The sampling room is a den of relaxation with plenty of comfy leather-bound chairs.

Widmoser Smuckatelier
Falckensteinstrasse 45, Kreuzberg, tel 030 69 56 42 19. Closed Sunday to Wednesday. Jeweler Sigrid Widmoser dreams up dazzling amorphous shapes in attractive colors, from chunky silver rings with rose quartz to inlaid earrings of nonallergenic metals. These are classy, tailor-made items at reasonable prices.

ENTERTAINMENT

Nowhere else in Germany does the cultural scene bubble with more energy or abandon than in Berlin, the non-stop capital. It's no exaggeration to say there's something for everyone, usually at any time of day or night.

Excellent opera, dance, and theater productions thrive next to literally hundreds of venues offering music and dance of every conceivable ilk, with no shortage of watering holes along the way. The scene in the west is well established, with mostly upscale venues in Charlottenburg, although the clubs and bars around Winterfeldplatz in Schöneberg and along Kreuzberg's Oranienstrasse have a pleasantly grungy feel. The theater district is centered around Savignyplatz and the streets leading off the Kurfürstendamm (Ku'damm).

On the other hand, the eastern parts of town (Mitte, Prenzlauer Berg, and Friedrichshain in particular) are a laboratory of the latest trends in bars and clubbing, despite a creeping commercialism in such popular tourist zones as Hackescher Markt and around Kollwitzplatz. Venues in "F-Hain" are the place to visit for deep-set grunge with its gloves off. But no matter the pursuit, there's a palpable attitude among Berliners that entertainment is an inalienable right. Chances are you'll find yourself staying out later than usual.

BEER GARDENS
Cafe am Neuen See
Lichtensteinallee 2, Tiergarten, tel 030 254 49 30. On hot summer days, the leafy, open-air café in the Tiergarten is the closest Berlin gets to a bona fide Munich beer garden. Line up for half liters of Bavarian wheat beer, *leberkäse* (spicy meatloaf), and pretzels before plumping down at the tables under shady chestnut trees. There's a sandbox for the kiddies, and you can rent a boat on the adjacent pond. On weekends the place fills to within an inch of its life.

Prater
Kastanienallee 7–9, Mitte, tel 030 448 56 88. This is one of Berlin's oldest beer gardens, founded in 1837. It hasn't lost its drawing power: All 600 seats are often taken in summer at the tightly packed tables under big chestnut trees. Apart from foaming mugs of beer, there's rib-sticking grub on offer (steak sandwiches, bratwurst, and the like). It includes an old-fashioned restaurant, open-air theater, and the famous Bastard Club nights.

Strandbar
Montbijoustrasse 3, Mitte. Why jostle for rays in some tropical tourist trap? Instead try a worry-free afternoon at Berlin's greatest beach bar, a real-life mirage complete with carted-in palm trees, golden sand, and gulls shrieking over the Spree River. Do like the natives: Grab a deck chair, quaff a brew, and raise a smug hand to the passing tourist boats. Other such oases include Mühlenstrasse 24–26 in Friedrichshain, next to the East Side Gallery.

CLASSICAL MUSIC & THEATER
Berlin Philharmonic
Herbert-von-Karajan-Strasse 1, Mitte, tel 030 25 48 80. The Philharmonie is undoubtedly the best place in Berlin to hear world-class classical music performances, conducted by Sir Simon Rattle. It has ultra-modern facilities, and its fine acoustics can be enjoyed from anywhere in the house—the concert podium is in the center, with seating on all sides. Tickets can be booked online at www.berliner-philharmoniker.de.

Chamäleon
Hackesche Höfe, Rosenthaler Strasse 40–41, Mitte, tel 030 40 00 59 30, closed Mon. This variety theater stands out from the pack with a dazzling array of events of consistently high quality. A changing procession of gala nights, concerts, circus acrobatics, and plays are performed in this intimate art-nouveau hall with 300 seats. There's good food, too.

Konzerthaus
Gendarmenmarkt, Mitte, tel 030 2030-92101. Home to the very capable Berlin Symphony Orchestra, the handsomely restored Konzerthaus is dripping in musical heritage. It was here that Weber's *Der Freischütz* had its world premiere and Wagner directed his *Fliegender Holländer*. Every year the hall holds more than 550 concerts and other events.

Schaubühne
Leniner Platz, Kurfürstendamm 153, Charlottenburg, tel 030 89 00 23. Berlin's (some would say Germany's) cutting edge of drama and choreography is honed here. Drawing on a deep well of material, the German-language productions feature some of the country's most accomplished actors (such as Bruno Ganz, who played the lead in the film *Hitler: The Downfall*).

Staatsoper
Unter den Linden 5–7, Mitte, tel 030 20 35 45 55. The oldest and best of Berlin's three opera houses, the Staatsoper is located in a stunning building, a copy of a neoclassic court opera house from 1742. Its driving force is renowned musical director Daniel Barenboim, who draws top talent to classy events like the annual Festival Days (see p. 234). Walk-ins are welcome, and barring shorts and sneakers, there's no real dress code.

CINEMA
Arsenal
Potsdamer Platz, Potsdamer Strasse 21, tel 030 26 95 51 00. An antidote to the mainstream films of the nearby Sony Center, this comfy duplex theater shows

a mélange of independent and classic movies, many of which figure prominently in the history of cinema. It's attached to the Filmmuseum next door.

CineStar Sony Center

Potsdamer Platz, Potsdamer Strasse 4, tel 030 26 06 62 60. This plush multiplex shows movies in their original language without subtitles—a rarity in Berlin, where films are typically dubbed into German. The eight screens are located in the Sony Center at Potsdamer Platz, the stage for many a movie premiere rolled out in the presence of glowing stars.

Hackesche Höfe

Rosenthaler Strasse 40–41, Mitte, tel 030 283 46 03. Expect discriminating, subtitled gems at this upstairs five-screen cinema. Filmmakers often turn up for preview chats.

CULTURAL COMPLEXES
Admiralspalast

Friedrichstrasse 101–102, Mitte, tel 030 47 99 74 99. In the roaring '20s the labyrinthine Admiralspalast was the focus of Friedrichstrasse's "entertainment mile," taking in a spa, grand café, theater, concert halls, and a huge ice rink with several tiers of seating. Renovated with much fanfare in 2006, its reincarnation has added a jazz club and discotheque to its repertoire. A steam bath with original art nouveau tiles is located on the top floor.

Kulturbrauerei

Knaackstrasse 97, Prenzlauer Berg, tel 030 44 31 51 52. Once home to the Schultheiss Brewery, the "culture brewery" now hosts 20-odd venues for parties, movies, and food spread around an old industrial courtyard. If you're undecided, just wander through and choose from options including the Franzz nightclub, music venues such as the Kesselhaus, Maschinenhause, and Palais, as well as the atmospheric Pool &

Cigars, which offers fine smokes and whiskeys over the green baize.

Pfefferberg

Schönhauser Allee 176, Prenzlauer Berg, tel 030 443 83 342. Another converted brewery, the Pfefferberg delves deep into the alternative with a fascinating complex that includes a charity café and a rabbit's warren of art galleries. It hosts noteworthy concerts and special events like Flamenco Week and artist's markets. In summer there's a fabulous beer garden with views through old industrial arches over Senefelder Platz.

Tacheles

Oranienburger Strasse 54–56, Mitte, tel 030 25 89 890. This scary-looking, bombed-out rump of a department store has shifted from cult-artist status to self-conscious grunge, but is still plenty interesting. It has an active program that includes dance and concerts, a cinema, art galleries, and a very earthy beer garden out back.

NIGHTLIFE
A-Trane

Bleibtreustrasse 1, Charlottenburg, tel 030 313 25 50. Blue-ribbon talent plays contemporary jazz on a regular basis in this cozy little club, one of western Berlin's most venerable. You'll need to book a table, as it fills up fast. Special duo and Afro-Cuban nights are a regular feature.

Adagio

Marlene-Dietrich-Platz 1, Potsdamer Platz, tel 030 25 92 95 50. Open 7 p.m. Thurs.–Sat. If you've ever wanted to dance in a medieval banquet hall to the strains of Abba or INXS, then this outlandish place underneath the Theater am Potsdamer Platz is for you. The over-the-top interior includes Gothic tables, candelabras, and wooden balconies straight out of King Arthur's prop shop. It's a favorite with the

after-work crowd around Potsdamer Platz.

B Flat

Rosenthaler Strasse 13, Mitte, tel 030 283 31 23. Just north of Hackescher Markt, this is the best jazz club in Mitte, with live concerts most nights. The program covers everything from blues and mainstream jazz to tango dance nights.

Ballhaus Mitte

Auguststrasse 24, Mitte, tel 030 282 92 95. This venerable dance hall has been reincarnated for Mitte's insatiable party set. It has a split personality, with pizzas and Berlin *Bouletten* (hamburger) served during the day and a diverse diet of tango to funk after sunset.

Bar jeder Vernunft

Schaperstrasse 24, Wilmersdorf, tel 030 883 15 82. This elaborate '20s-style marquee stages a whimsical program somewhere between theater and cabaret. The venue itself is worth the admission: art deco mirrors, theater boxes decked out in red velvet, and hand-carved wood paneling. After the performance you can retire to the bar or beer garden.

Galerie Bremer

Fasanenstrasse 37, Wilmersdorf, tel 030 881 49 08. Closed Mon. For four decades Rudolf van der Lak has been running this art gallery and intellectuals' salon where time seems to stand still. Bow-tied art critics and ladies in furs are part of the furniture, which includes a massive wooden bar served by the octogenarian owner himself.

Green Door

Winterfeldtstrasse 50, Schöneberg, tel 030 215 25 15. Renowned among lovers of retro architecture and fine, expensive cocktails, Green Door is a high-class parody of itself with a marvelous wavy bar, screaming wallpaper, and patrons escaping the meat-market clubs

ENTERTAINMENT

around Nollendorfplatz. To enter, ring at the green padded door.

Joseph Roth Diele
Potsdamer Strasse 75, Schöneberg, tel 030 26 36 98 84. Closed Sat.–Sun. With its French café furniture, aged wainscoting, and gilt-edged crockery, not to mention local patrons, this café in the heart of the theater district takes you back to a Berlin still found in black-and-white picture books. Named after a prolific Jewish writer whose quotes and book covers decorate the walls, it's famous for its readings of deep Germanic literature as well as its rolls filled with smoked-sausage spread.

Künstliche Beatmung
Simon Dach Strasse 20, Friedrichshain, tel 030 29 44 94 63. The name means "artificial resuscitation," and the interior is certainly breathtaking. Some 70 cocktails provide the lubrication in futuristic '70s style: A tunnel shaped like a trachea provides padded seats facing one another, separated on each side by beams of light.

Newton Bar
Charlottenstrasse 57, Mitte, tel 030 20 61 29 99. A magnet of the high-society types around Gendarmenmarkt, the bar was named for Berlin-born Helmut Newton, a frequent guest before his death in 2004. Newton's black-and-white "big nudes" grace the glassy walls of the downstairs bar. A well-stocked, walk-in humidor is located upstairs, next to the comfy lounge with gold-leaf ceiling.

Oxymoron
Hackesche Höfe, Rosenthaler Strasse 40–41, Mitte, tel 030 28 39 18 86. By day this baroque café-restaurant serves Italo-French cuisine, but after sunset, it morphs into a '70s-era bar-lounge and then a dance club into the wee hours. The monthly "Pasta and Opera"

nights feature Italian arias between the courses.

Sage Club
Köpenicker Strasse 76, Mitte, tel 030 278 98 30. The Sage is one of the trendiest clubs in Berlin, featuring house thumps over three dance floors with an outdoor swimming pool to prevent overheating. The legendary DJs host charity party nights with proceeds going to the Sage Hospital in Senegal.

Spindler & Klatt
Köpenicker Strasse 16–17, Kreuzberg, tel 030 69 56 67 75. This sprawling club-restaurant is on the A-list of Berlin's dinner-and-dance spots. Located on the waterfront, most of its beautiful guests are entranced by the cool white dining futons and the tasty pan-Asian menu. The music reinvents itself virtually every night, swerving from hip-hop to jazz in the blink of a stylish eye.

Ständige Vertretung (STÄV)
Schiffbauerdamm 8, Mitte, tel 030 282 39 65. When Germany's capital moved from Bonn to Berlin in 1999, a market niche opened up for homesick Rhineland politicians on the banks of the Spree. The name means "permanent representation," after the Cold War label for West Germany's embassy in the East. In a sea of photos and assorted cultural-politico doodads you can order a *Kölsch* (Cologne beer) or a variety of Rhineland dishes and enjoy dance music later on.

Tajikistan Tea Room
Am Festungsgraben 1, Mitte, tel 030 204 11 12. Open evenings only. This is perfect if you're in the mood for a civilized tea with cookies and rum cake in Aladdin-like surroundings. A blast from the GDR's complex past, the entire interior comes from a Tajik display at a '70s trade fair in Leipzig that was presented to the East German government as a gift, back when Tajikistan was a Soviet ally.

Readings and music are a regular feature, and reservations are a good idea.

Trompete
Lützowplatz 9, Tiergarten, tel 030 23 00 47 94. Closed Sun.–Tues. A good distance from the hype of trendy Mitte, the Trompete is a relaxed, well-designed bar–concert lounge run by Ben Becker, one of Germany's top actors and entertainers. The program ranges from classic soul to disco, hip-hop, and of course jazz, sometimes led by the trumpet-tooting Becker himself. The action moves to the garden outside during the summer months.

Weekend
Alexanderplatz 5, Mitte, www.week-end-berlin.de. Located on the 12th floor of the socialist-era Haus des Reisens, the Weekend affords stunning views of the city through panorama windows, a particularly beautiful sight at sunrise after a hard night's churning to house and dance beats. The club draws jet-setters looking for the glitzy side of Berlin clubbing.

WMF
Café Moskau, Karl-Marx-Allee 34, Friedrichshain, tel 030 24 63 16 26. Open Fri.–Sun. For over 15 years the WMF has been at the throbbing forefront of Berlin's club culture. This prominence owes a lot to the latest venue, the communist-era Café Moskau. This café, decked out in red leather, is where People's Army officers came to ply themselves (and their night's date) with shots of vodka and schnapps. The WMF spins high-energy house music and sells CDs under its own label.

LANGUAGE GUIDE

USEFUL WORDS & PHRASES

Yes *Ja*
No *Nein*
Please *Bitte*
Thank you *Danke*
Excuse me *Entschuldigen Sie bitte*
Sorry *Entschuldigung*
Goodbye *Auf Wiedersehen*
Goodbye (informal) *Tschüs*
Good morning *Guten Morgen*
Good day (afternoon) *Guten Tag*
Good evening *Guten Abend*
Good night *Guten Nacht*

here *hier*
there *dort*
today *heute*
yesterday *gestern*
tomorrow *morgen*
now *jetzt*
later *später*
right away *sofort*
this morning *heute morgen*
this afternoon *heute nachmittag*
this evening *heute abend*

large *gross*
small *klein*
hot *heiss*
cold *kalt*
good *gut*
bad *schlecht*
left *links*
right *rechts*
straight ahead *geradeaus*

Do you speak English? *Sprechen Sie Englisch?*
I am American *Ich bin Amerikaner (m)/Amerikanerin (f)*
I don't understand *Ich verstehe Sie nicht*
Please speak more slowly *Bitte sprechen Sie langsamer*
Where is/are...? *Wo ist/sind...?*
I don't know *Ich weiss nicht*
My name is... *Ich heisse...*
At what time? *Wann?*
What time is it? *Wieviel Uhr ist es?*

NUMBERS

one *eins*
two *zwei*
three *drei*
four *vier*
five *fünf*
six *sechs*
seven *sieben*
eight *acht*
nine *neun*
ten *zehn*
twenty *zwanzig*

DAYS OF THE WEEK

Monday *Montag*
Tuesday *Dienstag*
Wednesday *Mittwoch*
Thursday *Donnerstag*
Friday *Freitag*
Saturday *Samstag/Sonnabend*
Sunday *Sonntag*

MONTHS

January *Januar*
February *Februar*
March *März*
April *April*
May *Mai*
June *Juni*
July *Juli*
August *August*
September *September*
October *Oktober*
November *November*
December *Dezember*
spring *Frühling*
summer *Sommer*
fall *Herbst*
winter *Winter*

IN THE HOTEL

Do you have a vacancy? *Haben Sie noch ein Zimmer frei?*
a single room *ein Einzelzimmer*
a double room *ein Doppelzimmer*
with/without bathroom/shower *mit/ohne Bad/Dusche*
key *Schlüssel*
porter *Pförtner*

EMERGENCIES

Help *Hilfe*
I need a doctor/dentist *Bitte rufen Sie einen Arzt/Zahnarzt*
Can you help me? *Können Sie mir helfen?*
Where is the hospital?/police station?/telephone? *Wo finde ich das Krankenhaus?/die Polizeiwache?/das Telefon?*

SHOPPING

Do you have...? *Haben Sie...?*
How much is it? *Wieviel kostet es?*
Do you take credit cards *Akzeptieren Sie Kreditkarten?*

When do you open/close? *Wann machen Sie auf/zu?*
size (clothes) *Kleidergrösse*
size (shoes) *Schuhgrösse*
color *Farbe*
brown *braun*
black *schwarz*
red *rot*
blue *blau*
green *grün*
yellow *gelb*
cheap *billig*
expensive *teuer*
I'll take it *Ich nehme es*
enough *genug*
too much *zu viel*
check *Rechnung*

SHOPS

bakery *Bäckerei*
bookshop *Buchhandlung*
pharmacy *Drogerie*
delicatessen *Feinkostladen*
department store *Warenhaus*
fishmonger *Fischhändler*
grocery *Gemüseladen*
self-service shop *Selbstbedienungsladen*
antique shop *Antikladen*
junk shop *Trödelladen*
library *Bibliothek*
supermarket *Supermarkt*
market *Markt*
newspaper kiosk *Zeitungskiosk*
shoe shop *Schuhgeschäft*
clothes shop *Bekleidungsgeschäft*
special offer *Sonderangebot*
stationery *Schreibwaren*

SIGHTSEEING

visitor information *Touristen-Information*
exhibition *Ausstellung*
open *geöffnet*
closed *geschlossen*
daily *täglich*
all year *ganzjährig*
all day long *den ganzen Tag*
entry fee *Eintrittspreis*
free *frei/umsonst*
cathedral *Kathedrale*
church *Kirche*
abbey *Kloster*
castle *Schloss*
country house *Landhaus*
museum *Museum*
staircase *Treppe*
tower *Turm*
town *Stadt*
old town *Altstadt*
town hall *Rathaus*

MENU READER

I'd like to order *Ich möchte bestellen*
I am a vegetarian *Ich bin Vegetarier (m) Vegetarierin (f)*
The check, please *Die Rechnung, bitte*
Cheers *Prost*
Enjoy your meal *Guten Appetit*
Was it tasty? *Hat es geschmeckt?*
dinner *Abendessen*
menu *Speisekarte*
snack *Imbiss*
knife/fork/spoon *Messer/Gabel/Löffel*
salt/pepper *Salz/Pfeffer*
mustard *Senf*
sugar *Zucker*
bread *Brot*
cheese *Käse*
wine list *Weinkarte*

DRINKS/GETRÄNKE
Apfelsaft apple juice
Bier beer
Berliner Weisse Wheat beer with fruit extract
Kaffee coffee
Milch milk
Orangensaft orange juice
Rotwein red wine
Sekt sparkling wine
Tee tea
Weisswein white wine

BREAKFAST/FRÜHSTÜCK
Brötchen bread roll
Eier eggs
   hartgekochtes hard-boiled
   weich gekochtes soft-boiled
Rühreier scrambled eggs
Schwarzbrot dark brown rye bread
Speck bacon
Spiegelei fried egg
Weissbrot white bread

SOUP/SUPPE
Erbsensuppe pea soup
Gemüsesuppe vegetable soup
Hühnersuppe chicken soup
Linsensuppe lentil soup
Ochsenschwanzsuppe oxtail soup
Pilzsuppe mushroom soup
Spargelcremesuppe cream of asparagus soup

MEAT/FLEISCH
Blutwurst black pudding
Bockwurst large frankfurter

Bouletten meatballs
Brathuhn roast chicken
Bratwurst fried pork sausage
Currywurst curried sausage
Eintopf stew
Eisbein knuckle of pork
Ente duck
Fasan pheasant
gebratene Gans roast goose
Hackbraten meatloaf
Hühnerfrikassee chicken fricassee
Kalbsbrust breast of veal
Kalbshaxe roast knuckle of veal
Kassler Rippen smoked pork chops
Lammkeule roast lamb
Leberknödel liver dumplings
Leberwurst liver sausage
Rehkeule roast venison
Rinderbraten roast beef
Sauerbraten braised beef, marinated in spiced red wine
Schinken ham
Schlachtplatte mixed cold meat
Schweinebraten roast pork
Tafelspitz boiled rump of beef
Wiener Schnitzel veal escalope
Wildschweinkeule roast wild boar

FISH/FISCH
Aal eel
Austern oysters
Fischfrikadellen fish cakes
Flunder flounder
Forelle trout
Garnelen prawns
Heilbutt halibut
Hummer lobster
Jakobsmuscheln scallops
Kabeljau cod
Karpfen carp
Krabben shrimp
Lachs salmon
Makrele mackerel
Matjes pickled herring
Schellfisch haddock
Scholle plaice
Seebarsch sea bass
Seelachs pollack
Seezunge sole
Steinbutt turbot
Tintenfisch squid

VEGETABLES/GEMÜSE
Aubergine eggplant
Blumenkohl cauliflower
Bohnen beans

Champignons/Pilze mushrooms
Erbsen peas
Feldsalat lamb's lettuce
Fenchel fennel
Gurke cucumber
Kapern capers
Kartoffeln potatoes
Kohl cabbage
Kürbis pumpkin
Lauch leek
Linsen lentils
Möhren carrots
Maiskolben sweet corn
Pfifferlinge chanterelle mushrooms
Reis rice
Rosenkohl brussel sprouts
Rotkohl red cabbage
Sauerkraut pickled cabbage
Sellerie celery
Spargel asparagus
Spinat spinach
Tomaten tomatoes
Wirsing savoy cabbage
Zwiebeln onions

FRUIT/OBST
Ananas pineapple
Apfel apple
Apfelsine/Orange orange
Aprikose apricot
Backpflaumen prunes
Birne pear
Blaubeeren blueberries
Brombeeren blackberries
Erdbeeren strawberries
Himbeeren raspberries
Kirschen cherries
Pampelmuse grapefruit
Pfirsich peach
Pflaumen/Zwetschen plums
Rote Johannisbeeren red currants
Schwarze Johannisbeeren black currants
Weintrauben grapes
Zitrone lemon

DESSERTS/NACHSPEISEN
Apfelkuchen apple cake
Bienenstich honey almond cake
Gebäck pastry
Kaiserschmarrn sweet pancake
Käsekuchen cheesecake
Kompott stewed fruit
Krapfen/Berliner doughnuts
Mandelkuchen almond cake
Obstkuchen fruit tart
Sachertorte chocolate cake
Schlagsahne whipped cream
Schwarzwälder Kirschtorte Black Forest cake

ILLUSTRATIONS CREDITS

Abbreviations for terms listed below: (b) bottom, (t) top.

Cover: All cover photos by Pierre Adenis.
Interior: All interior photographs by Pierre Adenis except the following:
24, Landesarchiv Berlin; 25, Gianni Dagli Orti/CORBIS; 26, Landesarchiv
Berlin; 27, Landesarchiv Berlin; 28-29, Hulton Archive/Getty Images; 30-31,
Hulton-Deutsch Collection/CORBIS; 32, Landesarchiv Berlin; 33,
www.berlin-tourist-information.de; 39, Stephanie Maze/CORBIS; 44,
Landesarchiv Berlin; 45, Landesarchiv Berlin; 46, Landesarchiv Berlin; 47,
Hulton Archive/Getty Images; 48, X Filme Creative Pool; 49, Landesarchiv
Berlin; 70, www.berlin-tourist-information.de; 72 (t), www.berlin-tourist-
information.de; 79 (b), Landesarchiv Berlin; 99, Lawrence M. Porges; 108-
109, Lawrence M. Porges; 113, Landesarchiv Berlin; 131, www.berlin-
tourist-information.de; 137, Bettmann/CORBIS; 142, Lawrence M. Porges;
151, Peer Grimm/epa/CORBIS; 152, CORBIS; 164-165, Arnd
Wiegmann/Reuters/CORBIS; 167, www.berlin-tourist-information.de; 170,
www.berlin-tourist-information.de; 180, Landesarchiv Berlin; 181 (t), Time
Life Pictures/Getty Images; 181 (b), Hulton Archive/Getty Images; 182,
Lawrence M. Porges; 186, Lawrence M. Porges; 194, Landesarchiv Berlin;
195, Landesarchiv Berlin; 215, Bettmann/CORBIS; 216, Royalty-Free/COR-
BIS; 217, Lawrence M. Porges; 218, Manfred Mehlig/zefa/CORBIS; 233,
Lawrence M. Porges.

The editors wish to thank the Berlin Tourist Information office for their
assistance in the production of this book: BTM–Berlin Tourist
Information, Berlin Tourismus Marketing GmbH. Reservations and information: 49-30/25 00 25; Internet: www.berlin-tourism.de

One of the world's largest nonprofit scientific and educational organizations, the National Geographic Society was founded in 1888 "for the increase and diffusion of geographic knowledge." Fulfilling this mission, the Society educates and inspires millions every day through its magazines, books, television programs, videos, maps and atlases, research grants, the National Geographic Bee, teacher workshops, and innovative classroom materials. The Society is supported through membership dues, charitable gifts, and income from the sale of its educational products. This support is vital to National Geographic's mission to increase global understanding and promote conservation of our planet through exploration, research, and education.

For more information, please call 1-800-NGS LINE (647-5463) or write to the following address:

National Geographic Society
1145 17th Street N.W.
Washington, D.C. 20036-4688
U.S.A.

Log on to
nationalgeographic.com;
AOL Keyword: NatGeo.

For information about special discounts for bulk purchases, please contact National Geographic Books Special Sales: ngspecsales@ngs.org.

Special Offer! Order today and get one year of National Geographic Traveler, the magazine travelers trust, for only $14.95. Call 1-800-NGS-LINE and mention code TRAC3A6.

Travel the world with National Geographic Experts: www.nationalgeographic.com/ngexpeditions

Published by the National Geographic Society
John M. Fahey, Jr., *President and Chief Executive Officer*
Gilbert M. Grosvenor, *Chairman of the Board*
Nina D. Hoffman, *Executive Vice President and President, Book Publishing Group*
Kevin Mulroy, *Senior Vice President and Publisher*
Marianne Koszorus, *Design Director*
Kristin Hanneman, *Illustrations Director*
Elizabeth L. Newhouse, *Director of Travel Publishing*
Cinda Rose, *Art Director*
Carl Mehler, *Director of Maps*
Barbara A. Noe, *Series Editor*

Staff for this book:
Lawrence M. Porges, *Project Editor*
Kay Kobor Hankins, *Designer*
John C. Anderson, *Illustrations Editor*
Patricia Daniels, *Text Editor*
Anthony Haywood, Sylvia Moehle, *Researchers*
Lise Sajewski, *Editorial Consultant*
XNR Productions, *Map Research and Production*
Chapel Design & Marketing, Ltd., *Map Art*

R. Gary Colbert, *Production Director*
Mike Horenstein, *Production Manager*
Rebecca Hinds, *Managing Editor*

Teresa Neva Tate, Abby Lepold, *Illustrations Specialists*
Robert and Cynthia Swanson, *Indexers*
Jack Brostrom, Steven D. Gardner, Leonie Rubiano *Contributors*

Artwork by Maltings Partnership, Derby, England (pp. 56–57, 86–87, and 212–213)

ISBN-10: 0-7922-6212-3
ISBN-13: 978-0-7922-6212-1

Printed and bound by Cayfosa Quebecor, Barcelona, Spain.
Color separations by North American Color, Portage, MI.

The information in this book has been carefully checked and to the best of our knowledge is accurate. However, details are subject to change, and the National Geographic Society cannot be responsible for such changes, or for errors or omissions. Assessments of sites, hotels, and restaurants are based on the author's subjective opinions, which do not necessarily reflect the publisher's opinion. The publisher cannot be responsible for any consequences arising from the use of this book.

NATIONAL GEOGRAPHIC
TRAVELER

A Century of Travel Expertise in Every Guide

- **Alaska** 0-7922-5371-X
- **Amsterdam** ISBN: 0-7922-7900-X
- **Arizona** (2nd Edition) ISBN: 0-7922-3888-5
- **Australia** (2nd Edition) ISBN: 0-7922-3893-1
- **Barcelona** (2nd Edition) ISBN: 0-7922-5365-5
- **Berlin** ISBN: 0-7922-6212-3
- **Boston & environs** ISBN: 0-7922-7926-3
- **California** (2nd Edition) ISBN: 0-7922-3885-0
- **Canada** (2nd Edition) ISBN: 0-7922-6201-8
- **The Caribbean** ISBN: 0-7922-7434-2
- **China** ISBN: 0-7922-7921-2
- **Costa Rica** (2nd Edition) ISBN: 0-7922-5368-X
- **Cuba** ISBN: 0-7922-6931-4
- **Egypt** ISBN: 0-7922-7896-8
- **Florence & Tuscany**
  (2nd Ed.) ISBN: 0-7922-5318-3
- **Florida** ISBN: 0-7922-7432-6
- **France** ISBN: 0-7922-7426-1
- **Germany** ISBN: 0-7922-4146-0
- **Great Britain** ISBN: 0-7922-7425-3
- **Greece** ISBN: 0-7922-7923-9
- **Hawaii** (2nd Edition) ISBN: 0-7922-5568-2
- **Hong Kong**
  (2nd Edition) ISBN: 0-7922-5369-8
- **India** ISBN: 0-7922-7898-4
- **Ireland** ISBN: 0-7922-4145-20
- **Italy** (2nd Edition) ISBN: 0-7922-3889-3
- **Japan** (2nd Edition) ISBN: 0-7922-3894-X
- **London** ISBN: 0-7922-7428-8
- **Los Angeles** ISBN: 0-7922-7947-6
- **Madrid** 0-7922-5372-8
- **Mexico** (2nd Edition) ISBN: 0-7922-5319-1
- **Miami & the Keys**
  (2nd Edition) ISBN: 0-7922-3886-9
- **New York** (2nd Edition) ISBN: 0-7922-5370-1
- **Paris** ISBN: 0-7922-7429-6
- **Piedmont & Northwest Italy**
  ISBN: 0-7922-4198-3
- **Portugal** ISBN: 0-7922-4199-1
- **Prague & the Czech Republic**
  ISBN: 0-7922-4147-9
- **Provence & the Côte d'Azur**
  ISBN: 0-7922-9542-0
- **Rome** (2nd Edition) ISBN: 0-7922-5572-0
- **San Diego** (2nd Edition) ISBN: 0-7922-6202-6
- **San Francisco** (2nd Edition) ISBN: 0-7922-3883-4
- **Sicily** ISBN: 0-7922-9541-2
- **Spain** (2nd Edition) ISBN: 0-7922-3884-2
- **Sydney** ISBN: 0-7922-7435-0
- **Taiwan** ISBN: 0-7922-6555-6
- **Thailand** (2nd Edition) ISBN: 0-7922-5321-3
- **Venice** ISBN: 0-7922-7917-4
- **Vietnam** ISBN: 0-7922-6203-4
- **Washington, D.C.**
  (2nd Edition) ISBN: 0-7922-3887-7

AVAILABLE WHEREVER BOOKS ARE SOLD